THE
POWER
AND THE
GLORY

THE
POWER
AND THE
GLORY

LIFE IN THE ENGLISH COUNTRY
HOUSE BEFORE THE GREAT WAR

ADRIAN TINNISWOOD

BASIC BOOKS
New York

Basic Books
Hachette Book Group
1290 Avenue of the Americas, New York, NY 10104
www.basicbooks.com

Printed in Canada

First Edition: November 2024

Published by Basic Books, an imprint of Hachette Book Group, Inc. The Basic
Books name and logo is a registered trademark of the Hachette Book Group.

The Hachette Speakers Bureau provides a wide range of authors for speaking
events. To find out more, go to hachettespeakersbureau.com or email
HachetteSpeakers@hbgusa.com.

Basic books may be purchased in bulk for business, educational, or promotional
use. For more information, please contact your local bookseller or the Hachette
Book Group Special Markets Department at special.markets@hbgusa.com.

The publisher is not responsible for websites (or their content) that are not
owned by the publisher.

Print book interior design by Bart Dawson.

Library of Congress Cataloging-in-Publication Data

Names: Tinniswood, Adrian, author.
Title: The power and the glory : life in the English country house before
    the Great War / Adrian Tinniswood.
Description: First edition. | New York : Basic Books, 2024. | Includes
    bibliographical references and index.
Identifiers: LCCN 2024019616 | ISBN 9781541602793 (hardcover) |
    ISBN 9781541602786 (ebook)
Subjects: LCSH: Gentry—England—History—19th century. |
    Country life—England—History—19th century. | Country homes—
    England—History—19th century. | Manors—England—History—
    19th century. | England—Social life and customs—19th century.
Classification: LCC HT658.G7 T56 2024 | DDC 305.5/232094209034—
    dc23/eng/20240618
LC record available at https://lccn.loc.gov/2024019616

ISBNs: 9781541602793 (hardcover), 9781541602786 (ebook)

MRQ-T

10 9 8 7 6 5 4 3 2 1

For Helen

CONTENTS

Contents

INTRODUCTION

ALL THAT GLITTERS

CONVERSATIONS DIED TO silence as the princess took the floor, her diamonds shimmering in the light of a cluster of enormous chandeliers. And as she curtseyed to her partner and the orchestra struck up an Offenbach quadrille, the elite of British landed society looked on with complacent pride at this young woman whose father was a king and whose husband was heir to the largest empire in history. The ball had begun, and the assembled company—dukes and generals, politicians and society dames—watched and waltzed and two-stepped until dawn, happy in the knowledge that the night, and the world, belonged to them.

The day was Friday, December 2, 1870. The place was Sandringham House. And the occasion was both a housewarming and a birthday party. Alexandra, Princess of Wales, was celebrating her twenty-sixth birthday; and she and her husband of seven years, Prince Albert Edward, known in the family as Bertie, had just moved into Sandringham after a long programme of rebuilding which saw this modest Norfolk mansion transformed into a vast and imposing

Jacobethan palace—a building which, like Alix and Bertie and their guests, radiated prosperity and an unbridled confidence in the future.

Was it misplaced? In the 1870s, bad weather, poor harvests, and outbreaks of foot-and-mouth disease and liver rot, combined with foreign competition which undercut prices on the home market, had a devastating effect on British agriculture. Grain came in from America, and a dramatic fall in prices in the 1880s proved disastrous for cereal growers, particularly in the east and southeast of England. Livestock and dairy farmers weren't quite so badly affected: although steamships brought refrigerated lamb and butter from New Zealand, demand remained high for dairy products, and home producers were able to take advantage of that. Nevertheless, British farmers struggled with falling prices, and as prices fell, so rents fell, and that meant that incomes fell for the big rural landlords. Statistics for the period are incomplete, but what is clear is that some parts of the country suffered more than others, and some landowners were better than others at investing in improvements.

Between the early 1870s and the early 1890s, the Duke of Richmond found that his income from his Goodwood estate fell by 25 per cent. The Earl of Leicester's net income from Holkham went down by more than 20 per cent. The Duke of Bedford sold off a fifth of his estates in Bedfordshire and Buckinghamshire, and this combined with falling rents meant that his income from land dropped by more than 40 per cent. Some country house owners, like Bedford, reduced their land holdings; others had done so already, putting their money into mining or manufacturing or stocks and shares.

But other factors also contributed to the breakup of large estates, and one of the most far-reaching was the relaxation of the laws governing family settlements. A country house owner in the 1870s may have wanted to sell off parcels of outlying land to fund improvements on his farms. He may have wanted to have a quiet talk with a representative from an auction house about that van Dyck of his ancestor in the dining room or the First Folio in the library. He may even have yearned to put the entire estate, ancestral seat and all, on the market and decamp to Paris with his mistress and the proceeds. But in nine cases out of ten he couldn't: the terms of the family settlement prevented him.

And that was just what it was meant to do. A strict family settlement turned the "owner" into a tenant for life, able to enjoy his estates and the income they generated but unable to dispose of any part of them without the consent of the trustees. If the van Dyck and the First Folio had been deemed at some point to be heirlooms, he couldn't flog those, either. And the settlement entailed the estate on the landowner's eldest son, a move guaranteed to keep everything together, in contrast to European practice, which split land holdings among children on the death of the parent.

Long-established landowners supported the system—after all, if young Johnny came down from Cambridge with a chorus girl for a wife, or gambled away his allowance, at least the settlement would limit the damage to the family finances—while simultaneously railing against the shackles which prevented them from doing exactly what they liked with their own property. Reformers argued that the settlement was an outdated feudal practice, hampering the working of the free market, and that the agricultural depression justified their demands for change. In 1882 agricultural improver James Caird told a royal commission, "[Landowners] will find it necessary to have utmost freedom of action in view of the great competition upon which we are entering with America, and anything that prevents that freedom of action is undesirable."[1]

A series of Settled Land Acts were passed between 1882 and 1890. They allowed the tenant for life to sell land, although the capital remained part of the settlement, but it made an exception of the principal mansion and park, the sale of which still required the consent of trustees or, failing that, a court order. There was some ambiguity about this: the act stipulated that the tenant for life must "have regard to the interests of all parties entitled under the settlement," without going into detail about how those interests might be defined.[2] And that ambiguity was tested in 1892 in the Savernake Hall case.

Savernake Hall, more correctly known as Tottenham House, was a large late-Georgian mansion in Wiltshire built on the site of, and incorporating parts of, two earlier houses, one from the 1570s and the other, designed by Lord Burlington, from the 1720s. It stood at the heart of a forty-thousand-acre estate which included a vast swathe of Savernake Forest, an ancient royal hunting forest; ninety-five separate farms; about a thousand houses; and land in the nearby town of Marlborough. All this belonged to the Brudenell-Bruces, Marquesses of Ailesbury and Wardens of Savernake. In 1878 the title and the estate, along with several others in Yorkshire, including Jervaulx Abbey, were inherited by the sixty-seven-year-old Ernest Brudenell-Bruce. The agricultural depression, and some lavish spending by his two predecessors, meant that the family fortunes were at a low ebb, and the situation wasn't helped by the fact that the new marquess had to make provision for his five surviving children while finding jointures for his stepmother, his sister-in-law, and a widowed daughter-in-law. His eldest son, George, had been better at spending than saving and had died of drink in Corsica in 1868, leaving a daughter, Mabel, and a son, George William, known in the family as Willie. Because he was the heir to the marquessate, the Savernake estates were entailed on Willie, although the family's Yorkshire estates were not part of the family settlement.

And Willie—"Ducks," as he was called by barmaids throughout the East End of London—was exactly the kind of heir that a family settlement was designed to guard against. Amiable and not too bright, he had, in the words of one of his biographers, a passion for "fast women, wine and slow horses."[3] The horses proved to be even more of a drain on his resources than the women and the wine; but whenever he had run through his allowance there were moneylenders who were willing to advance him large sums. He was expected to come into money when he was twenty-one, and it was also generally known that the Savernake entail would come to an end when his elderly grandfather died, leaving him the absolute possessor of an enormous estate. By 1884, his debts amounted to an astonishing £175,000, many millions in today's money. He was once heard to say, as he emerged from an East End boxing gym, "Ain't it strange that such a blessed fool as I am should be a lord?"[4]

The conventional course in situations like these would have been for his grandfather to find him a wealthy and unsuspecting bride. That course wasn't open to him because on May 6, 1884, a month before his twenty-first birthday, Willie had married Julia Haseley, better known as the music hall artiste Dolly Tester. He was said to have won her at a racecourse in a fistfight with the wealthy gentleman jockey George Alexander Baird.

Ailing, and appalled at the thought of what would happen after his death, the elderly marquess did three things. First, he sold his Yorkshire estates to pay off Willie's debts, a move that broke his heart. "Another nail in my coffin and one of the last it must be," he confided in his diary when he heard that the sale of Jervaulx was going through.[5] Second, he had a new settlement drawn up, by which Willie had only a life interest in the estate, which would then be passed on to his heir. "Thank God for it!" he wrote.[6] And third, he died.

Willie didn't spend much time at Tottenham House, preferring life in London and at the racecourse. He continued to drink prodigious amounts and to spend prodigious amounts; he borrowed heavily; and he became involved in some dishonest practices, which culminated in his being publicly warned off the turf by the Jockey Club. (He had acquired a bad habit of ordering his jockeys not to win their races.) As a result he was ruined, socially and financially, by the age of twenty-five.

Willie's creditors, led by a Birmingham-born moneylender to the nobility named Samuel Lewis, who was charging Willie interest at a rate of 100 per cent, pressed him to sell up the Savernake estate. When he pointed out that under the terms of the recent family settlement the estate wasn't his to sell, they advised him that there was a way to get round that. Under the terms of the Settled Land Acts he could still sell, they argued, but any proceeds would be for his trustees to invest. If he got a high enough price, there would be an income for him and the settlement of his debts for them.

And this is where the ambiguities surrounding the Settled Land Acts came in. The law stipulated that he could sell the agricultural land as long as he didn't touch the capital from the sale, but he couldn't sell the mansion, gardens, and park without the prior consent of his trustees. Then there was that phrase about having regard "to the interests of all parties."

There were two trustees. One, Hugh Mewburn Walker, was also Willie's solicitor, and he thought the pragmatic course was to sell off the entire estate, country house and all. But the other was Willie's uncle, Lord Frederick Brudenell-Bruce, and Frederick was on close terms with his older brother, Lord Henry, who, unless Willie produced an heir, stood to inherit and who was, therefore, very definitely an interested party. Uncle Henry would never agree to the sale. Nevertheless, Mewburn Walker quietly let it be known that Savernake was up for sale, and three potential buyers emerged: an unnamed English peer; an unnamed American millionaire; and the brewer Sir Edward Guinness, who offered £750,000 for the entire estate. It was a generous offer; rental income from the estate over the past few years had fallen from £25,500 a year to £21,000, and outgoings and repairs amounted to a lot more than that. The interest on the capital from the sale would give Willie an income and would go some way towards paying off his debts, which now stood at something like £230,000, £200,000 of which was owed to Sam Lewis.

Lord Frederick was shocked. Lord Henry was outraged, and he vented his spleen not on his useless nephew but on Guinness, "a mere upstart merchant, a *nouveau-riche* Irishman."[7] He duly mobilised family opinion against the sale. And with one trustee in favour and the other against, Guinness refusing to go ahead with the deal unless the mansion was included, and Willie desperate to liquidise his assets, the matter went to court, allowing Willie a stay of execution on imminent bankruptcy proceedings "in the expectation that a settlement satisfactory to all parties might be arrived at."[8]

The case of the Ailesbury Settled Estates came before Mr Justice Stirling in the Chancery Court on August 7, 1891. Willie's counsel argued that the sale of the estate, "together with the mansion-house, known as Savernake-hall, and the pleasure grounds, park, and lands, usually occupied therewith," was in the interests of all concerned. For Uncle Frederick, Uncle Henry, and the rest of the family, Sir Horace Davey QC cleverly said there was no objection to the sale of the land, just the mansion (knowing that Sir Edward Guinness wouldn't take the one without the other). He put Willie in the witness box and made him admit he was living on an allowance from Sam Lewis and that Lewis was "very anxious" for the sale to go through. The proposed sale of an historic mansion was against the wishes of the family, and its only purpose was "to pay off the money-lenders who had preyed upon the extravagance of this youthful tenant for life."[9]

Mr Justice Stirling dismissed Willie's petition. "Every living person interested under the settlement is opposed to the sale," he noted. Everyone except Willie, anyway. "Each is actuated by the desire, recognized by common feeling in this country as worthy of respect, to enjoy in his turn this unique historic possession, the home of his family for more than 200 years." As tenant for life, Willie had a duty to act in the interests of all parties concerned, and Stirling decided he had not done so.[10]

Supported by Samuel Lewis, Willie took his case to the Court of Appeal—and won. The three judges were in no doubt about his character: he was, said one of them, Lord Justice Lindley, "a spendthrift who has ruined himself by his own extravagance and folly and who has brought disgrace upon the family name, and exposed the family estate to destruction for the rest of his life."[11] But if they prevented the sale of Savernake Hall, the consequences for the estate would be even worse than if it went through. Willie and Lewis could cut down all the timber. They could sell off everything bar the mansion. And they could ignore the welfare of the five thousand or so tenants on the estate.

The rest of the family took the case to the House of Lords, and lost. Uncle Henry accused Willie of fraud, and lost. (He also accused Guinness of offering him a £50,000 bribe to drop his opposition to the sale.) But by a series of legal manoeuvres over the fate of heirlooms in the house, the priority of other creditors on the Savernake estate, and the future of the jointures owed to Ailesbury dowagers, he managed to delay the sale until May 1893, when Guinness, now Lord Iveagh, finally lost patience and bought Elveden Hall in Suffolk instead. Willie, who was drinking even more heavily than before and living on Clapham Road with another actress, Bessie Bellwood, fell ill and died in April 1894, the day before he was due to be declared bankrupt. He was thirty. A carefully worded and on the whole rather generous obituary in the local paper said he was nobody's enemy but his own. Savernake passed to Uncle Henry. It isn't clear what, if anything, passed to Samuel Lewis. The doctor who attended Willie in his last illness sued Bessie for his bill.

The Savernake case left the country house world both relieved and slightly uneasy. The judgment in the Lords meant that a tenant for life could run up huge debts and then force through the sale of his ancestral seat on the grounds that he had done just that. Nor did it do much to clarify the legislation, and entails and family settlements continued well into the twentieth century, with lawyers growing rich on the resulting confusion. On the other hand, the Settled Land Acts certainly did make it easier for landowners who were struggling with falling rents and useless heirs to sell off their estates, country houses included. And not every possessor of an ancient ancestral seat was as attached to it as Willie's Uncle Henry.

The agricultural depression put pressure on some owners to sell, and the Settled Land Acts made it easier for them to do so. But there was a third factor, more harmful to the status quo than these and more far-reaching in its impact on the country house.

In his 1894 budget, Chancellor of the Exchequer Sir William Vernon Harcourt introduced an inheritance tax on estates valued at more than one hundred pounds. The heirs of those who died with estates at this bottom end of the scale would have to supply the Treasury with a sum equal to 1 per cent of the value of their estate. But the tax was graduated, hitting the wealthy harder the more they owned. Landowners with estates valued at over £100,000, for example, had to find 6 per cent; at the top end, the duty was 8 per cent on estates of over £1 million. Harcourt's announcement in the House of Commons caused "a buzz of amazement, corresponding to the whistles of astonishment heard at a public meeting when some unusually strong sentiment is delivered."[12] Unsurprisingly, the response in the House of Lords to a tax on inherited wealth was more vigorous. The Duke of Devonshire, owner of nearly two hundred thousand acres in England and Ireland, was described by one observer as giving a "manly and vigorous" speech against the tax but also as being "somewhat antiquated in his arguments," which revolved around the familiar idea that it would deter people from accumulating wealth, and since they would have less to spend, they would be less able to employ workers—ergo, it was the working classes who would suffer most.[13] More credibly, the duke prophesied that the new tax would force the owners of great estates to sell off large libraries and collections of art, and that some precious items would inevitably leave the country. It would "reduce the stately splendour of great houses":

> If you increase taxation upon the owner of personal property and reduce his income it is probably not very difficult for him to change in some degree his mode of life, to live in a smaller house, to maintain a smaller establishment, to effect econo-mies in a great many directions without experiencing any great wrench in either his own existence or that of the peo-ple dependent upon him. The case of the owner of a landed estate is entirely different. He is bound to the estate, and to a certain scale of expenditure upon it, as long as he remains there. For him it is no question of certain minor economies; for him the question is whether he shall go or stay, whether he will stay as a pauper, unable to discharge the duties which he has hitherto fulfilled, or whether he will go and abandon altogether the occupations to which he has been accustomed and the obligations which he has undertaken. . . . If a man has to reduce his expenditure he will keep fewer servants and horses, and will diminish his tradesmen's bills, the servants having to find other places, the tradesmen other customers. In the case of a man who is compelled by the operation of this measure to close his country place and to reduce his expendi-ture upon the estate, the immediate effect will be the absolute cessation of the employment of a large number of people who probably will not readily find employment anywhere else, and the deprivation for hundreds of families of, at all events, their present means of subsistence.[14]

Nobleman after nobleman rose to attack Harcourt's bill. The Earl of Feversham, owner of thirty-nine thousand acres of Yorkshire, asked the Earl of Rosebery if he really supposed that "a measure fraught with so much injustice to the landed interest in this country could be so passed." Lord Halsbury, a previous (and future) Lord High Chancellor, called the bill "an illustration of the hostile spirit towards the landed aristocracy."[15] Still, the bill passed into law later that year, and those who had predicted it was the thin end of an antilandowner wedge felt themselves vindicated, but poorer for it, when fifteen years later David Lloyd George's budget raised the rates: the duty on estates over £100,000 went up to 9 per cent, the heirs of estates over £1 million now had to find 15 per cent, and, even worse, Lloyd George's land taxes provided the foundations for an annual tax on estates. The increases in death duties weren't a vast amount compared to the 50 per cent top rate imposed by Clement Attlee's Labour government in 1950. But they were enough to hurt.

Some country house owners embraced change. In 1889, for example, the radical young Hugh Fairfax-Cholmeley took over the running of his 3,200-acre family estate at Brandsby in Yorkshire, and the £33,000 of debt that went with it, filled with a desire to upset "the old order," as he put it.[16] Spurning Brandsby Hall, his eighteenth-century family seat, he commissioned the Arts and Crafts architect Detmar Blow to build him a much more modest place. He "wanted a house of extreme simplicity," wrote Lawrence Weaver in *Country Life* in 1915, "and to adopt the more primitive standard of comfort that is nowadays usual."[17] Having earned the wrath of his conservative neighbours and the even more conservative local vicar by turning one of his vacant cottages into a reading room for his tenants (and starting it off with a subscription to *The Star*, a socialist newspaper), he set up a cooperative and turned part of the coach house at Brandsby Hall into a dairy. He improved estate cottages, built piggeries, held lectures in his drawing room for the local farmers with titles such as "The Principles of Manuring," and built a goods depot in the village which connected to the North Eastern Railway so that the farmers on his estate could transport produce to various markets more efficiently.

Modern farming methods like these could stave off the worst effects of the agricultural depression, for a time at least. In any case, by 1914 it seemed that most of the changes in country house life that had taken place over the past forty-four years had been for the better. The country house was still a central feature of rural life. The great ducal mansions—Chatsworth, Blenheim, Welbeck, Woburn, Badminton, and the rest—were just as much a part of national and local life as they had always been. For those who preferred something new in the way of an ancestral seat, the paint was barely dry on some of the period's greatest architectural achievements: Richard Norman Shaw's Cragside, Philip Webb's Clouds, and the same architect's Standen. Edwin Lutyens had hardly begun on Castle Drogo, his medieval-modernist magnum opus. Ernest Barnsley was still watching the walls go up at his Arts and Crafts masterpiece, Rodmarton.

With a vast national railway network to get you into the country in an hour or two and back to town just as swiftly, the country house Saturday-to-Monday had become an integral part of the social rounds for the elite. Now you could invite your guests by telephone, although admittedly that still wasn't quite the thing in the best circles. You could send your chauffeur in your Daimler or your Renault to pick up those guests at the station: if King George and Queen Mary owned motorcars, why shouldn't you? You could offer guests hot and cold running water, water closets and a bathroom or two, electricity to illuminate their ten-course dinner and, when bridge and billiards were over, to light their way to one of your forty bedrooms. Perhaps it was the one they were supposed to sleep in, or perhaps it belonged to someone else.

In 1914 the country house was still an essential adjunct for the ruling class, a class that now admitted outsiders into its ranks—Jewish bankers and American millionaires and Indian princes. It was still a hub in local and national politics, still an object of desire for the ambitious manufacturer or mill owner eager to join county society and to achieve the longed-for baronetcy, or at least to marry off his daughter to a baronet. It was still true that an Englishman's home might quite literally be his castle, ancient or modern, or if not a castle, then a modest but tasteful mansion on a couple of hundred acres. Confident and secure, country house society basked in the light of a last, best golden age.

ONE

POWER AND PRIDE

IT WAS LATE afternoon, and the December light was already failing when the fast train from King's Cross pulled into Worksop station in Nottinghamshire. It was bitterly cold, too, but that didn't deter the crowd who had gathered outside the station entrance. They raised a cheer as a little family group emerged and climbed into three waiting coaches: the mother, middle-aged but still beautiful, with raven-black hair, and her five children. The youngest was a little girl only six years old; the oldest was twenty-one, a rather self-important young officer in the Coldstream Guards. This was William Cavendish-Bentinck. Seventeen days earlier, on December 6, 1879, an elderly cousin, the 5th Duke of Portland, had died, leaving William the title, a house, Welbeck Abbey, estates of over 162,000 acres, and an annual income which was estimated at the time to be well over £140,000. And now, two days before Christmas, William had come to take up his inheritance.

The 5th Duke of Portland had been something of a recluse. "He was a member of four London clubs—Boodle's, Brook's, Travellers' and White's," claimed one newspaper report, "but we believe he never attended any of them. He was a deputy lieutenant of Nottinghamshire, but we never heard of him acting in that capacity or wearing the official uniform; he was a member of the House of Lords, but the benches of that august assembly never held his tall and slender form. But he had a little world to preside over at Welbeck."[1]

That little world was in an alarming state. When the new duke wrote to the resident agent to inform him of his plans to bring his mother, brothers, and sister (actually his stepmother and half siblings—his own mother had died shortly after his birth), the man did his best to discourage him, saying that the place was in a state of chaos and the furniture was all in storage. That didn't stop the duke: encouraged by his stepmother, Augusta, who sent up the furniture from the family's town house in Grosvenor Square, and notwithstanding the fact that one of his brothers was still so weak from the aftereffects of peritonitis that he had to be carried, he announced that come what may, the Cavendish-Bentincks were going to spend Christmas in their new home. Hence their arrival at Worksop station, five miles from Welbeck, on that cold, dark December afternoon.

When they arrived at Welbeck itself, the reasons for the agent's reluctance to welcome them were quickly apparent. The drive was covered in builder's rubble, and planks had been laid down so that the carriages could reach the front door. A reception committee was waiting to greet them in the hall: Thomas McCallum, the house steward; the agent, F. J. Turner; the clerk of works, a Mr Tinker; and some of the senior servants. But there was no floor: temporary boards had been put down to enable the party to enter, and after a short and, one imagines, rather strained conversation, the family, still wearing mourning for the late duke, was ushered into the west wing, towards the four or five habitable rooms that made up the 5th duke's private apartment.

And privacy was the key to Welbeck's recent history. As its name suggests, it had once been an abbey, and a few medieval fragments remained, although they were buried deep in centuries of remodelling and rebuilding by a succession of architects—some distinguished, others less so—until by the nineteenth century the abbey had evolved into a vast if rather disjointed ducal mansion. As a young man the 5th duke, who inherited Welbeck from his father in 1854, had led the normal life of a privileged aristocrat, but around 1860, for reasons which remain rather obscure, he began to develop an exaggerated passion for privacy. For the next two decades he indulged what one contemporary commentator described as "a fancy of truly remarkable intensity for solitude and seclusion." (The writer added rather primly, "One cannot but wonder that the nobility in such a man did not find issue by somewhat worthier channels.")[2] The gardens of his town house on Cavendish Square were overlooked by his neighbours, so he wrapped them in an enormous high screen of frosted glass. He didn't like the idea of meeting others when he travelled up and down to London by train, so he had his carriage lifted onto a railway truck and kept the green silk blinds tightly drawn for the entire journey.

At Welbeck, this obsession with privacy manifested itself in strange ways, as the new duke and his family soon found out. The day after their arrival they began to explore the house. The doors in the 5th duke's apartment, where they had spent the night, were equipped with double sets of brass letter boxes, one for "in" and one for "out." Most of the other rooms in the house had bare floors, pink walls, and no furniture, except that each boasted a ducal water closet, with water laid on and in good working order—yet "not enclosed or sheltered in any way," recalled the 6th duke's little sister Ottoline (the future Bloomsbury hostess Lady Ottoline Morrell).[3] Only the fan-vaulted Gothic Hall, designed in 1747–1751, showed signs of occupation: it was filled with "a vast gathering of cabinets all more or less in a state of disrepair."[4]

It was when the family ventured below ground that the full extent of the 5th duke's ambitious eccentricity became apparent.

Like children in a fantasy novel by E. Nesbit, they descended into an underground passage and then up through a trapdoor into the seventeenth-century riding school, one of the largest in the world, to find it lined with mirrors, hung with crystal chandeliers, and filled with paintings, many of them unframed and unnamed, stacked two or three deep. A building which had once housed stables now held the kitchens, from which food was lowered by a lift onto a heated truck, which one of the menservants pushed on rails along another underground passage for 150 yards until it reached the main house. A farther passage ran off this one into a range of enormous chambers, all underground, heated by hot air and lit by skylights during the day and thousands of gas jets by night. (One room alone had one thousand jets.) The largest of these rooms, 154 feet long by 64 feet wide, had originally been conceived as a picture gallery but was later known as a ballroom: at the far end was a second hydraulic lift which was said to be able to take a carriage, so that guests could arrive in the ballroom without having to leave their coach. There never were any guests.

The technology involved in the 5th duke's subterranean creations was impressive. In addition to the gas lighting (the duke had built a gas plant on the grounds) and the hydraulic lifts and the hot-air heating, the walls were lined with layers of asphalt to keep out the damp; cast-iron columns supported the ceiling in one room, while the ballroom had an uninterrupted span achieved by the use of box girders concealed in the roof structure.[5] Cut-and-cover tunnels and passages were brick vaulted and surprisingly long. The great driving tunnel, which was the only direct road to Worksop, ran for more than a mile. It was wide enough for two carriages to pass side by side and was lit during the day by "small mushroom windows which threw a ghostly light," recalled Ottoline, and at night by hundreds of gas jets.[6]

There were two tunnels from the house to the stables and gardens, each about a mile long: one was for the duke, the other for gardeners and workmen. The duke didn't want to meet anyone walking in the same tunnel as himself, remembered Ottoline. There was a skating rink in the garden, where the old duke employed a man just to look after the skates of various sizes. Apparently he liked his servants (there were eighteen living in, including a baker and a confectioner) to use the facilities, so much so that if he came across one of the maids sweeping the corridors or the stairs, he packed them off to the skating rink whether they wanted to go or not.

When the new duke arrived at Christmas 1879, his predecessor had worked on Welbeck for nearly twenty years. But much of that work was still unfinished. There were wheelbarrows and shovels lying around in the underground chambers; no rooms were furnished apart from the private apartments; and the grounds looked like a building site, which of course they were. Welbeck was weird and depressing. "This vast place," said Ottoline, "denuded as it was of all grace and beauty and life, cast a gloom over us." It was filled with the personality of its last duke; and that personality was problematic, troubling, evidence of a man intent on "banishing grace and beauty and human love and companionship."[7]

The 5th duke's architectural peccadillos can't have come as a complete surprise to his successor. They were common knowledge in the district—how could they not be, when the duke was employing an army of workmen on his projects and when, in the words of one of the many newspaper accounts of the works, "Welbeck was like an industrial village"?[8] The whole world was talking about the tunnels and underground chambers at Welbeck Abbey. "The late duke led a retired life, devoting a large portion of his time to building and making improvements at Welbeck Abbey, on which he expended an enormous amount of money," ran his *Telegraph* obituary.[9] Less measured descriptions of the works appeared in dozens of journals and newspapers all over the country in the weeks following the 5th duke's death.

But the extent of these works, and their unfinished state, came as a shock. The new duke kept up the usual Christmas customs, since arrangements were already in place. All the poor and widows of the district received their usual gifts of prime beef and plum puddings on Christmas Eve, the day after the family's arrival; and when the duke, his stepmother, and his half siblings attended morning service at Worksop on the following Sunday, the county turned out to inspect them and the church bells were rung in their honour.

But what Portland really wanted to do, as soon as it was decently possible, was to shut up the house and go back to London. As he confessed in his memoirs years later, he was already annoyed with his predecessor for the inconsiderate timing of his death, which had ruined the young man's plans to spend Christmas hunting in Buckinghamshire. Who wanted to live in such a peculiar house? Not him.

Luckily for Welbeck—and for the duke, whose home it turned out to be for the next sixty-four years—his stepmother had other ideas. Augusta told him it was his duty to remain in Nottinghamshire, and she was going to stay with him and knock the house into shape. Shocked that the 5th duke had demolished the family chapel, she announced that "it was extremely wrong that [they] should all live as heathens," so she screened off one end of the old riding school with a red baize curtain, had a temporary altar and a lectern set up, installed a resident chaplain and a harmonium, and got up a choir from the workers on the estate. A painting by Sir Joshua Reynolds, *Angel in Contemplation*, hung over the altar, but as a chapel it wasn't a success. "At night, when its multitude of gas jets in glass chandeliers are lit, the suggestion of a foreign café in a large city might be at least strong, if not overpowering," commented one visitor.[10] It was remodelled in the early 1890s by architect Henry Wilson, who created a remarkable Byzantine interior with an equally remarkable altar frontal of electroplated silver.

For the duke's young half brothers and half sister, the attempt to make sense of the mansion and its contents was exciting, even if it was exhausting for their mother. They found cupboards full of socks and silk handkerchiefs and dark-brown wigs. They watched as Gobelins tapestries were taken out of their tin cases and unrolled, and they rummaged around in what looked like a dressing-up chest but actually held a set of robes worn for George I's coronation in October 1714. Ottoline remembered standing in a dark chamber one evening while a servant held a candle and her brother went through the drawers of a cabinet filled with snuffboxes and watches and old miniatures, when he found a green silk purse. It was stuffed with £2,000 worth of banknotes. "The little green purse—but without the notes—was given to me to keep, and still when I look at it I see myself again a small child peering up at those dim treasures lit by a solitary candle."[11]

From these unconventional beginnings, the 6th duke soon established a conventionally ducal way of life at Welbeck. He began to entertain, with his stepmother acting as his hostess: In the summer of 1881 Prince Leopold, Duke of Albany, came to lunch, with the Duke of St Albans. Later that year the Prince of Wales, who according to Portland "had himself proposed the visit," descended for two days' pheasant shooting.[12] An impressive clutch of aristocrats was invited to meet him, including the Duke and Duchess of Manchester, the Marquess of Hartington (heir to the Devonshire dukedom), Lord and Lady Castlereagh, later the Marquess and Marchioness of Londonderry, and the widowed Mary, Marchioness of Ailesbury, who, having found her style in the early Victorian period, continued to cling to it, wearing her hair in unfashionable ringlets until her death in 1895. The prince himself was surprised to be driven to the abbey through the 5th duke's long, gas-lit tunnel, escorted by a troop of the Yeomanry Cavalry. His hat fell off and was trampled by one of the Yeomanry horses.

In 1889, the duke married Winifred Dallas-Yorke, daughter of a Lincolnshire JP. It was a happy marriage which lasted until Portland's death (Winifred always called him "Portland") in 1943, and the duchess produced an heir, a spare, and a daughter named Victoria, the elderly queen's last godchild. They divided their time between the Grosvenor Square house and Welbeck, where they lived in some state. They kept an indoor staff of twenty-eight, including ten housemaids. Six footmen worked in shifts, and at dinner their day livery of black tailcoat, dogtooth-check waistcoat with monogrammed buttons, wing collar, and white bow tie, gave way to state livery: a claret-coloured velvet cutaway coat, a shirt of Nottingham lace, white doeskin breeches, white silk stockings, black shoes with silver buckles, and a silver wig.

Portland was a fanatical sportsman. He owned and bred racehorses: his St Simon won the Ascot Gold Cup in 1884. He laid out his own golf course in the park at Welbeck. He was a great supporter of the local cricket club: his chaplain and his secretary organised a Welbeck eleven, "which was seldom beaten."[13] And he held a succession of shooting parties every winter. On one notorious occasion in 1913 a loader tripped and one of his guns accidentally discharged, narrowly missing one of Portland's guests. It was Archduke Franz Ferdinand. As Portland recalled, "I have often wondered whether the Great War might not have been averted, or at least postponed, had the archduke met his death there and not at Sarajevo the following year."[14]

When a nursery maid accidentally left an electric iron switched on at the socket in October 1900, the mansion was badly damaged by the resulting fire and the drenching it received from the four steam fire engines called out to extinguish it. Portland commissioned repairs and remodelling from the firm of Ernest George and Yeates, recommended to him by Bertram Mitford (grandfather of the Mitford sisters), who had just employed George to restore his own seat, Batsford Park in Gloucestershire. There was another connection: in 1881 George had designed the Ossington Coffee Palace in nearby Newark for the 5th duke's temperance-mad sister. Portland originally asked the Earl of Wemyss to recommend an architect, but Wemyss, who had just had the Scottish architect William Young carry out work at Gosford House in East Lothian, replied that although he was satisfied with Young's work, they had had a falling out when he "ventured to suggest that Inigo Jones and Sir Christopher Wren were *almost* as great architects as himself." That was enough to put Portland off.[15]

Ernest George was a safe pair of hands, a conventional architect who until 1892 had been in partnership with the more gifted Harold Peto. Between them they had built up a big practice turning out an eclectic mix of Queen Anne, Jacobethan, Wrenaissance, and neo-Georgian country houses, and when Peto retired and E. G., as he was known in his office, brought in Alfred Yeates as a business partner, the practice continued. E. G. didn't disappoint when it came to repairing fire-damaged Welbeck, producing some solid but not unattractive work in an English baroque style. It suited Portland, who was himself solid but not unattractive.

How typical was Portland's lifestyle, the constant round of house parties and shooting parties and public duties? (He was lord lieutenant of Nottinghamshire for forty-one years, and master of the horse to Queen Victoria and Edward VII.) In 1875 George Routledge and Sons published *The Upper Ten Thousand: An Alphabetical List*. Drawing on a phrase first used about New York high society and by then in general use to describe any elite, it was compiled by a journalist and ex–colonial official, Adam Bisset Thom, who explained that he had set out to list "*all those who have any definite position* [his italics] arising either from hereditary rank, or from any recognised title or order conferred up them by the Sovereign, or from any of the higher grades of the military, naval, clerical, or colonial services of the State."[16] Thom clarified "forms of epistolary address," gave tables of precedence, and provided helpful explanatory notes:

The daughter of a peer does not lose her own rank should she marry a commoner or a bishop; but if she marries a peer her title and precedency are merged in his, e.g., if the daughter of a duke marries a baron, she sinks to the rank of a baroness. But if the widow of, for example, a duke marries a baron, she retains her own rank of duchess. The widow of a peer or knight may retain her title notwithstanding her second marriage, but she does so only by courtesy. The widow of a baronet, however, enjoys her precedence for life by right. Official rank and precedence is not communicable to the wife, but the wife of the Viceroy of Ireland and of a lord mayor has precedence derived from her husband's office.[17]

Is everybody clear on that?

Then came the list, beginning with Major-General Sir Frederick Abbott, whose residence was given as Broom Hall in Kent, and ending with the Bishop of Zululand, Thomas Wilkinson, DD. There was no address for Bishop Wilkinson—the precise location in Zululand of his episcopal palace had obviously eluded Thom. And sandwiched between Abbott and Zululand were the great and the good of Great Britain and Ireland: the landed nobility and its offspring, the military men who commanded an empire, the politicians who ruled it. Entries were concise, giving names, titles (and when they were first created), brief personal details, clubs, and residences in country and in town. The entry for the 4th Marquess of Bath is fairly typical:

Bath, 4 marq. of (1789). John Alexander Thynne; b. 1831; m. dr. of 3 visc. de Vesci; 2nd tit. visc. Weymouth: dep.-lieut. Wilts and Somerset, knight grand cross of the tower and sword of Portugal, cap. Wilts yeomanry from 1850.

Boodle's, Carlton; Longleat, Warminster, Wilts; 48 Berkeley Square.

One of the more noticeable things about the list, once one has managed to decode all the abbreviations, is that most families deemed by Thom to have a definite position in society also had a country house or two. It might be a palace (although interestingly, the Duke of Marlborough's house was given as "Blenheim House" rather than "Blenheim Palace'); it might be something quite modest, like Abbott's Georgian Broom Hall. There might be more than one house. Portland's predecessor, the eccentric 5th duke, kept two other country houses besides Welbeck: Fullarton House and Langwell Lodge, both in Scotland. Sudbury Hall in Derbyshire was the Vernon family's main seat, but the 6th Lord Vernon also listed Poynton Hall in Chester and Widdrington Castle, Morpeth, as well as having a town address at 34 Grosvenor Street. The 7th Duke of Devonshire listed Chatsworth, of course, but also Bolton Abbey in Yorkshire; Holker Hall in Lancashire; Compton Place, Eastbourne; and Lismore Castle in County Waterford, Ireland. And there was a town house, given as "78 Piccadilly," which scarcely does justice to the enormous scale of Devonshire House, which had been at the heart of London Society since 1696.

The Upper Ten Thousand was a great success. It was swiftly taken over by Kelly and Company, the publisher of trade directories for every county in England, and it was regularly updated under its new name, *Kelly's Handbook to the Titled, Landed and Official Classes*. But the criteria for inclusion began to broaden. By 1909, when *Kelly's* was into its thirty-fifth edition, the original entrants had been joined by a new category: "the chief landowners being also occupiers of one of the principal county seats."[18]

Even in the early editions of the work, there were names that seemed somehow out of place among all the noblemen and women, the generals and bishops and MPs who made up Adam Bisset Thom's Upper Ten Thousand. Take Sir William George Armstrong, for example. Apart from his knighthood, sixty-five-year-old Armstrong possessed none of the usual qualifications for entry—he had no hereditary title, no pedigree, no landed estate, no high political office. He was a solicitor turned engineer—an industrialist who in the 1850s had invented a rifled breech-loading artillery piece known as the Armstrong gun, with a factory, the Elswick Ordnance Company, in his home city of Newcastle upon Tyne.

Take a closer look at the Upper Ten Thousand list, and one can see a few more intruders scattered around its pages, and their numbers grew with each new edition: William McEwan, described simply as "a brewer"; Sir Richard Biddulph Martin, "a banker in London"; Abel Buckley, "a cotton manufacturer at Ashton-under-Lyne."[19]

Armstrong, McEwan, and the others were shining examples of a new—or newish—class of country house owners, men who had earned their own fortunes in trade or manufacturing; and the orthodox narrative is that having earned it, they set about acquiring a country mansion and estate of their own on which to spend it—although the truth was more complicated than that. William McEwan bought a country house not for himself but for his daughter, Mrs Ronald Greville, and lived with her at Polesden Lacey in Surrey until his death in 1913. Abel Buckley inherited two country houses from uncles, Ryecroft Hall in Lancashire and Galtee Castle in County Cork. The banker Richard Martin already had an ancestral seat: Overbury Court in Worcestershire, a handsome house acquired in 1723 by a banking forebear, rebuilt in 1739, and remodelled by Richard Norman Shaw at the end of the nineteenth century and again by Ernest Newton at the beginning of the twentieth.

William Armstrong fit the mould more happily. The son of a Newcastle corn merchant and town councillor, he trained as a lawyer before embarking on the career as an engineer and inventor which was to make his fortune. In 1835 he married Margaret Ramshaw, daughter of a County Durham builder and engineer, and the couple set up home in a new house, Jesmond Dene, which stood, rather confusingly, in the Newcastle neighbourhood of Jesmond Dene. The Armstrongs were generous with their home, opening the grounds to everything from the local floral and horticultural society's annual show of produce to grand civic occasions. They entertained on a big scale, too, but this also tended to be directed towards civic or philanthropic ends. In the summer of 1864, for example, the Armstrongs hosted a grand dinner for about 150 visiting members of the Royal Agricultural Society in a "banqueting hall" they had built two years earlier. The *Newcastle Journal* noted approvingly that the "*cuisine* was *a la Francaise*, and in the newest *mode*," and the guests were entertained between the many toasts by the Newcastle Corporation organist and members of Durham Cathedral Choir, whose repertoire ranged from William Byrd to a glee titled "Life's a Bumper."[20]

By then Armstrong, who was in his midfifties and who had been knighted in 1859 for his services to the British armaments industry, had begun to withdraw from the management of his industrial empire. In 1863, on a visit to Rothbury and the Debdon valley, where he had spent many happy childhood holidays—his earliest memories consisted of paddling in the river there, gathering pebbles on its gravel beds, and climbing amongst the rocks of the Crag—he decided to build a small shooting and fishing lodge. His first purchase, in November of that year, consisted of no more than twenty acres, but by systematically acquiring more and more land as it became available, he eventually owned 1,729 acres of pleasure grounds and twenty or so farms.

Armstrong's decision to extend this lodge, which he called Cragside House and which would eventually become one of the greatest of all Victorian country houses, came about in rather a roundabout way. In 1869 he bought a history painting by John Callcott Horsley to hang in the Banqueting Hall at Jesmond Dene. *Prince Hal Taking the Crown from His Father's Bedside* was enormous—twelve feet high—and, realising it wouldn't fit, Armstrong invited Richard

Norman Shaw to design an extension to the hall. Shaw had remodelled Horsley's early Georgian house, Willesley in Kent, in his distinctive Old English style some five years earlier, and it was probably Horsley who suggested the young architect.[21]

While Shaw was staying with the Armstrongs to discuss the project, Sir William mentioned that he was also thinking of extending the lodge at Rothbury for his retirement. That was enough for Shaw: according to legend, he sketched out the entire plan of Cragside over a weekend, while the other guests were out shooting, and presented it to Armstrong complete. (Shaw was a fast worker. There is another story that when he went to out to dinner, he wore a dress shirt with extra-long cuffs. If he found himself sitting next to a rich man in need of a new country house—whether that rich man realised it or not—he would sketch the design on a cuff, and by the time the gentlemen joined the ladies, he would have a new client.)

In any event, Shaw was given the commission, and in three stages between 1869 and 1884 he more than trebled the size of Armstrong's original lodge. The first phase, an extension to the northwest, consisted of an inner hall, dining room, and library, with a suite of hot and cold baths beneath and bedrooms above. But by 1872, when these works were nearing completion, Armstrong had grown more ambitious. So Shaw created a new east-west wing to the south of the main block, containing a new staircase, a long gallery (which originally served as a museum for Armstrong's collection of geological and scientific specimens), and the Gilnockie Tower, the design of which was based on the stronghold of John Armstrong of Gilnockie, a border raider and supposed ancestor who was hanged by James V of Scotland in 1530. Shaw also raised the tower of the original house and crowned it with a half-timbered gable. His last set of designs, carried out from 1883 to 1885, involved the building of yet another wing, this time on a roughly north-south axis and to the east of the Gilnockie Tower.

This wing housed a large top-lit drawing room which also served as a gallery for the display of Armstrong's paintings.

To weld the little 1863 house and the additions, spanning more than fifteen years, into a unified whole would have been well-nigh impossible. But much of the magic of Cragside stems from just this lack of cohesion. Gables jostle with crenellations; towers strive to outreach tall Tudor chimney stacks; cavernous Gothic arches compete with mullioned bay windows; and half timbering stands side by side with dressed ashlar and rough stonework.

At first sight, these juxtapositions create a feeling that Cragside gradually evolved over centuries rather than years. But this soon fades: if anything, the building's irregularities owe more to Georgian theories of picturesque beauty than to the full-blown historicism of the Victorian Gothicists. This is the key to the success of the house. Against all odds, Cragside succeeds precisely because all of those periods, all of those styles, have been ransacked and then ruthlessly subordinated to visual impact, to spectacle and excitement.

Given this additive building history, one might expect that the internal planning of Cragside would be equally complex and challenging. And so it is, although here the variety and irregularity which produce such a powerful effect in the exterior can on occasion feel confused and tiresome. The dark, narrow corridor which originally formed the spine of the 1863 house seems out of keeping with the scale of the new Cragside. And the route from the drawing room to the dining room, admittedly a feature that Victorian architects tended to make as impressive as possible, is nearly sixty yards in length. As Armstrong's guests, who included the Prince and Princess of Wales and an impressive array of foreign potentates eager to purchase warships and weaponry—the king of Siam, the shah of Persia, the crown prince of Afghanistan—went down to dinner, negotiating the gallery, six flights of stairs, and a long passageway, one suspects that admiration of the grandeur of their host's new house must have been tempered by the prospect of the return journey.

But while the circulation spaces at Cragside may seem to ramble interminably, the individual interiors are among some of the finest of the period in Britain. The main living room was the library—an elegant high-art interior, with Morris and Company stained glass, light oak panelling, and a beautiful beamed and coffered ceiling with inset walnut panels and carved bosses by James Forsyth, one of Shaw's favourite craftsmen. Here, unlike the later interiors—the library belongs to Shaw's first set of alterations and was completed in 1872—the architect seems to have either selected or designed many of the furnishings. Chief among these is a set of ebonised mahogany Queen Anne chairs made by Gillow, with cane seats and leather backs stamped with a pomegranate motif.

Next door to the library is the dining room—and when Armstrong's guests finally did arrive here, their surroundings, as well as the meal, must have made the journey seem worthwhile. Heavy but somehow still intimate, it is the quintessential Old English interior, a quaint farmhouse parlour refined and stylised and enlarged until it met the requirements of a great Victorian industrialist, while still retaining an air of comfortable old-world domesticity. Ceiling and walls are panelled in light oak, with carvings of flowers, birds, and animals by Forsyth, who may also have been responsible for the richly carved stone inglenook, a feature which, with its connotations of cosy yeomen homesteads, was to become a commonplace feature of Arts and Crafts and Old English country houses.

Compare that dining room with the other great set-piece interior at Cragside, the drawing room, begun in 1883 and finished just in time for a visit from the Prince and Princess of Wales in August 1884. During the twelve years which separate the two rooms, Shaw moved away from the atmospheric intimacy of his Old English work and towards a more self-indulgent opulence, an ostentation symbolised in the Cragside drawing room by the colossal Renaissance marble chimneypiece designed by his chief assistant, W. R. Lethaby. Said to weigh ten tons and smothered in elaborate carving, this brilliant but cold monument surmounts another inglenook. But, in contrast with the one in the dining room, this one is lined with fine marble, and its settles are covered in red leather. It expresses wealth rather than welcome, power rather than peace.

The drawing room was Richard Norman Shaw's last job at Cragside. Further work—competent but lacking Shaw's flair—was carried out in the 1890s by the Gloucester architect Frederick Waller, who added a billiard room to the east of the drawing room wing. There was no smoking room in the house, and according to a 1901 article in *The Onlooker*, before the billiard room was added it was not unusual to see "a row of Japanese or other foreign naval officers, in charge of some war vessel building at the famous Elswick works, sitting in a row on the low wall outside the front door, puffing away for all they were worth."[22]

Lord Armstrong of Cragside, as he now was, having been raised to the peerage in 1887, gave Jesmond Dene and its Banqueting Hall to the people of Newcastle in 1884, having already presented them with ninety-three acres of gardens which formed the nucleus of a public park named after him. In 1893 Lady Armstrong died, and as a memorial to her he bought and began to restore the twelfth-century Bamburgh Castle, using the Cumberland architect Charles John Ferguson. Armstrong intended Bamburgh as a convalescent home, but he died in 1900, before the work was completed.

The Victorian nouveau riche outsider came in many forms. Armstrong's heart was in the Northeast rather than London, and his values were essentially bourgeois. Far from being an intruder, eager to break into Society, he was content to let Society come to him. Cragside, his kindest monument, is a softly lyrical building, evoking the past but not laying claim to it, and it is revealing that in the most characteristic portrait of him, by Henry Hetherington Emmerson, he sits reading a newspaper in the dining room inglenook at Cragside, his two dogs at his carpet-slippered feet and a quintessentially domestic inscription over the inglenook fireplace prominently displayed: "East or West, Hame's Best." It would be hard to imagine the Duke of Portland choosing to be memorialised in such an informal fashion.

TWO

MONEYBAGS

THE BRASH, VULGAR captain of industry, whether brewer or banker or cotton lord, was a stock figure of fun in novels and plays, an inept social upstart with no ancient responsibilities, no traditions to keep up. His own servants despised him as one of the jumped-up rich. Newspapers and magazines used him (and her, because his brash, vulgar, and socially ambitious wife was also a target) as fodder for their lamentations about all that was wrong with modern society. Eton, it was said in the 1890s, "is a school painfully infected with nouveaux riches whose fathers' and grandfathers' names are not to be found on the lists of that or indeed any other public school." They were laughed at for overtipping, since "the best people are not the people who give the best tips," and for giving their brand-new country houses names like "Court" or "Grange" or "Abbey" or "Priory," names "smacking of feudalism and a stirring historic past." They were pitied because they "have not had time to be educated to the use of wealth." They were condemned for their want of taste and their want of breeding—

criticisms which were often bound up with an unconcealed and unpleasant disdain for Jews and foreigners, exemplified by the pushy upstart who was, in the words of one commentator, "without one grain of culture," but "who [sought] to thrust himself forward by the mere force of his money-bags."[1]

"Sometimes," wrote Augustus Jessopp in 1890,

> the newcomers are a grievous infliction. Town-bred folk who emerge from the back streets and have amassed money by a new hair-wash or an improvement in stocking-plaster. Such as these are out of harmony with their temporary surroundings: they giggle in the faces of the farmers' daughters, ridicule the speech and manners of the labourers and their wives, and grumble at everything. . . . They introduce a vulgarity of tone quite indescribable.[2]

Jessopp, the rector of a rural parish in Norfolk, was scathing in his condemnation of the incomer, the Burton brewer or the Birmingham button manufacturer who blundered into the rural idyll and wrecked it. Nor was it just the vulgarity that grated: Jessopp was convinced that these intruders, these "come-and-go people who hire the country houses which their owners are compelled to let," upset the natural order of things.[3] Their footmen and ladies' maids gave themselves airs and made the rustics jealous. When word got round that the newcomers were engaging in antics up at the hall, such as daring to play tennis on Sunday afternoons, the old villagers felt unsettled, while the youngsters began to think that if the hall could do it, why couldn't they? And worst of all, the puritans in the community began to think like socialists, looking forward to the day when the rich got their just deserts.

That was a caricature, of course. But it was one which played to the fears of landed society, high and low. In his 1906 satire *The Country Life*, T. W. H. Crosland complained that the countryside was plagued by "fat Jews, wealthy brewers, swagger Members of Parliament, record breakers, company promoters, and their ill-bred wives, sisters, cousins and aunts."[4] Antisemitism, snobbery, and reactionary values went hand in hand.

Yet there were more considered responses to the nouveaux riches' invasion of the countryside. Thomas Hardy's "Architectural Masks" is one notable example:

> *There is a house with ivied walls,*
> *And mullioned windows worn and old,*
> *And the long dwellers in those halls*
> *Have souls that know but sordid calls,*
> *And dote on gold.*
>
> *In a blazing brick and plated show*
> *Not far away a "villa" gleams,*
> *And here a family few may know,*
> *With book and pencil, viol and bow,*
> *Lead inner lives of dreams.*
>
> *The philosophic passers say,*
> *"See that old mansion mossed and fair,*
> *Poetic souls therein are they:*
> *And O that gaudy box! Away,*
> *You vulgar people there."*

Less eloquent but just as telling was an *Illustrated London News* article of October 1882, "Le Nouveau Riche," which rejected the stereotype of the "vulgar obstreperous nabob of farces and comedies" in favour of a much more sympathetic picture of the type.[5] Its fictitious subject, "Mr. Capper," was a builder who had grown rich, "partly the result of enterprise guided by great shrewdness, partly of sheer good luck." His income "would have made a handsome fortune for an English Duke, or a Continental King." Yet there was nothing vulgar or brash about him. He was a quiet man who tended to avoid Society because he preferred his own company.

Everything about him spoke of quiet good taste, and that was never as clear as when it came to buying a country house. He brought in an architect to modernise it "in accordance with the last mandates of science and art." His wife "found one of the queens of fashion very ready to help her furnish it with quiet and convenient splendour." A distinguished academic chose the books to go into his library; a hard-up peer who understood these things filled his stable and his wine cellar. His head gardener came from Chatsworth; his head groom from Newmarket: and his coachmen had learned their trade in the royal stables.[6]

This rehabilitated, salt-of-the-earth member of the nouveaux riches still required the advice and support of his betters; but the implication was that quiet good sense and the ability to ask for advice—and to take it—were qualities to be sought after, and they could be found in the country houses of the nouveaux riches.

There was certainly an increase in the numbers of country houses that were being sold or, more often, let furnished around the turn of the century. By 1900, dozens of them were coming onto the market every week, sometimes with substantial estates, sometimes not. "A beautiful English home, one of the principal seats in the Midland Counties, suitable for a wealthy gentleman, fond of sport, to be let, furnished, for a term of years," ran a typical advertisement from June of that year for a mansion with thirty bedrooms "in the Tudor style," with its own private racecourse, shooting on over four thousand acres, and excellent hunting in the district. For 500 guineas a year you could have yourself a "fine old country house" with twenty-five bedrooms and three thousand acres of shooting. For 550 guineas, you could rent three thousand acres of excellent shooting and fishing in the hunting country of Northamptonshire, together with stabling for fifteen horses, two miles of river frontage, and a "beautiful old Country Seat," furnished and containing "billiard room, handsome ballroom, saloon or music room, drawing room, dining room, library, conservatory, about 25 bed and dressing rooms." (Don't you love that "about"? It is as if there were so many that the agent kept losing count.)[7]

Many of these advertisements emphasised the sporting potential of the estate: the size of the stables; the proximity to hunts ("hunting with four packs"); the fact that there were golf links nearby. Architectural merits tended to be played down, although there were exceptions. An advertisement announcing the sale of the medieval Priory in Orpington, Kent, was addressed to "Antiquarians and Others" and waxed lyrical about this "charming old Family Mansion, forming a really beautiful and genuine specimen of the early English domestic architecture." That was a rarity: the presence of modern conveniences, electric lighting, and decent plumbing was usually seen as a more telling selling point. "Sanitation said to be perfect" ran one not entirely convincing example.[8]

"The story of the owner and creator of the splendid mansion and gardens of Impney is typical of much that is best in this country," declared *Country Life* in 1901.[9] That owner was John Corbett, a real-life Mr Capper, a quiet, genial man with a wide forehead, inquiring eyes, and the kind of rags-to-riches story which the Victorians loved. Having joined his father, a Shropshire farmer with a fleet of canal boats, as a young man, John saw that the railways were going to be the death of canal traffic. In 1852 the family business was sold and John turned his attention to the salt industry, buying the Stoke Prior Salt Works in

Worcestershire and turning it into a huge and very lucrative business. In 1869 he began building a new country house, Impney Hall, on the outskirts of Droitwich in Worcestershire for his wife Anna and their five children. It was completed in 1875.

The French origins of Impney Hall—it did not acquire the name by which it is known today, Chateau Impney, until the 1940s, when it was being operated as a bar and restaurant—give it an affinity with those houses we shall look at in chapter 6, Oldway and Waddesdon and Halton, but the story of its building fits here. The explanation usually given for Corbett's choice of style, an ornate and high-roofed Louis XIII, is that his wife was French and he did it to please her. Neither is true: she was an O'Meara from County Tipperary, although she was living in Paris in 1855 when John met her, the daughter of a minor Irish diplomat; and as we shall see, by the late 1860s pleasing his wife was low on John's list of priorities. Another explanation is that Corbett, a Liberal, was locked in political battle with his Conservative rival for the constituency, Sir John Pakington, whose own seat, Westwood, had a touch of France about it, having been built in the early seventeenth century as a homage to the Château de Madrid near Paris.

Whatever the reason, Corbett wanted a French Renaissance palace, designed by a French architect. His in-laws suggested the Paris-based Auguste Tronquois, whose work included a number of town houses, at least one of which, a mansion on the rue Murillo in the eighth arrondissement, was in a neo–Louis XIII style. Tronquois wasn't prepared to supervise the building work himself; that task was handed over to an Englishman, Richard Phené Spiers, who had studied at the École des Beaux-Arts between 1858 and 1861.

No expense was spared on the new house. Corbett's biographers reckoned that as many as three thousand people were employed on the building and that the total cost was around £200,000.[10] Craftsmen were brought in from Europe to execute the internal plasterwork; there was carved oak and stained glass and gilt cherubs; and the doors to the main ground-floor reception rooms were decorated with phrases of music from Mendelssohn's "Spring Song." The ceiling of Corbett's octagonal study was filled with allusions to the seven sciences. One particularly nice feature was the provision of cat runs in the cavity walls and behind the wainscots, with cat flaps in the skirting—a precaution against mice and rats.

With its spiky turrets and steeply pitched roofs, Impney still looks remarkable in the twenty-first century. "It looks what it is," said *Country Life* at the time of its construction, "a magnificently built palace, intended to look splendid, and succeeding in that object."[11] And if the writer's prediction, that in three hundred years' time Impney would be as much admired as that Elizabethan masterpiece Wollaton Hall, is a little wide of the mark, the house is still a delight. Corbett also had another country house and estate, the Georgian Ynysymaengwyn in Merionethshire, which he bought in 1878, perhaps because it had once belonged to the Corbet family (with one "t") and he believed, wrongly as it happened, that he was resurrecting an old family connection.

But Impney was not what the people of Droitwich first thought of when John Corbett's name was mentioned. He was much better known for bringing employment to the district with his saltworks, for introducing better working conditions, and for distributing largesse on an impressive scale.

One Tuesday afternoon in April 1879, for example, with church bells ringing and flags flying all over the town, John Corbett presided over the opening of Salters Hall in Droitwich. Intended as a focus for the whole town and designed in a half-timbered style to fit with the older surrounding buildings, it was a meeting place, a venue for dances and concerts, and an opportunity to practise rational recreation, complete with a library and a reading room.

And it was built entirely at Corbett's expense. The official opening was a civic occasion, and it attracted the crowds: the mayor, Frank Holyoake, who gave the first of many speeches, apologised for his nervous delivery on the grounds that he had never before had to address "such a vast assembly"—there were more than 1,500 people in the hall. He then proposed a motion "that the thanks of this assemblage, and the thanks of the whole town and trade, be given to Mr Corbett for his extreme kindness and liberality in erecting this most magnificent hall." Everyone gave three cheers, and Corbett, whose coat of arms was placed over the stage as a reminder of his munificence, responded with a short speech in which he said that he thought it "the duty of every man, according to his means and position, to endeavour to do some amount of good in his day and generation."[12] The speeches were followed by a concert given by the Worcester Vocal Union, and afterwards Corbett, the mayor, and the performers went next door for supper in the Raven Hotel, which Corbett had recently bought.

He remodelled the Raven and built two more hotels in the town, the Worcestershire and the Royal. All three were meant to service another of his schemes, turning the town into a popular health spa. In 1882 he bought Droitwich's old saline baths, rebuilt them, and opened them as St Andrew's Brine Baths. Advertisements declared that they were "now rendered more effectual than ever by the recent erection of Baths on the most scientific principles, including Massage, Douche, Needle, Vapour, and Swimming Baths."[13] He gave land for a new railway station and paid for the construction of two new wide roads. They were named Corbett Road and Corbett Avenue.

These were sound business ventures. (When Corbett's will was read, the people of Droitwich were upset to discover that although he had given them to understand he was donating Salters Hall to the town, he had actually hung on to it and bequeathed it to his trustees.) But he also lived up to his desire to "do some amount of good in his day and generation." He gave the gardens surrounding his brine baths to the town as a public park. There were almshouses for twelve "decayed salt workers" or their widows in the village of Wychbold, a couple of miles northeast of Impney, with Corbett ravens perched in every half-timbered gable, and an eighteen-bed hospital in Stourbridge "for the treatment and relief in sickness or accident of poor persons," together with a £10,000 endowment.[14] As president of Bromsgrove Cottage Hospital, Corbett laid the foundation stone and footed a good part of the bill; he contributed £4,500 to the restoration of the church of St Michael in Stoke Prior, where his saltworks were situated, and £2,500 towards the repair of St Michael, Brierley Hill, where his parents were buried. In Towyn on the North Wales coast, he laid out an esplanade, laid on a water supply, founded a school, and built a hotel, the Corbett Arms.

There was a strong tradition of philanthropy among Victorians who had come up through trade. Michael Thomas Bass, besides being an immensely rich brewer with a substantial country house, Rangemore Hall in Staffordshire, where the gardens and conservatories by Joseph Paxton were described by a contemporary as "a veritable paradise," was a generous donor to civic causes, contributing a hefty £30,000 to the building of Derby Public Library.[15] (In a marvellous piece of theatre, a woman clutching her baby dashed out of the crowd at the official opening of the library in 1879, crying, "God bless you, Mr Bass. May you live to be a hundred years old.") In Scotland, William McEwan built a graduation hall for Edinburgh University at a cost of £115,000 plus £6,500 a year for maintenance. His generosity was recognised in 1897 at the opening of the new hall, which was named after him: he was given an honorary doctorate and the freedom of the city of Edinburgh. And in Ireland, the Guinness family gave fabulous sums to their chosen charities. Their support for the restoration of St Patrick's Cathedral in Dublin cost them a quarter of a million pounds, around £100,000 coming from Arthur Guinness, who stepped back from the day-to-day running of the family firm in 1876 to focus on his Ashford Castle estate in County Galway but who also laid out St Stephen's Green in Dublin as a public park and built a new wing at the Coombe Lying-In Hospital in the city. Arthur's brother Edward famously contributed vast sums for the creation of decent housing for workers in London and Dublin, and by the end of his life he was reckoned to have dispensed well over £1.2 million to charitable works.

Philanthropy comes in many forms. On a scale which boasts a donation to the local Sunday school at one end and the charitable works of the Corbetts and Guinnesses of this world at the other, it is notoriously hard to isolate motives. Edward Guinness let it be known to the government in London that he "certainly [did] look forward to a peerage as a natural object of his ambition," and he achieved that object in spades, receiving a baronetcy in 1885 and being made Lord Iveagh in 1891, Viscount Iveagh in 1905, and Earl of Iveagh in 1919.[16] Michael Thomas Bass didn't receive a peerage, although his son did; William McEwan turned one down. Were such men moved by simple altruism? A sense of social responsibility? A hunger for fame and a title? All three, perhaps, at different times and for different men. But in Corbett's case there may have been something else: a drive to lose himself in his good works, a determination to leave a legacy which didn't involve his family.

When Corbett and his wife Anna moved into Impney Hall in 1875, they had two sons and three daughters, the youngest of whom was nine years old. Anna was forty-four, John was fifty-eight, and if family stories are correct, their physical relationship was virtually nonexistent.

So when, in the spring of the following year, Corbett realised that his wife was pregnant, it came as something of a shock. And his surprise was compounded by reports from the servants that Anna's priest was a frequent visitor to the house. John was a firm if conventional Anglican, Anna was a practising Roman Catholic, and the couple's religious differences had been a bone of contention for most of their married life. They took the not-unusual step of agreeing that the boys would be brought up as Anglicans and the girls as Catholics.

In spite of Anna's denials, Corbett leaped to the conclusion that the baby was the priest's bastard. He refused to have anything to do with his wife or the child, a girl named Clare; and with the paint scarcely dry on their fabulous new chateau, the couple agreed to keep out of each other's way, although they maintained a civilised appearance of domestic harmony in public. That lasted only until 1879, when Anna and her daughters moved to Ynysymaengwyn. They kept up a substantial household which, in 1881, included the two Corbett boys, who sided with their mother. There was a Swiss governess for Clare, a lady's maid, a cook, four maids, a footman, and a coachman. Corbett, on the other hand, sat brooding in his enormous French palace with just a married couple as butler and general servant, and maid. The couple's four-year-old daughter lived in, an unusual arrangement for the time.

In August 1884 Corbett's lawyers drew up a legal deed of separation, according to which, because of their unhappy differences, the couple agreed to live separately and apart from each other. Anna had to leave Ynysymaengwyn and could not live within forty miles of either of Corbett's country houses or of his London residence in Mayfair. In return, he agreed to pay her £1,100 a year, plus a one-off payment of £1,000 to enable her to set up her own household. The deed stipulated that if Anna ever tried to have her conjugal rights restored or tried to persuade John to live with her, the £1,100 annuity would stop. For a while she drifted from one seaside town to another—Folkestone, Ilfracombe—before settling at Fowey in Cornwall.

John Corbett continued to live at Impney Hall. By the time of the 1901 census his household had expanded to a more normal size. In addition to two attendant sick nurses, he employed a butler, a cook, two housemaids, a footman and a pantry boy, and a "lady house keeper," Annie Dungey. The census was taken on March 31. Three weeks later he died, at Impney Hall, and the obituarists devoted pages to his memory. "He was exceedingly generous," said one.[17] Not a bad epitaph.

THREE

KINGS OF THE GILDED AGE

W E TOOK OUR piper with us when we returned to New York," recalled Andrew Carnegie in his autobiography.[1]

Carnegie's Scottishness was dear to him. Born in Dunfermline in 1835, the son of a handloom weaver, he and his family emigrated to America in 1848. While still a young man, he began to make astute investments in oil, railways, the telegraph, and, most famously, steel. Those investments made him very rich indeed, and when in 1901 the Carnegie Steel Company merged with J. P. Morgan's Federal Steel and nine other companies, Andrew Carnegie walked away from the deal with $225 million. He was sixty-six, with a wife, Louise, who was twenty-two years younger than him, and a five-year-old daughter. Not particularly interested in paintings or the decorative arts, he turned in earnest to the private philanthropy for which he is still known today.

But he also turned to his Scottish roots. The Carnegies had honeymooned in Scotland in 1887, renting Kilgraston, a solid neoclassical

45

country house in Perthshire built around 1800. And there Louise, who had been born and raised in New York, fell in love with Scotland, to Andrew's delight. "She soon became more Scotch than I," he wrote. "All this was fulfilling my fondest dreams."[2]

The honeymoon was quite a social affair: that summer they entertained Robert Browning, Lord and Lady Rosebery, the author Edwin Arnold, and the Gladstones. (Mary Gladstone had first met Andrew Carnegie in London five years earlier, calling him "a Scotch American rolling in gold"; a fortnight later he sent her a thousand pounds for one of her good causes, the Royal College of Music.) John Hay, the American diplomat (and future secretary of state under William McKinley and Teddy Roosevelt) who joined a sixteen-strong house party at Kilgraston for a few days that August, reported to journalist Henry Brooks Adams that "Carnegie likes it [here] so well he is going to do it every summer and is looking at all the great estates in the county with a view of renting or purchasing." The newlyweds found their piper, John Macpherson, and the following year they began a regular pattern of spending every summer in Scotland, renting Cluny Castle in Inverness-shire, a playful Scotch Baronial concoction built in 1805.[3]

Louise, in particular, loved Cluny. "I just revel in it," she wrote to her mother.[4] It was more homely and comfortable than Kilgraston, and it was surrounded by spectacular scenery—brooks and waterfalls and heather-covered mountains. Every morning at eight their piper woke them and their many houseguests; every evening at seven he piped them in to dinner; and afterwards he played while the company danced Highland flings on the lawn in front of the house.

The Carnegies' only child, a daughter named Margaret, was born in 1897, and Louise decided it was time for them to have a Scottish country house of their own, instead of being obliged to move in and out on certain dates. That summer she tried to persuade the Macphersons, owners of Cluny, to sell, but negotiations faltered after Mr

Macpherson explained that he was soon to be married and he and his bride intended to take up residence. So while Louise spent one last summer at Cluny with their baby, Andrew went house-hunting in the northern Highlands.

He found Skibo, a run-down estate of twenty-two thousand acres on the banks of the Dornoch Firth, forty miles north of Inverness. Skibo came with a twenty-five-year-old Gothic Revival house that was too small for the Carnegies' entertaining needs. The owner, Evan Sutherland-Walker, had bankrupted himself in a series of lawsuits intended to assert his entirely fictitious feudal rights over his neighbours, and the estate was in the hands of court-appointed trustees. There was also a collection of decrepit outbuildings, an entire village, and several hundred crofters and labourers. Bringing the place up to scratch would be an enormous and enormously expensive project; and the Carnegies decided to rent Skibo for a year with an option to buy while they pondered whether or not it was right for them. Andrew's health was poor that year, and instead of returning to the United States as they usually did, they took a villa in Cannes for the winter.

They moved into Skibo Castle in the summer of 1898 and promptly fell in love with the place. Andrew bought it for £85,000 and they set about enlarging the house and remodelling its surroundings. Their architects were the Inverness firm of Alexander Ross and Robert John Macbeth, better known for churches, schools, and public buildings than for high-status country houses, and the main contractors were Messrs D. & J. Milligan of Ayr, who quoted a contract price of £50,000 for the building work. Working closely with Louise Carnegie, and keeping Evan Sutherland-Walker's house as the core of the new building (and installing a pipe organ in his entrance hall), they added a south range containing a drawing room with a mahogany dado and, above it, panels of rose-coloured silk; Louise's boudoir; a great library; and, next to it, Andrew's study and his secretary's office. A new servants' wing was built to the north, and to the west, there was a breakfast room and a formal dining room panelled in carved oak. The upper floors were filled with bedroom suites.

In the grounds, there were new lodges, an electric plant, a private telephone exchange, and a glass-roofed marble swimming pool which doubled as a ballroom, where guests could dance to the music of "Mrs Logan's dance band from Inverness" beneath huge arc lamps.[5] The Carnegies created a nine-hole golf course and two new lochs, one stocked with trout and the other with a salmon ladder. Landscape architect Thomas Mawson was brought in to lay out new terrace gardens, and the various outbuildings and tenants' cottages were modernised. It was said that the Carnegies' henhouse was better equipped than any of the private houses in the neighbourhood, because, unlike them, it had electric light.

Most of this work was completed by the summer of 1902, when the Carnegies arrived to take possession of their new home. The local population turned out in force (and in a cold driving rain) to welcome their new laird. Several hundred workmen, tenants, and estate workers gathered at the entrance from the public road to the newly laid-out avenue to the house, and they erected a floral arch with the Union Jack and the Stars and Stripes flying from it and the inscription "Welcome home to Skibo." There were speeches, shorter than normal on account of the bad weather, from the contractor and from Andrew Carnegie, who delivered his from the shelter of his closed carriage. A brass band from Dornoch, the nearest town, competed with a pipe band made up of workers on the estate, and when the speeches were over the crowd cheered, the horses were unyoked, and, in a traditional gesture of welcome, the Carnegies' carriage was dragged by the men of the estate all the way to the door of the castle, a distance of some two miles.

There is no doubt that the new laird of Skibo and his family were made welcome. They were a pleasant change from Carnegie's litigious and difficult predecessor, and they offered the prospect of employment in what was an economically depressed area. Louise had eighty-five servants in her household, and then there were the estate workers, the labourers and builders and landscapers. In any case, why would the local people *not* welcome an impossibly rich philanthropist with a reputation for doling out vast sums on any cause which seemed good to him?

There was something undeniably theatrical about life at Skibo. The Carnegies had a huge carved oak overmantel made for the Great Hall by the West Steam Joinery Works of Aberdeen: seven feet six inches wide by five feet high, it had a frieze carved with the motto "Hame is hame, but a Heilan Hame is Mair than Hame." One bedroom suite was named for Sigurd, a Viking warlord who was said to lie buried at Skibo. Another, the Montrose Room, commemorated the moment in 1650 when the royalist Marquess of Montrose was held prisoner at Skibo on his way to be hanged at Edinburgh. It was designed "in the Elizabethan style, which is entirely of wainscot, the ceiling, frieze, cornice and walls being most elaborately and beautifully carved in high relief." The Carnegies found another piper, Angus Macpherson, brother of John, who doubled as groom of the chambers and court jester, dancing Highland flings and sword dances for the Carnegies' houseguests. "This gave great pleasure to the American guests," Macpherson recalled, "and Mr Carnegie in his own kindly way never forgot to say something nice about the performer." Every morning at eight o'clock precisely guests were awakened by Macpherson, in full Highland dress, playing his bagpipes on the terrace.* They ate their kippers to the sound of Wagner bashed out on the pipe organ in the hall—Louise's large staff included an organist.[6]

---

* Skibo's guests were lucky. At Glen Tanar, the Aberdeenshire country house belonging to Manchester MP Sir William Cunliffe Brooks, the piper started at seven. Thomas Mawson, who stayed there in the 1890s, recalled that the wailing began as the piper left his cottage and got steadily louder, until by five minutes past "he was going the rounds of the house, piping as if to wake the dead." Mawson, *English Landscape Architect*, 47.

And there always *were* guests. Andrew Carnegie entertained constantly and relentlessly, rather to Louise's despair. "The castle is like a luxurious hotel," wrote Woodrow Wilson, who was staying there in the summer of 1908. "Some 20 or 25 persons sit down to every meal."[7] There were local dignitaries and relatives of Andrew's mixing with statesmen and celebrities, both British and American. Margaret Carnegie later remembered sitting on Rudyard Kipling's knee while he told her his "just-so stories." The Liberal statesman John Morley was an old friend and a frequent visitor. Whitelaw Reid, the American ambassador, was happy to make the six-hundred-mile trek from London to spend a few days at Skibo. So was David Lloyd George.

The African American educator Booker T. Washington spent three days at Skibo, which he called "three of the most interesting and restful days I have ever had." A novelty in the Scottish Highlands, which were not noted for their ethnic diversity, he spent his time discussing race relations with Morley, who was then secretary of state for India. "What he said about the matter was the more interesting," said Washington, "because he was able to draw parallels between racial conditions . . . between the Indians in India and the Negroes in the United States."[8]

One can't help wondering whether it was the Carnegies who were socially accepted at Skibo or just their money. One thinks of Mary Gladstone and her slighting reference to the "Scotch American rolling in gold." And while Andrew Carnegie was undoubtedly a good, kind man, he was always hovering on the edge of buffoonery, lacking that stiff British sense of what was appropriate and what was not. One afternoon in October 1902 the Carnegies' housekeeper got a message from the Duke of Sutherland at Dunrobin, fourteen miles away, to warn them that Edward VII was on his way over, having heard about the Carnegies' transformation of Skibo and being keen to see the results for himself. There was a general panic: Macpherson struggled into his Highland costume, and the organist, who had been in the swimming pool when the news broke, barely had time to dress and belt out "God Save the King" on the organ in the hall as Edward arrived. There is a story, which I rather hope is true, that a slightly flustered Carnegie received the king in his library and by way of welcome read to him "Usland to England," a poem by the eccentric American poet Joaquin Miller. It was, in its naked hostility towards the British, rather an odd choice, ending with these lines:

> *And if your king, Edward the Fat,*
> *Should signify he don't like that,*
> *Why, we'll annex old England too—*
> *We yearn for islands, doan-cher-knew!*

Carnegie paused after the words "Edward the Fat" and said, "That's you, sir!" The king, always sensitive about his weight, was not amused. It was left to the Carnegies' five-year-old daughter Margaret to restore Anglo-American relations. She presented the king with a single rose and said without ceremony, "Here. This is for you." Then she handed him another, saying, "Give this to the queen when you get home."[9]

There were sneers. The satirist T. H. S. Escott wrote of

Norfolk suits, of patterns loud enough to be heard a good league into the Atlantic, shooting-coats of plaid tweed, chequered on so large a scale as to do duty for chess-boards, coaching attire that might have taken away the elder Weller's breath, with mother-of-pearl buttons the size of saucers . . . These articles are in season the outward and visible signs of the pursuits dear to the lord of Skibo Castle.[10]

But perhaps the most telling story came from the pen of the impeccably correct courtier Almeric FitzRoy, who noted in his diary that one day in 1911, when John Morley was staying at Skibo, Morley took his detective down to see Carnegie's glass and marble swimming pool and asked him what he thought. "Well sir," said the detective, "it seems to me to savour of the *parvenoo*." "Impudent fellow!" exclaimed Morley—while privately agreeing with him.[11]

"There are many old families," said Lady Dorothy Nevill, "which, both in mind and pocket, have been completely revivified by prudent marriages with American brides." The notion of the bartered bride as the reluctant saviour of landed society around the turn of the century has become embedded in British and American social history, cropping up everywhere from Consuelo Vanderbilt's 1952 autobiography, *The Glitter and the Gold*, in which she gave a rather self-serving account of her disastrous marriage to the 9th Duke of Marlborough in 1895, to the television series *Downton Abbey*, whose Cora, Countess of Grantham, is heiress to the fortune of her father, a Cincinnati dry-goods millionaire. There was certainly a spate of aristocratic and gentry Anglo-American marriages between 1870 and 1914: 134 American women married into the peerage; 129 married baronets or their heirs; and 176 married into what might loosely be termed the landed gentry.[12] The phenomenon was commented on at the time: "The House of Lords is getting a good many American mothers," noted the *Times*, while *Punch* declared unkindly that

> 'Tis her fortune, not her face,
> That captivates the British peer.[13]

There was a flood of popular novels with titles like *Transplanted Daughters*, *American Wives and English Husbands*, and *Lord Loveland Discovers America*. "Gilded prostitution" was the phrase used by journalist W. T. Stead, who lamented the British tendency to regard the

American girl "as a means of replenishing the exhausted exchequer, a kind of financial resource, like the Income Tax."[14] And there was certainly an element in British high society which welcomed the dowries American brides brought with them but would have preferred them to just send a cheque instead of crossing the Atlantic in person.

American men came over to Britain, too—not in such numbers, admittedly, and not usually with the idea of marrying a British girl, wealthy or otherwise. Soon after Edward VII came to the throne, he decided he couldn't afford to keep up Osborne House, the Italianate mansion on the Isle of Wight where his mother had died. A rumour soon began circulating in the American press that three American millionaires were vying with each other to buy it. The "Copper King" of Montana, Senator William A. Clark, had written to the king to ask him how much he wanted for the house. Clark, whose response to being caught up in a political bribery scandal in Montana was to say "I never bought a man who wasn't for sale," was said to be bidding against the Chicago financier Charles G. Yerkes and William Waldorf Astor, who wanted to present Osborne to his daughter Pauline on her forthcoming marriage to the English soldier Herbert Spender-Clay.

There was no truth in the story: the king gave Osborne to the nation on the day of his coronation, and it was put to use as a Royal Navy training college. But American millionaires certainly were renting and buying British country houses. The New York financier Bradley Martin rented the Balmacaan shooting estate and the country house that came with it from the Earls of Seafield from 1885 until his death in 1913, entertaining there on a grand scale: local dignitaries and sportsmen regularly mingled with foreign ambassadors and English aristocrats. It was at Balmacaan that Martin's daughter Cornelia met the 4th Earl of Craven, who was one of her father's houseguests and who became her husband in a lavish ceremony at New York's Grace Church in April 1893, when the groom was twenty-four and his bride sixteen (or fifteen, according to some accounts).

Henry Phipps Jr., Andrew Carnegie's business partner in the Carnegie Steel Company, leased the Earl of Lytton's Knebworth in Hertfordshire for several years in the 1890s before taking Beaufort, the Lovat family's Scotch Baronial castle and shooting estate in the Highlands, about forty miles south of Skibo. After an unfortunate incident in 1905 when two of Phipps's sons found themselves in court, having shot three of Lord Lovat's men after coming upon them netting salmon in the middle of the night (Phipps's rent for Beaufort included the fishing rights), he moved instead to the fifty-thousand-acre Glenquoich, Scotland's finest deer forest. "Only a millionaire can be a tenant of Glenquoich and its lodge," said one newspaper at the time, "as the rent and expenses amount to about £100,000 a year."[15] An exaggeration, but the point was well made.

Sensing an opportunity, British estate agents began to target Americans as potential buyers. Advertisements for houses to let or to buy began to appear, directed at the American who was on the lookout for a prestigious country house. In 1903 an eleven-bedroomed Thameside villa at Windsor ("Royal Windsor," as the agent was careful to point out) was offered for sale "to Americans, wealthy city gentlemen, and others." Four years earlier the estate agents Knight Frank and Rutley went overboard in their efforts to persuade "Americans and men of wealth" that they should take "one of England's ancestral homes . . . the most beautiful seat in this country." There was no accompanying photograph in their advertisements, and it isn't clear exactly which country house was on offer—perhaps Compton Wynyates, perhaps Apethorpe? But the agent certainly pulled out all the stops when it came to the description, calling it "the finest example of the Tudor period in existence," with gardens that were "the most lovely in the Midland counties."[16]

Such was the reputation of the wealthy American that at the beginning of the twentieth century a man calling himself James Adams was able to pose as a retired Boston lawyer and a relative of the American ambassador, looking for a country house for his elderly mother, who accompanied him and told everyone she was a personal friend of the mayor of Boston. In fact, they were a pair of confidence tricksters from Londonderry, Benjamin and Emily Alcorn, who talked their way into leases on a succession of country houses in Ireland, Scotland, and England. Even though they had no bank account and could produce no references, the landed gentry handed over house after house on the assumption that because they were (or claimed to be) American, they must be "rolling in gold," to use Mary Gladstone's expression. They had each house redecorated and expensively furnished; they opened accounts with local shopkeepers; and then, when tradesmen began to ask for their money, they moved on to the next mansion. When Ireland grew too hot for them, they went to Glasgow and then down to Yorkshire, where the law finally caught up with them. After narrowly escaping a beating from a mob of irate tradespeople, they appeared at Armagh Assizes, where, in spite of their counsel arguing that "there was a species of lunatic hallucination" about them, Benjamin Alcorn was sentenced to eighteen months' hard labour and his mother went to jail for a year.[17]

The British were happy to accept American money, but they were not so happy to accept Americans. An embarrassing air of snobbery hung about most comments on Americans and country houses—not only in relation to the bartered brides, but also on a perceived absence of good taste and what the Edwardians thought of as good breeding. The Chicagoan Minna Field, struggling with her mount at a meet of the Quorn Hunt in 1908, embarrassed her escort, Algernon Burnaby of Baggrave Hall in Leicestershire, by saying very loudly in front of the hunt, "I'm doggawned if I don't cable for half a dozen from America where of course I can ride anything ever foaled." The gallant Mr Burnaby said that for such a magnificent horsewoman as she, it was hard to find a horse difficult enough to ride. "I think he's coming on!!" Minna wrote in her diary. As indeed he was: the couple were married five months later. And the British press noticed, with its nose firmly in the air, that George Westinghouse, founder of the Westinghouse Electric Corporation, was building himself a massively expensive country house in Massachusetts: "It is to be largely composed of marble. . . . Mr Westinghouse has purchased an Italian title for his son and heir, a lad of tender years." Clearly not quite the thing.[18]

So perhaps it was just as well that American entry into the world of the British country house never amounted to much more than a trickle, although the entrants were always interesting. Walter Hayes Burns of Newark, New Jersey, was a partner in the merchant banking firm of J. S. Morgan and Company, having had the good sense to marry J. S. Morgan's daughter Mary. The bank had offices in New York and London, and the Burnses came to England in the 1880s, buying 69 Brook Street (now the Savile Club) in 1884.

Nine years later, deciding that they needed their own place in the country, they bought the beautiful North Mymms estate in Hertfordshire for £67,000. North Mymms was the quintessential E-shaped Elizabethan country house: built around 1600 of soft red brick with tall chimneys and spiky gables, it had remained substantially intact until the nineteenth century, when it passed through a number of hands before ending up as the home of the Burns family. And it had royal connections: Queen Elizabeth I was said to have stayed at North Mymms as a girl, although, annoyingly, that was in an older house which this one had replaced. Since then, the only substantial alterations had been made in 1846–1847, when the workmanlike architect Edward Blore added an entrance vestibule flanked by two rather odd double-height bays, and some lovely ogee-capped turrets. Within months, Walter and Mary had commissioned Ernest George and Yeates to get rid of the bays, but not the turrets, as well as to add a new domestic wing, modernise the interiors in a broadly sympathetic Jacobethan style, and lay out the gardens, which were then planted by Irish gardener William Robinson. Within a few months the contractor,

Simpson and Company of Paddington, had two hundred men working on the site, and they remained there for the next three years, after which the decorators moved in.

Walter Hayes Burns did all the right things, providing employment to local people, subscribing to local charities, opening the grounds to Sunday excursionists. His wife and daughter were presented at court. But he could sometimes be high-handed in a way that suggests he didn't quite understand local life. North Mymms House was described, not altogether happily, as a "palatial mansion" by the parish council, which in 1895 got into a heated debate with Walter and his agent over some new gate piers which were apparently encroaching by a few feet onto the public highway. At an angry council meeting at which several of the councillors, led by a local carpenter called Aslett, were plainly spoiling for a fight with Burns, one of the more conciliatory members gave them pause for thought when he said, "We do not want to fight with a man like him."[19] The council backed down; although when Burns tried to alter a right of way through his park a few years later, Aslett succeeded in preventing it.

In February 1897 Simpson's men were back, carrying out further work in the grounds. But at the end of that year, after ailing for some months, Walter died at North Mymms, aged only fifty-nine. A private service for family and household was held in the hall of the house, before more public ceremonies at St George's, Hanover Square, and in New York, where he was buried. His wife, who was left a life interest in North Mymms, stayed on at the house and continued the work begun by her husband. When her daughter Mary became engaged, there was a presentation in the courtyard in front of the house, with a crowd of estate workers and villagers in attendance. The foreman gave a commendably brief speech and handed over to Mary a hand-carved gilded clock with the inscription, "Presented to Miss Burns by 165 workmen on the North Mymms Estate." The local headmaster gave a rather longer speech in which he said, "How pleased we all are, as

English folk, to hear of your engagement to a typical Englishman—a representative of a great and historic English house." Mary's fiancé, Lewis Vernon Harcourt, was continuing a tradition established by his father, the distinguished Liberal politician Sir William Vernon Harcourt, whose second wife had also been an American heiress. Lewis—Loulou to his friends—was also a sexual predator with a collection of child pornography and what one of his victims described as an "ungovernable sex desire for both sexes." When rumours began to spread about his activities in the years after the First World War, he took an overdose of a sleeping draught and was found dead in his bed at 69 Brook Street, the town house his father-in-law had bought back in the 1880s. Whether or not Loulou was a "typical Englishman," we can perhaps let America decide.[20]

In 1893 another American millionaire entered the British property market. Cliveden House, a majestic Italianate mansion rebuilt in 1851, after an 1849 fire, by Charles Barry for the 2nd Duke of Sutherland and standing in an even more majestic setting on the banks of the Thames in Buckinghamshire, looking towards Windsor Castle, was put up for sale by the Duke of Westminster, who had bought it from his mother-in-law twenty-five years earlier.

The buyer was one of the richest men in America: William Waldorf Astor, whose extended family's property empire gave them the epithet "the landlords of New York." Astor's purchase of Cliveden, a country house with a history that stretched back to Charles II's time, sent ripples through high society. "Another well-known English home of sylvan beauty has passed into the hands of the American capitalist," declared one newspaper, rather churlishly. Others chose to suggest that it didn't really matter because the house was ugly. "A heavy mass of masonry . . . not in any sense picturesque," said one. "The present

edifice was built from designs by Barry . . . with an effect unfortunately the reverse of picturesque," said another. Americans might
rent a mansion or a shooting lodge, or even buy up a country house
from an impoverished nobleman desperate to decamp to Bognor or
Baden-Baden on the proceeds of the sale. But an American millionaire who bought an important country house from one of the richest
men in Britain, someone who certainly didn't need the money? That
went against the order of things.[21]

Astor was a hard, complicated, and immensely rich man, with
money enough not to care what people thought of him and a sensitive
ego which cared very much indeed. After a bruising foray into American politics, he had decamped to England in 1890, declaring that
America was no place for a gentleman and thus earning the endur-
ing contempt of the American press, which delighted in reminding
everyone of his humble origins. His great-grandfather, he said later,
would always be regarded in New York society as a Dutch sausage
peddler, "and my fate promises to be the same if the American press
can make it so."[22] Unlike Andrew Carnegie, who never lost his American identity in spite of all the faux-Scottish playacting at Skibo, Astor
took British citizenship in 1899, further alienating himself from the
land of his birth, and found a refuge of sorts in British and European
history. That year he published a family tree which was aspirational
rather than accurate in tracing the Astors back to an eleventh-century
Castilian, Pedro d'Astorga, who was killed in the First Crusade at
the taking of Jerusalem. Astor founded the *Pall Mall Magazine* in
1893 as an offshoot of the *Pall Mall Gazette*, a popular evening paper
which he also owned, and used it to publish his own self-conscious
and mildly embarrassing historical stories, with titles like "The Red
Dwarf of Rabenstein" and "The Wraith of Cliveden Reach." A couple
of lines from "The Wraith" are enough—some may say more than
enough—to give one the flavour of his writing:

The Dore being ajar, I heard the sweete fainte sownde of the old virginall touched exceeding slow, and my harte smote me at what seemed a mysticall greeting, for the musique was a sad tune my lady deftly played in bygone days of happy memorie.[23]

Astor's wife Mary died in 1894, and with the death in 1902 of his thirteen-year-old daughter Gwendolyn, he lost his taste for Cliveden, and he gave it to his son Waldorf in 1906. In the meantime, he turned his attention and his fortune on a more romantic and undoubtedly more picturesque slice of British history, a moated medieval castle dating back to the fourteenth century. This was the ancestral seat of the Boleyn family, the place where Henry VIII was said to have courted Anne Boleyn, the place where her ghost was said to still walk. He decided he wanted Hever Castle in Kent.

Hever had had an unhappy time of it in recent years. It was owned by the ornithologist Edmund Meade-Waldo, but when he wasn't engaged in collecting birds in southern Europe and North Africa, he focused his resources on his family's other estate, four miles away, and Hever became a working farm.* In 1896 Guy Sebright, an officer in the Coldstream Guards, and his wife Olive took a ninety-nine-year lease on Hever; they moved in with their eight domestic servants and began to repair some of the worst damage. But they didn't have the resources to complete the work, and they soon came under fire from the Society for the Protection of Ancient Buildings, whose members thought it would be a good idea if they were invited to advise him on how to proceed. "This view is not shared by Captain Sebright," they reported.[24]

---

* Meade-Waldo is best known for his sighting of a sea serpent off the coast of Florida in 1905, while aboard a scientific research vessel. His report to a gathering of the Zoological Society the following June caused quite a stir.

In 1901 Astor opened negotiations with Meade-Waldo to buy the freehold and with Captain Sebright to buy out the remaining years of his lease. Finally, on July 27, 1903, the deal was done, and Hever and its 640 acres of grounds belonged to Astor.

The dilapidated castle immediately became the subject of another of Astor's historical romances. In "Free in a Faraway Land," which appeared in his *Pall Mall Magazine* the month after the sale went through, he played out a fantasy common to just about everyone who ever bought an historic house: the discovery of a secret chamber behind the panelling. In his story, this hiding place contained a rapier, "a crystal divining ball of remarkable brilliancy," and a roll of paper, on which was written a memoir by Sir Thomas Boleyn's fencing master. Astor even went so far as to illustrate a specimen of this manuscript, along with several highly imaginative pictures of Henry VIII and Anne Boleyn together.[25]

"Free in a Faraway Land" was only one example in a little flurry of Hever-related articles that appeared in Astor's magazine. A couple were written by others: the novelist William Outram Tristram contributed a long account of Hever and Anne Boleyn, complete with a dozen photographs, most showing bare, empty rooms, while Olive Sebright wrote "A Haunt of Ancient Peace," which was, somewhat inevitably, all about Hever and Anne Boleyn. Astor contributed another story, again based on his favourite literary device of a manuscript found hidden at Hever, this one in an old leather box containing the deeds to the castle. "A Dragon in the Garden of Eden" was set in 1618 and described the experiences of Silvertip, an imaginary Native American who came over with Pocahontas (although Astor still managed to get in plenty of references to Anne Boleyn, including the legend that the Hever dandelions turned crimson the moment her blood fell on Tower Green and remain so to this day).

The most interesting contribution was "Hever Restored," which appeared in January 1907. Signed simply "A Visitor," it was probably

by Astor himself, and it offered a guided tour of the works which he
and his architect, Frank Pearson, had carried out over the past three
and a half years, with the aid of 750 workmen who lived in a temporary encampment on the site. Astor had a stone cottage specially built
for his own use while he was down to view the works. Eight detectives
worked in shifts to keep an eye on things.

The exterior came through the restoration relatively unscathed,
with ivy stripped away and stone and brick replaced only where necessary, along with a new working drawbridge of English oak. But the
interiors were transformed, filled with intricately carved panelling and
furniture, any one piece of which was museum quality. Two suits of
Tudor armour, pikes in hand, stood at the entrance to the house, "and
at once attuned one to the proper mood for sympathetic exploration."
The outer hall had a huge fireplace of Verona marble, and the inner
hall was panelled from floor to ceiling with Italian walnut, and carved
walnut columns supporting the minstrel gallery were reputed to come
from a tree which stood on the estate of Count Louis Salome at Isola
in 1747. A piece of an ancient rapier was apparently found embedded
in the wood, "a romantic circumstance which our imaginations may
interpret as they will," wrote Astor.[26]

The romance of the past was the key to Astor's Hever. The long
gallery where Henry and Anne "paced and whispered" was filled with
cabinets and coffers and spinets and harps. The walls were hung with
sixteenth-century portraits including a Holbein of Anne Boleyn and
another of Anne of Cleves, who was given Hever by Henry VIII as a
consolation prize after their divorce. In the hall, "the long table, the
buffet, the tapestry, the coffers, the chairs, the armour, the heraldic
emblazonments in the lofty windows, are eloquent of the period when
Hever was in its glory." The unnamed author was curiously reticent
about Anne Boleyn's bedchamber, but in the room where Henry VIII
was supposed to sleep during his visits to Hever, Astor had placed a
four-poster bed and "a throne-like chair."[27]

Less prominent in the narrative were the modern conveniences— the bathrooms, the hot and cold running water, the electricity generated by a purpose-built power plant on the site. These would have intruded on the dream.

Astor was happy with his dream, but it didn't quite come off. It was too new, too opulent. Astor was elevated to the peerage as Lord Astor in 1916 and was made Viscount Astor of Hever the following year. But he and his castle of romance never quite fitted in. They just weren't *English* enough. His biographer reckoned that the whole feel of the place was idealised Tudor—"a harsh, crude age viewed through later rose-tinted spectacles." The architect Philip Tilden was even less sympathetic, saying it had become "a miniature Metropolitan Museum of New York." When Astor employed psychic researchers to find the ghost of Anne Boleyn, who was reputed to wander disconsolately through the gardens, unkind critics said she had left Hever in disgust when she saw what he had done to her ancestral home.[28]

But there were strokes of architectural genius. The author of "Hever Restored," whoever he or she was, described mounting the top of the keep and looking down on an "assemblage of quaint roofs, gables, and chimneys which clustered round the end of the Castle." This was the most remarkable addition to Hever: a range of timber-framed stone guest cottages grouped around a series of courtyards just outside the castle wall so as to seem like a little Tudor village. It is a wonderful composition, the result, so Astor claimed, of a wish to entertain his friends while not interfering with "the very chambers he was bent on preserving intact."[29] Pearson later said that it was because Astor, who could be paranoid at times, didn't want other people wandering round in his castle. He liked to see them off at night and pull up the drawbridge.

FOUR

COSMOPOLITANS

THE ARCHITECT EUSTACE Balfour, brother of the Conservative politician Arthur Balfour, was not impressed with Alfred de Rothschild's faux-French Renaissance Halton House. "I have never seen anything more terribly vulgar," he wrote. "A combination of French chateau and a gambling house. . . . Oh the hideousness of everything, the showiness! The sense of lavish wealth thrust up your nose!"[1]

It is hard to know whether the underlying cause of Balfour's diatribe was Alfred de Rothschild's status as a prominent member of the nouveaux riches or his Jewishness. Probably both, since a casual antisemitism and a disdain for the ostentatious display of wealth went hand in hand among the established landed elite, and its members had a tendency to close ranks against both. "Money is a vulgar thing and money is what rules us now," said Countess Cowper in 1874. "What right have those people to force themselves into our society!" Half a century later another countess, Daisy Warwick, recalled, "We resented the introduction of Jews into the social set of the Prince of

Wales; not because we disliked them individually . . . but because they had brains and understood finance."[2]

But enter the Prince of Wales's set they did, although not in any great numbers. Among the seventy-odd characters who socialised regularly with the prince at one time or another as part of his Marlborough House Set, only Reuben Sassoon, Arthur Sassoon, Maurice de Hirsch, and Ernest Cassel were Jewish.

Reuben, Arthur, and their half brother Abdullah were the sons of David Sassoon, a Baghdadi Jew who had moved with his family to India around 1830 and who had founded a vast business empire trading in everything from Indian cotton and Chinese opium to Lancashire textiles, with hubs in Bombay, Shanghai, Hong Kong, and London. Abdullah, who changed his name to Albert, moved to London in 1875 to oversee the firm's operations from there. Reuben and Arthur were already living in England, and Reuben in particular became one of the Prince of Wales's intimates, often staying at Sandringham, accompanying Edward to Goodwood or Ascot or Epsom, and appearing at one house party after another when the prince was also a guest.

The brothers all had substantial houses in London—Albert in Kensington Gore, Arthur in Knightsbridge, and Reuben on the corner of Belgrave Square. Arthur also kept a shooting lodge in the Highlands. But none of the three brothers maintained large country houses. Instead, their weekends were spent at villas in Brighton: the MP Henry Labouchère, a noted antisemite, sneeringly described Brighton as "a sea-coast town, three miles long and three yards broad, with a Sassoon at each end and one in the middle."[3] These villas were large enough to play host to Edward both as Prince of Wales and as king, although they were not large enough to accommodate his court, who grumbled at having to lodge in nearby hotels.

If the Sassoons didn't embrace country house life, the same can't be said for another of the prince's Jewish intimates, Maurice de

Hirsch. Descended from a family of court bankers in Bavaria and with a personal fortune reckoned at around £20 million, Hirsch had a country house near Sandringham and another, Grafton House, at Newmarket. He also owned Bath House, a substantial mansion on Piccadilly (named for a previous owner, the 1st Earl of Bath, rather than for an ablutionary past); a town house on the rue de l'Élysée in Paris; an enormous neoclassical mansion, the château de Beauregard, a few miles north of Versailles; a medieval castle, hrad Veveří, in what is now the Czech Republic; and St Johann, a vast shooting estate in Hungary, where he regularly entertained. "I never saw so much game in my life," the Prince of Wales told his son after a shooting party at St Johann in 1890 which killed twenty thousand head of game in ten days.[4]

The notion that a Jew like Hirsch should be accepted in royal circles was incomprehensible to European aristocracy. While Edward was staying at St Johann, a neighbouring Hungarian count invited him over, but the invitation pointedly excluded Hirsch. The prince refused, and the count explained, "I should be glad to receive you on any other occasion, but not when coming from that Jew's." There was prejudice against Hirsch in Britain, too, even if it was not so overtly expressed. Queen Victoria refused to invite him to Buckingham Palace, much to her son's annoyance, and the Earl of Derby confided to his journal that Hirsch's influence over the prince was "a puzzle to society, since he is neither a gentleman, nor reputed altogether honest."[5]

The prince enjoyed the company of Jews like the Sassoons and Hirsch. But he also enjoyed their money at a time when his own finances were precarious and he was regularly spending a good deal more than the £112,000 a year granted to him through the Civil List. Lord Rothschild advanced the prince £100,000 in 1889 and another £60,000 four years later. When another of the prince's lenders died in 1890 and his trustees called in the debt—rumoured to be a colossal

£250,000 and secured against the Sandringham estate—Hirsch paid it off, putting Edward in his debt and, according to Hirsch's detractors, thus securing for himself a place in the prince's set.

When Hirsch died in 1896, rumours flew that he had left a million pounds to the Prince of Wales in his will. His executor was his protégé Ernest Cassel, a forty-four-year-old merchant banker from a family of Ashkenazi Jews. Cassel took over Grafton House in Newmarket; more significantly, he also took over the management of the Prince of Wales's financial affairs from Hirsch, who had left instructions that the prince's debts to him, said to amount to more than £300,000, should be written off. It was a one-sided arrangement: the prince took the profits from his investments while Cassel took the losses.

There was some speculation about Cassel's religion. The courtier Sir Almeric FitzRoy was eager to discover if he was in fact Jewish—not out of any particularly base motive but simply because as clerk to the Privy Council he had to oversee the swearing-in of new privy councillors, and Edward VII had made Cassel a councillor in his coronation honours in 1902. "I am still without exact information whether Cassel is a Jew or a Christian," complained FitzRoy. "Further, there are rumours that he may turn out a Roman Catholic."[6] Just in time for the swearing-in ceremony, he discovered from Lord Rothschild the carefully guarded secret of Cassel's religious beliefs: he had converted to Catholicism in 1881 at the request of his dying wife. So he was sworn in accordingly, but most people who knew him—and even more who didn't—still regarded him as Jewish.

The agonies FitzRoy suffered on that occasion were as nothing compared to his tribulations in swearing in two new privy councillors in 1909. One was the Jewish financier Sir Edgar Speyer; the other was Syed Ameer Ali, an Indian lawyer and the founder of the London Muslim League. When it came to the ceremony, Speyer was quite happy to take the oath on the New Testament, but, punctilious as ever, FitzRoy insisted he use the Pentateuch, "and thus saved the

Gospels from outrage."[7] Syed Ameer Ali brought along his own copy of the Koran.

Like Hirsch, Cassel accumulated homes. Besides Grafton House, he owned Moulton Paddocks, a racing stable in Newmarket formerly known as Fidget Hall, with stabling for forty horses, a stud farm, and a country house containing twenty bedrooms and thirteen more for the servants. He lived in a town house in Grosvenor Square before taking on Bath House in Piccadilly, and then in 1907 he bought Brook House, a huge French Renaissance mansion on Park Lane. (The dining room could seat one hundred: "There is no need for dwellers in Brook House to dream that they dwell in marble halls," said one visitor. "They do dwell in them.")[8] He had Les Cèdres, a villa in forty-two acres of gardens at Cap Ferrat which had once belonged to King Leopold of Belgium; a flat in Paris; and the Villa Cassel in the Swiss Alps. He also owned the 1,100-acre Hare Park estate in Cambridgeshire, which included part of Newmarket racecourse, and Branksome Dene, a seaside villa in sixty acres in Bournemouth. Cassel was also a discriminating collector of French furniture, old English plate, Italian bronzes, and porcelain. When his collections came up for auction after his death, the sale of his Meissen alone took a whole day.

Cassel was liked by those who knew him. They invited him to their country house weekends; they accepted his hospitality in return at Brook House or Moulton Paddocks. Margot Asquith called him "dignified, autocratic and wise; with a power of loving those he cared for which I find rare."[9] But others accepted him because the king's patronage meant they had no choice. The suspicion that the Rothschilds and the Sassoons and Hirsch and Cassel, all of whom were conventionally regarded as outsiders, could buy their way into an inner circle from which they were themselves excluded, inflamed a nasty strain of antisemitism already common among the country house–owning classes, as it was common almost everywhere in turn-of-the-century Britain.

Cassel's close relationship with Edward, both as prince and as king, caused jealousy among courtiers and among those both outside and inside the Marlborough House Set. When the king held a garden party at Windsor in 1905, for example, and "tea was served to the royalties in a private tent to which only a very few intimate friends were bidden," Cassel was one of them. When the king inspected horses at Newmarket, "Windsor Cassel" was by his side. The two men even looked alike. The Marquês de Soveral, Portuguese envoy and a member of the set, was once asked by Edward VII whether he knew *The Importance of Being Earnest*. "No, I cannot say that I do; but I have long since known the importance of being Ernest Cassel."[10]

The legal status of Jews in Britain changed significantly over the course of the nineteenth century. In 1889 the prime minister, Lord Salisbury, wrote to Nathan Rothschild to say that he wished to appoint him lord lieutenant of Buckinghamshire. Nathan had already been raised to the peerage four years earlier as Baron Rothschild of Tring, but this still marked a significant step towards social acceptance: he was the first Jew to take on the historic position of the monarch's personal representative in the county. The Prince of Wales felt it necessary to apologise to Nathan's neighbour, the 3rd Lord Carrington, who might conceivably have expected to fill the post: "It would have been strange ten years ago, but times change. He is a good fellow and a man of business, and he and his family own half the county."[11]

British Jewry had been disappointed by the emancipation acts of the 1820s, which had allowed Roman Catholics and Protestant Dissenters into public office but which had inserted a declaration that candidates for Crown or corporate office must promise not to injure the Church of England "on the true faith of a Christian," a phrase which effectively barred Jews from obtaining public office. Baron Lionel de Rothschild stood for one of the four City of London parliamentary seats in the general election of 1847 and was returned, only to be denied his seat because he refused to use the words "on the true faith of a Christian" while taking his oath. After a decade of to-ing and fro-ing in which Rothschild resigned his seat, stood again, was elected again, and was rejected again, the Jewish Disabilities Act of 1858 finally allowed MPs to take their seat without using the contested phrase, and on July 26, 1858, Rothschild became the first openly Jewish MP. By the early 1900s, the lord chief justice, Sir Rufus Isaacs, was a Jew; so was the postmaster general, Herbert Samuel; and the permanent under-secretary of state for India, Edwin Montagu.*

And yet antisemitism remained endemic in British society—not to the same extent as in mainland Europe, perhaps, but there was still a sense that Jews were somehow "other." Medieval arguments that the Jews had killed Christ were still being routinely resurrected in Edwardian England, while more subtle criticisms centred on fears that, once allowed to hold positions of authority, Jews would de-Christianise the nation. "Do you still believe the Messiah is coming, Lord Natty?" Lady Ribblesdale once asked Lord Rothschild at a dinner party. Nor could they be trusted to show loyalty to the Crown: they would inevitably put race before country. According to Lord Winchelsea, speaking in the House of Lords in 1848, the Jews were "a distinct and peculiar people, bearing their nationality of character in whatever part of the world they were dispersed."[12]

In 1853 Rev. John Mills published *The British Jews*, which claimed to be "a faithful account of the domestic, social, and religious conditions of the Jews in this country." This relatively positive, albeit racist,

---

* Isaacs had been involved in some shady insider dealing over a government contract given to the Marconi Company, and this, together with his appointment as lord chief justice, inspired Kipling to write a particularly nasty poem, "Gehazi," ranting against "that Jew boy on the bench." Pinney, *Letters*, 4:208–209.

review of the condition of British Jewry focused mainly on explanations of Jewish religious practice. But Mills ended with an attempt to sum up "national traits of character." On the one hand British Jews were, he decided, industrious, abstinent, clean, decent, and hospitable. On the other, they were rather too fond of balls and plays; they were "proud and self-approving," congratulating themselves "upon being still the chosen people of Heaven"; and they were far too fond of jewellery, bright colours and finery in general—"a relic of their oriental taste."[13]

This kind of racist stereotyping served to confirm the otherness of British Jews, even as they were taking their place in the highest of high society. In 1880 a biographical sketch of the prime minister, Benjamin Disraeli, who had become an Anglican when he was thirteen years old, said that he was "an outsider in our social and public affairs. . . . A stranger and a sojourner in this land of his birth and his adoption, this Egypt of which he has taken possession in the name of his brethren of Judaea." Others found it perfectly acceptable to refer to Disraeli as "alien," "un-English," "the Jew," "Shylock," or "the Hebrew." "Lord Beaconsfield [as Disraeli became in 1876] has never turned European. . . . He remains as purely Asiatic as if he had never left Ur of the Chaldees." "He is among us, but he is not of us."[14]

Disraeli was born in London. So was his father.

This emphasis on racial and cultural difference showed itself in varying degrees of intensity. Sometimes it was casual, although no less unpleasant for that. One evening at Mentmore Towers, the country house in Buckinghamshire which had come to Hannah de Rothschild on the death of her father in 1874, her husband, Lord Rosebery, wished the female houseguests, most of whom were Jewish, good night by saying to them in solemn tones as they gathered at the foot of the great staircase, candles in hand, "To your tents, O

Israel."* Almeric FitzRoy mentioned in passing in his diary in the summer of 1914 that his fellow houseguests at Broadlands House, the Hampshire home of Lieutenant Colonel Wilfrid Ashley, included not only Molly Forbes-Sempill, a divorcée who was just about to become Ashley's second wife, but also "a clever little American German Jew."[15] FitzRoy didn't bother to name him, but he was referring to R. D. Blumenfeld, the distinguished editor of the *Daily Express*. Ashley's first wife, incidentally, was Ernest Cassel's daughter Amalia, who died in 1911; their daughter Edwina would marry Louis Mountbatten.

More serious than these nasty little private slights was the institutional racism which actively discriminated against Jews. Queen Victoria refused to grant a peerage to Lionel de Rothschild because he was a Jew, in spite of Gladstone's urging. "I shall have to refuse on the score of his religion," she confessed in her journal. "To make a Jew a peer is a step she *could not* consent to," Gladstone was told. That attitude was still prevalent in the years leading up to the First World War. When Sir Richmond Ritchie, permanent under-secretary of state for India, died unexpectedly in 1912, there was no question of his assistant, Lionel Abrahams, being considered for the post. "With one Jew Parliamentary Under-Secretary," wrote Sir Almeric FitzRoy, referring to Edwin Montagu, "the claims of another to the permanent secretaryship are obviously inadmissible." And when Lieutenant Colonel Sir Matthew Nathan was suggested as secretary to the Treasury, FitzRoy, who was not unusual in his racism, urged against the appointment: "As a soldier and a Jew I thought him impossible." (Nathan, who had a long track record as a colonial administrator in Sierra Leone, Hong Kong, and Natal, was made under-secretary of state for Ireland

---

* Hannah died in November 1890 and was buried with full Jewish rites in the Jewish cemetery in Willesden. Queen Victoria noted in her journal that "Ld Rosebery had felt very painfully the Jews having taken complete possession of the remains." Victoria, journal entry, December 5, 1890.

in 1914, which may not have betokened a relaxation of institutional antisemitism but which did say much for the Asquith government's attitude to Ireland at the time.)[16]

Then there was the suspicion that British Jewry put its own interest before that of the kingdom. The Boer War crystallised anti-Jewish feeling among those who held that British soldiers were fighting and dying to protect the interests of the predominantly Jewish Randlords, who had made their fortunes in the Kimberley diamond mines and the goldfields of Johannesburg, while the popular press voiced the suspicion that these Randlords, most of them still speaking with heavy German accents, were somehow manipulating the markets and the British government for their own ends.

Was there such a thing as an Anglo-Jewish country house? On one level the answer is an obvious yes. Plenty of Anglo-Jewish families built or remodelled country houses in the decades before the First World War: the Rothschilds at Waddesdon, Halton, Tring, Mentmore, Ascott; stockbroker Ludwig Messel's Germanic Nymans in Sussex; Randlord Sir Frederick Eckstein's Italianate Ottershaw Park in Surrey.

The diamond magnate Julius Wernher, of whom Bertrand Russell wrote that "though Balfour [the prime minister] governs the Empire, Wernher governs Balfour," rented Luton Hoo in Bedfordshire in 1899 and bought it in 1903. It was remodelled for him by the architects Charles Mewès and Arthur Davis, who were in the middle of designing the Ritz; and the Ritzy opulence of Mewès and Davis's Louis XVI–style Luton Hoo was the perfect expression of Edwardian new money, "the finest country-house evocation of this new age of confident, cosmopolitan wealth," in the words of *Country Life*. "Cosmopolitan" was code for "Jewish."[17]

That wealth was not limitless. Wernher was anxious about keeping his architects—and his wife Alice, nicknamed "Birdie"—from going over their budget, although without much success. He sailed for South Africa on business at the end of 1903, just as the building work began, leaving Birdie to deal with the contractors, George Trollope and Sons; with Maison Leys, the Paris-based decorators and furnishers, whose men were staying on-site; and with the architects. Mewès battled against any attempt to economise while he and Davis racked up bills for site visits. Davis charged two guineas per visit and made 102 visits. "Mewès's rough estimate was £100,000," Wernher told Birdie. "I reckoned knowing what rogues they are £150,000 and now you make it £250,000. A fine pickle. . . . You must settle as best you can. Have as little done in France as possible."[18]

That said, the impetus for the new building came from Birdie. "You bought the place under protest," she told her husband. "(I persuaded you), you alter it under greater protest (again I persuaded you) therefore you are naturally less inclined to spend large sums on it."[19] The couple already had Bath House, once the London home of Maurice de Hirsch. But Birdie was socially ambitious, and for any socially ambitious hostess, a place in the country for weekend entertaining was de rigueur. Luton Hoo was to be that place.

The final bill was £147,000. For that, Julius Wernher, a big, imposing man, got a big, imposing house, dripping with opulent detail: a white-and-gold Louis XIV ballroom; a dining room hung with glittering crystal chandeliers and walled by Mewès in two shades of marble to frame three Beauvais tapestries bought by Julius in the 1890s and originally woven for the comte de Toulouse, son of Louis XIV; and an oval Louis XVI staircase hall of white marble, described by architectural historian Nikolaus Pevsner in 1968 as "French *Beaux Arts* at its most convincing and indeed its most splendid."[20]

The Wernhers spent most of their time at Bath House, visiting Luton Hoo at weekends or staying there for a couple of months for the shooting in the autumn. Early visitors included Grand Duke Michael of Russia, Prince Albert, Duke of Schleswig-Holstein, and, in February 1907, Edward VII, who arrived to lunch two hours late after his car suffered a flat tyre.* Making only occasional use of their place in the country wasn't unusual for members of the landed elite in Edwardian England, although perhaps the fact that the Wernhers kept fifty-four gardeners, ten electricians, and twenty or thirty indoor servants was. The Fabian Beatrice Webb, who with her husband Sidney was invited by the Wernhers to use a house on the estate, felt a frisson of guilt at the proximity and plight of the poor town of Luton, as she sat under the Wernhers' trees and enjoyed the fruit and vegetables and flowers from their gardens. She reckoned that the Wernhers were spending around £30,000 a year just to keep the place up.[21]

Luton Hoo was one of the great Anglo-Jewish houses, and it came in for some nasty antisemitic gibes. "South African gold mines are not paying so well as formerly," declared the left-leaning *Clarion*.

> But the patriotic Anglo-Saxon-cum-Semitic millionaires manage to make ends meet. At Luton Hoo a quarter of a million is to be spent on the work. It is not true, however, that Mr Wernher is going to turn the mansion into a retreat for maimed and out of work soldiers who fought [in the Boer Wars] for him and his brother-plutocrats in South Africa.[22]

But such attitudes weren't universal. Going to lunch at Ernest Cassel's Park Lane house in the summer of 1913, Almeric FitzRoy was impressed. The house, he wrote in his diary, was splendid. The dining room, hung with four van Dykes, was magnificent. "It is the great merit of your Jew of taste that he never overloads his walls with pictures: selection in excellence is his aim."[23]

---

* The king borrowed one of Wernher's cars for the journey back to Buckingham Palace. When a policeman stopped him for speeding and demanded his name and number, the king cheerfully said, "My name is Wernher, the number you can see on the car, and my address is Bath House, Piccadilly." Trevelyan, *Grand Dukes*, 248.

FitzRoy's views on Jewish taste ran counter to the prevailing wisdom. To a landed elite which habitually mistrusted Jews, foreigners, nonconformists, foreigners, people who had grown rich through trade, foreigners, and anyone who spoke with a foreign accent, the Jewish country house was defined by the ostentatious display of wealth. After a visit to Nathan Rothschild's Tring, Lord Crawford was so appalled by what he called the "overpowering ostentation and vulgarity" that he swore he would never stay again at one of the "big Jewish houses." It is hard not to think that Beatrice Webb, who belonged to no such landed elite, was expressing stereotypical anti-Jewish behaviours when, after a dinner at Bath House in July 1905, she offered a critique of Birdie Wernher which began softly with faint praise and built to a crescendo of contempt. She was not a bad sort, said Beatrice, but she had become a slave to her wealth. "Consequently both in person and manners and speech she was essentially ugly. . . . Her talk of nothing else but herself and her possessions."[24]

Beatrice was equally scathing about Bath House. Nothing pleased her: the room settings, the flowers, the food, the wine, the paintings on the walls—everything was overdone, she declared. "Wealth—Wealth—Wealth, was screamed aloud wherever one turned."[25]

But here's the thing. Birdie Wernher was Jewish. Charles Mewès was Jewish. Arthur Davis was Jewish. But Julius Wernher was not Jewish, having been born into an old established Protestant family in Hesse. In English upper-class society, that didn't matter. His name, his German accent, his role as one of the biggest players in the diamond mines and gold mines of South Africa, were enough to convince the world that he was Jewish. Therefore, Luton Hoo was a Jewish country house.

Clearly, if there was such a thing as a Jewish country house in the period 1870–1914, definitions must rely on something more than heritage and ownership. But what would a quintessentially Jewish architecture look like? "It is as difficult to answer that question as it is to

sort out what is Jewish about the Jews," wrote the architectural historian Fredric Bedoire in 2004.[26]

Looking back on the period, it seems as though the opulent personal tastes of a very few people, mainly members of the extended
Rothschild family, defined the Jewish country house. Yet many more
wealthy Jews bought or rented quite modest off-the-peg mansions.
Sir Ernest Cassel took a short lease on Walworth Castle near Darlington, then on Compton Verney in Warwickshire, then on Dalby
Hall in Leicestershire. In 1902 Sir Frederick Eckstein's business partner, Alfred Beit, leased the seven-hundred-acre Tewin Water estate in
Hertfordshire, along with all of its furniture, pictures, and servants.
Rufus Isaacs and his wife Alice leased Foxhill just outside Reading,
an exercise in Gothic Revival polychromy designed in 1867 as his
own country residence by Alfred Waterhouse, architect of Manchester
Town Hall, the Natural History Museum, and the Duke of Westminster's Eaton Hall in Cheshire. Compared to those buildings Foxhill
was modest, as was the domestic staff of nine, who, like their employers, moved between Foxhill and the Isaacses' Mayfair town house.

In the late 1870s Sir Julian Goldsmid restored and sensitively
extended Somerhill Park, a quietly beautiful Jacobean country
house near Tunbridge Wells in Kent which had been purchased by
his grandfather Sir Isaac Lyon Goldsmid in 1849. Also in Kent, Sir
Edward Sassoon, whose wife Aline was a Rothschild, had a modest
mid-nineteenth-century Gothic house, Shorncliffe Lodge, in Sand-
gate. Sassoon was MP for Hythe, a seat which had been held for fifteen years by Mayer de Rothschild.[27] In 1905 he described the lodge
as one of his two seats, although admittedly he gave as the other Sans
Souci, a palatial neoclassical mansion in Bombay where his mother
Hannah—who preferred to live in India while her husband Albert
made his home in England—had hosted a visit from the Prince of

Wales back in 1876. Sir Edward's main residence was 25 Park Lane, later made famous by his son Philip and the influential series of exhibitions of British art he held there in the 1930s.

There was a small cluster of Anglo-Jewish country houses in Kent around the turn of the century. Marcus Samuel, the banker, merchant, and founder of the Shell Transport and Trading Company, was knighted in 1898 and served as lord mayor of London in 1902–1903, after which he was made a baronet. He was raised to the peerage after the First World War, first as Baron Bearsted of Maidstone and then as Viscount Bearsted. And he established himself at the Mote in Maidstone, a big square country mansion in two thousand acres which he bought in 1896 from the Earl of Romney, for whose family it was built between 1793 and 1801 by the architect Daniel Alexander. Here he did all the right things and was immensely popular as a result: he hosted the Kent Agricultural Association's annual summer shows; he gave work to the unemployed and supported the local hospital; he gave £1,000 to the Mote Cricket Club and built them a new pavilion. A little "Kentish cameo" in the local paper in 1909 praised his "beautiful country seat," his love for Kent, his kind heart and generous spirit and happy manner.

But difference, and the public proclamation of difference, remained. That same cameo was also swift to point out that Marcus Samuel "is a Jew, and possesses to the full the supreme ability of his remarkable race, and its aptitude for the acquirement of wealth."[28]

FIVE

BRITISH RAJ

A MODEL ENGLISH GENTLEMAN," said the press. "A first-class shot," said the aristocracy. "A sound Churchman," said his tenants.[1] Queen Victoria stood godmother to one of his children, and the Prince of Wales invited him to his wedding. His portrait by Winterhalter hung at Buckingham Palace. He sent his sons to Eton and Sandhurst, and played host to the cream of the aristocracy on his vast estates in Suffolk.

Yet Maharajah Duleep Singh, the last ruler of the Sikh Empire, was always an outsider in his adopted country—although perhaps "adopted" suggests a degree of choice which was absent from his life story. In 1843, when he was five years old, the assassination in Lahore of his brother Sher Singh propelled him to the throne, with his mother as regent. Six years later the East India Company annexed Punjab and relieved him of that throne, along with his private estates and, incidentally, the fabled Koh-i-Noor diamond, which was handed over to Queen Victoria. Duleep Singh was placed in the care of a Scottish surgeon in the Bengal Medical Service, John Spencer Login, who encouraged him to convert to Christianity and took him into exile in Britain, where he was welcomed into the court by Queen Victoria and Prince Albert.

There is a little watercolour of around 1854 in the Royal Collection. It shows a turbaned youth in European clothes kneeling to dress a small, rather anxious-looking child in an Indian costume. The artist was Queen Victoria; the youth was Duleep Singh; and the little boy was the four-year-old Prince Arthur, Victoria's seventh child and third son. Duleep Singh was, said the queen, "truly amiable [and] so kind to the children, playing so nicely with them."[2]

Throughout the later 1850s and 1860s Duleep Singh drifted from one shooting estate to another, living on a pension of £25,000 a year from the India Office and trying half-heartedly to adapt to elite cultural norms. Login's wife Lena recalled that although he continued to wear the traditional costume of a Sikh emperor when he was at court, he adopted European dress in everyday life, combining it with a Sikh turban and a quantity of jewels. He "was never without the three rows of enormous pearls round his neck, and a pair of large emerald and pearl earrings." To begin with, Login leased for him Castle Menzies, a forbidding sixteenth-century stronghold in Perthshire, where he wore Highland dress and earned himself the title of "the Black Prince of Perthshire." He also alarmed his guardian by flying falcons against grouse, a skill he had acquired as a child in Lahore. "The Sikhs, like most Orientals, are keen falconers; and the Maharajah at one time went at the sport with great vigour," reported a gossip columnist in 1880. "His mews was full of hawks from every part of the globe: gyr-falcons and peregrines from Iceland and Norway; eyasses from the nest, and haggards caught in Holland; goshawks famous for dashing straight at their quarry, and a few Indian varieties not well known to European

falconers."* But falconry lacked the immediate excitement of shooting, and the maharajah eventually gave it up.[3]

At nineteen he demanded his own household, and after spells at
Grandtully Castle, also in Perthshire, and Mulgrave Castle in North
Yorkshire, in 1862 he bought Hatherop Castle, a recently remodelled
country house in the Cotswolds, for £105,000. But Hatherop "was
not a success," recalled Lady Login.[4] After he had been in the Cotswolds for barely a year, he found that Elveden, an established sporting estate in Suffolk, was on the market (and that his neighbours
would include the Prince of Wales at Sandringham), and he sold up
and bought Elveden instead. The British government advanced him
£198,000 for the purchase and subsequent building work, but it was
an advance against his allowance, and he was made to pay yearly
interest of £5,654, which reduced his annual income to around
£13,000—still quite a hefty sum, but a good deal less than the
£40,000 he claimed to have been promised when he relinquished his
throne. A sense of grievance that the British government had reneged
on its promises, exacerbated by an unfortunate determination to live
well beyond his means, was to dog him for the rest of his life, souring
his relations with the India Office and eventually with the queen
herself.

Most country house owners with connections to India advertised
those connections with nothing more than an elephant's-foot umbrella
stand in the entrance hall or a moth-eaten tiger-skin rug in the library.

---

* "Gentlemen are respectfully requested NOT TO SHOOT or INJURE his Highness the Maharajah Duleep Singh's TRAINED HAWKS, which are flown in the
neighbourhood. They may be known by having Bells and Leather Straps to
their legs. Elveden Hall, December 8, 1863." *Bury and Norwich Post*, January 5, 1864, 8.

Others brought home more spirited souvenirs: Robert Sterndale, an Indian Civil Service official who had been born in Bengal, retired to Surrey with his wife and two daughters, all of whom had also been born in India, and took with him a Bengali servant, Abdul Azim. Queen Victoria's attachment to Abdul Karim, one of two Indians brought over as servants to enhance the spectacle of her Golden Jubilee in 1887, is well known. Karim acted as her *munshi*, or teacher, and her Indian Secretary, much to the annoyance of just about everyone in the royal household. Prince Arthur was furious at Karim's closeness to his mother, and the courtier Frederick "Fritz" Ponsonby declared him to be "a thoroughly stupid and uneducated man, [whose] one idea in life seems to be to do nothing and to eat as much as he can. . . . If he had been kept in his proper place," Ponsonby told his wife, "there would have been no harm done."[5]

Duleep Singh had two Indian valets at Elveden, Amroor Singh and Hookum Singh, both Punjabis, like him. (As an aside, North African servants were also in vogue: Louise de Rothschild kept a Nubian footman, Abdul Roffman, at Aston Clinton in the 1880s, while George Tangye of Heathfield Hall employed a thirteen-year-old Berber "valet" named Mahommad Saleh.)

Georgian architects had played with the idea of India, most famously at Sezincote House in Gloucestershire and its offspring, the Royal Pavilion at Brighton. Sezincote, designed at the beginning of the nineteenth century by Samuel Pepys Cockerell for his cousin, the East India Company nabob Sir Charles Cockerell, is essentially a classical English country house cloaked in Mogul ornament, much of it inspired by the Indian aquatints of the artist Thomas Daniell, who had spent some years working in India and who also had a hand in the design. A big central onion-shaped copper dome flanked by *chhatri*, the distinctive open domed pavilions which are a feature of Indo-Islamic architecture, proclaims its debt to Muslim India and at the same time introduces, according to Christopher Hussey's 1939 *Country Life* article on the house, "the glamour of the strange and remote." Its connection to the architecture and culture of India was just as remote: as Hussey noted, at the time the term "Indian" comprised Chinese, Turkish, Persian, and the Orient generally by reason of the fact that products from all these places were imported by the East India Company.[6]

John Nash's "Hindoo" Royal Pavilion at Brighton, built between 1815 and 1822 for the Prince Regent, later George IV, exemplified this eclectic approach to exotic Eastern glamour. It was a magnificently flamboyant melange of Islamic, Chinese, and Gothic elements, all Indian domes and *chhatri* and red lacquer interiors and silvered dragons. "As a matter of fact it is vulgar." (Architectural historian Nikolaus Pevsner's verdict, not mine.) What it wasn't was a serious attempt to evoke India. Or if it was, it failed. As Thomas Daniell said after it was completed, "There is not a feature, great or small, which at all accords with the purity, grandeur, and magnificence, that characterise the genuine Oriental style." And he would have known.[7]

But that wasn't the point of these whimsical early attempts at cultural appropriation. They weren't scholarly essays on orientalism. Nor were they conscious expressions of imperial might. (Whether they were *un*conscious expressions of that might is another matter.) They were lighthearted evocations of the glamour of the strange and remote. And remoteness was a relative value: Dromana Gate in County Waterford was an exotic Hindu-Gothic gate lodge of timber, canvas, and papier-mâché put up in 1826 by tenants to welcome home Lord Stuart de Decies and his bride after the newlyweds had honeymooned, not in India, but in Brighton. They liked it so much that in 1849 they commissioned the Irish architect Martin Day to build it in stone. Their country house is long gone, but the architectural souvenir of a holiday in Brighton still survives.

When Duleep Singh bought Elveden in 1863, he found himself with a seventeen-thousand-acre sporting estate which was regarded as one of the finest shooting properties in the kingdom, and a dull eighteenth-century country house which, according to *The Builder*, "had nothing interesting about it, being altogether devoid of architectural merit, having a flat and prison-like appearance, illustrating one of the worst periods of English architecture."[8]

Nevertheless, he settled down to the life of an English country gentleman, attending church on Sundays (a fact which made news all over the country) and celebrating Christmas 1863 by giving coal to the poor of Elveden village, supplying a supper for the estate workmen, and entertaining the local children. And he turned his thoughts to the future. In Egypt in 1864, while returning from depositing his mother's ashes in Bombay, the maharajah met and married the fifteen-year-old Bamba Müller, the illegitimate daughter of a German banker and an Ethiopian slave. Bamba was teaching in the American Presbyterian Mission School in Cairo and was unable to communicate directly with her husband, since she didn't speak English and he didn't speak Arabic. The Countess of Leven, who met the girl at Roehampton in July 1864, reported to Lady Login that "she is most submissive, and if asked if she would like to do anything, answers: 'Maharajah wish—I wish!'"[9] After they returned to Elveden she bore him three sons and three daughters before taking to drink and dying of renal failure when she was just thirty-nine.

It isn't clear exactly when the maharajah decided to rebuild Elveden. Some accounts say that work started while he and the maharanee were on their honeymoon; others say that it began much later. The account in *The Builder*, which was published in 1871, is probably the one to be relied on. It reported that in 1869 (by which time Bamba had borne two living sons, Prince Victor Albert and Prince Frederick Victor, and another boy who died at birth), Duleep Singh commissioned John Norton to add a wing to the "flat and prison-like" house, and that before it was completed, he changed his mind and decided to pull down the entire mansion and start again. To be honest, at first sight the end result doesn't seem to be much of an improvement: Norton was a respectable architect rather than a sparkling one, most comfortable when he could show a little brio by introducing asymmetrical Tudor-Gothic facades peppered with flèches and turrets. (Tyntesfield in Somerset is his best work in this vein.) At Elveden he produced an Italianate block which looked rather like a gentleman's club on Pall Mall, except that it was built in red brick, with Ancaster stone dressings.

The real excitement lay behind the facade, where "Mr Norton had the gratification of being instructed to decorate the interior with pure Indian ornament."[10] Using models prepared by the main contractor, Cubitt and Company, pictures taken by the well-known photographer Samuel Bourne, who had just returned from seven years of photographing Indian architecture and landscapes, and details from the maharajah's own collection of watercolour drawings from Lahore, Norton and an army of English craftsmen created a remarkable group of Anglo-Indian interiors. The main reception rooms were filled with marble inlays, coloured cements, and encaustic floors specially made by Maw and Company. The ceiling of the drawing room, still to be completed in 1872, was covered with silvered convex glass, glittering fragments of mirror from the stained-glass manufacturer Powell of Whitefriars. There were characteristic multifoil arches everywhere, acting as screens or lining the walls or leading the eye from one space to another. Plaster panels were filled with poppies and irises and lotus flowers; cast-iron balustrading was painted bright red. The risers of the stone staircase were carved with a tulip motif. Only Bamba's boudoir bucked the trend: it was decorated in a French Renaissance style. By his own account, the maharajah spent £22,000 on rebuilding Elveden and a further £8,000 on furniture.

For a while, Elveden provided everything that Duleep Singh desired: status, a family home where he could entertain on a royal scale, a base from which he was able to slaughter vast quantities of game. In a good season—good for him, if not for the wildlife of Suffolk—his bag consisted of 9,600 pheasants, 9,400 partridges, 3,000 hares, and 75,000 rabbits. The Prince of Wales was a regular visitor; Elveden, he said, offered "the most wonderful shooting I ever saw," after his party bagged 6,000 birds in two days.[11] Bamba hosted fashionable tennis parties and entertained not only the county but a fair cross-section of British nobility. Their boys went to Eton; court circulars announced the couple's presence at state balls and royal drawing rooms. Their eldest son was christened in the private chapel at Windsor Castle, with Queen Victoria standing as one of his sponsors.

There were other ways in which Duleep Singh conformed to the expectations of elite British society. He gambled, he drank, he womanised. Donald Shaw, the author of a scurrilous collection of reminiscences titled *London in the Sixties*, painted a devastating picture of the maharajah at play. He was to be found every night at the Alhambra, wandering around backstage and waving some piece of jewellery while he asked, "What nice little girl is going to have this?" For a time he was obsessed with Polly Ash or Ashted, a dancer at the Alhambra: he set her up in a flat in Covent Garden and settled £3,000 a year on her. After that it was a sixteen-year-old chambermaid in Cox's Hotel named Ada Wetherill. "Her manners were admirable," recalled an acquaintance, "but her voice had the unmistakeable Whitechapel accent, and her pronunciation and the expressions she used were, to say the least, abnormal."[12] Duleep Singh was obsessed with her. When he was at Elveden he insisted she telegraph him twice a day to let him know what she was up to, and in 1886 he decamped to Paris with her.

By then he had alienated most of his old friends. There had always been an edge to society's acceptance of an Indian, even a royal Indian. Sir John Login overheard a woman saying that there was something about the young man's expression which was cruel and indicative of Oriental character. And Shaw's racist mockery of Duleep Singh in *London in the Sixties* was not unusual. "Every evening found him at the Alhambra graciously accepting the homage of the houris in the green-room, and distributing 9-carat gimcracks with Oriental lavishness." He may look grand in his court finery, said Shaw, but put him in evening dress "and a podgy little Hindoo seemed to stand before one . . . only requiring, as it were, a chutnee-pot peeping out of his pocket to complete the illusion."[13]

Repellent and racist. All the same, the last maharajah of the Sikh Empire did himself no favours. His conviction that the British government had cheated him led him to a series of damaging and rash declarations. He got into a very public quarrel with the India Office, writing angry letters to *The Times* claiming officials had swindled him out of his inheritance. He announced that he was going to return to Punjab and take up his birthright. He renounced Christianity and returned to Sikhism. He mixed with Fenian revolutionaries and shady Russians while British agents tracked his every move. He and Ada went to Moscow, where he offered his services to the czar of Russia, who didn't want them. In the meantime, he deserted Bamba and his children and settled in Paris with Ada, eventually marrying her after Bamba's death in September 1887. Elveden was dismantled. By the spring of 1886 he had sold tapestries, jewellery, a quantity of plate, and some embroidered hangings; and in May most of the remaining contents of Elveden came under the hammer in a sale which lasted for seven days. A suite of carved sandalwood furniture inlaid with ivory and embroidered with Indian needlework was broken up, the armchairs fetching twenty-one guineas each and eight chairs fetching between fourteen and seventeen guineas each. A Tudor bedstead with embroidered Indian silk hangings went for thirty-two pounds. The house and the shooting were advertised to let, but there were no takers until 1894, when the estate was bought by Sir Edward Guinness.

It might be stretching things to claim that Queen Victoria's son Prince Arthur's interest in Indian culture was due to his early encounters with the "truly amiable" young maharajah. One might just as accurately put it down to the distant influence of Morris and Webb and the other pioneers of the Arts and Crafts revival. Stationed in India in the 1880s as a recently married young soldier, the prince, who was created Duke of Connaught and Strathearn in 1874, together with his wife Louise, daughter of Prince Friedrich Karl of Prussia, visited the Calcutta International Exhibition of 1883–1884, where the couple met John Lockwood Kipling, the principal of the Mayo School of Arts in Lahore (and father of Rudyard). Kipling was an ardent promoter of traditional Indian crafts, which had suffered from competition from cheap imports and a tendency in India to value European design at the expense of native products. Kipling was particularly eager to raise the profile of the famous woodcarvers of Punjab, and it was probably at his prompting that the duke and duchess visited Lahore in the autumn of 1884. The result was that the duke's comptroller of the household, Sir Howard Elphinstone, suggested that if Indian royalty cared to give the duke and duchess a late wedding present (they had been married for five years at this point) then perhaps they might pay for the creation of an Indian room at the couple's country seat, Bagshot Park in Surrey.

The paint was barely dry on Bagshot. A much-altered and frequently remodelled seventeenth-century house had been demolished in 1877 and replaced by a huge and rambling Tudor-Gothic mansion designed by the elderly architect Benjamin Ferrey, whose last building it was. But the Connaughts had already decided their new home wasn't huge and rambling enough: they wanted an extension to house a billiard room and a smoking room, those exquisitely gendered male adjuncts to the Victorian country house. The idea of decorating the extension with examples of Punjabi wood carving appealed to them both, and they were determined that the new interiors should be authentically Indian and should showcase traditional Indian crafts.

Panels, 241 of them, were carved in Lahore and shipped over to England, where their installation was supervised by three men: Caspar Purdon Clarke, keeper of the India Museum at South Kensington and designer of the "Indo-Saracenic" Indian Pavilion at the 1878 Paris Exhibition; John Lockwood Kipling; and one of Kipling's protégés, a Sikh master carver and architect named Bhai Ram Singh. Of the three, Purdon Clarke was the manager, Lockwood the facilitator, and Singh the major creative talent. He had just designed a new building in Lahore for the Mayo School of Arts, and in 1910 he would become the first native principal of the school. (And as the architect of Punjab University's Senate Hall, he was also the only native to be credited with the design of a colonial building.) Lockwood reserved the task of making some of the intricately carved panels for the wood-carving class at the school. The rest of the panels were contracted out to carpenters in Amritsar, who worked directly under Bhai Ram Singh.

The result was one of the most exciting Indian interiors to grace an English country house. Carved wall panels filled the billiard room, depicting Indian and European plants and animals—roses and daffodils, cobras and elephants, mango trees and willows. Two of the panels paid homage to the duke and duchess: Prince Arthur's showed an intricately carved throne surmounted by two yak's tails, symbols of royalty; his wife's panel consisted of her initials, L. M. for Louise Margaret, with parrots and a seated Ganesh, the Hindu elephant god of wisdom and good fortune. Kipling designed the "Indian" scoreboard and cue rack.

The installation took years: inscribed panels over one of the billiard room fireplaces crediting Kipling and Singh give the dates 1885–1887, but in March 1888 Elphinstone was writing to ask for the panels to be transported, along with a written explanation of the various motifs. Kipling was still overseeing the finishing touches in 1890, and Singh was back to carry out unspecified work on the interior in 1892. When Queen Victoria visited her son and daughter-in-law in June 1894, she was impressed. After taking tea in a *shamiana*, an Indian tent which the Connaughts had put up in the gardens, she went into the house "and looked at the beautiful Indian room designed by Ram Singh, much of the carving having been executed by him," as she wrote in her journal.[14] The billiard room, the adjoining smoking room, and the corridor connecting the extension to the main house were filled with objects the Connaughts had brought back with them from India.

By the time of her visit, Queen Victoria had an Indian room of her own. Interest in Indian crafts and culture had been piqued by the Colonial and Indian Exhibition in South Kensington, which was opened by the queen, flanked by the Prince of Wales and Prince Arthur, on May 4, 1886. The national anthem was sung in Sanskrit (the middle verse, anyway), and Tennyson composed a poem for the occasion—not, one has to confess, his best work:

> *Britain's myriad voices call*
> *"Sons, be welded, each and all,*
> *Into one Imperial whole,*
> *One with Britain heart and soul!*
> *One life, one flag, one fleet, one Throne!"*
> *Britons, hold your own!*[15]

Prayers were led by the Archbishop of Canterbury, Edward White Benson; a massed choir sang the "Hallelujah" chorus; and the famous Canadian soprano Emma Albani treated the audience to renditions of "Home, Sweet Home" and "Rule Britannia." Although, as its title suggests, the exhibition was intended to showcase the products of the entire British Empire, the largest the world had ever seen, imperial India was given fully one-third of the exhibition space—about 103,000 square feet in all. There were elaborate gateways from Jaipur and Gwalior, displays of silks and carpets, and demonstrations of weaving and silversmithing and other skills by a group of "native artisans" (actually inmates of Agra Gaol who had been brought over to England for the occasion by the gaol's British superintendent, Dr J. W. Tyler, who was described as "Officer in charge of Native Artisans"). The highlight was the Indian Palace, designed by Purdon Clarke and intended, as the souvenir guide put it, "to represent a typical Royal Residence in feudal India, with its great fortified entrance gateway, forecourt with shops for the service of the Rajah, and, beyond, the Hall of Audience and public portions of the Palace."[16]

One of the most remarkable objects in the entire exhibition was this "hall of audience," or durbar room. Made of wood, it was carved "in the Punjab style" by two Punjabi carvers, Sunni Muslims named Muhammad Baksh and Muhammad Juma, who came over to England in June 1885 and worked on the hall for the next ten months. When it was finished, every surface was covered with a mass of intricate ornament, "so rich is the fund of design possessed by these native craftsmen."[17]

This was just the effect that the Connaughts were aiming for with their Bagshot Park billiard room—a seemingly infinite variety of ornaments covering every inch of space and giving the lie, in its individuality and creativity, to all those soulless, machine-made duplications that were swamping traditional crafts both in Britain and in India. Thomas Brassey, the Liberal politician and an inveterate traveller, was so taken with the durbar room that after the exhibition was over he bought sections of it and had them re-erected by Purdon Clarke as an extension to his Park Lane mansion.* Muhammad Baksh and Muhammad Juma stayed on after the exhibition, such was the demand for their one-off pieces, and they may well have been involved in the installation of the Duke of Connaught's billiard room and smoking room.

---

* After Brassey's death in 1918 the durbar room was gifted to Hastings Museum, where it can still be seen today.

Queen Victoria's relationship with India was close and complicated. On New Year's Day 1877 she was proclaimed empress of India
at Calcutta, Bombay, Madras, and Delhi, where the viceroy, Lord Lytton, presided over a vast gathering of ruling chiefs and their entourages
and assured them that the queen had assumed this title as "a symbol
of the union of their interests and a claim upon their loyal allegiance;
the Imperial power giving them a guarantee of impartial protection."
As a reminder of what that "protection" involved, each of the more
important chiefs was given a banner with the inscription "From Victoria, Empress of India," and the viceroy presented it to each one saying,
"Whenever this banner is unfurled, let it remind you of the relations
between your Princely House and the Paramount Power."[18] Never forget who is boss, in other words.

In 1890 Victoria decided that she needed a large reception room at
Osborne, the Italianate country house on the Isle of Wight designed
in the 1840s by Prince Albert and the builder and developer Thomas
Cubitt. And she wanted it to have an Indian theme, like Arthur's new
work at Bagshot. That August, while staying at Osborne, she noted in
her journal:

> I went with Louise [her daughter], Arthur, Louischen [Arthur's
> duchess] & Mr Kipling, (a gentleman Arthur knows well, who
> is at the head of the School of Art at Lahore, & who arranged
> things for him), to the new building. I want Mr Kipling to
> design the decoration of the interior of the new room, which is
> to be Indian. We agreed upon what was to be done.[19]

Bhai Ram Singh worked on the designs in Lahore over the
autumn, and after some to-ing and fro-ing over the details, it was
agreed that he should come to England to see the room he was designing. Kipling gave him one month's leave of absence from the Mayo
School of Arts, which seems rather stingy considering the voyage from

India to Britain took a good deal longer than that; in the event, he was away for well over two years. The queen agreed to pay one hundred pounds for his passage to England and back with P&O, to give him five pounds a week, and to provide him with a cottage near Osborne. He wasn't invited to stay in the house, not least because there was some anxiety about his dietary requirements. "The feeding of Mahammadans is always troublesome," wrote Sir Henry Ponsonby, the queen's private secretary.[20]

Bhai Ram Singh was at Osborne by the beginning of February 1891, showing the queen his "really beautiful drawings." She thought he was "a very intelligent, pleasant, nice man." Two weeks later he presented her with more designs, including "a cast of the small model of the chimneypiece with a peacock." And in March he visited her at Windsor, again bringing his "beautiful drawings."[21] From then on, work progressed quite quickly: Victoria was soon in her new Indian room, which she was now calling the Durbar Room, and discussing cottons to hang on the walls with "the principal man from Proctor's Oriental Shop." Authenticity wasn't paramount, as it had been at Bagshot; in any case, although Kipling and Singh had initially suggested the same delicately carved wooden panelling, that was ruled out on the grounds of cost: there were no Indian princes offering belated wedding presents this time. Moulded plaster and papier-mâché were a great deal cheaper, and the plasterworking firm of George Jackson and Sons (which coincidentally had worked on the decoration of the "Hindoo" Brighton Pavilion seventy-five years earlier) set up a studio on-site to make fibrous plaster ornaments, working directly from moulds and templates made by Singh. Their working relationship was rather fractious, and they eventually fell out over Singh's modifications to the original design, which took Jackson well over its £2,250 budget.

Bhai Ram Singh also had to contend with Victoria's daughter Princess Louise, who was actively involved in the whole process. The princess had pronounced views. She fretted about the lack of an oriental tone. She vetoed Singh's suggestion that the colour scheme should be light blue and gold, declaring that anything other than white and gold would look common. She complained that his design for the chimneypiece was clumsy and too heavy, suggesting that it should display an "Indian flower, a peacock or something of that sort."[22] It was this which led to his presenting a model of the peacock chimneypiece to Victoria, and in the end the peacock in high relief became the focus of the chimneypiece, dominating the space. It took Singh's team of craftsmen more than five hundred hours to make.

That space still has the power to astonish today. The deeply coffered ceiling is filled with intricate moulded floral designs, with four birds circling each other at the centre. A first-floor gallery is flanked by a pair of *jharokhas*, projecting balconies of carved teak. There are birds and deer and fish and lion heads and sunflowers. Ganesh appears over a door, together with lesser deities, while in a nice piece of ecumenism, the phrase *Wala Ghalib Illal Lah*, "There is no conqueror but Allah," appears on a gilded wall panel.

The queen was delighted with "my Durbar room." Bhai Ram Singh was invited to design furniture for the room, including thirty-six dining chairs carved with a pheasant motif, sideboards and matching side tables, stands for the electric lamps, and brass handles for the doors. Victoria commissioned a portrait of the craftsman from the orientalist artist Rudolf Swoboda, who had already painted two pictures of her *munshi*, Abdul Karim.

While Elveden was meant to comfort an exile and Bagshot had been a serious attempt to demonstrate how traditional Indian crafts could be transported to Britain and used more or less authentically— give or take a rose and a daffodil or two—the Durbar Room at Osborne had an element of theatricality about it. "The room is Orientalised to the height of the most cultivated Indian Rajah's imagination," declared one popular magazine shortly after Singh's decorative scheme was complete. "And with such surroundings, when the Queen dresses in Indian costume and enters her Imperial Room at Osborne, Her Majesty will look a real Indian Empress." In fact, while it may have served to remind her guests that the queen was also an empress, her Durbar Room also acted as backdrop to a bewildering procession of events, from a dinner for fifty at which the guest of honour was her grandson, Kaiser Wilhelm II, to plays, tableaux, recitals by Italian virtuosi, and concerts: "We went over to the Durbar Room, where a Welsh Ladies Choir, 35 in number sang. . . . They all wore their national dress, with those curious pointed hats over caps."[23]

In the summer of 1891, when the seventy-one-year-old queen empress was staying at the Grand Hotel at Grasse on the French Riviera, she had a distressing interview with Maharajah Duleep Singh, who had come over from Nice with his second son, Frederick. The queen noted that he was hatless and "in European clothes." (What did she expect him to wear in the south of France?) Broken, broke, and partially paralysed after a stroke, he was unable to kneel as he kissed her hand. She invited him to sit, and he burst into a fit of weeping, begging her to "excuse me and forgive my grievous faults." "That is all forgiven and past," said the queen; but the interview lasted only a few minutes, in which the pair discussed his sons and daughters. Then "I wished him goodbye and went upstairs . . . very thankful that this painful interview was well over."[24] The last maharajah of the Sikh Empire was given some refreshments and packed off back to Nice.

Two years later, in Paris, on the night of October 21, 1893, he had a second stroke, and he died the next evening. He was fifty-five. His body was taken back to England and he was buried next to Bamba in the Elveden churchyard. Ada sent a wreath in the form of a cross of white flowers, with ADA picked out in violets. Ada herself died in 1930 in Tunbridge Wells, having spent her last years writing to the India Office to ask for a loan to open her own hat shop.

How did Duleep Singh's children fare in a society which still deferred to nobility (and especially to royalty) but was ambivalent, to put it mildly, towards nonwhites? In 1898 Victor, the maharajah's heir—Eton, Cambridge, Sandhurst, and a commission in the 1st (Royal) Dragoons—married Lady Anne Coventry, youngest daughter of the 9th Earl of Coventry, of Croome Park in Worcestershire. In an article headlined "Fashionable Marriage" the *Daily Telegraph* gave a long account of the wedding at St Peter's, Eaton Square, referring obliquely to the fact that this was the first time a member of the British aristocracy had married an Indian. "What difficulties were to be overcome, what obstacles surmounted, before the Hindoo Prince could so triumphantly lead to a Christian altar his British bride."[25] According to one account, the Earl of Coventry only allowed the marriage after the Prince of Wales intervened on Victor's behalf. And there was a persistent rumour that Victoria only consented to the match on the understanding that the pair would have no children.

Victor and his bride, now Princess Victor Duleep Singh, set up home at Hockwold Hall in Norfolk, an attractive Jacobean country house which had been frequently altered and rearranged. *The World*, which included Victor in its "Celebrity at Home" series the year they were married, visited the couple at Hockwold and portrayed the prince as a typical country squire—his appearance gave "but little hint of his Oriental origin"—who loved to show visitors his kennels and stables, while his wife liked nothing better than to chat about horses and hunting.[26] (Lord Coventry's wedding present was a hunter called Pegasus.)

This rural idyll didn't last. "Prince Victor Duleep Singh . . . is an Englishman in his tastes," declared the *Daily Mirror*. The trouble was that those tastes were expensive: in 1902 Victor was made bankrupt, and at the subsequent court hearing he disingenuously explained that he had been financially embarrassed ever since his father's death and that a £50,000 loan from the Prudential Assurance Company had gone "for betting, money-lenders, and so forth." Even more disingenuously, he told the court that he attributed his situation to his expenditure having exceeded his income. Quite. An attempt to gift the contents of Hockwold Hall to his wife to prevent them from falling into the hands of creditors failed, although she kept a flat in Paris in her own name, and that remained safe. Hockwold was put up for sale in 1902; and an action against the India Office, claiming that the allowance awarded to his father should have been transferred to him on his father's death, was unsuccessful.[27]

The prince's financial embarrassments don't seem to have had much of an impact on the couple's social life. They were seen at the opera and at various big county balls. They were frequent visitors to Highclere Castle—Victor was one of the 5th Earl of Carnarvon's closest friends—and the prince also spent time as a guest of the Iveaghs at his father's old house, Elveden Hall. In later years they lived in Paris in an apartment on the avenue du Trocadéro, playing bridge and playing the tables at Monte Carlo, where Victor died in 1918. His princess stayed in France, making only occasional visits to her family in Worcestershire; she died in Paris in 1956 and was buried next to Victor in the Cimetière de Monaco.

Bamba, the eldest of Victor's sisters, settled in Lahore, where she married the principal of the medical college there, Dr David Waters Sutherland. Catherine, the next, lived partly in Switzerland and partly in Kassel with her German governess and lifelong companion, Lina Schäfer. Sophia was a campaigner for votes for women and an active member of the Women's Tax Resistance League.

Alone in the Duleep Singh family (and there were two more half sisters, daughters of Ada Wetherill), Victor's brother Prince Frederick was the one who settled down quietly to a conventional life in an

English country house. Frederick lived first at Old Buckenham Hall, a 340-acre estate in Norfolk, twenty miles from Elveden, and then, after a temporary move to a modest house in Breckles, he went to Blo Norton Hall, also in Norfolk, an attractive Tudor country house which he leased in 1909 and which remained his home until his death in 1926. There he devoted his life to his antiquarian interests: heraldry and genealogy, old furniture, and stained glass. At Cambridge he had, said his sister Bamba, indulged in "his love of the picturesque dress of the eighteenth century."[28] He had a passion for Stuart relics: the drawing room at Blo Norton was filled with Stuart portraits and mementos, including a seal belonging to Bonnie Prince Charlie's brother, Henry, Cardinal York, which he picked up in Italy. Also at Blo Norton, Frederick created an oratory dedicated to King Charles the Martyr.

He was an ardent preservationist and a member of the Society for the Protection of Ancient Buildings. He read papers on church restoration to the Norfolk and Suffolk Archaeological Societies, appealing "to those who live in the country, to those who live in our old villages who are interested in the lives and histories of their predecessors . . . to preserve every little bit of tangible history that still exists."[29] He had a huge collection of Norfolk and Suffolk portraits, and he was the author of a posthumously published two-volume work titled *Portraits in Norfolk Houses.*

He was, in fact, the epitome of the antiquarian country squire. Lord Dufferin called this last surviving male heir of the last maharajah of the Sikh Empire "a thorough Englishman."[30]

SIX

FIRE FROM FRANCE

"T HAT SUMMER WE went to Devonshire," wrote the dancer Isadora Duncan, "where he had a wonderful chateau which he had built after Versailles and the Petit Trianon, with many bedrooms and bathrooms, and suites, all to be at my disposition, with fourteen automobiles in the garage and a yacht in the harbour."[1]

Duncan's generous lover was a sewing machine millionaire, Paris Singer. And the "wonderful chateau" where they spent the late summer of 1910 was Oldway in Paignton, one of the most remarkable country houses in Edwardian England.

Oldway has a colourful history. Its connection with the Singer family began in 1871, when Paris's father Isaac bought a twenty-acre estate overlooking the little seaside town of Paignton and the modest Victorian villa, Oldway House, that went with it. Born in New York State in 1811, Isaac Merritt Singer pursued a career as an actor and manager of a travelling theatre troupe, the Merritt Players, while all the time trying to make his fortune by patenting various mechanical devices. In 1851 he took out a patent on the first practical sewing machine—there were others in America at the time, and the early years of I. M. Singer and Company were fraught with litigation—and within a few years his firm was the leading manufacturer of sewing machines in America, and Isaac Singer had amassed a huge fortune.

He had also amassed a huge family. Singer fathered at least twenty-four children by two wives and three mistresses, managing to blur the conventional boundaries between marriage and cohabitation so successfully that after his death his widow was involved in a messy court battle with one of the mistresses, who argued that as Singer's common-law wife she should take precedence and thus, of course, his money (some $15 million). The mistress lost, but it was what the newspapers called Singer's "frightfully misshapen life" that had driven him to leave New York. He married his second wife, Isabella, whose English mother and French father ran a pension in Paris, in 1863 when she was newly divorced and heavily pregnant. The couple's attempts to gain a foothold in conservative New York society fell afoul of Singer's scandalous reputation. "Hundreds were invited. Few went," was the comment of one newspaper on their first big party together.[2]

So in 1865 Isaac and Isabella moved to Europe, first settling in Paris and then, when the Franco-Prussian War broke out in 1870, decamping to England. By now they had six children under the age of eight—Isaac was nothing if not prolific—and after a brief stay at Brown's Hotel in Mayfair the family moved to Torquay for the sake of Isabella's health. They liked South Devon so much that they decided to settle there, moving into Oldway House in 1871. But it was neither big enough nor grand enough, and Singer soon commissioned a young local architect, George Soudon Bridgman, to build him a rather large and rather French country house in the grounds, with a private theatre and curving carriage ramps leading up to a spectacular first-floor porte cochère. Bridgman also built a massive circular indoor riding school, known at the time as the Arena but later renamed the Rotunda. Singer nicknamed the main house "the Wigwam" and topped it off with a carving of a bow-and-arrow-wielding Native American perched on top of a flagpole—both intended as statements of his American origins, according to his children.

Isaac Singer died in July 1875 with the new Oldway still unfinished, and a few months later a bitchy article appeared in local newspapers, claiming he had been ostracised by the county. "He tried to get into society by giving a grand ball, to which all the aristocracy of the neighbourhood were invited. But they mercilessly snubbed him, and in revenge he asked all the tradesmen of the place, and gave them an entertainment the like to which for magnificence has hardly ever been seen in England." There is no other evidence to suggest either that the Singers were kept out of Torbay high society, such as it was, or that they made any efforts to enter it—except, perhaps, that the guests at the grand parties he threw in the grounds or in the Arena tended to be resolutely middle class rather than landed gentry, "the better-class residents and the wives and daughters of the leading tradesfolk of the district."[3]

Isaac Singer cut quite a figure at these parties and balls, standing up in the gallery of the Arena to give a speech of welcome, wearing a long coat of royal blue velvet lined with primrose satin. His flamboyance, no less than his foreignness, marked him out as "other," while his generosity endeared him to the local community. He made sure to give his custom to local businesses, distributed food to the poor at Christmas, invited all and sundry to celebrate the Fourth of July with him at Oldway, and handed out expensive pieces of jewellery to every girl who took his fancy. Old habits died hard.

One can get an inkling of just how complicated is the problem of defining the "Jewish country house" when the cultural historian Thomas Stammers argues that, although there is no evidence that the Oldway Singers were Jewish, if they were of "probably Jewish heritage" they didn't attach much importance to the fact; and that no one in Edwardian England spoke of Oldway as a Jewish country house; yet "if it was not a Jewish country house in its own right, studying the social world to which the Singers belonged, and some of their cultural choices, can illuminate how many rich Jews around 1900 invested in French styles of housebuilding and home-decorating."[4] Isaac and Paris Singer may not have been Jewish, in other words, but they acted like they were Jewish country house owners, and that can shed light on how Jewish country house owners behaved. A circular argument.

Oldway, which was left to a family trust, was completed after Isaac Singer's death. His widow Isabella soon found another husband, a Dutch musician who falsely claimed to be the vicomte d'Estenburgh but who did eventually enter the Italian peerage as Duke of Camposelice. Her two daughters also looked to the European aristocracy for husbands: Isabella Blanche became the Duchess Decazes (and, incidentally, the mother of the socialite Daisy Fellowes), while Winnaretta married, first, Prince Louis de Scey-Montbéliard—a union that was annulled after a particularly unsuccessful wedding night during which the bride took refuge on top of a wardrobe and threatened to kill the groom if he came near her—and, second, Prince Edmond de Polignac, a *mariage blanc* which left both partners free to pursue their own same-sex relationships.

Meanwhile, back in Devon, the Singer boys—Mortimer, Washington, Paris, and Franklin—took houses in and around Paignton, the older ones occasionally using Oldway as a party venue. Paris's coming-of-age party there in November 1888 was a particularly lavish affair. Weeks of celebrations kicked off with a performance of Gounod's *Faust* in Oldway's private theatre, with Paris taking the role of Mephistopheles himself and the famous soprano Marie van Zandt singing Marguerite. Then there was a fancy-dress ball in the Arena, which was converted into a ballroom for the occasion: "The guests numbered over 200, and comprised the elite of the neighbourhood," said the local paper, without going into details of the guest list. Paris went as a Louis XIV courtier, and his wife Lillie (the couple had married while both were still underage in Tasmania the previous year) was a Girton Girl. Washington Singer came as a Spanish toreador, and his wife was Robinson Crusoe. Two nights later Paris hosted a tradesman's ball for three hundred, and at the end of the week there was a third, private ball at the mansion.

In 1892, with no sign of any members of the family choosing to live at Oldway, the Singer trustees decided to put it up for auction. It didn't sell, but the prospect of losing it prompted Washington Singer to buy the house and estate from the trustees. Paris Singer went halves with him and then bought him out, moving in permanently in 1897. He took out British citizenship three years later.

If Isaac Singer didn't go out of his way to woo the nobility and gentry of Devon, his son didn't need to. A lot had happened in the quarter century since Isaac's death, and now, if money didn't *quite* matter more than breeding, it certainly ran a close second. Lillie Singer was presented at court, "her white satin gown embroidered in gold, and wearing a pale blue train." She presided over charity bazaars in London and hosted charity balls at Oldway. Separately and together the couple was asked to Buckingham Palace drawing rooms, levees, and courts, while Paris played a role—admittedly a minor one—in Edward VII's coronation, and he appeared in gossip columns driving Queen Alexandra "in one of his horseless carriages." (Paris was an enthusiastic and entrepreneurial motorist, a founding member of the Automobile Club of Great Britain and Ireland, later the RAC, and an advocate for electric cars: in 1902 his City and Suburban Electric Carriage Company bought a skating rink in Westminster and converted it to a "charging centre for electric broughams.") They kept a box at Covent Garden and entertained at Henley Royal Regatta on their houseboat, the *Minnehaha*, "a pretty white and green boat, most tastefully treated with white and pink." "Paris Singer, who has recently made his mark in the social world of London," declared the *Daily Express* in 1901, "is rich, clever and successful."[5]

Paris had homes all over Europe: a house on Sloane Street and a mansion flat on Kensington Court; an apartment on the place des Vosges in Paris, where he was treated like a king in all the best restaurants. "All the Maitres d'Hotel and all the cooks vied with one another to please him," recalled Isadora Duncan. The "yacht in the harbour" she referred to earlier was the *Lady Alicia*, a steam yacht with a crew of fifty in which Paris cruised the Mediterranean. A regular visitor to the French Riviera, Singer bought land at Cap Ferrat and built himself a villa fortress there, Les Rochers. When he took it into his head to winter on the Nile with Isadora, he chartered a *dahabeah* with thirty native sailors, a first-class cook, and sumptuous en suite cabins. "We had with us a Steinway piano," she wrote, "and a very talented young English artist, who played for us every night Bach and Beethoven, whose solemn measures harmonise so well with the space and the temples of Egypt."[6]

Within months of becoming the sole owner of his father's Wigwam in 1897, Paris embarked on a huge scheme to modernise the mansion and its grounds. He always referred to it as Oldway House, which might suggest a desire for conformity, but at the same time his choice of style and architect emphasised his cosmopolitan background, his otherness. He commissioned a master plan from the French father-and-son team of Henri and Achille Duchêne, who surrounded Isaac's Wigwam with formal avenues and parterres, pulling in references to Versailles and the Petit Trianon. A new entrance to the house was announced by a triumphal arch copied from the Porte Saint-Antoine, which forms the entrance to the Trianon gardens, while a new south front forming the backdrop to the formal gardens took inspiration from the Trianon's Pavillon Français of 1750. Isaac's rather bland east front gave way to a colonnaded facade which references the place de la Concorde in Paris.

The centrepiece of Paris Singer's new Oldway, and possibly the inspiration for it, was a vast (thirty-two feet by twenty) painting by Jacques-Louis David of the coronation of Napoleon and Empress Josephine. Paris bought the picture at auction in 1898, and to provide a suitably grand setting for it, he did away with his father's private theatre at the heart of the mansion and replaced it with a top-lit hall. This was an accurate replica of the monumental L'escalier des Ambassadeurs, designed in 1668 by Louis Le Vau as an awe-inspiring approach to Louis XIV's apartment at Versailles. The fact that the staircase had been destroyed in 1752 only added to its legendary status, and a scale model and engravings survived to enable Singer's workmen to reproduce it with remarkable accuracy, except for the addition of the colossal David painting, which filled one wall. Marble for the floors came from the quarries used for Versailles. The original colours and techniques were faithfully copied. It was, and it remains, one of the wonders of Edwardian country house architecture.

What motivated Paris Singer to take his inspiration from France? Apart from the fact that he was born in Paris, named after his birthplace, and had a mother who was half French and two sisters who were living in France and married to French nobility, he was also following a distinct fashion for all things French in late Victorian and Edwardian Britain. "The French styles of Louis XV and XVI are eminently suitable for a drawing room," declared the author of *Our Homes and How to Beautify Them* in 1902.[7] The following year, art historian Émile Molinier declared that

during the past forty years or so, the French styles of the eighteenth century have experienced a remarkable fortune; one after the other they have come back into fashion and at this very time, should one wish to furnish, in a sumptuous manner, a mansion or even a more modest residence, it would seem that his choice lies between the styles of the Regency Period, or the reign of Louis XV or that of Louis XVI.[8]

In 1907 the society hostess Lady Dorothy Nevill noted that "within the last twenty years French eighteenth-century art has become highly appreciated in England . . . [and] rooms fitted up entirely in the French style have recently been increasingly popular."[9]

Not only rooms: entire country houses. John Corbett's Louis XIII–style Impney, designed by a Parisian architect and executed by a Beaux Arts–trained Englishman, is an obvious example, but there are several dozen more. One of the pioneers in this field was Thomas de Grey, 2nd Earl de Grey, who inherited Wrest Park in Bedfordshire in 1833 and proceeded to build an enormous new house in the style of Louis XV, of his own design but drawing heavily on French architectural literature. His new entrance front was based on Jean Courtonne's Hôtel Matignon in Paris, which was illustrated in Jacques-François Blondel's *French Architecture* (1752), while the garden front came from Blondel's *On the Designing of Country Seats* (1737–1738). "I had my French books always under my hand," wrote de Grey, "[and] referred to them for authority whenever I could find anything to suit me."[10] The theme was continued in the rococo decoration of the principal staterooms, with French wall hangings, French panelling and wallpapers, and, in case anyone was in any doubt, a decorative cartouche perched over a door in the staircase hall, with emblems of the arts and architecture flanked by books whose spines bore the names of Blondel, François Mansart, and Antoine Le Pautre.

An interest in French art and interior decoration was common enough by the 1830s, fostered first by the Prince Regent's taste for French furniture and then by the British aristocracy's empathy with the Bourbons, who had been deposed in the July Revolution of 1830. But Earl de Grey's desire to build a French country house in the middle of Bedfordshire—rather than simply buying a Boulle cabinet, a

Sèvres breakfast service, or a couple of rococo pier glasses—seems to have been motivated by a simple passion for French architecture.

But what counted as an oddity, albeit a rather elegant oddity, in the 1830s was by the 1870s becoming almost ordinary. English architects began to borrow from France, introducing spiky rooflines and round turrets with conical roofs while their clients raided chateaux and *hôtels* to find authentic panelling and chimneypieces. French architects were also in fashion: Impney and Oldway were both designed by Frenchmen, although in both cases the supervising site architect was English. So was the remarkable Bowes Museum (1869–1871) in County Durham, the work of Jules Pellechet for John Bowes, the illegitimate son of the 10th Earl of Strathmore, and his actress wife Joséphine Benoîte Coffin-Chevallier. Bowes had retreated to Paris in 1847, partly to avoid the social stigma attached to his parentage: his father had married his mother the day before he died, which may have left him socially embarrassed but also left him with forty thousand acres and an income of £20,000 a year.

He met his wife when he bought the Théâtre des Variétés in Paris, where she was appearing; after he bought her the Château de Madame du Barry at Louveciennes as a wedding present, they began collecting pictures and antique furniture. Eventually they sold the chateau and hit on the idea of building a museum in Bowes's native Teesdale to house their collection. Pellechet's Second Empire creation looked rather like a French town hall and was in fact based on the recent Hôtel de Ville at Le Havre (1855), designed by Charles Louis Fortuné Brunet-Debaines. Begun in 1869, the Bowes Museum wasn't completed until 1892, by which time Bowes and Joséphine were both dead, and speakers at the official opening couldn't resist the opportunity to take a dig at the French. The couple had decided on siting the museum in England rather than France, declared the local MP to cheers from the crowd, because England, "with its more sober progress in the political path, was more likely to hold in reverence works of art and keep them in safety than was the country which had been desolated from time to time by what was called patriotism, but which resulted at last in the terrible outrages of the Commune."[11]

This ambivalent attitude towards all things French—nice furniture, shame about the politics—raises the question of motive. John Corbett was always said to have chosen a Louis XIII style for Impney to please his French wife. However, she wasn't French, and their relationship was already fractured beyond repair when building began, so that seems unlikely. Paris Singer's love affair with France began in childhood, and his mother *was* French, or half-French, at least.

When it comes to the most famous, and arguably the greatest, of faux-French country houses, we have the builder's own explanation for why he favoured an alien style. "Having been greatly impressed by the ancient Chateaux of the Valois during a tour I once made in Tourennes," said Ferdinand de Rothschild of the origin of his ideas for Waddesdon Manor, "I determined to build my house in the same style. . . . The French sixteenth century style, on which I had long set my heart, was particularly suitable to the surroundings of the site I had selected [on a Buckinghamshire hilltop], and more uncommon than the Tudor, Jacobean or Adam of which the countryside affords so many and such unique specimens." Rothschild was equally clear about his choice of architect, the Parisian Hippolyte Destailleur: he "considered it safer to get the design made by a French architect who was familiar with the work, than with an English one whose knowledge and experience of the architecture of that period could be less thoroughly trusted." Destailleur, who had recently restored the spectacular Renaissance Château de Mouchy in northern France, produced a design which pulled together elements from different historic French chateaux: external staircases from Blois, towers from Maintenon. The grounds were landscaped by a comparatively unknown French designer, Elie Lainé. Even the horses which carted building materials to the site were French: Percheron mares imported from Normandy.

"They travelled faster over the ground and were much cheaper than Shire horses," Ferdinand recalled.[12]

Destailleur didn't play a big part in the interior decoration of the chateau, perhaps because, although Ferdinand insisted that during their eighteen-year collaboration they never fell out, his architect paid scant regard to the necessities of daily life. Looking back on the project in 1897, Ferdinand claimed that Destailleur "had not the faintest conception of the needs of a large establishment, sacrificed the most urgent household requirements to external architectural features, and had the most supreme contempt for ventilation, light, air, and all internal conveniences."[13] Conceiving Waddesdon as not only a country house but also very much an appropriate setting for his astonishing collections of art objects, Ferdinand used various English and French decorators to create interiors which either replicated French models or made use of materials recycled from French houses. Chimneypieces came from old houses in Paris. Ornamental ceilings were copied from those still in existence in Parisian town houses. The panelling in Ferdinand's Grey Drawing Room came from a town house in Paris Saint-Germain that was built for the financier Abraham Peyrenc de Moras between 1728 and 1732. The neoclassical panelling in the Tower Drawing Room was made in 1773 and once adorned a country house designed by Étienne-Louis Boullée. Even the heavily carved Renaissance panelling in the Billiard Room in the Bachelors' Wing dates from the 1560s and is thought to have begun life in the Château d'Acquigny in Normandy.

The overall effect—room after room filled with the best of French eighteenth-century decorative arts, furniture made for the French royal family, carpets made for the Louvre in the Savonnerie workshops, replicas of seventeenth- and eighteenth-century silks, brightly coloured Sèvres porcelain, and clocks by Boulle—was opulent, almost overwhelmingly so. "So full of fine things that it is difficult to particularise," said Lady Dorothy Nevill. Mary Gladstone, daughter of the prime minister, William Ewart Gladstone, confided to her diary during a weekend at Waddesdon in 1885 that she "felt much oppressed with the extreme gorgeousness and luxury," adding that "the pictures in his sitting-room are too beautiful, but there is not a book in the house save 20 improper French novels." But then she was suffering from a head cold and feeling rather grumpy.[14]

Waddesdon was one of a cluster of country houses in Buckinghamshire and Hertfordshire built or remodelled for the Rothschild banking clan between 1851 and the 1890s. Not all took their inspiration from France: Aston Clinton House, modernised by George Devey for Anthony Nathan de Rothschild in the 1850s, was a sprawling, vaguely Italianate mansion. Others looked back to a very English past: Mayer Amschel de Rothschild's Mentmore Towers, for example, designed by Joseph Paxton in 1851 and the first of the great Rothschild mansions, was based on the Elizabethan Wollaton Hall in Nottinghamshire. Ascott House, Leopold de Rothschild's picturesque Jacobean manor house, was rendered more picturesque by George Devey, who from 1874 onwards provided it with half timbering, tall chimneys, and leaded casements, until when Mary Gladstone visited the "palace-like cottage" and ate strawberries and cream there in 1880, she thought it "the most luxurious and lovely thing I ever saw."[15]

Yet if a visit to a Rothschild house gave one an impression of overpowering opulence, it was usually French opulence. Even George Devey, who was much more at home with Old English half-timbered palace-cottages, was prevailed upon by Nathaniel Mayer Rothschild to give Tring Park a mansard roof and a French air. And, perhaps inspired by Ferdinand's Waddesdon, in 1881 their cousin Alfred de Rothschild built himself a spectacular French Renaissance mansion at Halton, next door to Aston Clinton and only ten miles or so from Waddesdon.

Ferdinand and Alfred were both serious collectors of French art (as were most of the Rothschilds, come to that) and both were enthusiastic hosts, so it was no surprise that a certain rivalry existed between them. Notwithstanding Ferdinand's impressive collections, Lady Dorothy Nevill thought that "amongst living collectors of fine French furniture, china, and pictures, in England, Mr Alfred Rothschild undoubtedly takes first place." After listing some of Alfred's treasures—the *Toilette of Venus* by Boucher, a bureau in mother-of-pearl that once belonged to Marie Antoinette, two Sèvres marriage chests—she noted merely that at Waddesdon there were "also many beautiful specimens of French art." And although Alfred kept most of his best pieces at his Mayfair town house, he was proud of Halton and its contents, commissioning a set of twenty-four photographs of the exterior and interior from Aylesbury photographers Samuel Glendening Payne and his wife Maria ("Photographs of Mansions, Groups, Schools, Families, &c . . . Every likeness guaranteed"). The photographs were bound in blue leather albums and given to friends and acquaintances. One went to his architect, William Rogers, "with every expression of sincere gratitude." Another was given to Alfred's illegitimate daughter Almina, later to become the Countess of Carnarvon and chatelaine of Highclere Castle in Hampshire. The albums open with a photograph of Alfred lounging in a Louis XV armchair upholstered with Beauvais tapestry and gazing proprietorially into the distance. Jean-Baptiste Joseph Pater's *Les Amants heureux* hangs on the wall behind him. As one distinguished historian recently noted, this prefatory photograph "not only gave a crucial indication of Rothschild's collection aspirations but also presented the viewers with an image of him as a man of taste reigning over the exquisite surroundings he had devised."[16]

The Prince of Wales was the guest of honour at Alfred's first house party at Halton. Ferdinand de Rothschild was also there, as was Daisy Greville, Countess of Warwick, who admired the way that "the whole place was furnished in the period of Louis Quinze with French pictures cunningly framed in the walls." Ferdinand behaved badly, finding fault with everything. "He was," she thought, "really jealous of his cousin, because he feared that Halton would rob him of his house-parties." It was generally agreed that Alfred was the more socially accomplished host, if a little eccentric. He kept a private orchestra at Halton, which he used to conduct himself with a diamond-encrusted baton; he also had a private circus, and he enjoyed taking visitors for rides around his estate in his four-in-hand, which was pulled by zebras. During the housewarming he showed off his troupe of performing Japanese dogs, with qualified success. According to Daisy Warwick, "Great confusion was aroused by the fact that, although the chief little dog performed, it was not according to the programme."[17]

If Ferdinand enjoyed his cousin's discomfiture, it was returned in spades when the Prince of Wales fell down the stairs and broke his kneecap during a stay at Waddesdon in 1898.

Both Hippolyte Destailleur and landscape designer Elie Lainé also worked for other members of the Rothschild clan. In the 1880s Lainé laid out the grounds of the Château d'Armainvilliers in Seine-et-Marne for one of Ferdinand's many cousins, Baron Edmond de Rothschild. Lainé's career is still something of a mystery, but it has been suggested that in 1905 he may also have designed the gardens at the Villa Ephrussi in Cap Ferrat for yet another cousin, Béatrice de Rothschild. And between 1876 and 1884, whilst still working on Waddesdon, Destailleur created a palatial (and very French) mansion in Vienna for Ferdinand's cousin, Baron Albert von Rothschild.*

Destailleur was also responsible for one more tongue of fire from France burning brightly and incongruously in the English

---

* After the Rothschilds were forced to leave Austria in the wake of Germany's annexation of the country in 1938, the Palais Albert Rothschild became the headquarters of Adolf Eichmann's notorious Central Agency for Jewish Emigration in Vienna.

countryside. In 1871, after losing the Franco-Prussian War, Emperor Napoleon III went into exile in England with his wife, Eugénie, and their teenage son, the Prince Imperial. They settled at Camden Place, a big country house at Chislehurst in Kent, which was offered to the emperor for £500 a year by its owner, a close friend of Napoleon's one-time English mistress. The emperor died there in 1873, and his widow employed the architect Henry Clutton to design a mortuary chapel for his remains in the local Catholic church.

Six years later, in the summer of 1879, the Prince Imperial was killed fighting in the British army against the Zulus, and the grieving Eugénie decided she must have an extension to the chapel to house her son's tomb. She commissioned Destailleur to do the work, but their plans were rather too much for the church authorities, and in any case, Eugénie had decided that she and her small court of faithful retainers needed a place of their own.

In 1880 she paid £50,000 for the 257-acre Farnborough Hill estate in Hampshire. There was a new house, all high roofs and tall chimneys and jettied timber framing, designed by Henry E. Kendall Jr. in his own version of Old English for the previous owner, the publisher Thomas Longman, in about 1862; it was "an outrageously outsized chalet with . . . a lot of bargeboarding," as Nikolaus Pevsner described it.[18] But it wasn't big enough for an empress, and Eugénie asked Destailleur to alter and extend it while he continued to work on the designs for the mausoleum, which was now to be situated across the park. (Eugénie also built the Premonstratensian priory of St Michael, now a Benedictine abbey, to house the canons regular who would act as custodians.)

The mausoleum was completed by January 1888, when the embalmed bodies of Napoleon III and the Prince Imperial were moved from Chislehurst to their new resting place, watched by thousands of curious spectators. Destailleur's building is an eclectic essay in historicism, with a Romanesque crypt, a Gothic upper church inspired by royal funerary chapels of the late fifteenth and early six-teenth centuries at Toledo and Granada (where Eugénie was born), and a Renaissance dome or cupola which owes something to Tours Cathedral. The interior of the mausoleum was fairly restrained, with a white marble altar, a stained glass rose window, and a red-and-white Corsican marble floor. The ornate exterior didn't meet with everyone's approval, however: "A conspicuous object in the landscape for many miles round," said the *Morning Post*, while the *Evening Standard* declared that "the outward decoration, with its prominent gargoyles and other pronounced ornaments, may not commend itself to a severe taste," before adding, "but it is undoubtedly effective and picturesque."[19]

The house was something of a mausoleum, too. Destailleur kept much of Kendall's exuberant Old English exterior: Eugénie believed that "in any house you have to leave some remnants and mementos of the previous owners."[20] And he added a new service wing which, while holding to the idea of picturesque massing, managed to impart something of the French vernacular. As a result, although the house was never a Waddesdon or an Impney, there is undoubtedly some-thing un-English about its Old Englishness. The interiors were more overtly French: Louis XIV in Eugénie's *grand salon*; Blois, Chambord, and the sixteenth century in the cloister gallery, which formed part of the processional route from *salon* to dining room; Louis XVI in that dining room.

Opulent though the interiors were, they were made more opulent still by the empress's collection of Gobelins tapestries, Second Empire furniture, and dozens of portraits and busts, in which her husband and her son figured prominently. She had a deal with the French gov-ernment whereby she was paid compensation for items in the royal palaces which belonged to her family rather than to the state, but she also managed to negotiate the transfer to Farnborough Hill of the entire contents of the Villa Eugénie in Biarritz, which formed the core of the collection. It is also possible that some of the richest stateroom furniture was specially designed by Destailleur.

But there was no escaping the fact that Farnborough Hill was a retreat from the world and an *hommage* to the dead. The empress would join them in Destailleur's mausoleum in 1920, after a widowhood that had lasted nearly half a century. Augustin Filon, an old courtier and a frequent visitor to Farnborough Hill when Eugénie was alive, called it a mansion in mourning:

> The house constitutes an incomparable record of history, and in the evening, when a single ray of electric light leaves the spectator in shadow and sheds its white radiance over pictures and statues, a vanished world springs again into life, peopled with those once well-known figures who are the real inhabitants of the dwelling, and when the Empress passes in the midst of them one is almost tempted to believe that she, too, is a shadow of the Past.[21]

Isadora Duncan's visit to Paris Singer's "wonderful chateau" at Oldway in the summer of 1910 wasn't a great success. The couple had met the previous year when Paris, who was separated from his wife, came backstage at the Gaîté Lyrique, where the dancer was performing. He whisked her and her school of young dancers off to the south of France, where what had been a reasonably platonic relationship turned into something more serious. (According to Isadora, it happened in a telephone kiosk while they were trying to get hold of a doctor for one of the child dancers who had croup.) There followed the Mediterranean cruise in the *Lady Alicia*, the trip down the Nile. The couple made love in Singer's apartment on the place des Vosges (in a Louis XIV bed). Isadora toured America, and Singer, who had never been there, went with her. "Travelling with a millionaire does simplify things," she said, with entirely unconvincing *naïveté*. They had to cut short the tour when the results of those happy hours in the Louis XIV bed began to show.[22] She gave birth to Singer's child, a boy named Patrick, in May 1910.

Paris Singer's lifestyle was very different from that of a conventional Edwardian country house owner. Where his Devon neighbours might be content to host hunt balls or charity concerts, Singer threw wildly extravagant parties. He took over the park at Versailles and held a fete there. While his guests sipped champagne and slurped caviar, the famous Concerts Colonne played Wagner, conducted by the equally famous composer Gabriel Pierné, who conducted the world premiere of Stravinsky's *Firebird* with the Ballets Russes in June 1910. When he decided he wanted to see Isadora dance in one of the fabled temples in Paestum by moonlight, he hired an orchestra from Naples to accompany her.

But he still played the traditional country house host when he was at Oldway, and Isadora found life there dull by comparison. For one thing, it rained a lot. She looked on in horror as Singer's houseguests ate huge breakfasts before donning mackintoshes and trudging around the countryside until lunch, "when they eat many courses, ending with Devonshire cream." The really important business of the day, she thought, was dressing for dinner, "at which they appear in full evening dress, the ladies very décolleté and the gentlemen in starched shirts, to demolish a twenty-course dinner."[23] Singer, who was recovering from a stroke, was unwell. Noticing her boredom, he suggested she turn the great ballroom into a dance studio, and he sent to France for her backdrops to hide the priceless Gobelins tapestries which hung on the walls, her carpet to cover the waxed floor, and a pianist from the Concerts Colonne to accompany her.

Unfortunately the pianist did rather more than accompany her: after they were literally thrown together in the back of one of Singer's fourteen automobiles in the course of a bumpy ride, she "suddenly felt my whole being going up like a pile of lighted straw." Back at Oldway, the pianist and the dancer nipped behind a convenient screen in the ballroom, and while Singer lay ill in his bed, they spent the next weeks alone together "in the conservatory, in the garden, even taking long walks in the muddy country lanes."[24]

Isadora blamed her lapse on the fact that Singer ordered his butler to present his guests every day with a stimulant that his doctors had prescribed for him. The correct dose was a teaspoonful, but Singer insisted that everyone should drink it by the wineglass. So her indiscretion was obviously his fault.

SEVEN

MANSIONS OF
OLD ROMANCE

O N FRIDAY, JANUARY 8, 1897, a new weekly magazine hit train
station bookstalls. Priced at sixpence, Edward Hudson's *Country Life Illustrated* looked at first sight to be a racing paper, full of
reports on recent meetings, profiles of promising horses, and articles
on equally promising young jockeys. But after a long piece called
"Racing in Australia" the tone changed: there were articles on the
Devon and Somerset Staghounds, on the wild cattle of Cadzow Forest in Lanarkshire, on the Princess of Wales's pet dogs. And quite a
motley bunch they were, including Princess Alexandra's borzoi, Alix,
"from the Imperial kennels in Rusia," a collie called Newmarket Tip, a
crooked-legged basset hound, a Pekinese, and a chow called Plumpy.[1]

Tucked away among all these accounts of dogs and horses and
their various activities was a short article under the generic title "Country Homes," on Baddesley Clinton in Warwickshire, a moated manor
house dating back to the Middle Ages. The author, John Leyland,

managed to leaven his history of the house and its owners with a big dollop of atmosphere:

> Romance lingers in these stately chambers, round the walls of which hang many old portraits, each with its individual history, and in the mind's eye dead men loom out of the shadows when the moonlight falls through the tinted glass, and in imagination's ear the rustle of kirtles and farthingales, of brocaded silks and satins is heard anon as the wind whispers through the galleries and the rain patters down on the storied pane.[2]

There were swans gliding gracefully by on the moat. There was a romantic yearning for a comfortable and mythic past.

In the second issue of *Country Life* Leyland stayed in Warwickshire, turning his attention to a house with another, more famous mythic past: Charlecote Park, the home of the Lucy family. Charlecote's Elizabethan owner, Sir Thomas Lucy, was said to have had young William Shakespeare flogged for poaching deer on the estate, an incident which caused the youth to decamp to London and take up the slightly less precarious occupation of writing plays. There was so much to see, and so much to say, that Leyland left his description of the interior of the house until the next week, when he lingered over a visit by Elizabeth I, rather better documented than the Shakespeare episode:

> Picture the high state in which she came and was received. A young queen then, with many a lord and lady in her train, meeting a gay cavalcade as they approached the door. The long-lineaged squire kneels at her coming, to rise a knight, and never to forget that day. Prouder man there was not in Warwickshire.

Leyland lamented the fact that nineteenth-century Lucys had carried out some restoration work on the house, leaving it "less dilapidated, perhaps . . . [but] something of the old picturesqueness may
have departed." He consoled himself with a visit to the Lucy tombs
in the Charlecote church, admiring effigies of the 3rd Sir Thomas and
his wife, which were carved, he noted, "by the famous Bernini." They
weren't.

When he wasn't contributing to *Country Life* John Leyland was a
prolific writer of guidebooks with titles like *The Peak of Derbyshire: Its
Scenery and Antiquities* and *The Thames Illustrated: A Picturesque Jour-
neying from Richmond to Oxford.* (He also wrote extensively on naval
history, which seems to have been his main interest.) He had obviously made a tour of Warwickshire for these early *Country Life* articles, and in 1900 Country Life Ltd published his *Shakespeare Country
Illustrated,* which rehashed them in a slightly different form. His next
piece was on Warwick Castle, and the following two described a couple of good Georgian mansions in the county: Guy's Cliffe House,
which loomed over the legendary hermitage to which Guy of Warwick
was said to have retreated; and Stoneleigh Abbey, a fabulous piece of
British baroque designed—most of it, at least—by Francis Smith of
Warwick. In neither case did Leyland show much interest in these
buildings. Of Guy's Cliffe he remarked that "the house itself has no
architectural features calling for attention," and he preferred instead
to focus on the legends and the setting.[3] At Stoneleigh, Smith of Warwick's masterpiece, he wallowed instead in a pre-Dissolution "world of
mediaevaldom, of barons and men-at-arms, of the silent cloister, and
of white-robed men labouring in the fields," before taking the abbey's
staterooms at a generic gallop:

Within its spacious chambers—the entrance hall, library, silk
and velvet drawing-rooms, saloon, dining-room, breakfast-
room, and chapel—are nobly adorned, oak-panelled and

richly ceiled, with storied glass in their panes. Beautiful furniture and rare works of decorative art are within them, and
a splendid collection of family, probably, and other pictures is
upon their walls.[4]

That "probably" says it all.

In *Country Life*'s first year Leyland produced all but two of the
weekly articles in its Country Homes series. (The exception was a
more learned two-parter on the landscape garden at Painshill near
Cobham, which was unsigned.) Glamis and Hever, Holkham and
Hardwick, Leeds Castle and Castle Ashby, all came in for his ful-
some, if not particularly searching, praise. From early 1898 onwards
the tone of the Country Homes articles began to vary, and most of
the pieces, now under a distinctive masthead by Byam Shaw and
titled "Country Homes and Gardens Old and New," were unsigned.
Leyland may well have continued to contribute, but so did others,
including H. Avray Tipping, who became the magazine's architectural editor in 1907. Yet Leyland's little group of articles on Baddesley Clinton, Charlecote Park, Warwick Castle ("to which ivy fondly
clings"), Guy's Cliffe, and Stoneleigh Abbey marked a milestone in
the history of the country house. They confirmed a supremely attractive, if mythic, vision of the past and placed the country house at the
heart of that romantic vision.

The Country Homes articles became more scholarly in the early
twentieth century, combining genealogy and landscape history with
art history and architectural history. And they extended their reach
beyond Merrie Englande and moated manors to take in more recent
country houses. Edward Hudson was famously fond of the architecture of Edwin Lutyens, commissioning him to design or remodel
Deanery Garden (1899–1902), Lindisfarne Castle (1902), the *Country Life* offices on Tavistock Street, Westminster (1904), and Plump-
ton Place in East Sussex (1927). *Country Life* promoted Lutyens

relentlessly: between 1897 and 1914 his name appeared in the magazine 172 times. His new houses were the subject of articles, as were his gardens and even his furniture. *Country Life* published a laudatory ten-page review in 1913 of Lawrence Weaver's *Houses and Gardens by E. L. Lutyens*. Weaver was the architectural editor of *Country Life*, and *Country Life* published the book.

Yet in publicising and praising contemporary country house architecture (and Lutyens wasn't the only living architect to appear in its pages—Richard Norman Shaw and Philip Webb, who died in 1912 and 1915 respectively, were two more examples among many), the Country Homes articles still maintained the centrality of the country house in British—or, more accurately, English—culture. They were still underpinned by the conviction that the country house was not only woven into the fabric of English society but represented all that was best about that society: good taste and leadership, hierarchy and community and, above all, country life.

Celebrating the thousandth issue of *Country Life* in March 1916, H. Avray Tipping looked back on around seven hundred loving and respectful descriptions of country houses. He was clear that the intention had always been not only to inform and entertain but to educate. The accounts of those seven hundred houses showed "that our ancestors had, except in the matter of convenience, housed themselves more excellently than ourselves, and that there was much to learn in every one of the succeeding styles into which they had translated their changing requirements."[5]

There were two sections of society that found such an approach particularly attractive. One was the country house–owning class. It was rather nice, rather reassuring after years of agricultural depression and industrial unrest and rural depopulation, to be told that you were custodians of greatness, that your way of life represented all that was best about England, that your Adam library or Charles II staircase or Elizabethan great hall epitomised the peak of civilisation.

The other was the outsider, who was not quite part of the county set but who saw ownership of a country estate as a way of belonging. As one historian put it, *Country Life* "glamourised the country, made successful businessmen long to live in it, secure in the knowledge that by selling up and buying land one became at least a sort of gentleman."[6]

The turn-of-the-century appeal of the country house was enhanced by an uneasy feeling that some of the most romantic examples were in danger of disappearing. Allan Fea suffered from what he called "the epidemic of Manor House hunting." An earnest young clerk in the Bank of England (where he indulged an interest in photography by using the bank's safes as darkrooms), he spent weekends and summer holidays tramping around the countryside with an old school friend, William Satchell, in search of history and romance. They turned up at Baddesley Clinton, where they were shown round by the ancient owner, Marmion Ferrers, "a fine old gentleman, more like a Vandyck picture than a nineteenth-century squire." At Littleberries in Mill Hill, then a village but now a London suburb, they broke in through an open window one Sunday and wandered through "empty wainscoted and gilded chambers," imagining that they walked in the footsteps of Charles II's mistress Louise de Kérouaille, who was said to have lived there.[7]

Fea discovered that one of his fellow clerks was a cousin of the owner of Rushbrooke Hall in Suffolk, and he procured a personal tour. He was distressed to find evidence of neglect everywhere. There was damp and mildew on the walls, and "invaluable Stuart relics were hauled out of chests and cabinets for our inspection as if they were discarded garments awaiting the ragman; yet the Royal Stuarts had worn these treasures."[8]

Fea was simultaneously attracted and appalled by the neglect he found as he trekked around the mansions of old England. At

Chastleton in Oxfordshire, then unoccupied, he wallowed in it, roaming through the deserted rooms "and in the dusky twilight fancy[ing] all kinds of mysterious footsteps and spiritual shadows," although the colony of bats which occupied the long gallery at the top of the house proved a little too much for him; their "squeaks and flappings were calculated to work one's nerves up to concert-pitch." But when he visited Ockwells, a stunning late-medieval manor house in Berkshire which was described in the 1960s as "the most sophisticated timber-framed mansion in England," he was so shocked at the state of the place—the great hall in use as a barn, with sheep and cattle wandering in and out—and the rumour that it was about to be pulled down, that he fired off a letter to the newspapers, which started a national campaign to rescue it.[9]

Fea regularly published short articles about the examples of domestic architecture he met with on his travels, and in the 1890s he began to put his search for history and romance to use in a series of popular books about picturesque old cottages, manor houses, and mansions. They were so successful that by the beginning of the twentieth century he left the Bank of England, moved to Kent, and concentrated on a gentle and undemanding antiquarianism.* *Secret Chambers and Hiding-Places: The Historic, Romantic and Legendary Stories and Traditions About Hiding-Holes, Secret Chambers etc.* (1901) was followed in quick succession by *Picturesque Old Houses, Nooks and Corners of Old England, Old World Places*—the titles say it all, really. Ghostly damsels and mailed knights figured largely.

Fea's writing possesses an interest which goes beyond his inconsiderable literary talents. He recorded an old England of tumbledown cottages and rickety timber-framed manor houses that was

---

* Fea also published extensively on the Stuarts. His first book, which brought together both interests, was *The Flight of the King: Being a Full, True and Particular Account of the Miraculous Escape of His Most Sacred Majesty King Charles II After the Battle of Worcester* (1897).

fast disappearing, and "who does not feel a pang of regret at parting with something which linked us with the past?" He showed a disdain, shared by most of his contemporaries, for anything much later than the seventeenth century. The "battlemented towers . . . and Georgian and Victorian Gothic sash-windows" of Hinton House in Somerset meant that it was "by no means beautiful," unlike the nearby Sandford Orcas manor house, "a gem of early-Elizabethan architecture." Derbyshire's Haddon Hall was well-nigh perfect: "the enchanted castle of the fairy story," a country house whose "picturesqueness [was] enhanced by its lack of uniformity." Elizabethan Hardwick Hall was "peculiarly majestic and stately"; whereas baroque Chatsworth's interest for Fea lay largely in the fact that Mary, Queen of Scots, had been held prisoner in an earlier version of the house.[10]

But perhaps the most significant feature of Fea's books is the fact that in what is supposed to have been the golden age of the English country house, so many of the places he visited *were* in such a state. In November 1897 *Country Life* published an article titled "Deserted Houses." The author, Lucy Hardy, said how curious it was how often, especially in rural England, one found houses "which look deserted as well as empty; tenantless houses which display no bill 'To Let,' and which appear to have been unoccupied for many a long year." Hardy came up with various reasons for this: the owners might be abroad, or the place might be too remote; there might have been a recent murder or suicide there. Or there might be ghosts, which seemed to prefer country houses to more mundane suburban villas. "The sheeted ghost . . . which drags a chain, or playfully disengages its head and rolls it down the grand staircase at midnight, usually appertains to the castle, or to the baronial hall, and does not deign to 'walk' in houses of meaner degree."[11]

A few weeks later *Country Life* carried an article on Emral Hall, one of the great houses of Wales. Built for the Puleston family in the early seventeenth century, Emral's glory was its first-floor drawing room or great chamber, with a remarkable plasterwork ceiling filled with scenes from the life and labours of Hercules. The hall had been extended in the early eighteenth century, but profligate Victorian owners had mortgaged the estate up to the hilt and then deserted the house. By 1897 it had been standing empty for more than thirty years, and it was in a sad state. Floorboards and stairs were rotting dangerously, oak wainscotting was coming away from the walls in the bedrooms, and everywhere there were signs of neglect. Murals on the grand staircase had faded to nothing. Oak carvings had been ripped out and stolen, and the panelling that was left was "much disfigured with names and dates cut by unthinking visitors who used to visit the hall without permission," clambering in through broken windows.[12]

Soon after the article appeared, Catherine Puleston, the widow of the last Puleston baronet, came to the rescue, restoring Emral and repairing much of the damage inflicted by time, neglect, and "unthinking visitors." The reprieve was only temporary, however. Emral Hall was demolished in 1936.*

Perhaps the most famous encounter with a country house in decline, and the melancholy thrill which came with it, was described by Augustus Hare. In November 1879 Hare, a professional country house guest and a prolific writer—his *Story of My Life*, which runs to 3,029 pages and six volumes, has a claim to being the longest autobiography in the world—was staying at Osterley Park in Middlesex. One afternoon his hosts took him over to Ham House on the Thames south of Richmond, the ancestral home of the Tollemache family, then owned by the twenty-year-old William Tollemache, 9th Earl of Dysart. It was, said Hare, "a most curious visit."[13]

---

* The wonderful plasterwork ceiling was bought by Welsh architect Clough Williams-Ellis, along with the house's panelling, oak floor, and mullioned windows. They were all incorporated into Hercules Hall, a new town hall at Williams-Ellis's fantasy village of Portmeirion in North Wales.

Rather too many of the earl's ancestors had been either wildly profligate or neurotically reclusive, and Ham—once the opulent home of
one of the Restoration's most formidable power couples, the Duke and
Duchess of Lauderdale—had suffered for it. Already in the eighteenth
century Horace Walpole, whose niece was married to the 5th earl,
found the place rather depressing: "The old furniture is so magnificently ancient, dreary and decayed," he wrote, "that at every step one's
spirits sink, and all my passion for antiquity could not keep them up."[14]
Matters were made worse by the behaviour of the 9th earl's father, a
former horse dealer and bankrupt, who had amassed huge debts on
the strength of an inheritance that he never lived to enjoy, dying before
his own father, the 8th earl. He also had amassed a small army of illegitimate children, nine in all, by two different mistresses, as well as
William, his heir, and William's three legitimate sisters, before dying
in 1878 and leaving the family to meet his considerable obligations.
When Hare saw the house in 1879, it was occupied by a colourful
gaggle of relations, including the young 9th earl, his widowed Roman
Catholic mother and two unmarried and legitimate Protestant sisters,
two great-uncles, and a great-aunt.

Like Walpole before him, Hare was struck by Ham's poor state
of repair, although unlike Walpole, he found that it gave the place an
aura of romance. Ham was, he said, a "palace which looks like that of
the Sleeping Beauty in the Wood." A donkey grazed on the lawn in
front of the house. As a door at the top of the stairs opened, its handle
went through a portrait by Reynolds of a Dysart ancestor: "It always
does go through it." One of the great-uncles, Algernon Tollemache,
received the visitors in a room which managed to combine richness
with austerity: his bed was hung with embroidered Chinese silk while
the floor was uncarpeted; a mirror with a silver frame stood on a
rough pine scullery table; and Algernon's washstand was a board with
a white jug on it. As the party was shown round the house, Hare wondered that almost everything was precious and decrepit. Delicate silk

hangings were "mouldering in rags"; old Persian carpets were worn to shreds; solid silver chandeliers were as black as ebony from want of cleaning.[15]

The Tollemache clan kept few servants and no carriage. They never repaired or restored anything, Hare claimed. And they ate bread and cheese for lunch. Yet he was sure they had money. (He was right about that: after the 9th earl reached the age of twenty-five in 1884 and came into his inheritance, he quickly set about modernising the house, making structural repairs, fixing the dilapidated furniture, and redecorating the state rooms.) This was crucial: if Hare and his friends were simply witnessing poverty, a family forced to live in reduced circumstances, their reaction would have been embarrassment. They needed to know that the decay and decrepitude was a deliberate act; that made it somehow both romantic and eccentric. In 1900, when Hare published his account of his visit twenty-one years earlier, he commented in a footnote that the house "has been greatly, perhaps too much restored since this."[16]

There was a ghost at Ham. Augustus Hare ended his account of the Sleeping Beauty palace with the tale of the butler's little daughter, who during a stay in the house woke at dawn to see an old woman scratching at the wall near the fireplace. The child sat up and the old woman stopped what she was doing and came to the foot of the bed. "So horrible was her stare, that the child was terrified, and screamed and hid her face under the clothes." People ran in to see what the trouble was, and when she told them, they made a careful examination of the wall. "And concealed in it were found papers which proved that in that room Elizabeth, Countess of Dysart, had murdered her [Tollemache] husband to marry the Duke of Lauderdale."[17]

Hare was partial to a good ghost story, and his inveterate country house visiting provided plenty. At Rufford Abbey in Nottinghamshire, he heard of the phantom of a girl who was shut up in a little chamber and starved to death; she frightened the family's pug dog out of its wits. Baddesley Clinton boasted ghosts of a woman and a child, as well as a "murder-room, stained with the blood of a priest whom a squire of Edward IV's time slew when he caught him chucking his wife under the chin."[18]

But it was generally agreed among the chroniclers of country houses that haunted mansions were a thing of the past, so to speak. "Steam-engines and speculative builders are rapidly diminishing these lingering relics of the past," declared John H. Ingram, a writer who divided his time between championing the literary reputation of Edgar Allan Poe and collecting tales of ghostly apparitions. Fea agreed with him. "The ancestral ghost has had his day," he wrote. "The search-light of science has penetrated even into his sacred haunts"—a reference to the Society for Psychical Research, founded in 1882 with the aim of investigating mesmeric, psychic, and spiritualist phenomena in a purely scientific spirit.[19]

And yet the country house ghost was more popular than it had ever been. Henry James's frightening 1898 novella, *The Turn of the Screw*, was set at Bly, a turreted mansion in Essex filled with empty chambers and crooked staircases and inhabited by two children, Miles and Flora, who were possessed by the ghosts of the manservant Peter Quint and his lover, Miss Jessel. The mezzotint which provided the title for one of the tales in M. R. James's first collection, *Ghost Stories of an Antiquary* (1904), depicted Anningley Hall, "a not very large manor-house of the last century, with three rows of plain sashed windows with rusticated masonry about them, a parapet with balls or vases at the angles, and a small portico in the centre." It also depicted a figure, muffled in black and fresh from the grave, who seemed to be creeping closer and closer to the house every time the mezzotint was viewed, before slipping in through an open window and making off with the young heir. And in Oscar Wilde's "The Canterville Ghost"

(1887), an American family bought Canterville Chase and frustrated the best attempts of its resident ghost, Sir Simon de Canterville, to scare them. The father, Hiram B. Otis, pressed a bottle of Tammany Rising Sun Lubricator on the ghost and urged him to oil his noisy chains. The young Otis twins dressed up as a ghost and scared him so much that he ran back to his room and hid under the bedclothes. They caught him with a butter-slide "from the entrance of the Tapestry Chamber to the top of the oak staircase."[20] And when he burst into their bedroom dressed as Reckless Rupert or the Headless Earl, a carefully placed jug of water soaked him to the skin:

> At the same moment he heard stifled shrieks of laughter proceeding from the four-post bed. The shock to his nervous system was so great that he fled back to his room as hard as he could go, and the next day he was laid up with a severe cold. The only thing that at all consoled him in the whole affair was the fact that he had not brought his head with him, for, had he done so, the consequences might have been very serious.[21]

Tales of real country house ghosts—if "real" is quite the right word—were just as popular. The painter John Seymour Lucas stayed at Raynham Hall in Norfolk one Christmas. The Townshend family, who owned Raynham, weren't in residence, but Lucas, a convinced sceptic, persuaded the house steward to let him sleep in Raynham's haunted chamber, notorious for the appearances of the Brown Lady, Dorothy Townshend, who had died in the house in 1726 after being imprisoned there by her husband on account of her adultery. "Having little belief in the supernatural, [Lucas] thought it would be something to swank about if he had slept in a genuine haunted chamber." A friend, the barrister Alfred Harmsworth (father of the newspaper tycoon), came with him but slept in another part of the house. It was a wild night, and having clambered into his "great funereal four-poster,"

Lucas was kept awake by the wind and by the tapestries on the walls, which shivered disconcertingly. Eventually his nerves got the better of him and he was just about to go in search of his friend when the door opened and Harmsworth crept in, having—so he claimed—actually encountered the Brown Lady.* "Deciding that two was company and three none, they locked and bolted the door and did their best to cheer one another until break of day."[22]

The mania for ghosts wasn't confined to country houses. Phantoms, headless and otherwise, popped up in country towns and suburban villas, in woods and fields and modern service flats. Supernatural sightings tapped into a strain in the late Victorian psyche which reacted against the rationalism of the age; which, hearing the melancholy, long, withdrawing roar of the sea of faith, reached for any evidence that death was not the end. Perhaps they bore out the truth of G. K. Chesterton's dictum that "the first effect of not believing in God is to believe in anything." But country houses were typical settings for eerie manifestations, and turn-of-the-century descriptions of country houses are full of ghosts. They cry for vengeance, they warn of impending doom, they announce their recent—sometimes very recent—death as they shimmer down staircases and float through walls. The drama of their appearance is often enhanced by the fact that they show themselves to unbelievers. Or the person describing these incidents would declare themselves to be an utter sceptic about all things supernatural before recounting "a strange incident" told to them by a third party. At East Denton Hall just outside Newcastle upon Tyne, a woman dressed in a white silk dress would appear, her hand outstretched in warning, in bedrooms or in the gardens.

---

* Sightings of the Brown Lady continued into the twentieth century. In 1936 *Country Life* published what the photographers Hubert Provand and Indre Shira claimed to be a photograph of her gliding down the staircase at Raynham. Others suggested it was a clever piece of double exposure or, more prosaically, grease on the camera lens.

"A death in the family, however distant, or a warning of good or ill fortune, is frequently marked by her sudden appearance, apparently indiscriminately, to anyone in the house"—which covers most eventualities. At Newstead Abbey in Nottinghamshire, ancestral seat of the Byrons, Little Sir John Byron with the Great Beard was said to descend from his portrait at midnight and stalk through the state apartments. Also at Newstead, a Black Friar walked the cloisters, a harbinger of doom to whichever member of the family saw him. The poet Lord Byron confirmed this: he saw the friar shortly before what he called "the greatest misfortune of his life"—his marriage. At Wentworth Castle in Yorkshire, the Earl of Strafford, who lost his head on Tower Hill in 1641, was supposed to walk through the castle with that head under his arm, "which strangely enough, seems to be the fashion with decapitated ghosts," noted one Edwardian commentator.[23]

A decapitated head figures largely in one of the stranger country house ghost stories of the period. It centres on Burton Agnes Hall, a spectacular manor house in East Yorkshire built in the first decade of the seventeenth century and probably designed by the brilliant Robert Smythson. In 1903, after *Country Life* ran a series of articles on Burton Agnes in its Country Homes and Gardens Old and New series, a correspondent wrote with details of a haunting head. According to legend, the youngest of three sisters extracted a promise from the other two that when she died, her head should be placed on a table in the hall. The writer wasn't specific about the reasons for this request, which, if it had been complied with, would have provided unwary visitors with an unusual introduction to the house. But it wasn't: she died, and her sisters buried her, head and all.

That night she appeared to them with her head tucked under her arm and scolded them for neglecting their promise. Then she placed her head on the hall table and disappeared. The next morning it was still there; the body was exhumed and found to be headless. "Any attempt to remove the head was followed by disturbances during the night; it was even buried at a distance from the house, but was restored by the ghost." Eventually the head disappeared, said the writer rather vaguely, before adding that "the disturbances continue nightly in the hall."[24]

"A really well-authenticated ghost fetches a big price," reckoned Fea; and if that ghost was identifiable as a figure from history, so much the better.[25] The ghost of Anne Boleyn (headless, of course) was said to appear at Blickling Hall in Norfolk on the anniversary of her execution in 1536. She also patrolled the grounds of Hever Castle in Kent, the Boleyn family's seat. And Sir Francis Drake was reputed to appear near his old home, Buckland Abbey in Devon, driving a hearse drawn by headless horses and followed by a pack of headless hounds. His own head remained firmly on his ghostly shoulders, in a departure from the usual routine.

In 1560 Amy Robsart, wife of Sir Robert Dudley, was found dead at the foot of a staircase in Cumnor Place. Dudley, who harboured ambitions to marry Elizabeth I, was suspected of having arranged her death, but nothing was proved against him. For centuries, Robsart's ghost was said to haunt the park, looking for justice, until it was laid to rest by nine parsons from Oxford and packed off to a pond in the park, which afterwards was never known to freeze over. Her death was made famous, first by an eighteenth-century poem by William Julius Mickle, "The Ballad of Cumnor Hall"—"For ever since that dreary hour / Have spirits haunted Cumnor Hall"—and then by Sir Walter Scott's *Kenilworth*, which featured it prominently. American tourists came to see the spot where Amy died and to try for a glimpse of her ghost.

In 1892 William Scott-Hall, "a gentleman of historical tastes," bought Cumnor Place from the Earl of Abingdon for £2,010, on the understanding that he was getting the house, or at least the site of the house, where Amy Robsart died and the chamber which was traditionally supposed to be haunted by her. In fact, at the auction, he only decided to raise his bid beyond his £2,000 limit after "remarks had been made with reference to the rumoured ghostly and other associations of the place."[26] But after the sale, Scott-Hall found he had bought a relatively modern house on a different site. The old Cumnor Place had been demolished in 1810, and hardly a stone remained. The aggrieved Scott-Hall (who had in fact viewed the property before the auction) now refused to hand over the purchase price, arguing that the Earl of Abingdon's agents had misrepresented the property. He sued the earl, and the earl sued him for full payment.

The case came to the High Court in April 1894, with archaeologists and antiquarians and surveyors appearing as expert witnesses. And the press had a field day. Scott-Hall styled himself "Reverend" and dressed "in clerical attire," although under questioning from the judge, Mr Justice North, he confessed that he wasn't actually a clergyman, a point which did not count in his favour. The *Pall Mall Gazette* reported that Scott-Hall "consider[ed] that in purchasing from the Earl of Abingdon the house known as Cumnor Place he was defrauded of the mass meeting of ghosts which he believed to be haunting the place, with the apparition of Amy Robsart in the chair," and went on to say that "Mr Swinfen Eady, Q.C., [led] for the Earl; and Mr Augustine Birrell, Q.C., was for the defendant. The ghosts were not represented." Mr Justice North inquired whether having a haunted house was an advantage. Birrell's reply, that he thought it was, "to a gentleman of his client's taste," caused laughter in the court. Having established that Scott-Hall had upped his bid from £2,000 to £2,010 when he heard of the haunting, North caused more laughter when he pointed out that Scott-Hall had only given another ten pounds for the ghost—or rather ghosts, since Amy Robsart's supposed killers were also said to haunt Cumnor Place.[27]

The case lasted for two days, at the end of which Mr Justice North decided that since Scott-Hall had seen the house before the sale he must have realised that it wasn't the one haunted by the phantom of Amy Robsart. Nor had he asked to see the room in which Robsart was killed or the stairs down which her body was thrown. North regarded this as conclusive evidence that Scott-Hall knew beforehand that he wasn't buying the house where Amy Robsart died. He gave judgment to the Earl of Abingdon, with costs. The question of the existence or otherwise of Robsart's ghost was left for others to decide.

EIGHT

GENTLEMEN'S HOUSES

MOST LANDED FAMILIES around the turn of the century lived in mansions built by their own, or somebody else's, ancestors. Brand-new country houses were in the minority, while for those who wanted something off the shelf, the agricultural depression and the Settled Land Acts continued to bring some big estates onto the market. Those who wanted a big house without the responsibility of a big estate found plenty to choose from, too. Take one example: Breadsall Priory in Derbyshire, a nineteen-bedroomed stone mansion built in about 1600 and gothicised in the 1850s, was sold in 1899 with pleasure grounds, flower gardens, "a romantic wilderness walk through which a stream flows"—and not much else, except for a home farm, six cottages and some stables. The quaint half-timbered Jackwood House in Kent was sold around the same time with a park of twenty acres and twenty-two acres of woodland. Even more manageable was the fourteen-bedroomed Holcombe House in Devon. Fitted and decorated by London firms and containing a noble suite of reception rooms and a three-manual organ "of magnificent tone," it stood in gardens of just six and a half acres.[1]

But what about men and women who rejected antiquity and headless history in favour of sensible planning of their own making, complete with central heating and plenty of water closets?

Between 1870 and 1914 around 270 significant country houses were either built or so drastically remodelled as to present an entirely new face to the world.[2] They included everything from an archaeologically correct Gothic Revival castle, Edward Godwin's Dromore in County Limerick, for the 3rd Earl of Limerick (1866–1873), to Heathcote in Yorkshire, a bizarre reinterpretation of a Palladian villa designed by Edwin Lutyens for a Bradford wool merchant, John Thomas Hemingway, and his wife Emma. Most new houses fell somewhere between these two stylistic extremes. Some were so dull and formulaic that they leave one crying out for such extremes.

There were certain things that a late Victorian or Edwardian client had come to expect from his or her new country house, besides efficient heating and decent plumbing. Since the early nineteenth century, when the introduction of an effective bell-pull system allowed an owner to move servants and domestic offices out of a raised basement beneath the main house and into a wing of their own, it was usual to have living rooms grouped at ground level and bedrooms on the first floor. Those living rooms typically included a dining room at a reasonable distance from the kitchens (architects and clients were both very sensitive about the prospect of cooking smells drifting into the main house); a drawing room; a morning room, which should ideally face east or southeast to catch the early sun; and a library. A hall might be cavernous; it might be little more than a lobby. No one seemed quite sure what to do with it until the beginning of the twentieth century, when there was a vogue for living halls as spaces in which to socialise and relax, and the great hall came back into fashion and hence back into use.

There were endless variations. The library, traditionally seen as a male domain, might be grouped with a billiard room and a smoking room, although some country house owners disapproved of tobacco to such an extent that their houseguests were expected to decamp into the gardens if they wanted to smoke; others held such advanced views that anyone could smoke where they liked and women could join in with the smoking and the billiards.

A business room and/or study was useful for interviewing tenants and discussing estate business with one's agent. There might be a boudoir, where the mistress of the house attended to her correspondence and discussed menus with her chef or housekeeper. Grander houses, especially those built for couples with an eye to entertaining the county, boasted a ballroom and a saloon. The pious required a chapel; the sportsman needed a gun room.

It has become almost obligatory for any discussion of Victorian country house design to begin with what has long been regarded as a seminal text on domestic planning: Robert Kerr's *The Gentleman's House; or, How to Plan English Residences, from the Parsonage to the Palace.* Born in Aberdeen in 1823, Kerr settled in London in 1845 and became an important figure in the British architectural establishment, but as a polemicist and an educator rather than as an architect. He published a stream of pamphlets, lectures, and books, beginning in 1846 with *The Newleafe Discourses,* in which he managed to attack both the classicists and the medievalists—"the Greek and the Goth"—as well as take a swipe at the newly formed Royal Institute of British Architects. He was a founding member (and first president) of the Architectural Association, and from 1861 to 1890 he was professor of the arts of construction at King's College, London. A 1904 notice of his death in *The Builder* celebrated his oratorical talents before noting that "he may not always have made the most judicious use of this gift, but he kept things alive at meetings." The anonymous obituarist went on to say, in his cheerfully undermining fashion, that Kerr "never had an extensive practice, nor can he be said to have accomplished much in actual architecture."[3]

As we'll see, that isn't quite fair, although it is pretty close. But Kerr's most lasting achievement was *The Gentleman's House* (1864), which went through three editions in seven years and became—for historians, if not for contemporaries—the go-to manual of High Victorian country house planning. Kerr explained his purpose in his preface to the first edition: it was, he said, to provide a "systematic exposition" of the ideal gentleman's house—"a convenient and comfortable English residence of the better sort."[4]

Such a house, the arrangements of which reflected "the domestic habits of refined persons," could be divided into two zones: one for the family and another for their servants. Kerr wasn't interested in style, except to rail against it.* In discussing the dining room, for example, where he was quite specific about the layout—"A small Dining-room ought never to be less than 16 feet wide. . . . Allow from 4 to 6 feet for the width of the table; 20 inches on each side for the company seated; from 24 to 30 inches in length as the sitting space of each person"—he asked whether the arrangements would be affected by the choice of modern classic or modern medieval. The answer was an unequivocal no. "Any English gentleman of the present day who would consent to sacrifice the characteristics of a comfortable Dining-room for the sake of imitating the manners, whether of ancient or modern Italy on the one hand or Gothic or Tudor England on the other, would be charged on all sides, amongst his acquaintance, with something very much akin to eccentricity."[5]

---

* Ever eager in his pursuit of categories, Kerr listed ten architectural styles suitable for a gentleman's house: Elizabethan and Elizabethan Style Revived; Palladian; Rural-Italian; Palatial-Italian; French-Italian; English Renaissance; Medieval or Gothic; Cottage; and Scotch Baronial.

Kerr's uncompromising approach to country house design continued throughout his book, as he took prospective builders (and prospective clients, assuming they could put up with his intransigence) on a tour of the perfect gentleman's house. A minstrel's gallery was allowed in his great hall, so long as it functioned as a passage across the hall at first-floor level. A properly organised house needed a main entrance, of course, and a garden entrance. It probably also needed a luggage entrance, a business entrance, a nursery entrance, and perhaps a second garden entrance for the private use of the family or to give access to an invalid's suite of rooms. This compartmentalisation of the country house, with each element serving a different, defined purpose, was fundamental to Kerr's thinking. A principal staircase was for certain members of the family only, and even then they would need a private family staircase up to their bedroom suites and on up to the nurseries. The servants needed their own staircase, of course; it wouldn't do for members of the family to bump into a footman carrying up coals to the bedrooms or a maid bringing down the contents of a commode. Single men needed a bachelors' stair; young ladies needed a young ladies' stair. As if five staircases weren't enough, "there may also be occasionally other *Special Stairs*," although to what end he didn't specify.[6]

Always mindful of hierarchies, both within the country house and between country houses, Kerr devoted a chapter to "a few Mansions of very superior class . . . [which] the high position of the owners in rank and wealth requires to be maintained in palatial state." Even here, he didn't depart from his dogmatic, even puritanical, approach. Architectural effect can easily tip over into bad taste, he said. Any departure from the rectangular box—a circular or cruciform plan, a domed ceiling—"mar the very purpose of the apartment."[7]

When it came to a big room of entertainment, like the state drawing room, adequate ventilation was a priority, as it was for the ballroom, where size mattered. In passing, he advocated the addition of a great hall, "so that 'the good old English Gentleman,' when he desires to entertain his tenants, perhaps his constituents, need *not* have to choose between a tavern and a marquee." And, warming to his topic, he urged the prospective builder of a palatial mansion to consider a great library or suite of libraries, perhaps with sculptures or paintings, and glass cabinets for collections of curiosities; "elaborate effects, however . . . ought not to be encouraged." There should be a picture gallery, anywhere up to a hundred feet long, and a chapel, with separate entrances for the family and the servants and seating arranged to reflect the relative status of the worshippers: family and guests at the front, "strangers of position" next behind them, then the upper servants, then the lower servants, together with visitors of their classes. "Private chantries, stalls, and so on, are all affectation."[8]

As the *Builder*'s obituarist noted rather unkindly, Kerr didn't actually design much: a Congregational church in Essex, the offices of a friendly society in the City, and a handful of country houses, including Dunsdale near Westerham in Kent (1858), all towers and turrets and tall chimney stacks, and Ford Manor (1868), a jumble of a building with a facade which, as Pevsner's *Surrey* says, "seems to contain one of everything, starting with a tower at one end, ending with a French pavilion at the other, and with Dutch and English gables in between." Architectural historian Mark Girouard described it as "appalling."[9]

Kerr was a hard man to work with. One client, John Thadeus Delane, editor of the *Times*, was unimpressed with the house Kerr designed for him, Ascot Heath in Berkshire, and even more unimpressed with the man himself. "My architect has no notion of aspect or prospect, and not much of respect," he wrote in 1867.[10]

Delane came across Kerr through his boss, John Walter, proprietor of the *Times*, for whom the architect was building his best-known country house, Bear Wood in Berkshire (1864–1874). And Walter had in turn picked Kerr as a result of the latter's *Gentleman's House*.

Bear Wood was the most complete expression—indeed, just about the *only* expression—of Kerr's rage to have a place (and a staircase) for everything and to put everything in its place. The planning of the main house was unexceptional: dining room, entrance hall, drawing room, morning room, library, and gentlemen's room, all grouped around a central, top-lit picture gallery which accommodated Walter's collection of Flemish art, handed down to him by his father. But when it came to the domestic offices, Kerr revelled in segregation and demarcation. There were separate corridors for male and female servants, two more for the housekeeper and the butler, another for the cook, and another for the nurseries. There was not only a principal staircase, housed in a spiky square tower with an arrangement of windows that declared its purpose by climbing along with the stair, and a back stair. There were also separate staircases for the bachelors and the young ladies and for women servants (the menservants presumably used the back stairs). And there were six entrances to the house, each one dedicated to a particular purpose: garden, business, luggage, and so on. By the time Bear Wood was finished it had cost John Walter £120,000—twice Kerr's estimate. Kerr suggested that Walter might pay him something extra over and above his agreed-on fee, to compensate him for all his hard work. Walter disagreed.

If Kerr was a minor country-house architect with a reputation that rested on a single commission and a book, then who were the big hitters in late Victorian and Edwardian Britain?

In 1870, the leading figures of the mid century—Edward Blore, Anthony Salvin, William Burn, George Gilbert Scott—were either nearing retirement or well past it. Blore, whose commissions included the completion of John Nash's Buckingham Palace between 1831 and 1838 and the addition of an east wing to the palace for Queen Victoria in 1847–1850, was eighty-three. Anthony Salvin was seventy-one, and his last great country house commission, Thoresby Hall in Nottinghamshire (1864–1875, for the 3rd Earl Manvers) was in a Tudor style which was already coming to seem rather dated. Burn died in 1870, ending a career whose prolific output—196 country houses in styles ranging from Jacobethan to Italianate to Scotch Baronial to Greek Revival—meant it was hard to find any place in the British Isles *without* a mansion he had built or extended or remodelled.

The acknowledged giant of the architectural establishment in 1870 was the fifty-nine-year-old George Gilbert Scott—Sir Gilbert Scott, as he styled himself in 1872, after Queen Victoria knighted him at Osborne House in recognition of his design for the Albert Memorial in Kensington Gardens. Fellow architect T. G. Jackson remembered his time as a pupil in Scott's office in 1858–1861 when, as he said in his memoirs, "the fervour of the gothic revival was still at its full blast."[11] There were twenty-seven men working in the office, and Scott himself rarely put in an appearance, spending his time instead tearing round the kingdom visiting one or other of his projects. The stories of his busy life are legion: how he admired a new church, to be reminded that he had designed it; how his office received a telegram from him one day which simply read, "Am in St Albans. Why?"

Yet in spite of his dominance and his prolific output of around four hundred commissions, which included dozens of churches and masterpieces like the Midland Grand Hotel at St Pancras Station, the Albert Memorial, and—less of a masterpiece, perhaps, but still interesting—the Italianate Foreign Office building on King Charles Street, Westminster, Scott designed only a handful of country houses, mostly in the late 1850s and early 1860s. They weren't among his best work: the most successful is perhaps Kelham Hall in Nottinghamshire, a heavy and delightfully ostentatious piece of domestic Gothic, designed for a collateral branch of the Manners family and built from 1858 to 1861. And although Scott would serve as president of the

Royal Institute of British Architects from 1873 to 1876, a bout of ill health in 1870 saw him withdrawing from practice.

In the next generation of architects, the ones who were at their peak in 1870, the most interesting is George Devey, whom we'll meet again later, designing a new service wing and estate buildings for the 6th Lord Vernon at Sudbury Hall in Derbyshire. Devey's early career was spent working on estate cottages, stables, and lodges, and it was only in 1866 that he was given a commission to design a new country house: Akeley Wood in Buckinghamshire, for the landowner and JP Captain Charles Pilgrim. After that there came a steady stream of country house commissions right up to his early death from a chest infection after he caught a chill visiting the Earl of Dunraven's Adare Manor in County Limerick to discuss a new commission.

Devey was interested in the architecture of the past—not the earnest past of the Gothic and Tudor revivals, but the softer, more lyrical past as exemplified in the vernacular buildings of southern England: the farmhouses and cottages and small manor houses of Kent and Sussex. His country houses were gentle, rambling assemblages of timber-framed gables set off by the occasional stone tower, tall chimneys, and soft, diapered brickwork. They were, above all, romantic rather than scholarly.

Unlike Scott, Devey had a small practice. He was a private man, and he didn't publish his designs. As a result, he remained relatively unknown in his lifetime. But his buildings helped to demonstrate that there were alternatives to the Jacobethan mansion on the one hand and the classical-cum-Italianate palace on the other. And he inspired a generation of young architects who began to experiment with an exuberant range of different styles. William Eden Nesfield did Queen Anne Revival at Kinmel Park in Denbighshire (1868–1874). Richard Norman Shaw cornered the market in Old English at Leys Wood in Kent (1868) and Cragside in Northumberland (1869–1884). With Wightwick Manor in Staffordshire (1887–1893), Edward Ould produced a completely half-timbered mansion for the paint manufacturer and aesthete S. T. Mander, the perfect setting for Mander's collection of Morris and Company textiles and antique furniture.

By the end of the century the country house scene was eclectic, to say the least. There were French chateaux and Gothic fantasies; vast Italianate houses and florid neo-Caroline monsters and quaint little manor houses which looked as though they were centuries old instead of having been built yesterday. Having pioneered the Old English house and excelled at the Queen Anne Revival, Norman Shaw, whose career spanned almost the entire period between 1870 and the First World War (he died in 1912), discovered a kind of classicism by the end of the century, revelling in what was called, half-jokingly, the "Wrenaissance." Inspired by the redbrick walls with stone dressings and white woodwork of Sir Christopher Wren's Hampton Court Palace, Shaw and fellow enthusiasts like Reginald Blomfield and Edwin Lutyens designed a series of country houses which harked back to the early Georgians. Shaw's vast and wonderful Bryanston in Dorset (1889–1894) for the 2nd Viscount Portman is one of the best of the genre, along with Blomfield's Moundsmere Manor in Hampshire (1908), the exterior of which exhibits an almost slavish loyalty towards Wren's domestic architecture.

Edwin Lutyens, whose early country houses owed a lot to the Arts and Crafts movement and the vernacular buildings of Surrey and Sussex, turned to Queen Anne and George I in the first years of the twentieth century. "In architecture, Palladio is the game!" he told his partner Herbert Baker in 1903. "The way Wren handled it was marvellous. Shaw had the gift. To the average man it is dry bones, but under the hand of a Wren it glows." Lutyens didn't have quite the gift that Shaw and Blomfield had when it came to the Wrenaissance—although he was the greatest architect of the three—but as an example of the style, his Ednaston Manor in Derbyshire (1912–1919), designed for W. G. Player of Player's tobacco, is still a triumph of quiet good taste, with its dormer windows and hipped roof. Lutyens's early biographer, A. S. G. Butler, thought it the most perfect country house the architect produced. In 1923 historian Christopher Hussey declared that "it is not too much to say that Ednaston is as nearly perfect a modern country house of its size as can be found in England," and Lutyens himself reckoned it as one of his favourites.[12]

And then there was Philip Speakman Webb. Webb's career as a designer of country houses began with a building that would change the world. While others were building classical palaces and Gothic castles and vast Jacobethan monsters, he found his inspiration in the vernacular buildings of southern England. The result was Red House in Bexleyheath, designed in 1859 for William Morris and his bride, Jane. Like Webb himself, Red House is quiet and understated. As a setting in which Morris and his friends—Dante Gabriel Rossetti, Edward Burne-Jones, Ford Madox Brown, and Webb himself—could make furniture and decorate the walls and dream their dreams of a preindustrial Eden, it was the first Arts and Crafts house in the world.

Webb was principled, with simple tastes and a gift for making complicated architecture seem modest and unassuming. "I never begin to be satisfied until my work looks commonplace," he liked to say. He is often called "puritanical" by modern critics, quite unfairly. Ill health led him to retire from practice in 1900, and in his career he designed relatively few country houses, mainly because he kept a small office and preferred to supervise projects himself instead of delegating. But the houses he did build were remarkable. A strong Morrisite socialist, he insisted on giving the servants comfortable quarters when he designed Clouds in Wiltshire for the Wyndham family; finished in 1886, the main block was gutted by fire three years later and the family moved into the servants' wing while it was being rebuilt. "It is a good thing that our architect was a socialist," observed Madeline Wyndham. One of his last country houses, Standen in Sussex, which was built for a prosperous solicitor, James Beale, and his family in 1891–1894, reflects Webb's abiding love for the English rural landscape. To Webb, recalled architect W. R. Lethaby, "the land was not merely 'nature,' it was the land which had been laboured over by the generations of men; buildings were not 'architecture,' they were builded history and poetry." Standen is a supremely satisfying mix of materials—weatherboarding and roughcast and brick and tile hanging and stone. It looks as though it belongs in the landscape, as though it has always belonged there, and Standen's interiors are plain and filled with light. Pure? Yes. Puritanical? Never.[13]

NINE

CAMELOT

I F YOU CANNOT at once laugh at a thing and believe in it," declared G. K. Chesterton, "you have no business in the Middle Ages."[1]

If a little self-deprecating laughter was in short supply among late-Victorian country house builders, belief in the power of the Middle Ages to conjure up chivalry and romance was there in plenty at the end of the century. It meant different things to different people, and it was fed by different and interlocking strands of thought: the anti-industrialism of John Ruskin, William Morris, and the early Arts and Crafts movement; a wave of Roman Catholic evangelism in the wake of the 1850 restoration of the Catholic diocesan hierarchy in England, which looked longingly back to a pre-Reformation age of faith; the Romantic movement's love affair with the past, embedded in the works of John Keats, Sir Walter Scott, and their contemporaries; and a conviction that the chivalric ideal was something which could profitably be applied to turn-of-the-century Britain. In 1897 G. F. Watts's great portrait of Sir Galahad, the perfect knight of Arthurian romance, was hung opposite the entrance to the chapel at

Eton College, so that the boys would see it as they filed into morning and evening prayers, "a lesson that is at once so very beautiful and so deeply Christian." Eighteen years later, when those boys were killing and dying in France and Flanders, Galahad was still being held up as a shining example to the nation's youth, urging them in patriotic pamphlets to enlist and to say "I also shall follow the Quest! I too shall serve the blameless King." (And, apparently, I'll also do my best not to masturbate or catch a sexually transmitted disease: "To be a Sir Galahad . . . means in the camp, and amid a thousand new temptations, to wear the white flower of a blameless life.")[2]

From the very beginning of Victoria's reign, this fascination with chivalry and the Middle Ages produced some curious results. In 1837 Sir Francis Sykes of Basildon Park in Berkshire commissioned a family portrait from the Irish artist Daniel Maclise. He chose to be depicted as a knight in full armour, his jousting lance carried on his shoulder as he stood proudly at the foot of a turret stair. His three young sons were dressed as pages, bearing his peacock helm, his sword, and his mace, while his wife, Henrietta, wore the flowing ermine-lined robes of a medieval queen. Two years later, a group of young noblemen led by Archibald Montgomerie, 13th Earl of Eglinton, decided to show the world that the age of chivalry was not yet past by staging a full-scale mock-medieval joust at the earl's Ayrshire seat, Eglinton Castle, in front of an estimated one hundred thousand spectators.

Real life has a habit of interfering with fantasies. Heavy rain turned the tourney field at Eglinton into a mud bath, and tempers became so frayed that several of the jousters had to be dragged apart when they began bashing each other for real with their maces. And while the Sykes family portrait was painted, Henrietta Sykes was sleeping with Maclise. The affair ended badly, with Sir Francis suing for divorce and placing an unchivalrous and unnecessarily detailed advertisement in the newspapers saying that he no longer held himself responsible for his wife's debts, because she "hath committed ADULTERY with DANIEL

MACLISE, of Russell-place, Fitzroy square, Portrait and Picture-painter (with whom she was found in bed at my house, No. 20, Park-lane, in the parish of St. George, Hanover-square, in the county of Middlesex, on the 4th day of July, 1837)."[3]

So seductive was the past that people went in search of its landmarks. Tutbury Castle in Staffordshire, an important centre in fifteenth-century England and famous as one of Mary, Queen of Scots' prisons in the sixteenth, was so popular that admission was by ticket only (one penny each, or half a crown for a family season ticket). At Ashby de la Zouch Castle in Leicestershire, the scene of the famous tournament in Walter Scott's *Ivanhoe* (1820), the enterprising proprietor opened the ruins to visitors, thinking to attract business to the Ivanhoe Baths, which he had built nearby. Ashby was given another boost in 1891 by the premiere of Sir Arthur Sullivan's grand opera, named after Scott's eponymous hero.

The arts played an important role in Victorian medievalism, something one can see in its by-product, the interest in all things Arthurian that swept the country in the second half of the nineteenth century. Tennyson's *Idylls of the King*, a retelling of Malory's *Le Morte d'Arthur* that the poet laureate began in the early 1840s and was still tinkering with in the late 1880s, set the tone, with its picture of an ideal community in decline:

> *O brother, had you known our Camelot,*
> *Built by old kings, age after age, so old*
> *The King himself had fears that it would fall,*
> *So strange, and rich, and dim . . .*[4]

Once one starts to look, the examples come thick and fast: Matthew Arnold's *Tristram and Iseult*; William Morris's *Defence of Guenevere*; Algernon Charles Swinburne's *Tristram of Lyonesse*. The visual arts have everything from Holman Hunt's *The Lady of Shalott* and Edward

Burne-Jones's *The Last Sleep of King Arthur in Avalon* to Aubrey Beard-sley's weirdly subversive illustrations for *Le Morte D'Arthur*, Julia Margaret Cameron's photographic illustrations for the *Idylls*, and, of course, Watts's *Sir Galahad*. "The British king [Arthur] is more ubiquitous in his resuscitation than even in the days of his mortality," declared a writer in 1860, and there was much more to come. In 1875 Minton produced a set of tiles depicting scenes from the *Idylls*, including one showing a surprisingly nubile Lady of the Lake handing Excalibur to Arthur. The new Trocadero Restaurant on Shaftesbury Avenue was decorated in 1896 by artists Gerald Moira and F. Lynn Jenkins with a remarkable ninety-foot-long frieze showing scenes such as "King Arthur's Round Table" and "The Coming of Guinevere to Camelot." The infatuation with all things Arthurian even crossed the Atlantic: a bemused public watched in November 1896 as a knight in full armour cantered down the streets of Boston carrying a standard advertising King Arthur Flour. "As King Arthur was a champion without fear and above reproach," ran the accompanying advertisement, "so is King Arthur Flour the peerless champion of modern civilisation."[5]

The fact that Arthur was a figure from folklore didn't stop people from seeking out real-life landmarks associated with him. When the Cadbury estate in Somerset came on the market in 1889, it was advertised as including "the important British Encampment, the 'Camelot of King Arthur,' now known as Cadbury Castle. . . . Tradition says that the hill is full of treasure, suggesting a great field for investigation and, mayhap, most important national discoveries."[6] And by the end of the century Tintagel—identified by Geoffrey of Monmouth in his twelfth-century *History of the Kings of Britain* as the place where Arthur was conceived when his father, Uther, sneakily took the form of Igraine's dead husband and slept with her—was the hub of a major tourist industry. A little cove known for centuries as the Haven had become King Arthur's Cove. A cavern at the base of the island on which Tintagel Castle stands was Merlin's Cave. The local hotel, designed in 1895 by Cornish architect Silvanus Trevail—a name which itself seems to belong at the Round Table—was King Arthur's Castle Hotel. By then, Tintagel had become known as Arthur's birthplace and residence, conception being an unwelcome concept to tender Victorian sensibilities.

This takes us rather a long way from the country house. But when the past—even a fictitious, folkloric past—was so congenial, then why not live there? Especially if the ownership of a castle confirmed, or perhaps even conferred, long lineage and ancient pedigree.

So much so that most late-Victorian castles weren't castles at all. Between 1875 and 1878, for example, the textile manufacturer Henry Isaac Butterfield and his architect, George Smith of Bradford, remodelled the Butterfield family mansion, Cliffe Hall in Keighley. They added a castellated tower, a ballroom, and conservatories; put a painted hammer-beam roof in the staircase hall; and installed stained glass depicting the family in Elizabethan dress. Then Butterfield renamed the house "Cliffe Castle"—a misnomer it retains to this day, when it serves as Keighley's museum.

When it came to building the real thing, the prolific architect George Gilbert Scott, who ruled the Gothic Revival of the mid century, railed against what he called "the monstrous practice of castle-building." In 1857 Scott argued that while the Georgian predilection for sham castles and castellated follies was bad enough, that had given way in his time to the building of "a real and carefully constructed medieval fortress, capable of standing a siege from an Edwardian army. . . . This is the very height of masquerading." The fact that he felt the need to condemn castle building so strongly speaks to its popularity with socially ambitious country house owners. But in truth, the notion of building a brand-new castle from scratch was already going out of fashion when Scott was complaining about it. Much more common were the building projects which rescued or revived or restored fragments of medieval castles.[7]

The group that one might expect above all others to embrace medievalism in all its forms is something of a disappointment. When it came to the Arts and Crafts movement's architectural vision of the Middle Ages, William Morris and his followers tended to ignore the rich man in his castle in favour of the poor man at his gate, confining turrets and battlements to literature and the visual arts along with knights in armour and damsels in distress. They preferred the modest timber-framed manor houses of the fifteenth and sixteenth centuries, the rose-pink brick farmhouses of Surrey and Sussex, and the honey-coloured stone cottages of the Cotswolds—Wightwick, Standen, and Kelmscott rather than Windsor and Warwick.

Others, though, saw the reinstatement of a medieval tone—often with a good deal of poetic licence—as a reminder of ancient pedigree. In 1868 George Luttrell, whose family had owned Dunster Castle since 1404, decided that radical alterations by different generations had robbed Dunster of its ancient air, and he commissioned Anthony Salvin to return it to its roots in the past. Salvin, who was coming to the end of a long career as a builder of country houses, had a reputation for castles. Architect Alfred Waterhouse, writing in 1878, noted that he was "celebrated for the way in which he [could] combine the exterior and plan of an Edwardian castle with nineteenth-century elegance and comfort."[8] He had done just that at Peckforton in Cheshire back in the 1840s, providing his client, the 1st Baron Tollemache, with a strikingly authentic-looking castle in which the vaulted great hall, the family rooms, the domestic offices, the stables, and the chapel were all grouped round a large central courtyard behind a forbidding curtain wall which was punctuated, apparently at random, with crenellated towers of different breadths and heights. On the strength of his work at Peckforton, Salvin was given a string of castle commissions, the most notable of which was the work he carried out for the 4th

Duke of Northumberland between 1854 and 1865 at Alnwick, where, as with Luttrell and Dunster, he medievalised an already-medieval castle which had suffered at the hands of taste and fashion since the family bought it in 1309.

At Dunster, Salvin—who was particularly fond of towers as a means of adding picturesque effect and conjuring fantasies of feudalism—put up a high, irregular tower on the site of what *Country Life* in 1903 dismissed as "an incongruous chapel built in 1720" but which was designed and presumably decorated by the great baroque muralist Sir James Thornhill. The effect was completed by another tower over the kitchens, this time crowned with a conical roof, and by the judicious application of battlements, along with some internal alterations including an enlarged great hall, the heart of any great house in the Middle Ages. As Pevsner noted in 1958, "There is no question that the highly picturesque appearance of Dunster . . . is due more to Salvin's than to any previous age." By the early twentieth century Salvin's interventions had been all but forgotten, and Dunster was being described as a fine old castle of the time of Henry IV.[9]

The attraction of a castle to the wealthy newcomer seems obvious, and by the turn of the century it was much more common to buy one and make it fit for use than to build one from scratch. In 1906, the brewer F. J. Tennant bought the near-derelict Lympne Castle, a medieval fortified house in a spectacular setting, perched above Romney Marsh and looking out across the Channel to France. He brought in Robert Lorimer, "the Scottish Lutyens," to make it habitable. It was, said Lorimer, "a most attractive job" (no doubt made more attractive by the knowledge that Tennant had recently inherited £3 million from his father). Tudor linenfold panelling lined the walls, and the castle was filled with a mix of late-medieval tapestries and antique furniture, most of it dating from the seventeenth century.[10] An exception was a remarkable brand-new Steinway grand piano, with a case designed by Lorimer and panels painted by Phoebe Anna Traquair, who took as her inspiration the Song of Solomon and the antics of the god Pan. Eclecticism was a prominent feature of turn-of-the-century interior decoration, and it is worth emphasising that, like the rest of his fellows, Frank Tennant didn't want to live in a museum. Authenticity and fidelity to period detail took a back seat to comfort, if they were considered at all. A look which conjured up a nonspecific past was good enough.

As we saw in chapter 3, the Americans William Waldorf Astor and Andrew Carnegie both succumbed to the castle craze, buying and renovating one of their own: Carnegie with Skibo in the Scottish Highlands in 1898, and Astor with Hever in Kent in 1903. In 1910 the founder of the Home and Colonial Stores, Julius Drewe, bought 450 acres at Drewsteignton in Devon, and, convinced by a genealogist that the Drewes were descended from an Anglo-Norman knight named Drogo whose family had been lords of the manor in the twelfth century, he commissioned Edwin Lutyens to design an enormous granite castle on the site. Castle Drogo proved too enormous and less than half of it was actually built, although what survived from the original plans still rates as one of Lutyens's finest country houses, against the odds. "I wish he didn't want a castle," the architect confided to his wife in August 1910, "but just a delicious lovable house with plenty of good large rooms in it."[11]

At first glance, the explanation for the outsider's fascination with castles is obvious: a castle showed the world that the arriviste had arrived. Buying a piece of feudal England gave a sense of belonging; *building* a piece of feudal England might not satisfy one's antiquarian instincts, but at least the plumbing would work. And restoring a piece of feudal England to modern standards gave the best of both worlds.

But when it comes to individual cases, the truth is sometimes more complicated. Take the case of Devizes Castle and the Leach family.

In 1838 a nonconformist tradesman named Valentine Leach, who had started his career as a linen draper's apprentice, bought the ruins of Devizes Castle in Wiltshire. Originally a timber motte-and-bailey castle put up soon after the Norman Conquest, it was rebuilt in stone in the twelfth century, and for much of the Middle Ages it played host to kings and queens, before being held by royalists in the Civil War, taken by Cromwell, and partially demolished. By the eighteenth century there was little of the original castle left standing, and a couple of windmills had been put up on the site. Leach wanted a castle: he brought in the Bath architect H. E. Goodridge, who gave him a chunky neo-Norman mansion centred on a massive round tower on the site of one of the windmills. This may or may not have been completed by the time of Leach's death in 1842.

The following year his son Robert Valentine Leach tried to sell what the auction catalogue described as "the famed Castle of Devizes . . . selected by the monarchs of England as the dowry and palace of their queens." There were no buyers, so he let the place and decamped to Briton Ferry in Glamorgan, where he bought a large Georgian house that had once belonged to the Vernons of Sudbury and turned it into a "retreat for mental invalids"—a lunatic asylum, in other words. The project prospered—one of Leach's daughters married the supervising surgeon—and in 1860 Leach came back to Devizes, took possession of the castle, and over the next twenty years devoted himself to an altogether grander project, this time with the help of a local man, John Ashley Randell, whose career trajectory in the census returns showed him moving from "auctioneer" in 1861 to "auctioneer, estate agent and building surveyor" in 1871, "auctioneer architect and surveyor" in 1881, and simply "architect and surveyor" in 1891.* Between them Leach and Randell trebled the size of the earlier rebuilding, keeping the loosely neo-Norman look but adding more towers, more battlements, and a strangely attractive curved neo-Norman fernery-cum-conservatory. The final element of the

---

* The Leaches and Randells may have been old friends: in 1842 Valentine Leach's will was witnessed by a Devizes bookseller, Nathaniel Randle, and his wife Martha.

scheme was a rock-faced and determinedly asymmetrical gatehouse, with one large round tower and a lower square tower. A commentator in 1901 described Devizes Castle as "an admirable imitation of a feudal fortress," which of course it wasn't. Glazed quadrant ferneries were rarely to be found in feudal fortresses.[12]

That didn't stop the castle from being an impressive piece of make-believe. But why did Robert do it? Why should the proprietor of a Welsh lunatic asylum devote thousands of pounds and perhaps two decades of his life to Devizes Castle? The conventional view would be that he was establishing the Leaches as a power in the town and quite possibly the county—that, by enlarging the castle in a style which looked back to its origins, he was providing the family with an ancestral seat, a launchpad for a dynasty that in the space of two generations had moved from draper's apprentice to landed gentry. According to that view, the logical next steps would be for him to entertain the county, hire a genealogist to "discover" the Leaches' Norman roots, and make an application to the College of Arms.

That all might have been true for his father. The idea of a local draper who worshipped at the Congregational chapel in the town perched aloft in his neo-Norman eyrie suggests a degree of social ambition and upward (quite literally upward) social mobility. But it doesn't work for Robert. His first step on inheriting the castle was to try to sell it. He wasn't interested in founding a dynasty, or if he was, fate played him the wrong hand: although his poor wife bore him fourteen children, eight of them in eight years, they were all daughters. He didn't even end his days in the castle; instead, he bought a place on the Italian Riviera, and it was in the Villa Valentina in Bordighera that he died in May 1888, in his eighty-first year. His executors lost no time in getting rid of the castle. Within eight weeks "this grand old residential and historical estate . . . in the Norman castellated style of architecture and in perfect keeping with its surroundings" was up for sale. The auctioneer joked that "if some one would buy the castle and present it to the nation, the donor would certainly be made a baronet, and possibly a peer." It went for £8,000.[13]

So why? Filial devotion? A desire to fulfil his father's dreams of living in a castle in the air? Just because it was there—half of it, at least? Historians sometimes forget the vital role played by personal idiosyncrasy in the choice of building styles. Perhaps Robert Valentine Leach just fancied having a castle.

One group of country house builders who flirted with the castle craze were Roman Catholics, both old established families and new converts, swept along in the great Catholic Revival of the 1860s and 1870s and eager to demonstrate their conviction, newly acquired in some cases, that the Reformation had been a huge mistake. Henry, 9th Baron Beaumont, for example, came of age in 1869 and celebrated the fact by returning to the religion of his ancestors—his father had gone over to the Church of England on acquiring a barony in 1840—and commissioning E. W. Pugin, son of Augustus Welby Northmore Pugin and the preeminent Catholic architect of his day, to remodel his ancestral seat in Yorkshire. Carlton Towers, while not quite a castle, had enough of the castle air about it in Pugin's designs: all towers and battlements and turrets (some of which disguised chimneys), with a "hall of the barons" and a massive keep with round corner towers that held a grand staircase. Sadly, the hall of the barons and the grand staircase were never built, either because Beaumont fell out with Pugin or because he ran out of money—by 1879 he had debts of nearly a quarter of a million pounds and was living abroad to avoid his creditors. What was left was a castellated country house, nice enough but sadly devoid of the medievalising theatricality that Pugin was aiming for.

When it came to old established Roman Catholic families, no one could beat Henry Fitzalan-Howard, 15th Duke of Norfolk, hereditary Earl Marshal of England, and head of the most senior noble Catholic family in Britain. In 1868 the duke came of age and immediately began to think about completing the refurbishment of the family's principal seat, Arundel Castle in Sussex, which his father had begun in the 1850s. Money was no object—the electric lighting system alone at Arundel cost an eye-watering £28,652 6s. Nor was he interested in returning to pre-Reformation levels of comfort. He installed eight bathrooms and sixty-five water closets. Most of the principal bedrooms were en suite. There was a coal-fired central heating system, a system of electric bells to summon the servants, and a luggage lift to make life a little easier for them.

But what the duke did want was a castle that looked like a castle.

He had parts of one: a keep from circa 1140, a Norman gatehouse, a thirteenth-century barbican. But his forebears had tinkered: the 11th duke built a Regency Gothick mansion; the 12th stripped the castle and went to live elsewhere; the 13th had a go at refurbishing the interior in preparation for a visit from Queen Victoria in 1846. She was not impressed: "The Castle has not been restored in a good style, by Duke Charles, the last but one, & Saxon & Gothic architecture are mixed," she wrote in her diary.[14]

The 15th duke wanted a Catholic architect to design his Catholic castle, and he found one in Charles Alban Buckler, a member of a clan of artists and architects, of whom the most famous is perhaps John Chessell Buckler, who almost won the competition to rebuild the Palace of Westminster after the great fire of 1834. Charles Alban had converted to Catholicism in 1844, and since then he had established himself as a builder of Catholic churches, with well over a dozen to his name by the time work began on Arundel in 1877. It went on, in fits and starts, until 1904 (at a cost of some £300,000, excluding furniture and estate labour), with the duke involving himself every step of the way. He chose the subjects for sculptures and stained glass. He approved designs for towers and chimneys, and only after two-dimensional cut-outs had been hoisted to the roof so that he could judge their effect on the skyline.[15] His library was filled with the seminal texts of the Gothic Revival—by Viollet-le-Duc, Pugin, Ruskin. An enormous Barons' Hall had canopied chimneypieces derived from Viollet-le-Duc and a timber roof that was a composite of the hall roofs at Penshurst Place and Prior Wulstan de Bransford's Guesten Hall at Worcester (circa 1326). The chapel is based on Henry III's thirteenth-century Lady Chapel at Westminster Abbey.

Buckler wasn't a particularly inspired architect, and his work at Arundel provokes mixed emotions. Architectural historian John Martin Robinson described him as "one of the few nineteenth-century Catholic architects who tried to create a medieval glamour which was quiet, scholarly and English." Historian Geoffrey Tyack called Arundel "one of the last great achievements of the Gothic revival in English secular architecture." Others, though, thought it was plain boring. Writing in the 1960s, critic Ian Nairn declared Victorian Arundel "a great disappointment" and described Buckler's south front as "appalling." The chapel was characterised by "a complete lack of feeling"; the Barons' Hall was "quite dead."[16]

Contrast that with the impressions of the courtier Sir Almeric FitzRoy, who lived in a more deferential age. FitzRoy was heavily involved in the preparations for the coronation of Edward VII and thus was thrown into frequent contact with the duke, who as Earl Marshal was responsible for the whole show. When FitzRoy visited Arundel in 1902, he found the castle "a place where the traditions of a stately and reverent life still survive." It was impossible to praise the new work too highly, he wrote in his journal. "The assimilation of the spirit of the past has taken the place of the sterile reproduction of its letter, with the result of elevating and subduing the mind to the reception of the most living lessons of history."[17] Perhaps that is the problem: Arundel is a history lesson, earnest and true. But instead of taking in the dates and names and battles of the past, one finds oneself looking out the classroom window and wishing one could go out and play.

If it is play that we want, Cardiff Castle and its little cousin, Castell Coch ("Red Castle" in English), are the places to find it. In December 1868 John Crichton-Stuart, the twenty-one-year-old Marquess of Bute, who with an annual income of around £300,000 was said to be the richest man in the world, caused a stir when after months of rumours he was received into the Roman Catholic Church. He had been christened an Anglican and raised a Presbyterian—facts which made his journey to Rome even longer and more controversial than usual. A Glasgow newspaper referred to him as "his perverted Lordship," while the *Times* simply said that "for our part we are sincerely sorry for him."[18] Four years later Bute confirmed his place in Catholic high society by marrying Gwendolen Fitzalan-Howard, the granddaughter of a previous Duke of Norfolk.

Bute was a very serious man, scholarly rather than sociable, passionate about the Middle Ages, happiest when he was translating a medieval breviary or writing an article on ancient Celtic Latin hymns. Augustus Hare, who met him in 1874, wrote, "He talks incessantly. . . of altars, ritual, liturgical differences; . . . he often almost loses himself and certainly quite lost me."[19] Bute would have liked to live in the past, and in William Burges, the architect of his two Welsh castles, he found someone who could bring the past to him and who could paint it in such colours that it brightened even Bute's solemnity.

Burges and Bute made an odd couple. The architect's opium habit, his passion for rat hunting, his visits to the notorious Judge and Jury Club in London to watch salacious legal cases being reenacted with seminude *tableaux vivants*—all seem at odds with everything the earnest, almost monastic marquess held dear. Yet Burges was also a medieval scholar with an international reputation, a designer of genius whose buildings and decorative schemes, furniture, sculpture, and metalwork conjured up rare and magical Tennysonian dream worlds, combining absolute fidelity to the spirit of the Middle Ages with breathtakingly idiosyncratic fantasy, filling those dream worlds with chivalrous plaster knights and pious painted pilgrims, gilded ceilings, great castellated chimneypieces, and grotesquely carved corbels. That ability to make Bute's lost worlds real is what made their partnership so perfect. That, and Bute's enormous wealth.

The two men first met in 1865, when Bute was a shy eighteen-year-old and Burges was thirty-eight. The young marquess was already keen to do something with Cardiff Castle, an early medieval fortress which had been partially converted into a comfortable residence by Henry Holland in about 1776, and he asked Burges to come up with some options. In 1866 the architect suggested Bute could conserve the oldest parts of the fabric or remake what was missing, a piece of archaeological restoration which replaced "everything that a study of archaeology would lead us to suppose had been lost." Or he could preserve the older parts of the castle while making "sundry additions which are to a certain degree demanded by the fact of the castle being used as a nobleman's residence." Bute chose the "sundry additions," and from 1868, when he came of age, until 1881, when Burges died, the marquess's money and the architect's imagination transformed Holland's residential range into a group of five high, connected towers, each one different in style and shape.[20]

The Clock Tower, 150 feet high, housed bachelor accommodation for Bute (who was not yet married), consisting of the Winter Smoking Room, Bachelor's Bedroom, and Summer Smoking Room. Appropriately enough, the decoration played with the idea of time: the clock which gave this first tower its name was flanked by painted statues representing the seven planets; and personifications of the signs of the zodiac, the seasons, the days of the week, and times of day—dawn, noon, dusk, and night—are everywhere, sculpted, moulded in plaster, in stained glass, and in tiled scenes on walls and floors. The double-height Summer Smoking Room at the top of the tower, described by historian Mark Girouard as "perhaps the strangest and most wonderful of all Victorian rooms," has a ceiling spangled with gilded crystal stars, a ceramic frieze depicting mythological scenes, and an enormous gold chandelier in the shape of the sun with a gold Apollo perched in the centre.[21] Corbels in the four corners are supported by medieval figures representing the eight winds of Greek mythology. (Burges was not afraid to mix his sources: Odin and Thor pop up in the Winter Smoking Room, while one of his most spectacular interiors was the Arab Room, the gilded ceiling of which is like something seen through a child's kaleidoscope, an impossibly intricate pattern of alcoves and corbels and geometries.) The great hooded chimneypiece has a carved frieze of vaguely medieval figures representing the delights of love in summer, presided over by a winged god of love. The fact that the god has parrots perched on his wrists only adds to a sense of joyous bewilderment.

And that joy permeates the entire castle. Carvings in the library include a duck-billed platypus and an armadillo with a bookworm. The bell-push in the dining room is a carved oak monkey with a nut clenched between its ivory teeth: to summon a servant, the Butes had to shove the nut down the monkey's throat. Eight great parrots support the Arab Room ceiling. And all this in settings which constantly bring one back to the idea of the medieval. The Banqueting Hall, for example, with a vaulted hammer-beam roof, had murals depicting the story of Robert the Consul, a Norman owner of the castle; in a giant castellated chimneypiece he rides out from the castle while plaster heralds play a fanfare and his wife waves goodbye from the battlements.

Not everyone was impressed with Cardiff Castle. Some critics felt that decorating spaces was all Burges cared about and that the architecture had to be content with second place. Others rejected the idealisation of the past: one rather humourlessly called Burges's work "an art congenial to the tastes of an illiterate baron surrounded by his blood-stained ruffian retainers, who, when not engaged in fighting or plundering, spent their time in drinking and debauching in their fortified dens." But some understood. The *Architect* said Cardiff was a house for someone who "has more sympathy with the past than the present . . . and who, blest with vast hereditary possessions, chooses to make a little world of them and live in it."[22]

Among those vast hereditary possessions was Castell Coch, a ruined thirteenth-century fortress on a wooded hillside outside Cardiff. In 1871 Bute asked Burges once again to report on the options, and Burges said he could either leave it as a ruin or restore it as an occasional summer residence. He offered a series of attractive drawings showing what was possible if Bute went for the second option, which of course he did. Work began on the so-called restoration in the summer of 1875, and the structure was complete by 1879, although the interiors had yet to be done when Burges died in 1881, and they weren't completed for another ten years.

But the result is magical—vaguely French, entirely romantic, and not at all like the castle which originally stood on the site. If Cardiff Castle was a sanctuary, Castell Coch was a plaything, a toy with a working portcullis and drawbridge, a place intended for picnics and flying visits, but not a home. The Butes only spent a single night there. The accommodation consisted of four rooms overlooking a small courtyard. A great hall was decorated with murals of scenes from the lives of obscure British saints (so obscure, in fact, that the identities of some of them remain a mystery), with a statue of the legendary Lucius of Britain, who was said to have introduced Christianity there in the second century, hovering over the chimneypiece. Lord Bute's bedroom was austere, Lady Bute's rather wonderful, with crystal balls on the bedposts and a domed ceiling filled with monkeys, squirrels, and nesting birds. It is a room in which Sleeping Beauty might wait for her prince to wake her or the Lady of Shalott might weave the mirror's magic sights.

But the glory of Castell Coch is its octagonal vaulted drawing room. This was originally conceived as two rooms, one above the other, but Burges decided in 1879 that it would be more effective if it was thrown into one. Here, he said, "I have ventured to indulge in a little more ornament."[23] That is an understatement. The drawing room sparkles and hums with life: depictions of Aesop's fables cover the walls above panelling individually painted with fifty-eight different local flowers, each on a gold background. Snails, lizards, mice, and birds wriggle round the doorways. On the ribs of the vault, butterflies fly upward to a central sun, while between the ribs hundreds of birds wheel and flutter in a bright-blue plaster sky beneath the stars. The three Fates look down from the chimneypiece: Clotho spins the thread of life, Lachesis measures it, and Atropos cuts it off with her abhorred shears, as she would in 1900, when, with Cardiff Castle still unfinished and the paint barely dry on Castell Coch, the Marquess of Bute had an apoplectic fit and died, aged fifty-three.

There is nowhere in Britain quite like the two castles that Burges designed for Bute. They were without doubt the high point of the nineteenth-century castle craze, pushing it to its logical limits and beyond. Nothing else came close, and anything that followed was inevitably an anticlimax. At Cardiff and Castell Coch Burges made magic. He was, in the words of his biographer, J. Mordaunt Crook, "the most dazzling exponent of the High Victorian Dream." Pugin conceived it; Tennyson wrote poems about it. Ruskin and Morris philosophised about it. "But only Burges built it."[24]

By the early twentieth century the more flamboyant excesses of castle building were at an end. When Lutyens restored the Tudor Lindisfarne Castle for Edward Hudson in 1902–1912, he did away with battlements and chose instead to emphasise the gaunt, sheer severity of the silhouette and its organic relationship with the crag from which it emerges. That severity extended to the interiors, described by critic Lytton Strachey as "very dark, with nowhere to sit, and nothing but stone under, over and round you . . . not a comfortable place, by any means."[25] And Lutyens's Castle Drogo in Devon has the same raw ele-mentalism, establishing links with the medieval while at the same time rejecting Burgesian romanticism in favour of a wholly contemporary conception which is every bit as cold and hard-edged as the granite blocks from which it is built.

Flamboyance was largely confined to Scotland, where the Scotch Baronial tradition remained surprisingly strong, especially among those who weren't Scottish. It was usually combined with slightly predictable opulent good taste. In 1897 the Norfolk-born Randlord Charles Rudd, one of the founders of the De Beers Mining Company, bought part of the fifty-five-thousand-acre Ardnamurchan estate in the Highlands and commissioned the architect Sydney Mitchell to build guest accommodation in the form of the monumental Glenborrodale Castle, overlooking Loch Sunart. In the same year a Lancashire tex-tile magnate, George Bullough, built Kinloch Castle, a lavish shooting lodge on the Isle of Rum in the Hebrides, which his father had bought in 1888. Bullough was the archetypal late Victorian millionaire, with a country house in Herefordshire; another at Newmarket, where he owned two racing studs; and the *Rhouma*, a 221-feet-long steam yacht with a crew of forty, which Bullough used to transport himself and his guests to his island. The castle, designed by the Yorkshire and London firm of Leeming and Leeming, is solid rather than theatri-cal, quite low, but with corner turrets, battlements, and a tall central tower. There is a story that it was built by workers from Bullough's native Lancashire, who were paid a shilling a day on top of their nor-mal wages to wear kilts, although quite why is not at all clear. Guests who gathered before dinner in the galleried, double-height Jacobethan living hall were treated to a performance from Bullough's orchestrion, an electric barrel organ with drums, cymbals, and triangle which lived under the stairs and played the "Ride of the Valkyries."

TEN

A MODERN EDEN

IN 1877 THE writer Henry James was shown over a small country house in Shropshire, and he fell in love with the place, with its age and its landscape. It was raining heavily, but that didn't matter. The park, he said, was paradise, "a modern Eden, and the trees might have been trees of knowledge."[1]

But before the century was out, serpents were rearing their heads in Eden. In the spring of 1900 *Country Life* ran a series of five articles entitled Of Garden Making. The articles singled out for praise the formal gardens of the seventeenth and early eighteenth centuries, with their canals and fountains and long terraces terminating in pavilions, their covered allées and box-lined parterres—architectural gardens, which were designed to be extensions of the house. They were stately and dignified, in contrast to what came after: "the arrogant futilities of the landscape gardener and his satellites." The formal gardens of Hampton Court Palace, Versailles, and Herrenhausen were the supreme expressions of this type of designed landscape, which represented the acme of garden making, before "Pope and the sycophant epigram writers of his day [decried] the last remnants of a grand old tradition" and ushered in the random landscapes of Lancelot "Capability" Brown.[2]

Over the previous ten years or so the fashion for formal gardens had been enjoying something of a renaissance, the author argued. Once more "enclosure, subdivision, and change of level" were back in fashion, "the whole scheme being treated as a setting to the house. . . . Wherever we find them these principles are frankly applied with a definite object: masonry for the outer enclosures, hedges for the inner, and miniature hedges again to the compartments for flowers."[3] But the new formalism faced opposition, he said, not from the advocates of the Brownian landscape—their time had passed—but from a new breed of gardeners who seemed to think, absurdly, that gardening was all about plants.

There were two views on this, said the writer:

> There is that of the cultured man, who delights in harmonies of form and colour, who loves the seclusion of a walled garden and all that fancy may suggest in flower beds. And there is that of the scientific florist and collector, whose interest lies in the production of flowers for show purposes, in rearing exotic plants, and coaxing the growth of specimen trees.[4]

One could be cultured, artistic, romantic; or one could be a botanist. Not both.

The author of the Of Garden Making articles was a brilliant young architect and designer, Francis Inigo Thomas, and he was firing the latest salvo in a battle that had been raging for years over the creation of country house gardens. On the one side there was gardener William Robinson, the prolific Irish author of *The Wild Garden* (1870) and *The English Flower Garden* (1883) and founder of a string of gardening magazines, beginning with the weekly the *Garden* in 1871. Reacting against the endless vistas of carpet bedding and Tudoresque knot gardens which characterised the early Victorian garden, Robinson argued for a romantic reinterpretation of the traditional cottage garden, full of hollyhocks and foxgloves and honeysuckle. Instead of rearing acres of bedding plants in hothouses and filling carpet beds with them once or twice a year, the discerning gardener should rely on native plants, supplementing them by "naturalizing or making wild innumerable beautiful natives of many regions of the earth in our woods, wild and semi-wild places, rougher parts of pleasure grounds, etc."[5]

Robinson's emphasis on plants led to his raising up the plantsman as central to good garden design, and, unsurprisingly, plantsmen tended to agree with him. "The architect," he wrote in *The English Flower Garden*, "can help us much by building a beautiful house. That is his work. The true architect seeks to go no further."[6]

The architectural profession was never likely to accept talk like that without a fight, and in 1892 Inigo Thomas and his fellow architect Reginald Blomfield rose to the polemical challenge. *The Formal Garden in England*, with text by Blomfield and illustrations by Thomas (who carried out much of the research for the book), declared on its first page that "the question at issue is a very simple one. Is the garden to be considered in relation to the house, and as an integral part of a design which depends for its success on the combined effect of house and garden; or is the house to be ignored in dealing with the garden?"[7]

Blomfield cheerfully admitted in his preface that *The Formal Garden* ignored all questions of how to grow plants and flowers and trees, implying that the designer was above such mundanities: they were the province of the horticulturalist, who stood in the same relation to the garden designer as the builder did to the architect. (A necessary evil, in other words.) That enraged Robinson, who retaliated with a savage review of *The Formal Garden*, urging clients to abolish "the needless formality and geometry which disfigure so many gardens," sneering at "pretentious plans," and finally jettisoning all restraint to declare that "Mr Blomfield writes nonsense." There was ample proof, he claimed, "that the system [the formalists] seek to revive could only bring costly ugliness to our beautiful home-landscapes."[8]

Blomfield responded in the preface to the second edition of *The Formal Garden*, which appeared hot on the heels of the first: "Not being an artist, Mr Robinson does not understand the artistic importance of mass on the one hand, and of scale on the other"; "Mr Robinson has a lofty disdain for accuracy"; "Mr Robinson seems to conceive of a garden as a Botanical Museum." The public exchange of insults rumbled on for years, with others pitching in on both sides as the mood took them. The Arts and Crafts architect Edward Schroeder Prior argued that since people walked in a straight line from point to point, unless they were drunk, a bend or a curve required some justification. Inigo Thomas gave lectures bemoaning the way that old gardens had been destroyed by the landscape gardener, their walls thrown down, their terraces ruined, the whole thing converted into "a wilderness of specimen shrubs." (He provided magic lantern slides to illustrate his point.) That he was devoting time and energy to the fight in 1900, eight years after the first publication of *The Formal Garden*, is an indication of its staying power.[9]

The quarrel, entertaining and unedifying as it is, needs to be viewed in the context of the Wrenaissance, that rising interest in the architecture of the late seventeenth and early eighteenth centuries and the gardens that went with it. Interest had begun to stir with the appearance of A. H. Mackmurdo's *Wren's City Churches* (1883), which offered a fresh new design vocabulary in the so-called Free Classic style, a breath of fresh air after the pathological earnestness of the Gothic Revival, or what Inigo Thomas called "the dry bones of antiquarianism." Then in 1897 Reginald Blomfield published his *A Short History of Renaissance Architecture in England*, full of praise for Wren, "the most English of all English architects," in whose work he found "a singularly direct and unaffected method of expression, free from pedantry and foolishness, and, above all, pre-eminently English in its sober power." Country houses began to appear which borrowed heavily and very freely from Wren. Richard Norman Shaw's Bryanston and Reginald Blomfield's Moundsmere have both been mentioned earlier as important examples of this "Wrenaissance." Others on the list might include Stansted Park in Sussex (1900, by Reginald's cousin, Arthur Blomfield) and Ernest George's redbrick Ardenrun Place in Surrey (1906–1909) for the banker Hans Henry Konig, a splendid reinterpretation of domestic English baroque, complete with dressings of Portland stone, hipped roofs, dormers, and a cupola.[10]

Ernest George's partner in his architectural practice from 1876 to 1892 was Harold Peto, the son of the railway developer (and bankrupt) Sir Morton Peto. The firm of Ernest George and Peto made a name for themselves in the 1880s with big, opulent Mayfair town houses and even bigger, more opulent country houses, often in a heavy Tudor Gothic, for a mixed clientele. Batsford Park in Gloucestershire (1888–1893) was designed for a diplomat and civil servant; Shiplake Court in Oxfordshire (1889–1890) was for a stockbroker; Buchan Hill in Sussex (1882–1885) was for an ostrich feather merchant.

By the early 1890s Peto was growing bored with business and with London. In 1892 he split from George, agreeing that he wouldn't compete with him by practising architecture in England, and decided to travel, something he had always enjoyed, even during their partnership. He spent time in Italy and France, America, Egypt, and the Far East, while settling briefly in Kent and then outside Salisbury before buying Iford Manor, a country house with an early eighteenth-century facade masking some much earlier work, in a perfect setting by the River Frome on the Somerset-Wiltshire border. That was in 1899, and Peto quickly began to lay out new gardens on a steeply sloping site behind his new home. A series of formal terraces and borders was scattered with curiosities and architectural pieces: a Spanish loggia; a Greek sarcophagus and a Roman wine amphora; statues, columns, and terra-cotta plaques; and a cloister, intended, Peto wrote, "to contain . . . my collection of antique fragments which always interested me as an architect to buy when I came across them."[11]

The result is exactly the kind of formal, architectural garden that Blomfield and Thomas so admired. And Peto was of the same school, writing in *The Boke of Iford*, his account of the creation of Iford Manor gardens, that "for a garden to contain the highest development of beauty it must have a combination of architecture and plants. Old buildings or fragments of masonry carry one's mind back to the past in a way that a garden entirely of flowers cannot do."[12]

Starting around the time he bought Iford, Peto began to put theory into practise in a string of notable Edwardian gardens: he worked at Easton Lodge for Daisy Greville, Countess of Warwick, at Buscot Park in Oxfordshire for the 1st Baron Faringdon, at West Dean in Sussex for the big game hunter William James. One of his most notable designs was planned for the Belfast-born MP John Annan Bryce on Garinish, a little island in Bantry Bay, County Cork, just before the outbreak of the First World War. When Bryce bought Garinish in 1910 it had nothing but a Martello tower from 1805, reputedly the first of these Napoleonic defences to be built in Ireland, and a ruined garrison fort. By the time it was finished it was a little island paradise, surrounded by seals which flopped around on rocky outcrops and stared inquisitively at passing strangers come to admire the walks, the Grecian temple and the Spanish loggia, and the Italian garden—although not, unfortunately, the seven-storey country house that Bryce had intended to build if his ambition hadn't been curtailed by the war and a downturn in his fortunes caused by heavy investment in Russia.

If Henry James still looked for his modern Eden, Garinish was it: a paradise before the Fall.

Garinish and Iford made Peto famous, and rightly so. Inigo Thomas, whose reputation has been eclipsed by Blomfield, his more strident collaborator on *The Formal Garden*, didn't have a prolific output as either an architect or a garden designer. He wrote, he illustrated, he lectured on garden design. He was an accomplished artist: his pen-and-ink drawings helped to define the turn-of-the-century country house and garden as a place to reflect on the past in tranquillity, and in a self-portrait made in 1903 he depicted himself as every inch the country gentleman, clad in riding gear, with top hat and whip in hand. Architect Ninian Comper, who was a good friend of Thomas's, wrote much later that he was "the pioneer of modern times in gardens" and that his name "has not been known as it ought to be known."[13]

The renown of that name rests primarily on three fabulous projects in the 1890s, all involving the remodelling or extending of much older and rather run-down country houses. At Rotherfield Hall in Sussex, a Tudor ironmaster's house which Thomas restored and extended in 1897 for Lindsay Hogg, later Sir Lindsay Lindsay-Hogg, Bt, he made good use of a steeply sloping site, creating a paved terrace by the house which dropped eight feet to a long parterre which terminated in two tall pavilions, with cupolas fitted as dovecotes. (He also installed an example of that triumph of optimism over climate, the open sleeping loggia.) "Peaceful beauty, restful charm, should be leading qualities of normal [*sic*] gardens," wrote H. Avray Tipping. "All this we find at Rotherfield Hall."[14]

The same qualities of peaceful beauty and restful charm were in abundance in the gardens at Barrow Court in Somerset, a hopelessly dilapidated Tudor and Jacobean house which was bought by Henry Gibbs, son of the guano magnate William Gibbs of Tyntesfield, and restored for him in 1883–1884 by the architect Henry Woodyer. Thomas was brought in to lay out the gardens in 1893–1897, and his combination of terraced walks, clipped yew and statuary, iris pond and dovecote, stone pavilions and enclosed courts, with curving flights of steps flanked by tall stone piers topped with ball finials, led *Country Life* in 1902 to take a rather late swipe at the Robinsonians, declaring, "It is an architect's garden . . . and, *pace* those who would hold back the architect to the barrier of the house wall, it is not to be gainsaid that the effect is very fine."[15]

Thomas's finest garden, and the one which epitomises the achievements of the late Victorian and Edwardian formal school, is at Athelhampton in Dorset, a romantic late fifteenth-century manor house. In 1891, when it was bought by Alfred Cart de Lafontaine, an Anglo-French country squire with antiquarian interests, Athelhampton was in a sorry state: Lady Dorothy Nevill, who knew it as a child in the 1830s, remembered it as "a deserted and seemingly ruined building used as a farm." As for the gardens, they consisted of a plantation of larches and an open paddock scattered with trees, "a wilderness through which cattle roamed right up to the door."[16] Cart de Lafontaine restored the hall with some sensitivity and filled it with good period furniture, most of it oak, and some unlikely curios of exactly the type beloved by Victorian antiquarians: a fragment of Elizabeth I's dress, boots worn by Charles I.

Even before de Lafontaine had completed the purchase of Athelhampton, he consulted Inigo Thomas about laying out new gardens. The architect went down to see the site in the winter of 1890—two years before the publication of *The Formal Garden* brought him to public attention. A *Country Life* article of 1899 which was based on Thomas's own words noted,

There were felling, grubbing, and carting away of trees, the purchase and planting of yew and box, of turf and flowers and creepers. There were tons of gravel, twice sifted, and metalling for the garden baths. For many months waggons laded with russet stone from Ham Hill created down the Yeovil road.[17]

Thomas created a series of linked compartments. "There is more left to the imagination where the whole cannot be seen at a glance," he said in an 1896 lecture to the Royal Society of Arts. A paved terrace running along the southeast front of the hall was, said *Country Life*, "the very place to bask through a cigarette after lunch." From there steps led down to the first of three gardens, a plain lawned area with a lily pond placed centrally to catch the reflection of the hall. Next came a long, narrow garden which was intended to have a sundial as its centrepiece, and then a much bigger garden laid out with sixty-four symmetrical beds and a dozen pyramidal yews (though these grew so large that they overshadowed the beds, which had to be abandoned). That indispensable adjunct to a turn-of-the-century country house, the tennis lawn, lay behind this sunken area, and to one side was a long raised terrace, with stone summerhouses at each end. The effect was quiet, careful, and quite magical, giving weight to Blomfield's assertion that "to plan out a garden the knowledge necessary is that of design, not of the best method of growing a giant gooseberry."[18]

Thomas's gardens at Athelhampton lay mostly to the south of the old hall. In about 1904 de Lafontaine called in another designer, Thomas Mawson, to advise on the siting of a new stable and garage and to replan gardens to the north of the house. Mawson did nothing more than supply plans, some of which were executed by others, but he fits neatly here into the architect vs. plantsman debate because, perhaps more than any other Edwardian designer, it was Mawson who managed to steer a sensible course between the warring factions. In a 1908 article in the *Studio*, "The Designing of Gardens," he began in an uncompromising fashion by consigning Capability Brown and all his followers to the dustbin of history. Landscape gardens were nothing but "puerile attempts to imitate nature," he declared. They were neither nature nor art, and they must be "truly abominated by all good people with taste."[19]

But Mawson also acknowledged the importance of working with nature and urged a balance between art and horticulture. Neither could make a successful garden without the other. The architect provided the framework, and the gardener enriched it and made it complete. "This richness of dress, and a certain easy freedom therewith, is what every garden should possess." It is significant that Mawson started out as a nurseryman at Windermere in the Lake District, working with his two brothers in the family business before branching out into design during the 1890s. In *The Art and Craft of Garden Making* (1900), a book whose title promised a compromise between architect and gardener, Mawson wrote that his hero as a landscape designer, Humphry Repton, recommended "formality near the house, merging into the natural by degrees, so as to attach the house by imperceptible graduations to the general landscape." That's a fair summary of his own position, although, far less doctrinaire than either Blomfield or Robinson, he was happy to work with his client, giving them ultraformality if they wanted it or shrubberies and naturalistic woodland. Nor was he afraid to dwell on the selection of plants and shrubs. *The Art and Craft of Garden Making* contained lists of trees, shrubs, and conifers, of hardy climbers and roses, and of hardy perennials, aquatic plants, and ferns—all with helpful planting notes: "Buddle[j]a globosa . . . Orange-coloured flowers. It is an excellent shrubby climber for covering walls, and one which does well by the sea"; "Alyssums. The most useful for rock work are A. alpestre, montanum, saxatile compactum, all dwarf-growing varieties of a bright yellow, all do well in a dry sunny position."[20]

Mawson's two hundred or so commissions ranged from planting an entrance court to laying out an entire series of gardens. His country house contracts, which tended to be for self-made men rather than for the old aristocracy, included gardens at Skibo Castle for Andrew Carnegie; Bowden Hill near Lacock in Wiltshire, for Herbert Harris, a local JP; Breadsall Priory in Derbyshire for Sir Alfred Haslam, whose considerable wealth came from patenting a system of shipboard refrigeration for meat; Wightwick Manor near Wolverhampton, for paint manufacturer Geoffrey Mander; and Thornton Manor in Cheshire, for W. H. Lever, later Lord Leverhulme.

In fact, Mawson worked for Lord Leverhulme at several of his houses; according to his biographer, "All the schemes involved gardens of heroic proportions." At Lululaund in Hertfordshire, the strikingly muscular house designed for the artist Sir Hubert von Herkomer by the American architect Henry Hobson Richardson— "thirteenth-century Gothic with a Romanesque feeling" was von Herkomer's description—Mawson designed a rose garden, a pergola and a pavilion in 1912. As payment, von Herkomer painted Mawson's portrait, something for which he usually charged 600 guineas. (He had the same arrangement with Richardson.) At Graythwaite Hall in Lancashire, where Mawson worked on and off for years for the owner, Colonel Thomas Myles Sandys, MP, beginning in around 1889, he practised what he had preached in his reference to Repton, with tight formal features (and a tennis court) close to the house and more naturalistic planting in the park. There was a walk alongside a stream leading into this park, and "it is intended to naturalise Daffodils, Spiraeas of sorts, Iris, Japanese Anemone, and other hardy free-flowering plants."[21]

The most famous collaboration between architectural design and plantsmanship began in 1889, when Edwin Lutyens and Gertrude

Jekyll met at the Surrey home of a mutual friend, the rhododendron grower Harry Mangle. Lutyens was tall, trusting, and twenty, and had set up his own practice only a month or so earlier. Gertrude Jekyll was short, stern, and forty-five—"a bunch of cloaked propriety topped by a black felt hat," Lutyens called her—and was already beginning to establish a reputation for herself as a garden designer, an occupation she had taken up when failing eyesight forced her to give up a career as a painter, silverworker, and embroideress.[22]

The two got on immediately. During the early 1890s they spent weekends bowling along country lanes in Gertrude's pony cart, hunting for old farms and tumbledown cottages. And within months of their first meeting, "Aunt Bumps," as the young architect christened her, was advising on the layout of the gardens at Lutyens's first big commission, Crooksbury near Farnham (1890), a thoroughly Old English mixture of tile hanging, half timbering, and Tudor chimneys designed for Harry Mangle's sister and her husband.

Other ventures soon followed. At Chinthurst Hill in Surrey, a large country house begun to Lutyens's designs in 1893, Bumps created the terrace and a herbaceous border 180 feet long. And in the same year the two worked together to create a formal Italianate garden for the Dowager Duchess of Bedford at Woodside in Buckinghamshire. In what was to become a pattern for their many country house collaborations, Lutyens provided the architectural framework—terracing, brick paving, pergolas, and ponds—and Gertrude designed the planting.[23]

Garden designers of the period were swift to promote their own ideas, and their careers, in print. William Robinson's *The Wild Garden*, Blomfield and Thomas's *The Formal Garden*, and Mawson's *The Art and Craft of Garden Making* were only the tip of the horticultural iceberg. Robinson's *The English Flower Garden*, first published in 1883, went through fifteen editions, and he was also owner-editor of the *Garden* magazine, and later *Gardening Illustrated*, which competed with a growing number of magazines aimed at the middle-class gardener. Robinson's success as a writer enabled him to buy the late Elizabethan Gravetye Manor in Sussex in 1884, and his experience laying out the grounds there (in a surprisingly formal framework that would have given a great deal of pleasure to Blomfield and Inigo Thomas) was the source in 1911 for his *Gravetye Manor; or, Twenty Years' Work Round an Old Manor House*.

Gertrude Jekyll was no stranger to gardening journalism. In fact, she was perhaps the most prolific gardening author of her day. She was a regular contributor to Robinson's the *Garden* (at one stage she edited it), writing on everything from "The Pergola in English Gardens" to "Undesirable Plants."[24] She produced over a thousand articles for a variety of journals and newspapers, from *Country Life* and the *Ladies' Field* to the *Daily Mail* and the *Daily Express*. And she wrote fourteen books, beginning with *Wood and Garden* (1899), a collection of articles she wrote for the *Manchester Guardian*. With *Country Life*'s architectural editor Lawrence Weaver (whose *Houses and Gardens by E. L. Lutyens* featured several Lutyens-Jekyll collaborations), she wrote *Gardens for Small Country Houses* (1912), which had gone through four editions by 1920.

In *Colour in the Flower Garden* (1908), she set out her thinking on composition. "The possession of a quantity of plants, however good the plants may be themselves . . . does not make a garden; it only makes a *collection*." The great thing was to use them wisely. They were like a box of paints, she said, or colours laid out on a palette. The trick was "so to use the plants that they shall form beautiful pictures."[25]

Combined with this painterly approach to garden design, Jekyll had a love of and a respect for vernacular architecture, the farmhouses and cottages of the past, and it was this more than anything else which cemented her working relationship with Lutyens. Sir Herbert Baker, who worked with Lutyens in New Delhi, praised "her power to see, as a poet, the art and creation of home-making as a whole in relation to Life; the best simple country life of her day, frugal, yet rich in beauty and comfort, its garden united the house with surrounding nature." And Sir Robert Lorimer was full of enthusiasm for Munstead Wood, Jekyll's own garden in Surrey and the house that Lutyens designed for her there in 1897. It looked, said Lorimer, "so reasonable, so kindly, so perfectly beautiful that you feel that people might have been making love and living and dying there, and dear little children running about for the last—I was going to say, thousand years, anyway six hundred."[26]

The turn of the century saw a burgeoning market for all things related to the garden, its care, and its embellishment. Everything from silver sand and cold frames to bulk orders of orchid peat and forty-gallon dispensers of weedkiller could be despatched to the most convenient railway station. One enterprising coal mine in Swansea sold horticultural anthracite, as supplied "to the gardens of a great number of the Nobility, Gentry, and principal Florists, &c . . . Delivered by Rail to all parts with despatch direct from the colliery."[27]

Reproduction antique statuary was popular, so long as one had a big enough garden—and even if one didn't, which led to some distressing results. "Lead statue of Mercury on stone pedestal, total height 6ft 3in; a graceful addition to any garden, £7 15 0 each," ran one advertisement for lead garden figures, cherubs and urns and girls with flowers. Hughes, Bolcklow and Company, ship breakers of Blyth in Northumberland, offered a range of teak garden furniture, all of which was, they claimed, "made from battleships broken up." J. C. Vickery, "Their Majesties' Dressing Case Manufacturer," advertised a mahogany tea wagon with rubber tyres designed specifically for wheeling afternoon tea onto the lawn. Other firms offered glasshouses in every shape and size—orchid houses, ferneries, cucumber houses, melon houses, vineries—together with the boilers and pipework to heat them.[28]

Nothing, though, was quite as majestic as Joseph Paxton's Great Conservatory at Chatsworth, put up in 1836 and, at 277 feet by 123 feet by 67 feet high, less a glasshouse and more a cathedral to the horticultural profession. Still attracting praise and awe by the end of the century, it was situated at the end of a carriage drive, and for the favoured visitor, "the great doors will open, and the drive may be continued through what is, for all practical purposes, a tropical forest, or the best of many tropical forests rolled into one, without the wild beasts and the wilder men, and the snakes and other disagreeable accompaniments of the real thing."[29] There were palms, tree ferns, fig trees, and a first-floor gallery from which one could gaze down on an avenue of bananas. And in 1900 heating its six miles of hot-water pipes cost £1,500 a year, which is why the 9th Duke of Devonshire demolished it in 1920.

The lawn mower, patented in 1830 by the Gloucestershire engineer and inventor Edwin Beard Budding, was in general use by the 1870s and available in many sizes of blade, from six inches—"mere toys," declared William Robinson's *Garden* magazine—to three feet or more. There were one-man, two-man, and three-man machines; machines drawn by a donkey; machines drawn by a horse. The *Garden* recommended a full-size mower drawn by a donkey: "A donkey machine can cut even round small flower beds, and what it leaves the 12-in. machine can cut in a short time." By the 1890s Lloyd's, Lawrence and Company were advertising their "Lloyd's perfected 'Pennsylvania,'" an American lawn mower which won awards at the Chicago World's Fair of 1893: "Formerly with the old machine we used a horse," ran a testimonial from the Dowager Duchess of Wellington's steward at Bearhill Park in Surrey. "Now we can do the work better, and much quicker, with a man and boy." In the late 1890s,

Country Life was carrying prominent advertisements for Ransome's Lawn Mowers, with adjustable rollers and available in nine sizes from eight inch to twenty-four inch, "patronised by the Queen & Prince of Wales & in use everywhere." And by 1903 Ransomes, the market leaders, were offering motor mowers; four years later they were able to claim "nearly 200 supplied, including two to H. M. the King."[30]

It wasn't everyone who approved the arrival of the lawn mower. Gertrude Jekyll was quite excited at the thought of a brawny young man wielding his scythe: "Not only are the movements of the labourer full of vigorous grace and beauty, but so are also the subtly-curving lines of the scythe and sneathe [shaft]; while the splendid skill of the strong young man, often at work throughout the long daylight of middle June, makes light the lengthy hours of arduous toil."[31]

ELEVEN

ARRANGED WITH GREAT TASTE

I N THE AUTUMN of 1834 Lord Brougham, Lord High Chancellor, was travelling through the south of France on his way to Genoa when an outbreak of cholera meant he was stopped at the border and told he must either undergo ten days' quarantine or write to Paris for special permission to continue his journey. He chose the latter, and while he waited for an answer to his request, he looked around for somewhere to stay. It was recommended he go to Antibes, but instead, "finding the dirty cooking and inn of the garrison town by no means inviting," as he later recalled, he put up in the little fishing village of Cannes, just along the coast.[1] The beauty of the place didn't particularly strike him, but the climate did: he was told that the winters in Cannes were as mild as in Cairo and that frost and snow were almost unknown. He thought it would be an ideal place to stay with his invalid daughter, avoiding the cold winters and damp springs that sapped one's soul back in England, and on the spur of the moment he bought a plot of land and built himself a house.

The Villa Éléonore-Louise, a big and elegant Italianate mansion, was the work of French surveyor and engineer Louis Larras and a firm of local builders, the brothers Fleury Guichard. It was named for Brougham's fragile daughter, who died in 1839, before the house was finished; and this is perhaps why the interiors weren't fitted out for another ten years. In about 1850 Brougham added two wings and a first-floor terrace supported by a Doric colonnade which stretched the full width of the house, making the most of the views down to the sea.

Within decades, the Riviera was peppered with British country houses, as others followed Lord Brougham's example without necessarily exhibiting his quiet good taste. In 1852 Thomas Smith, a Hertfordshire architect who was more at home designing gaols and vicarages, was for some reason commissioned to design the Villa Victoria in Cannes for a Glasgow merchant, Sir Thomas Robinson Woolfield. Working with an English builder named Obadiah Pulham, Smith produced a defiantly English Tudor Gothic cottage orné which made no concessions whatsoever to local tradition. He also designed Protestant churches for the use of English visitors at Nice and Cannes, which were paid for by Woolfield; and in partnership with his son, Thomas Tayler Smith, he went on to plant several more English villas in French soil, of which the most remarkable was the Château Sainte-Ursule, an enormous neo-Gothic fortress with tall towers, battlements, and cruciform embrasures overlooking the Mediterranean just outside Cannes, again built for Woolfield in the 1850s but bought in 1856 by Lord Londesborough and sold on several times in quick succession. Woolfield explained the fact that he sold Sainte-Ursule to Londesborough for a "foolishly small price" by saying that his new church was just finished and he "was desirous that so large and influential a family [the Londesboroughs had twelve children] should help to fill it, and so increase our English colony."[2]

Smith's final work in Cannes was the Château Scott (1868–1872), yet another piece of English neo-Gothic. In 1883, when it belonged to the Liberal politician Lord Wolverton, it enjoyed a moment of fame when it played host to the prime minister, William Gladstone, who was holidaying on the Riviera with his wife and daughter. "The Scott Chateau, where the Wolvertons have perched themselves high above the sea," was how Mary Gladstone described it, before going on to note that at one of the English colony's at homes, a little girl asked Gladstone how a prime minister could govern England while drinking tea at Cannes.[3]

One of the best-known English homes on the Riviera was not new, nor did its reputation rest on its architectural merits. In 1867 Thomas Hanbury, a wealthy merchant and tea broker based in Shanghai, was holidaying in the Mediterranean when he came across a ruined palazzo in an extraordinarily beautiful position high above the sea. The Palazzo Orengo stood on a promontory, the Capo Mortola, a few miles along the Corniche from Menton on the Italian side of the frontier with France. Having started life as a watchtower and keep intended to protect its occupants from the Barbary pirates who used to raid the Mediterranean coast, it had been extended in the sixteenth century to form a large country house, with rubble and mortar walls four feet thick, limewashed and painted in bright colours. Now it was in a poor state, with daylight showing through the roof. One of the reception rooms was a stable for mules, while the hall was cluttered with oil jars and wine barrels, and bats and swallows occupied the piano nobile on the first floor.

Hanbury bought the Palazzo Orengo. He repaired the roof, ejected the mules and the bats and the swallows, and added two ranges, one containing a drawing room with bedrooms above and the other a service wing with kitchens and other domestic offices.

The main block, where Machiavelli was reputed to have stayed in 1511, was turned into a comfortable gentleman's house, with big Italianate chimneypieces, Chinese cloisonné, and, in the new drawing room, a mosaic floor based on several found in Roman villas in Leicester. The keep became a belvedere, commanding stunning views over the blue Mediterranean. A white marble terrace with a colonnade of spiral fluted columns faced south, overlooking the steeply sloping site which led down to the sea. Queen Victoria, who visited in 1882 while staying in Menton, was enchanted: "The house is a regular little old Italian Palazzo," she wrote in her journal, "and is arranged with great taste."[4]

But it wasn't Hanbury's palazzo that attracted Victoria. It was his garden, which was, she said, "planted with the most wonderful collection of flowers and shrubs, and plants from every part of the world." The Shanghai merchant's intention was to create a botanical garden on the fifty-acre site, with help from his eldest brother Daniel, a botanist with an interest in the pharmacology of plants. While Thomas went back to China to settle his business affairs (taking with him his wife Katharine, whom he had married in 1868 and who was, like the Hanburys, a Quaker), Daniel was left to develop the gardens at La Mortola, as the place became known. Thomas and Katharine left China in 1871 to settle in their palazzo, and after Daniel's death in 1875 they continued his work at the gardens. By 1889 there were 3,600 species growing there, and tourists flocked to pay their one-franc admission fee to see what the distinguished British botanist Joseph Dalton Hooker described in 1893 as a garden "which in point of richness and interest has no rival among the principal collections of living plants in the world."[5]

By the last years of the nineteenth century the stretch of coastline from Cannes up to Monte Carlo and Menton and into Italy had been transformed from a last resting place for consumptives into a playground for the wealthy of Europe and America. Nice's Casino Municipal, built in 1883, boasted a winter garden, a theatre, gaming rooms, and a café. In Monte Carlo, the entrance to Charles Garnier's Casino (1878–1881) was flanked by the statues *Dancing*, by Gustave Doré, and *Music*, by the actress Sarah Bernhardt, whose talent as a sculptor has been largely forgotten. Its gaming rooms were open daily from midday until 11 p.m. for roulette and Trente et Quarante. Entrance was free on presentation of a visiting card, and maximum stakes were 6,000 francs and 12,000 francs respectively—somewhere around £30,000 and £60,000 in today's values.

The coast's attractions were highlighted—and enhanced—by regular visits from Queen Victoria, who, as well as spending holidays on Lake Maggiore, in Aix-les-Bains and Florence, in Biarritz and San Sebastian, went to Menton in 1882 (when she visited La Mortola), to Cannes in 1887, to Grasse in 1891, and to Hyères in 1892. In 1895, travelling as she always did when abroad as the "Countess of Balmoral," she visited Nice, putting up at the Grand Hôtel, Cimiez. Her initial reception was not altogether to her liking: she thought the town was clean but uninteresting, and she was horrified when a deputation from the Fishwives of Nice arrived at her suite with a huge bouquet and their "fat spokeswoman" kissed her on both cheeks. "To avoid further kisses, I shook hands with all the others," the queen wrote in her diary.[6]

But the experience didn't deter her; she was back at the Grand Hôtel the following year, and the year after that. In fact she holidayed in Nice in 1895, 1896, 1897, 1898, and 1899, moving for the last three to the Regina, a huge new hotel with an electric lift where her party had a whole wing to themselves with a private entrance. On sunny afternoons she was driven out in the royal carriage on sketching expeditions and sightseeing tours, accompanied by her two Indian servants and the French detective who was responsible for her safety. At the end of her final visit, she mourned the loss of "this paradise of nature, which I grieve to leave." On her deathbed two years later she is reputed to have said that if only she were in Nice, she would get better. Up to her last week, she had planned another stay at the Regina. When she died the hotel charged an £800 cancellation fee.[7]

Her son and heir preferred bright lights and gaming tables to sketching expeditions. Bertie took to spending three weeks or so in Cannes in February and early March, sometimes staying in the town, sometimes on his yacht, often bringing his current mistress with him or arranging to rendezvous with her at one hotel or another. "The Prince of Wales spends most of his time walking and driving about, and visiting his friends," reported the *Times* in 1883, before going on to list the string of public and private balls he was expected to attend.[8]

And it was his presence, as much as that of the queen, that attracted the British elite to the Riviera; although the climate and the beauty of the area mattered as much, if not more. Some stayed in hotels—the Grand or the Hôtel de Paris in Monte Carlo, or César Ritz's Hôtel de Provence in Cannes. Others rented a villa for the season, where they could entertain their friends and misbehave discreetly. In 1895 Baedeker's handbook for travellers to southeastern France noted that "engagements are usually made for the whole season, the rent being 1200, 2000 fr and upwards," and it added a word of warning: "Cannes is considered a somewhat expensive place." Although the rents in Nice were not quite so exorbitant, there were clearly other things to worry about. Baedeker recommended that his readers consult a doctor before taking out a lease on a villa and insist on a notarized contract specifying the condition of the furniture, linen, and wallpapers. And, he wrote, "landlords sometimes make exorbitant demands on the death of one of their guests, in which case the aid of the authorities should be invoked."[9]

Now enjoy your holidays.

Some Britons liked the area so much that after a few seasons renting a villa (and not dying in it) they followed the example set by Lord Brougham and Thomas Robinson Woolfield and built their own country house, with varying degrees of success. They might go to a local architect: the Beaux Arts–trained Charles Baron, who settled in Cannes in 1863, just as the area really took off as an elite destination, is said to have designed around 150 villas and other buildings, mainly in an Italianate or Renaissance style. The widowed Bettina de Rothschild was one of his many clients: having rented the Villa Victoria, in 1881 she acquired a neighbouring property, demolished the house on the site, and commissioned a much larger neoclassical mansion, the Villa Rothschild, from Baron. Laurent Vianay, another Frenchman who saw the potential of Cannes and who set up in practice there in about 1870, designed at least ten villas in the following decade, several of which were intended from the outset as rentals.

The Riviera villas designed around the turn of the century were more competent and more quietly self-assured than the neo-Gothic excesses of Thomas Smith and his son—usually because they were the work of local men who understood the climate, the topography, and the social milieu. But there was one notable exception: Harold Peto.

Peto had agreed not to practise architecture in England when in 1892 he left Ernest George to continue their successful country house practice; and as we have already seen, he turned instead to garden design with great success. But the Riviera offered him a chance to be an architect again and, perhaps more important than that, it held out the possibility of his creating a unity of house and garden while working in the formal Italianate tradition that he loved.

In 1902 Peto was asked to design a villa and garden for Ralph Wormeley Curtis, the American impressionist painter, his wife Lisa, whom he had married in 1897, and their young daughter, Sylvia. After a rather nomadic existence in Paris, Rome, Venice, and the Netherlands, Curtis had decided to settle with his bride on the Riviera,

buying a long, steep plot peppered with old olive trees on the promontory of Saint-Jean-Cap-Ferrat, between Beaulieu-sur-Mer and
Villefranche-sur-Mer. Peto gave them a wonderfully understated
house, part Italian palazzo, part English Palladian country house,
with deeply projecting pantiled eaves, loggias carrying a first-floor balcony and an open sleeping porch, and a formal terrace leading to what
was, for Peto, a surprisingly naturalistic garden. He positioned the new
house right up against the retaining wall of the road that ran past the
site, rather than placing it farther down at the end of a drive; in this
way he extracted the maximum enjoyment out of the views and the
gardens. He kept the old olive grove, and although there was plenty of
colourful planting and that favourite device of his, the pergola, put in
an appearance, the overall feel of the Villa Sylvia was one of quiet good
taste and minimal interference with what was there already. "You have
realised the sentiment of our land!" a French artist told him.[10]

The Villa Sylvia was followed in 1904 by the Villa Maryland, also
at Cap Ferrat. Peto's clients this time were Arthur and Mary Wilson.* The Wilsons had bought a ten-acre site with great views but one
important disadvantage: a public road bisected it, and although that
road led to a cul-de-sac, so that there was a limited amount of traffic, there was no chance of having it closed or rerouted. Mindful of
a similar situation at his own house, Iford Manor, where a sunken
lane divided one half of his garden from the other, Peto turned it
to advantage. As at Villa Sylvia, he placed the entrance to the villa
straight off the road, but what an entrance it was! Guests immediately found themselves in a decidedly Moorish open court or cloister,
with vaulted walks on two levels and a fountain playing into a circular
pool in the centre. From the upper level of the house a bridge crossed

---

*   The Villa Maryland was named after Mary Wilson. There seems to have been
a very un-English fashion for naming Riviera villas after female members of
the owner's family. Was it begun by Lord Brougham and his Villa Éléonore-
Louise, or was Brougham merely following established French practice?

the offending road and flights of steps led down to a garden which contained rather more of the formal elements that usually featured in Peto's gardens: garden temples, formal pools, columns and statues and loggias, and a long pergola.

The interiors were cool and simple. The dining room had a vaulted ceiling and an enormous hooded chimneypiece; the saloon, reached through a pair of massive carved doors which originated in sixteenth-century Spain, was hung with red damask, loosely fitted so that it could be taken down and stored away from moths in the summer. Like the Villa Sylvia, the Villa Maryland combined English country house and Italian palazzo. "Just what an Englishman's Mediterranean home should be, that Maryland is," declared *Country Life* when the house was written up in the magazine in 1910. "It is a complete conception realised at every point, a difficult problem solved in all its details."[11]

In 1910 Peto designed a third villa overlooking Villefranche Bay on a two-and-a-half-acre site which his client, Arthur Cohen, had bought on his advice. The main house consisted at ground-floor level of four big rooms: a living hall with a raftered ceiling, plain whitewashed walls above walnut panelling, and an antique Italian hooded fireplace; a dining room; and, in projecting wings, a boudoir and a library. All four rooms faced south, and all opened onto a broad marble terrace with a rectangular pool at its centre. There was a loggia which supported a balcony on impossibly slender columns, and from there the Cohens could look down towards the southern boundary of their little estate, where Peto placed a double-arcaded loggia which gave spectacular views across the bay. And there was, of course, a pergola.

Peto worked on several more villas in the years before and just after the war. At Isola Bella in Cannes in 1910, he extended an existing house for the Baron van André and laid out new gardens, which were dominated by an enormous pergola of Ionic white-veined marble columns which curved around an oval reflecting pool a hundred feet wide. And in about 1920 he carried out some work at the Villa Salles-Eiffel, including the creation of a verandah and a long open cloister, for Adolphe Salles and his wife Claire, daughter of Gustave Eiffel, of Tower fame. Peto's contribution to the villas and country houses of the Riviera is small compared, say, to Charles Baron and his 150 buildings or Laurent Vianay and his rental villas. But it is perfectly formed. And absurdly, when I see the Spanish and the Italian and the Moorish influences that run through his Mediterranean houses and their gardens, it seems to me that there is something peculiarly English about his work. Perhaps it is the restraint, the sense of intellectual control. Or perhaps, embarrassingly, I've succumbed to a chauvinistic vein in British historiography which secretly still believes that we do these things better than Johnny Foreigner. I'm inclined to think it is a bit of both. As *Country Life* put it, discussing Peto's Villa Sylvia in 1910, the best modern architects were determined to create something that was beautiful,

> because it consents to discipline, because it belongs to an organised whole. . . . We are getting more and more to see this principle well carried out in England, and it is agreeable to our national vanity to find that its best and most satisfying manifestations on the Riviera are due to the initiative and taste of an English architect.[12]

"It is difficult to look upon the French Riviera as a purely foreign land," wrote the same *Country Life* critic in 1910. Two years later, on April 12, 1912, a statue of Queen Victoria by local sculptor Louis Maubert was unveiled in front of the Hôtel Régina in Nice: she stood accepting gifts from four young women, representing the four cities of the Riviera where she had stayed—Nice, Menton, Grasse, and Cannes—and in his speech the mayor of Nice reminisced fondly, if not entirely accurately, about how "she loved to wander the leafy paths of these green hills in a small carriage which she drove herself, often stopping at the house of some inhabitant in order to drink a glass of milk or to buy flowers and fruits that young girls from the countryside would ingenuously bring to her." The following day there was a second ceremony: a statue by sculptor Denys Puech of Edward VII, dressed as a yachtsman, was unveiled on the boulevard de la Croisette in Cannes, near the casino where he had loved to play and the Jetée Albert Édouard, the pier which was named after him. In front of a distinguished audience of local and national dignitaries, diplomats and admirals and politicians, the prime minister of France, Raymond Poincaré, gave a speech in which he paid tribute to "the great-hearted prince who under these skies at Cannes shed around him such a wealth of graciousness, of brilliance, and of winning charm." The French bands played "La Marseillaise" and then changed to "God Save the King" as "with one single motion the monument was laid bare and King Edward stood again as the people of Cannes knew him in yachtsman's dress smiling upon them," reported the *Times*. "It was really a very affecting moment."[13]

The anglicisation of the Riviera took different forms, from building Gothic follies and Protestant churches to taking afternoon tea and erecting monuments to the monarchy. The palm-flanked avenue by the sea at Nice was named the Promenade des Anglais. As well as the statues to Victoria and Edward, there was one to Lord Brougham in Cannes, near the Square Brougham, and there was an English Quarter in the same town. There were English churches at Menton and Cannes and Nice and Grasse. And there were those English villas—neo-Gothic, Jacobethan, Palladian, and baroque, Italianate and Moorish. But always and unmistakably English.

There must be dozens of substantial villas and country houses that were built by and for the British on the Continent and farther afield around the turn of the century. Harold Peto and Thomas Smith weren't the only British country house architects to try their hand. In 1871 the *Architect* published a design "for a mansion to be erected near Warsaw." The architects, Albert Hartshorne and George Somers Clarke Jr., set out to produce "an 'English Mansion,'" and the result was in the grand Jacobethan style—although with double-glazed windows throughout, a nod to Polish winters. In 1881 Edwin T. Hall, best known for designing Liberty's on Regent Street, published plans and an elevation for what the *Building News* described as a "Chateau in the Aegean." Anything less chateau-like, or less suited to the Aegean, would be hard to imagine. Like Hartshorne and Clarke's "English Mansion," Hall's chateau made no concessions to its surroundings. It was basically an old-fashioned piece of very English midcentury Gothic Revival, long and low, with turrets and battlements.[14]

The designer M. H. Baillie Scott was rather more innovative with his forays into Europe. He was well known in northern Europe around the turn of the century through the magazine the *Studio*, which was widely read in Germany and Austria and which regularly featured his work in Britain, and in 1904 architect Hermann Muthesius's *Das englische Haus* singled him out for praise as a poet among architects, one who had discovered an entirely personal form of expression. For Muthesius, Blackwell (1898–1900), the house Baillie Scott designed on Windermere, was "one of the most attractive creations that the new movement in house-building has produced."[15] The architect's reputation in Europe was further enhanced in 1901 when his competition design for a "House for an Art Lover" was awarded first prize by a jury of German architects.

But even before this, he had designed some remarkable Arts-and-Crafts-meets-Art-Nouveau-meets-Secession interiors for Ernest Louis, Grand Duke of Hesse (and grandson of Queen Victoria), who brought him to Darmstadt in 1899 to work at the Neues Palais. Ivory-white panelling and orange walls, electric light fittings (by C. R. Ashbee) in

grey pewter, and furniture in tones of green and blue. "This arrangement of white, orange, grey, green, and blue is supplemented by
touches of brilliant pink in the flowers," recalled the architect. A commission to design a music room and boudoir in Mannheim in 1900
followed: the panelling was again white, "and on the white ground of
frieze and ceiling are set trees and wreaths of mountain ash and rose
modelled in plaster, and painted their proper colours with flights of
silver birds."[16] The destruction of both the Darmstadt and the Mannheim interiors is greatly to be regretted, as is the loss of another of
Baillie Scott's European works: the interiors of Le Nid, commissioned
in about 1897 by Crown Princess Marie of Romania for her family's
summer estate in Sinaia. This was a grand and bizarre tree house, a log
cabin perched twenty-five feet high on eight stilts which were living
trees, and reached via a staircase in a wooden tower and a drawbridge.
Baillie Scott's own description gives a flavour of this so-called Nest of
the Princess:

> The apartment represents the room of the sun and sunflower,
> and in all its various decorations the same symbol is presented.
> The tiles, the seats and the windows all represent different
> treatments of this sunflower motif, while the ceiling rep-
> resents an attempt to convey in conventional terms something
> of the effect of glimpses of sky and sun seen through the upper
> branches of trees. In contrast to this golden room is the cool
> recessed *ercker* [a bay window], of which the lily is the symbol
> flower. Its floor is set with a mosaic of water lilies disposed
> in lines which converge to the shrine on which a dim light
> burns. Towards this shrine, too, the lilies of the frieze bend
> their heads, and the pictured Madonna is framed by branches
> intricately interwoven. On the opposite side of this little ora-
> tory is the organ enclosed by doors, the inner sides of which
> are bright with flights of angels painted on a gilded ground.[17]

"I arranged it with love," recalled Princess Marie, "and I spent many happy hours there between the earth and the sky."[18] But eventually she tired of it, and it fell down in a storm one night.

Baillie Scott designed houses in Canada, Switzerland, Belgium, Poland. The "House and Garden in Poland" he included in his 1906 *Houses and Gardens* was an accomplished piece of faux-medieval Arts and Crafts, a substantial country house with a timber-framed double-height great hall, a "studio" open to the rafters, and formal gardens with flower borders, a terrace, and a pergola. Like Hartshorne and Clarke, he acknowledged the fierce Polish winters and specified double glazing, extra-thick walls, plenty of open fires, and a complete system of water heating.

In 1912 he was approached by a Count Chludzinski to design a country house at Laskowice in Poland.* The count had three requirements for his new mansion: it should be protected against the weather; its interiors should express "something of the romance and free hospitality of country life in Poland"; and it must be "defensible against bands of robbers."[19] Baillie Scott's first design, published in the *Studio* in 1912, showed him at his best: a Byzantine building, all arches and white walls, crowned with a huge glass dome lighting a central courtyard and four winged victories. It looked to be much more at home in Vienna than in Laskowice. Clearly the count thought so, since the final design, again published in the *Studio*, showed a rather ordinary timber-framed courtyard house which wouldn't have looked out of place in Surrey or Sussex: no arches, no glass dome, no white stucco walls or winged victories. The timbers for its construction were all felled locally by the count's estate workers, in the best Arts and Crafts tradition. Someone warned Baillie Scott that he would have a problem extracting his fees from

---

* The late eighteenth-century neoclassical Chludzinski Palace in Laskowice was destroyed sometime before 1914. Was Baillie Scott being asked to design a replacement?

Count Chludzinski, and they were right. His client walked off with the plans and the architect didn't see the count or his money again.

Architectural commissions that crossed international frontiers often encountered local resistance, although wealthy Britons who built country houses abroad could often overcome them with liberal doses of philanthropy. Thomas Hanbury at La Mortola built two local schools and paid for their teachers; he was a generous benefactor to the local hospital; he gave plants to many towns along the Riviera; and in 1883 he installed a marble fountain in Menton, still called the Fontaine Hanbury, for the use of local people. The Italian government showered him with honours, and when he died at La Mortola in 1907, seven thousand mourners followed his coffin.

In 1895 Sir Ernest Cassel's doctor packed him off to the Swiss Alps for his health; he stayed at a hotel in the Valais, seven thousand feet up on the edge of the Aletsch Glacier, and he was so taken with the spot that some years later he bought a site a few hundred yards from his hotel and built himself the Villa Cassel, a tall, timber-framed, and turreted fairy tale of a house in a style which borrowed a little, but not much, from the Swiss. It was finished the following year. He was generous with his money, something that helped him to gain acceptance in the neighbourhood. Legend has it that when Winston Churchill was staying at Villa Cassel in 1904, he was driven mad by the clanging of cow bells as farmers drove their cattle past the villa. Cassel arranged for the bells to be stuffed with hay for the duration of Churchill's visit—for a suitable fee.

One of the more intriguing country house builders in mainland Europe was the Hon. Mary Isabel Portman, youngest child of the 2nd Viscount Portman. Raised at Knighton House in Dorset and then at Bryanston, the magnificent and enormous Dorset country house built by Richard Norman Shaw in 1890 for her father, Mary studied the violin in London under the German virtuoso August Wilhelmj before moving to Germany in 1906 or 1907 to continue her studies either privately or at one of the two Berlin conservatories, the Stern'sches or the Klindworth-Scharwenka. In 1900 she had been briefly engaged to a Captain Pelham, but she broke it off because, according to a contemporary, "she would not like to be always moving about wherever her husband was ordered."[20] That may not have been the whole truth: while in Berlin she met Amy Hare, a Somerset-born pianist who taught at the Klindworth-Scharwenka, and the couple moved in together, performing in various charity concerts and generally playing an active role in Berlin's cultural life.

In 1913, during a visit to the Bavarian Alps, they suddenly decided it would be nice to have a country house of their own, an artists' retreat complete with a fully fitted concert hall. Mary bought a piece of land at Kranzbach, south of Munich and near the Austrian border, and went to the great Arts and Crafts designer Detmar Blow and his rather less well-known partner, the Frenchman Fernand Billerey, for a design. They came up with a building that fitted perfectly into the Arts and Crafts tradition, with a dash of Scottish vernacular thrown in for good measure. Crow-stepped gables dominated both the main block, which contained a central hall flanked by dining room, billiard room, and two reception rooms, and two pavilions which were connected to the house by curving quadrant corridors. One of the pavilions contained the kitchens and servants' hall; the other was a single space—the concert hall, where Mary and Amy could perform with musical houseguests who came down from Berlin and Leipzig.

Work began on Schloss Kranzbach—"the English castle," the local people called it—almost immediately. It was still continuing when war broke out, and as enemy aliens, Mary and Amy had to leave Germany. And now Mary found herself in an awkward position. The castle was almost completed, and the builders were understandably keen to be paid before she decamped. In fact, they took out a warrant for her arrest for nonpayment of their rather large bills. And yet her cash was all in England, and wartime restrictions made it impossible for her to transfer money from England to Germany.

In the end two American diplomats came to her rescue. America was still neutral at this stage, and the US consul general at Munich, Thomas St John Gaffney, personally put up a bond of $40,000 as security for Mary's remaining in Munich. She was eventually allowed to go to Berlin on the understanding that the bond was transferred to the American ambassador to Germany, James Gerard, and after Gerard agreed to pay her workmen and she had signed a paper agreeing to send him stocks to cover the amount, she was allowed to go home at the end of 1914.

The weeks went by, and Gerard heard nothing from Mary. Gaffney went to London and had an interview with her in which she said the government wouldn't allow her father to send any money or securities out of the country. Gerard would have to wait until after the war for his $40,000. Gaffney reported back to Gerard, who cursed Mary "in language both picturesque and profane," the consul general wrote later. "I never learned how His Excellency was finally able to secure the return of the money from his titled friends."[21] Mary Portman never did live at Kranzbach; as far as we know, she and Amy Hare never saw it finished.

In the middle of the afternoon of Monday, March 27, 1876, a little convoy of carriages left Windsor Castle. They contained Queen Victoria and her youngest daughter, the Princess Beatrice; her friend and lady-in-waiting Janie, Marchioness of Ely; her lady of the bedchamber, Jane Churchill; her private secretary, Henry Ponsonby; her physician, Sir William Jenner; and her equerry, Henry Byng. Forty-eight hours later, as the queen noted in her journal, "we four ladies drove up in the waggonette, with the Grand Duke's old coachman, to my beloved Feodore's dear little house on the Friesenberg, which I call Villa Hohenlohe, and which now belongs to me."[22] And with that, the fifty-six-year-old Queen Victoria took possession of a rambling three-storey country house on the outskirts of Baden-Baden in southwest Germany.

The Villa Hohenlohe had been bought thirteen years before by Victoria's half sister Princess Feodora of Leiningen, with some financial help from the queen, after Feodora decided that her residence in Baden-Baden was too low-lying and that she would like a place with a garden and a view. The queen had visited her in her "charming little villa in the chalet style" when she had stayed at Baden-Baden in the spring of 1872, sampling the waters and seeing the sights like the town's famous spa resort and casino, the Kurhaus, which was opened specially for her one morning, its architectural delights overshadowed by the thought that it was "the scene of that dreadful gambling, which in the season, collects all the worst characters of both sexes in Europe" (including her own eldest son, she might have added).[23] Princess Feodora died later that year, and Victoria took over her villa.

The queen stayed at the Villa Hohenlohe for twelve days in late March and early April, with Beatrice, Janie Ely, and an assortment of domestic servants. Ponsonby, Jenner, and Byng lodged in a hotel in the town along with Jane Churchill, who had a dreadful cold. The queen could be demanding, so perhaps it came as a relief to them all to find that there wasn't room for them at the villa, where the queen had to make do with a drawing room, a dining room, a suite of four "very small" sitting rooms and a bedroom, "the same in which dear Feodora died."[24] She had a large writing table moved into the drawing room, where she attended to matters of state and kept up with the political news from home in the mornings, and in the afternoons she read on the sofa, sketched from her balcony, or drove out for excursions in the mountains. After dinner, Beatrice would play the piano.

Queen Victoria returned to her villa in the hills in 1880. That April she left "with regret the dear, pretty little Villa, where I can always be quiet, & all is so snug & nice."[25] It was her last visit.

TWELVE

GOD IS IN
THE HOUSE

C HRISTIAN WORSHIP, AND more specifically *Anglican* worship, was
an integral part of life in turn-of-the-century country houses.
Even those who were not particularly pious attended church on Sundays, if only to set a good example to the rest of the community; and
they certainly made sure that their servants did the same. Houseguests
were expected to be there, too, the women being driven and the men
walking across the park in the rain, clutching their prayer books and
their half-crowns for the offertory. The head of the household read the
lesson before settling back into the family pew, where his wife tried
vainly to stop him snoring during the sermon. The air would be heavy
with incense if the vicar and his patron were that way inclined. Otherwise, it was full of the smell of leather, wet Burberry, and hair oil.
Daisy Warwick recalled how, when she was a child, at the close of the
blessing she and her family filed out first, watched by their humbler
neighbours; then the estate steward and his family; then the farmers;

and last of all the cottagers. "One old lady even made a habit of getting up and curtseying as we passed down the aisle."[1]

In rural England, community, hierarchy, and religion remained bound together well into the twentieth century. (The situation was less clear-cut in Scotland and Wales, where dissenting Protestantism was stronger, and in Ireland, where the majority of the population was Catholic.) Yes, the cracks were starting to show: as a left-leaning adult, Daisy Warwick cured the congregation of their deferential habits by deliberately remaining kneeling, head in hands, until the cottagers grew tired of waiting and left. And as she grew older, she hardly went to church at all. But for most country house owners, a religious faith was part of the fabric of rural society, even if it was an unexamined faith.

Margot Asquith, who was born in 1864, wrote in later life that she never remembered her mother talking to her or her siblings about the Bible or hearing them at their prayers. "Nevertheless," she went on, "we were all deeply religious." She and her sister Laura said their prayers out loud to each other every night, and the whole family trooped off to Traquair Kirk every Sunday and sat in the family pew up in the gallery, watching the shepherds with their dogs take their places in the box pews below. Margot noticed how their father, the industrialist Sir Charles Tennant, kept his eyes tightly closed during the long sermons, leaning his head on his hand: no doubt he was listening intently. That brings to mind Lady Dorothy Nevill's account of attending services earlier in the century in the little church at Puddletown in Dorset, where her family had a country house and where, every Sunday, a motley village orchestra consisting of an old man with a trombone and another with a cracked fiddle accompanied children who sang hymns out of tune. "It seemed to me," she wrote years later, "that whenever Sunday came around, [my father] contrived to arrange an ache in some part of his body" which prevented him from attending divine service.[2]

Sundays could be quite intense. Sabbatarian organisations like the Lord's Day Observance Society, founded in 1831, were still something of a force, even if their targets were small traders and working people in towns rather than the landed elite, and restrictions on recreation and entertainment on Sundays were an accepted fact of life in many country houses. Staying at Whittingehame, the Balfour family seat, in 1871, Mary Gladstone found that a visit to the local church on Sunday morning ("the singing bad, very, but painstaking") was followed that evening after dinner by prayers in the house. There was a reading from Isaiah, and everyone sang hymns, starting with "Abide with Me."[3] At ten o'clock Mary and one of the Balfour brothers rounded things off by playing the entire *Messiah* right through as a duet.

The timing and format of morning prayers varied from country house to country house, depending on the piety of the owner, his or her High Church or Low Church proclivities and, perhaps, the patience of the listeners. A chapter from the Bible, a collective recital of the Lord's Prayer, and a closing prayer of grace were the bare minimum for morning prayers. Sometimes a hymn was sung, sometimes not. Although a conventional Anglicanism was the norm in the majority of elite households, the nuances were endless.

Ellen Twisleton, a bright young Bostonian who was newly married to the brother of Lord Saye and Sele of Broughton Castle, saw hypocrisy in the whole business. Introduced to an aristocratic parson who had just married into her husband's family (thereby securing a living and a pleasant parsonage that were Lord Saye and Sele's to give away), she noted, "He is a regular tory . . . and what sympathy can they have with their poor parishioners?" Every morning at 9:45 and every evening at 10:30 Mr Cholmondeley, the clergyman in question, officiated at family prayers with such a smug and self-satisfied air that it was as if he said, "Thou seest, O Lord, what well-dressed and well-connected people we are."[4]

Ellen was writing in the 1850s. Twenty years later, family prayers at John Hurleston Leche's Carden Park in Cheshire took place every day in the Great Hall, a big room about seventy feet long with staircases leading to the upper floors in the wings at each end. Each morning the menservants carried benches in from the servants' hall and the entire household assembled: Leche, his wife Eleanor, her five children and stepchildren, and her two sisters-in-law. They sat in chairs arranged anyhow around the room; so did the cook, the housekeeper, the lady's maid, and the governess. Mr Loges, the portly butler, bagged an armchair. The other seven servants ranged themselves on the benches and settled themselves as the head of the household led the prayers.

Leche was prone to outbursts of temper, and morning prayers at Carden could be quite eventful. On one occasion the household's devotions were interrupted by the arrival at the door of a travelling band of Italian musicians. Leche got up from his knees, using "very different language to that which he had been using just a few seconds before," and set the dogs on them. Another time Carden's chimneys were being attended to by a sweep and his climbing boy; the servants were told to lock all the doors leading into the hall before the service so that prayers wouldn't be interrupted by their comings and goings. Eight doors were duly locked (it was a big hall), but a ninth, through which the family arrived to begin the act of worship, was not, and so of course halfway through the proceedings the door handle turned and a small soot-covered youth in a cap stuck his head round the door, causing Leche's daughters to burst out laughing and Leche himself to scream at the boy to get out, once more using decidedly un-Christian language. Then, recalling himself, he said grace and dismissed the household, before venting his spleen on Loges, the butler.[5]

Interruptions like this were rare but memorable. One morning at Marchmont House in Berwickshire, Sir Hugh Hume-Campbell was leading the prayers. As he began the Lord's Prayer, his pet cat, of whom he was inordinately fond, sank her claws into his leg. Without moving a muscle, he did his best to continue. "Our Father—get away, cat!—which art in Heaven—go away, puss!—hallowed be Thy name—John, take the cat away!" and so on, until the prayer was finished. His wife had to stuff her handkerchief into her mouth to stop herself from laughing.[6]

Evening prayers were going out of fashion, although the practice was kept up in the more devout households, both High and Low. The novelist Charlotte M. Yonge recalled staying with the Anglo-Catholic Gibbs family at Tyntesfield in the 1870s, where William Gibbs, already an invalid, would preside in his wheelchair, wishing everyone good night when the prayers were over. "That beautiful house was like a church in spirit," she wrote.[7]

Periodic intrusions by wandering minstrels, soot-covered climbing boys, and importunate cats may not have been everyday occurrences. But they did highlight the drawbacks of using a quasi-public secular space like a great hall for regular acts of worship. At the Argory, an early nineteenth-century gentry house in County Armagh, the Mac-Geough Bond family held household prayers on an upstairs landing, where a lovely cabinet barrel organ by James Bishop of London could accompany their hymn singing without the need for an organist. Some country houses had parish churches so close at hand that they functioned as virtual household chapels: the church of All Saints at Sudbury in Derbyshire was separated by a door in the garden wall from the Vernon family at Sudbury Hall, earlier Vernons having had the foresight to keep the church close when they demolished the inconveniently situated village and moved it out of view. The same was true of another All Saints in Derbyshire: when the Curzon family swept away the local village in the eighteenth century in the course of rebuilding Kedleston Hall, they kept the church so that the household had a walk of no more than a few yards to attend divine service (even if the villagers had to trudge several miles).

Many of the grander and older country houses already had chapels dating back centuries, and they continued to be used for household prayers as well as other, more memorable events. When they visited Chatsworth in 1907, Edward VII and Queen Alexandra attended divine service in the Devonshires' magnificent baroque chapel, with its colossal alabaster reredos, its altarpiece by Antonio Verrio, and its walls painted with murals by Louis Laguerre. The service was conducted by Rev. Joseph Hall, the vicar of Edensor, who also served as the Duke of Devonshire's private chaplain. The choir came from Edensor church, and Albert Wragg, the local schoolmaster, played the organ. There was no sermon. The royal couple perhaps gave thanks for that. After lunch, the king and queen, the duke and duchess, and several of their other houseguests went out for a Sunday afternoon drive in the country—a decidedly un-Sabbatarian thing to do.

Twenty-five years earlier, in May 1882, the chapel at Chatsworth served a more sombre purpose. After the 7th duke's son Lord Frederick Cavendish, the new chief secretary for Ireland, and his under-secretary, Thomas Burke, were stabbed to death by Irish nationalists in Phoenix Park in Dublin, Lord Frederick's body was brought home to Chatsworth to lie in state in the chapel in an open coffin, "under the guardianship of the old housekeeper who nursed Lord Frederick as a child," noted the *Illustrated London News* in a special supplement devoted to the obsequies.[8] On the morning of the funeral, a special service was held in the chapel for members of the family and servants before the funeral procession left the house for Edensor churchyard, which lay half a mile away across the park. Fifty thousand people had come from all over the country to watch the cortege pass. The lanes were lined with the Chatsworth tenantry, and there were deputations from the Devonshires' other estates—Bolton Abbey, Hardwick Hall, Lismore Castle, and Holker Hall. Some three hundred ministers and members of Parliament arrived by special train, led by the prime minister, William Gladstone. Children from Edensor, wearing white armbands, sang the hymn "Brief Life Is Here Our Portion" as the coffin was lowered into the ground, and Lord Frederick's widow dropped onto it a wreath of roses sent that morning by the queen. The event was both medieval in its feudal loyalties and quintessentially Victorian in its grandiloquent celebration of death.

The ready availability of a household chapel—and a tendency to adhere to tradition—ensured that some country house chapels remained in use for both funerals and lyings-in-state throughout the late nineteenth and early twentieth centuries. While Lord Frederick Cavendish was interred in the graveyard at Edensor, the 7th and 8th Dukes of Marlborough were laid to rest in the chapel at Blenheim Palace in 1883 and 1892, with the rector of Woodstock officiating. This practice was more frequent at a long-lineaged level than it was among less-settled country house owners, but that isn't so surprising: burying members of one's family in the household chapel required an expectation of continuity, of permanence. It would be rather awkward if the ancestors had to be sold along with the ancestral seat, a thought which may help to account for the fact the practice all but died out after the Great War, when the country house entered a much more uncertain period.

The situation was rather more flexible when it came to christenings and weddings, neither of which was likely to leave bones behind, and there were few established country house chapels which didn't see one or the other or both, even if they were no longer used for daily family prayers. In December 1889, for example, the chapel at Castle Howard in Yorkshire was the venue for the marriage of Lady Mary Howard and Gilbert Murray, the professor of Greek at Glasgow University. Benjamin Jowett, the famous Greek scholar and master of Balliol, officiated, and Lady Mary's six bridesmaids were followed by a column of eighty girls chosen from the five villages on the Castle

Howard estate. The bride's father, the 9th Earl of Carlisle, who had only come into his inheritance earlier in the year upon the death of his great-uncle, hosted a wedding breakfast in the house before the newlyweds set off to honeymoon at Naworth Castle in Cumberland, another of the Carlisle estates.

The Castle Howard chapel was unusual for two reasons. For one, it dated only from the 1870s, and new country house chapels were something of a rarity in late Victorian and Edwardian Britain. Architectural historian Jill Franklin, in her survey of 380 country houses built between 1835 and 1914, noted that only twenty-one had new-built chapels, and seven of those were put up by Roman Catholics, who stood in greater need of dedicated places of worship than Anglicans, who could pop into the parish church when the mood or the need to keep up appearances took them. At Woodchester, Catholic convert William Leigh made sure that the chapel, the grandest part of the mansion and reputed to be the tallest in any country house, was finished first, as an homage to his new religion—although not, as local rumour still has it, as a sanctuary for Pius IX at a time when the Vatican was threatened by nationalists pressing for Italian unification.

Of the handful of new country house chapels built between 1870 and 1914, only three have a claim to greatness. The first and grandest is the private chapel at Eaton Hall in Cheshire, part of Alfred Waterhouse's creation of what Nikolaus Pevsner called a "Wagnerian palace . . . the most ambitious instance of Gothic Revival domestic architecture anywhere in the country." Built at a cost of some £600,000 for the 3rd Marquess of Westminster, who became the 1st duke in 1874, most of Waterhouse's Wagnerian palace lasted less than a century before being demolished; but the chapel survives, huge and yet dwarfed by its impossibly high freestanding clock tower. The artist Frederic Shields, who was commissioned to design mosaics and stained glass for the chapel based on the Te Deum, approached his task with a missionary zeal. "My soul kindled and flamed with the subject," he recalled. He wanted his work to "keep the heart hot, and the mind quick."⁹

Eaton Hall's chapel became a prominent private venue for concerts, services, and family weddings, and a centre for estate activities. There was an annual choral festival held in the chapel with choirs drawn from local villages and parishes. In 1890, at the sixth such festival, the centrepiece was a performance of Haydn's *Creation*, leading the local press to comment that "the advance in the competency of the choirs since His Grace first established these reunions six years ago is most marked."¹⁰ Each Christmas there was a children's carol service in the chapel in front of the duke and his family, their houseguests, and their servants, with young members of singing classes from the villages on the Westminster estate. The duke opened the hall and its superb chapel to the public at a charge of a shilling a head, with the proceeds going to local charities. When he died in 1899, a coffin containing his ashes stood in the chapel while his private chaplain conducted the funeral service.

The second notable new country house chapel was Arthur Blomfield's addition to Tyntesfield in Somerset. The architect of the house itself was John Norton, a capable local man whose West Country houses tended towards a chunky Tudor Gothic, all turrets and mild asymmetry. Tyntesfield was completed in about 1864 (the date on the drainpipe hoppers), but Norton's clients, William and Blanche Gibbs, both enthusiastic Anglo-Catholics, were not content with the oratory which was provided in the original scheme for daily prayers, even though it was equipped with an organ, a lectern, and oak stalls for fifty worshippers. They wanted a separate, dedicated, sacred space for the kind of ritualised worship that they favoured. Gibbs was fabulously rich, with a vast income derived from the family business shipping guano from South America for use as agricultural fertiliser. He and Blanche poured their fortune into a host of high-minded High

Church causes—everything from a home for incurables and the Western Counties Idiot Asylum in Devon to William Butterfield's magnificent polychromatic chapel at Keble College, Oxford (which Gibbs paid for in its entirety)—including huge contributions to the restoration or rebuilding of at least nineteen churches along the way. In 1873 Gibbs, now in his eighties and already employing a resident chaplain, decided that Tyntesfield needed a more imposing chapel. Instead of going back to John Norton, he commissioned a design from Arthur Blomfield, a Gothicist with a string of churches to his name and a father who had been Bishop of London and a stalwart of High Church Anglicanism.

Blomfield's chapel was tall, Gothic, and undeniably spectacular. Inspired by the medieval Sainte-Chapelle in Paris, it was filled with banks of stained glass by Powell of Whitefriars, and Powell was also responsible for the spectacular pavement, a mosaic composed of marble, Mexican onyx, and a vitreous material made by the firm "in which colours can be obtained, which are not found in any marbles," remarked the *Building News* approvingly.[11] William Gibbs died in 1875, shortly before it was finished.

The third great chapel belongs to a later generation. It is at Madresfield Court in Worcestershire, and it is one of Britain's great Arts and Crafts interiors, and a space immortalised by Evelyn Waugh's artist-narrator, Charles Ryder, in *Brideshead Revisited*:

Angels in printed cotton smocks, rambler-roses, flower-spangled meadows, frisking lambs, texts in Celtic script, saints in armour, covered the walls in an intricate pattern of clear, bright colours. There was a triptych of pale oak, carved so as to give it the peculiar property of seeming to have been moulded in Plasticine. The sanctuary lamp and all the metal furniture were of bronze, hand-beaten to the patina of a pock-marked skin; the altar steps had a carpet of grass-green, strewn with white and gold daisies.

"Golly," I said.[12]

Golly, indeed. Madresfield's chapel was built in 1867 as part of Philip Charles Hardwick's remodelling of the house for the 5th and 6th Earls Beauchamp. But it was decorated between 1902 and 1923, chiefly by Henry Payne and a team of artists from the Birmingham School of Art, as a wedding gift from the 2nd Duke of Westminster's sister, Lettice Grosvenor, to her husband, the 7th Earl. The decoration, a riotous union of arts and crafts in the best Morrisite tradition, took so long that Lettice was able to include their seven children in the design. They appear as angels and saints and knights in armour, drifting through an Arthurian romance or kneeling to adore the figure of Christ in Majesty as he floats serenely above the elaborate triptych which dominates the altar, the work of Charles March Gere. If Madresfield is one of the last country house chapels, it is also one of the best. A masterpiece, and the first act in a family tragedy which played out soon after it was completed, when Earl Beauchamp was outed as a homosexual, deserted by his wife, and forced to flee to the Continent to escape prosecution.

An expression of ducal grandeur, a statement of piety, an act of love: the country house chapel, rarity that it was by the end of the nineteenth century, could be all or any of these things. The chapel at Castle Howard was, arguably, an opportunity to display an advanced artistic taste as much as an example of religious fervour. Like the chapel at Madresfield, it was part of the house rather than a freestanding structure like Waterhouse's at Eaton Hall. It began life in the eighteenth century as a dining room, in fact, but by the late 1860s it had been converted into a chapel. In 1864 the 7th Earl of Carlisle died unmarried, and the Howard estates were inherited by his brother William, who was then living in a lunatic asylum in Sussex. Trustees were put in charge and another brother, Edward, moved into Castle Howard with his wife Diana. One of the improvements they made to the place was to completely remodel the chapel. They blocked up the lower parts of the windows to give the room a more ecclesiastical feel: "A great pity," said Rosalind Howard, who was married to Edward's nephew George, the heir to the Howard estates. "The view of the lake is a great reprieve during [a] tiresome sermon."[13] And, perhaps guided by George and Rosalind, who were having a house built for them in Kensington by the Arts and Crafts genius Philip Webb, with decoration by Morris and Company, Edward and Diana introduced stained glass by Edward Burne-Jones (with window frames designed by Webb) and frescoes by Charles Eamer Kempe. The work was completed by 1875, and for the next decade or so the Castle Howard chapel was used by the Howards, their household, and the local tenantry for Sunday services.

In 1889, though, George Howard's lunatic uncle died, and he inherited the Howard estates as the 9th Earl of Carlisle. A fierce advocate of temperance, one of his first acts was to empty the Castle Howard wine cellars and close down public houses on the estate. And one of the next was to close the family chapel, on the grounds that it was a private chapel and he was a Unitarian. "I consider that it is not necessary for me to maintain in my house the service of a Church to which I do not belong." And that was that, although the new earl came in for some sharp criticism, both on the grounds that he was happy to keep hold of various Anglican livings in his keeping, appointing ministers to those livings as he saw fit, and because the chapel at Castle Howard was a community resource. It belonged to him by law, but he had an obligation to maintain it for the benefit of his nondissenting tenantry.

"Lord Carlisle has acted within his rights," stormed *John Bull*. "But the closing of this beautiful chapel is none the less deplorable."[14]

The Church of England, and the rural church in England, were both marching as to war in the later nineteenth century. Historian Owen Chadwick, in his classic history of Victorian worship, *The Victorian Church* (1965–1970), described the scene in an ideal village church around 1860. The squire sat in his pew, well-to-do farmers sat in theirs, and on benches behind them sat "the labourers in smock frocks, delicately embroidered at front and back, their wives often in scarlet flannel shawls." Everyone was there, content in his or her place, because that was the way of things.[15]

By the beginning of the next century this idyllic scheme of things was becoming increasingly rare (if, indeed, the realities of rural life had ever quite matched up to the dream). And competition from dissenting churches, such as was seen at Castle Howard, was as nothing compared to the battles between High and Low factions within the Church of England. The Tractarian movement begun at Oxford in the 1830s by John Henry Newman, Edward Pusey, John Keble, and others, which sought among other things to restore elements of pre-Reformation liturgy, seemed to evangelicals and middle-of-the-road Anglicans alike to be steering dangerously close to Roman Catholicism, and when Newman left the Church of England and converted to Catholicism in 1845 their worst fears were confirmed. Some of the clergy followed Newman to Rome, but many more chose to remain in the Church of England while advocating the introduction of ritualistic elements into divine service. These elements varied from priest to priest, but the so-called Six Points were seen as clear indicators of a tendency towards Anglo-Catholicism. These were as follows: (1) the wearing of vestments; (2) the priest's habit of facing east at the altar, with his back to the congregation; (3) the use of wafer bread for the Eucharist; (4) the mixing of water with the Eucharistic wine; (5) the practice of having lighted candles on the altar; and (6) the use of incense during the service.

Resistance to these practices tapped into a long and not particularly nice strain of anti-Catholicism in British culture, and there were periodic attempts to clamp down on them. In 1874 the Archbishop of Canterbury himself introduced a private member's bill into Parliament to curb ritualism; it received the support of the government and passed into law, allowing disgruntled parishioners to petition their bishop if they thought their priest was introducing ornaments or decoration into the church, or wearing vestments, or deviating in the slightest from the directions set down in the Book of Common Prayer. It had little effect, since High Church clergy simply ignored it and bishops were loath to bring them to trial. There were a handful of prosecutions, but they represented a drop in the ritualistic ocean: by the beginning of the twentieth century nearly four hundred churches were regularly using incense.

The antiritualism movement underwent a resurgence at the end of the nineteenth century. A young David Lloyd George remarked that "ritualists were trying to substitute the Protestant doctrine of justification by faith with a system of salvation by haberdashery." Pamphlet wars were followed by militant action. Prominent among the militants was an East End bookseller, John Kensit, described by a future Bishop of Durham as "an obscure London fanatic," who founded the Protestant Truth Society and organised meetings and rallies up and down the country, interrupting church services and protesting loudly against ritualism in all its forms. Kensit's campaigning came to an abrupt and fatal end in 1902 when an Irishman in Liverpool took exception to his anti-Catholic stance and hit him over the head with an iron bar. But there were others to take up arms against ritualism: the Ladies' League for the Defence of the Reformed Faith of the Church of England; the

National Protestant Church Union; the Protestant Alliance. (The alliance, founded in 1845 as a coming-together of a group of smaller Protestant societies, is still going strong today, "firmly standing for the Reformed Faith; fervently preaching the Gospel; fostering knowledge of our Protestant history.")[16]

All of which is by way of providing some context for the unholy row that broke out in the autumn of 1889, when the twenty-five-year-old Henry Pelham Archibald Douglas Pelham-Clinton, 7th Duke of Newcastle, asked the Bishop of Southwell to dedicate the private chapel that the architect G. F. Bodley had built for him in the grounds of his ancestral seat, Clumber Park in Nottinghamshire. It was a masterly essay in High Gothic, 107 feet long, with stone vaulting and gilded bosses, a rood screen and rood, a marble high altar, stained glass by Charles Eamer Kempe, and seating in the nave for 270. The cost was widely reported to have been £40,000, perhaps somewhere around £5 million in today's money.

The young duke had decidedly Anglo-Catholic tendencies: earlier that year he had married Kathleen Candy, a breeder of fox terriers with similar tastes in worship, at All Saints, Margaret Street, "with all the pomp and circumstance which the Anglican ritual renders possible." And it was expected that the first service in his new estate chapel of St Mary the Virgin was going to be as imposing as "the whole paraphernalia of Ritualism can make it."[17]

The duke hosted quite a house party for the service, which took place on Tuesday, October 22, 1889. Guests included Edward King, the Bishop of Lincoln and a leading Anglo-Catholic, who had narrowly escaped prosecution under the Public Worship Regulation Act the previous year. Viscount Halifax, another prominent High Church man and the president of an Anglo-Catholic pressure group, the English Church Union, was there with his viscountess and upwards of thirty clergy, "most of the well-known High Church persuasion," according to the *Manchester Guardian*.[18] It was quite a spectacle for a ceremony in a country house chapel. The service, led by the Bishop of Southwell, George Ridding, was fully choral, with the duke's own twenty-eight-strong choir, supported by eight choristers from Lincoln Cathedral, and a sixteen-piece orchestra from St Agnes, Kennington Park, another bastion of Anglo-Catholicism. Clergy and choir processed around the chapel with a processional cross and banners; Ridding wore robes of scarlet and white, and Bishop King wore a cope of cloth of gold.

"It was generally acknowledged," said the *Guardian*, "to be the most magnificent display of extreme Anglicanism yet seen in the diocese." There was incense and wax candles on the altar; the Epistle and Gospel were sung; and at the close of the Communion the celebrant actually bowed to the cross. Bishop Ridding preached on Revelation 21, "And I heard a great voice out of heaven saying, Behold the tabernacle of God is with men."[19]

There was indeed a great voice. But it didn't come from heaven.

The Archdeacon of Lincoln wrote to the *Times* to protest the part played by his bishop and the Bishop of Southwell, and to say that the Lincoln choristers had been present at the service without his knowledge or permission. Questions were asked in the evangelical press about the bishops' presence at a service where every one of the notorious Six Points was observed. Much was made by the antiritualists of the fact that the duke had chosen to have the chapel dedicated but not consecrated, since consecration would have given the Church of England a say in the forms of worship that were in use at Clumber. Dukes still commanded deference, however, and most of the barrage of criticism was directed at Ridding and King for lending their support to such a blatantly popish plot. The Protestant Alliance complained to the Archbishop of Canterbury that the chapel was decked out with Romish devices: a crucifix over the rood screen, images of the Virgin and St John, a tabernacle for the reserved sacrament with a silver lamp burning in front of it, "and other Popish emblems." There was incense and there were banners, one of which was inscribed with the words "S. Maria Mater Dei." It was all too much. "The use of the idolatrous rites and ceremonies of the Church of Rome tends to alienate the affections of the people from the Church of England." If the archbishop didn't act swiftly to prevent the use of "such superstitious services and illegal practices," disestablishment was bound to follow.[20]

The row dragged on for several months, with various antiritualist groups denouncing Clumber and all its works as "outrages" and the Archbishop of Canterbury, Edward White Benson, politely fobbing off the strident protests of the Protestant Alliance. The Bishop of Southwell claimed, slightly disingenuously, that as a private chapel, Clumber was not under his control, and he flatly denied that there was anything Romish about the service. The duke, as dukes were wont to do, simply ignored the complaints. When he died in 1928, a solemn requiem mass was celebrated in his chapel, followed by a service of absolution for the dead. This time, there were no complaints.

THIRTEEN

MAGICIANS

Labour-saving devices come in all shapes and sizes. At Marchmont in Berwickshire, a large country house with large fireplaces, Sir Hugh Hume-Campbell designed a wheelbarrow with a solid rubber tyre and his family crest painted on the side, specifically for carrying logs around the house. "It was just the thing for the purpose and was more or less a sensation for staying guests," remembered one of Sir Hugh's servants.[1]

At the other end of the scale stood Thomas Thorneycroft, whose seat, Tettenhall Towers, was a sprawling, vaguely Italianate mansion near Wolverhampton. Thorneycroft, a retired ironmaster, brimmed over with bright ideas for new technology. In 1866 he proposed to form a Fresh Air Company, which would pipe healthy air from Brighton, say, to London, in the same way that water was piped long distances: houses would be fitted with fresh air meters and would pay for what they used. To his surprise, no one took him up on his plan, and he turned his attentions to improving life for his family and their eight domestic servants.* A gas flame burned at night on one of the towers which gave Tettenhall its name; it lit up the drive as visitors approached the front door, but its primary purpose was to burn sewer gases, which were piped up to the tower by an elaborate system of Archimedean screws. Sewer gas was one of Thorneycroft's pet hates: he had urged the major cities of Britain to have, in every street, "many pipes put from the sewers up the inside of the gas-lamps . . . and to bring the sewer gas close to the flame . . . these lamps to burn day and night."[2] Again, he was destined to be disappointed.

He also installed an internal telephone system with a second direct line from his bedroom to his coachman's bedroom over the stables, "where he [had] a means of communicating with the police station about 200 yards distant." There was a vastly complicated heating and ventilation system which, he proudly noted, incorporated a heated boot-rack cupboard, but which doesn't seem to have had his full confidence, since there was a backup: "Should the regular hot-air apparatus that heats the billiard-rooms [there were two] get out of order, then the two gas-stoves would do it."[3] And the house had ten "neck shower baths" of his own invention, designed to avoid wetting one's head—a dangerous practice which would inevitably lead to illness and death, according to Victorian medical orthodoxy.

After he failed to persuade his village to build a concert hall for community use, Thorneycroft built his own theatre at the Towers, which was licenced for public performance. It boasted a stage with a dance floor on India rubber springs and iron rollers, "like the Manchester ball-room," and a large magic lantern with a huge portable screen consisting of a sheet thirty-five feet by twenty-two on rollers: "On this sheet I lately showed my fellow directors from the Wolverhampton Hospital several views of the dangers of sewers leaking, and the dreadful effects of it." The theatre was fitted with large plate-glass

---

* Thorneycroft was reluctant to give up his big idea. By 1880 he was trying, without success, to bottle air.

windows through which coloured lights could be made to play on a fountain at the back of the stage, producing, he claimed, "such an effect as I never saw before." A telegraph in the dining room was connected to the smoking room in the main tower. And to cap things off, "there [was] also a flashing apparatus on the top of this large tower, like the one used in Zululand."[4]

Between these two poles—the crested wheelbarrow for logs and the flashing apparatus like the one used in Zululand—there lurked a vast array of technological miracles that transformed life in the country house around the turn of the century. In 1870, a house was lit with paraffin lamps, candles, and perhaps gas jets in passages and other circulation spaces, if the owner was enterprising enough to have a gas plant in the grounds. There was as yet no incandescent gas mantle, and gas was too hot and too smelly to be used in living rooms and bedrooms. Very few houses had hot and cold water piped to all floors and all bathrooms (if they *had* bathrooms): the first, or one of the first, is thought to have been Didsbury Towers, near Manchester, designed in 1865 by the architect Thomas Worthington for John Taylor, proprietor of the *Manchester Guardian*.[5] Cooking was usually done on huge coal-fired ranges or, in some of the more conservative households, over open fires. Stables, carriages, and grooms were a vital adjunct to every country house.

Forty years later, articles were already being written on how a country house owner might replace his aging electrical system and on the advantages of installing refrigerating plants, central heating, even electric clocks, "so connected that the clocks all over the house are synchronized and show the same time." The Earl of Ellesmere's Worsley New Hall outside Manchester, which wasn't particularly advanced for its time, had its own half-timbered electricity-generating plant providing power to 1,100 electric lights in the house (and another 210 to Worsley Old Hall, where his heir, Viscount Brackley, was living) and an automatic passenger and luggage lift. "This lift is actuated by

THE POWER AND THE GLORY

a series of push buttons clearly marked so that no lift attendant is necessary," marvelled a *Country Life* writer in 1908. "Anyone wishing to use the lift merely enters, closes the door and touches the button bearing the number of the floor which he wishes to reach and the lift will automatically stop itself at the desired level."[6]

One of the country house comforts that didn't show much in the way of technological advance was heating. Every country house had open fires in the principal rooms, the bedrooms, and pretty much every other room, and where central heating was installed—"concertinaed pipes looking like giant intestines," in historian Clive Aslet's memorable phrase—it was there to take the chill off rather than to replace those fires.[7] Electric convector heaters and portable electric radiators were available by the beginning of the twentieth century, but again, they were there to complement rather than to take the place of open fires.

In 1880 the architect J. J. Stevenson was convinced that an open fire was the best system for heating English houses, in spite of the fact that it produced dust and was terribly wasteful, most of the heat going straight up the chimney. "It has the advantage that we are used to it," he wrote. "It is a tolerably efficient mode of ventilation, and it is so cheery and pleasant that we are not likely to abandon it, as long as the coal lasts." More than thirty years later architect C. H. B. Quennell admitted ruefully that "the Englishman has remained wedded to the open fire" and that he condemned the enclosed stove as unhomelike and, worst of all, "Continental."[8]

The supply of water to a country house which was usually far from a town main and often sited on rising ground was a long-standing problem. "There are many picturesque country houses in which a convenient system of water supply is a marked deficiency," commented one writer in 1908, going on to propose the wind pump as a solution.

A complete wind-motor pumping plant for supplying a country house with five hundred to one thousand gallons of water per day would cost around fifty pounds, and "painted sky-blue on a latticed steel tower, or fixed on a pitch-pine mast upon the building, they are far from being unsightly."[9]

The wind pump was one of a host of different methods of raising water available to the turn-of-the-century country house owner. The Lancashire firm of John Blake Ltd sold patent self-acting rams and hydrams for raising water. Merryweather and Sons, a London firm established at the end of the seventeenth century as manufacturers of pumps and firefighting apparatus, described themselves as "specialists on all matters in connection with water supplies for country mansions." Country house owners could buy a Merryweather ram, worked by water from a running stream; a Merryweather windmill; a Merryweather electric pump ("if current is available"); a Merryweather horse or donkey pump; or Merryweather pumps driven by oil, petrol, steam, or hot-air engines.[10]

Once water arrived at the country house, the question arose of what to do with it. If you needed to soften it, then the makers of Maignen's Patent Automatic Apparatus for softening hard water declared with pride that it was supplied to the Prince of Wales at Sandringham, the Duke of Richmond at Goodwood, Leopold de Rothschild at Ascott, and Earl Radnor at Longford Castle. (And that "several large asylums have adopted the process with great satisfaction.") A ready supply was needed in the domestic offices for cooking and cleaning. And in spite of the fact that the advent of the motorcar made public laundries more popular with housekeepers, the purpose-built laundry was still a feature of many country houses, partly because their public counterparts had something of a reputation for making mistakes. "There will always remain the irresponsible carelessness associated with these establishments," declared one commentator in 1905.[11]

At Redleaf in Kent, architect Maxwell Maberly Smith designed a quaintly attractive Old English laundry building in the grounds for the Hills family, who had built themselves a large and vaguely Jacobethan country house in the 1880s.* Partly timber-framed, part sandstone, with tall chimneys and steeply sloping tiled roofs, it had a washhouse, drying chamber and finishing room, and water storage tanks, with a small living room and kitchen at the back and three good-sized bedrooms on the first floor, presumably for the chief laundrymaid and her family, or perhaps for a married couple who worked for the family as gardener and washerwoman. "It might almost appear to the casual passer-by to be fifty or sixty years old," wrote one commentator. "Half-timber work, if not oiled or varnished, will quickly turn a silvery grey, very much the colour of the genuine old work; and sandstone, where the joints are well pressed in, will rapidly cover with green lichen."[12] It was clearly an homage to George Devey's pioneering Old English cottages, which had been put up at nearby Penshurst in the 1850s. A certain vague yearning for a preindustrial past was always to be preferred, even in laundry buildings.

That yearning for antiquity didn't extend to the workings of a country house laundry. Although certain tasks still needed to be done by hand—the ironing of collars and cuffs, shirt fronts, women's blouses, and servants' aprons and caps—almost every other operation could be mechanised. In 1913 *Country Life* featured a cluster of country houses with up-to-the-minute laundries. All were in Scotland, oddly enough; perhaps it had something to do with the Scottish weather? At Carberry Tower in East Lothian the 16th Lord Elphinstone (brother-in-law to Elizabeth Bowes-Lyon, later Queen Elizabeth the Queen Mother) installed a modern steam-powered laundry at the beginning of the century. The boiler heated the water and powered an impressive array of equipment, including a rotary washing machine which rinsed,

---

* A George Maberly Smith was the local rector. He was also Maxwell's father.

washed, boiled, and final rinsed the contents in about forty minutes; a "decoudun ironer," which was basically a flatwork ironing machine with the operator feeding washed and dried linen through rollers; and a "hydro-extractor," which did the work of a wringer, extracting water by centrifugal force. An account of the 13th Duke of Hamilton's new laundry at Dungavel Lodge in Lanarkshire noted that his hydro-extractor was operated by hand and gave a helpful explanation of how this worked: "The action of the hydro-extractor may be understood when it is stated that if a rat or other animal were placed in the revolving cage all the blood would be sucked from its body."[13]

Dungavel also boasted drying horses of steel rails which could be pulled out, loaded with wet washing, and pushed back into a chamber heated by steam from the boiler, which fed heating coils in a pit beneath. "A temperature of about one hundred and fifty degrees Fahrenheit can be obtained in this chamber, which is capable of drying a load of linen in thirty to sixty minutes."[14] No mention was made of its effects on rats.

Laundries like these required a fairly hefty initial outlay. An operation like Lord Elphinstone's at Carberry Tower would cost around £550, excluding builders' and carpenters' work, and it required an engineer and two or three washerwomen to operate and maintain it. Equipping Dungavel cost more than £400, and because some of the operations were still done by hand, it needed seven people to run it: an engineer to look after the firing of the boiler and general maintenance, and six maids. On the other hand, "the average number of articles put through the laundry [at Dungavel] in a full week is eighteen hundred pieces, consisting of bed and table linen, body linen, wearing apparel, servants' garments, etc."[15]

"A very delightful and luxurious fitting to the basin," announced C. H. B. Quennell in a 1909 article on the country house bathroom, "is the combined hot and cold shampooing valve." This useful device—actually a small showerhead fixed to the washbasin—could also be used for spraying the face, "and refreshing indeed is the effect of this operation on the faces of those tried by the heat of a summer's day." And in case his readers remained unconvinced, Quennell assured them that "fittings similar to these have been installed for the King at Sandringham."[16]

Quennell's ideal country house bathroom was quite luxurious. It was provided with a roll-top bath, cast iron with a thin coating of porcelain; a separate shower bath, convenient "after a game of tennis in the summer"; a footbath; a washbasin equipped with that shampooing valve and with a mirror above it, lit by two gas mantles. There was also a heated towel airer, providing just enough heat "to make the bathroom pleasantly warm on a very cold morning," but no lavatory. A water closet "should never be placed in the bathroom." Instead, it should be situated in a separate room of its own.

Fittings were all nickel plated, and although marble might be used to line walls and floors, it should be used with great restraint. "If varied colours be introduced, the result is apt to be reminiscent of the cheap restaurant." Much better if bath, washbasin, and walls were all white, "so that by contrast our bodies may appear ruddy with health; and, looking well, we shall feel well."

Quennell's architectural output veered towards the gabled suburban villa rather than the stately home. Four Beeches, the house he designed for himself in Bickley Park, Kent, was typical. With a faint Arts and Crafts air, it was relatively small and cost well under £1,600. And his country house bathroom reflects aspiration rather than reality (although the small bathroom at Four Beeches did have its shampooer and towel airer). That reality was often rather more basic. Writing in 1880, J. J. Stevenson described an unnamed country house, recently built, where the owner placed earth closets "inside the house, arranged round a small back court, which a cart can enter with good results." That practice would not have appealed to Eardley Bailey-Denton, a civil engineer who made something of a career out of providing advice on drains to country house owners. In his *Water Supply and Sewerage of Country Mansions and Estates* (1901), he maintained vigorously that earth closets "are only advisable for the use of men, and . . . are usually placed in some secluded corner outside the house or out-buildings." And of course the mention of earth closets conjures up the famous three-seater garden privy at Kelmscott, and Edward Burne-Jones's rather cruel sketch of Jane Morris flanked by her husband on one side and her lover, Dante Gabriel Rossetti, on the other.[17]

Bailey-Denton had pronounced views on water closets. The traditional pan closet, with a container underneath, was no good "as it [was] merely a foul receptacle for the accumulation of filth."[18] Valve closets, which had recently come into favour and which had the outlet of the toilet bowl closed by a movable valve or plate held in place by a lever or spring, were unreliable on account of their complicated moving parts. No, the only possible choice for the discerning country house owner was the valveless closet, which is more or less the type of lavatory in use today. There should be no cabinet or wooden framework, so that one could easily detect any leakage.

When it came to the difficult question of how many water closets to provide, valveless or otherwise, there was a wide variation, from none at all (rare by the end of the century) to an embarrassment of riches. One thinks of the 5th Duke of Portland's insistence on having a water closet in every room at Welbeck, each crowned with a ducal coronet. Westonbirt in Gloucestershire, completed in 1870, was supplied with seven earth closets and water closets in the service wing for eighteen indoor servants, but that was unusual.

In that way he had of setting down the rules for everything concerning the gentleman's house, Robert Kerr explained his "rules for number and distribution" of water closets:

In the smallest house there will be one for the servants, separate from that for the family. As the next advance, there may be provided an extra one for the Bedchambers upstairs, the ordinary one being on the Ground Floor. The one on the Upper Floor will then come to be considered as appropriated to ladies. In the country an additional one is often provided in the Garden for gentlemen. The Cloak-room will have one attached to its Lavatory [here used in the Victorian and Edwardian sense of washing place or wash-basin]; if on a large scale, it may have two. Where there is no other provided in such a position as to be available for the purpose (as in the Cloak-room), there ought to be a special one so placed as to be readily accessible from the Dining-room. It is sometimes thought proper that the Billiard-room, if quite removed from the main house, should have one; so also with the Smoking-room; so also with the Library, if extensive, and used for study. One may also have to be provided in connexion with the Business-room and its adjuncts. In large establishments there will necessarily be several for the servants; chiefly in groups externally, for the sexes separately; but an odd one also here and there in connexion with outlying departments. Amongst the Bed-chambers again, when these are numerous, there must be a sufficient number properly distributed, for the family, guests, and servants separately, as obvious propriety will suggest. A suite of Nurseries must also be specially supplied; as also a School-room. Lastly, when the architect is arranging those private Bedchamber-Suites which have been described, each Suite ought to have one as an essential element of its own comfort; or the two Dressing-rooms of the same Suite may have one each.[19]

By my reckoning, that comes to somewhere between twenty and thirty water closets. Ample provision, one feels.

Bathrooms seem to have been in rather shorter supply, perhaps because the practice of bathing in one's bedroom was still considered to be safer for one's health than padding down icy corridors before and after a hot bath. When Hampton and Sons offered the twenty-two-bedroomed Brockham Park near Dorking for sale in 1913, it was advertised as having electricity, company water, modern sanitation—and just two bathrooms. Plas Tan y Bwlch in the Vale of Ffestiniog, a twenty-eight-bedroom pile thought to be the first country house in North Wales to be lit by electricity powered by its own hydro-electric station, was advertised for sale in 1909 along with an estate of 2,722 acres, at the low price of £36,000: Knight Frank and Rutley proudly pointed out in the particulars that it boasted two bathrooms. That seems to have been par for the course by the beginning of the twentieth century. Smallfield Place in Surrey, "one of the finest specimens of domestic Tudor architecture in the county" (according to the agent who was trying to sell it), had two bathrooms, and one on each of the bedroom floors was usual. And Blair Drummond, near Stirling, rebuilt in 1868–1872 but described by the selling agent in 1912 as a "stately pile [which] retains the style of the old Scottish Castles," had two bathrooms to service its twenty-seven principal bedrooms.[20] But plenty of country houses made do with a single bathroom, and a surprising number still had none, even by 1914. Danesfield in Buckinghamshire, on the other hand, had eight. But then Danesfield was built for a soap manufacturer.

Without doubt, the main driver in the technological revolution that transformed country house life was not the water closet, nor even the shampooer. It was electricity. Arc lamps were already in use for public lighting by the 1870s. Mary Gladstone commented on the "cheering and torches and electric light" that greeted her father on an electioneering tour of Scotland in the winter of 1879. But they were still a novelty: on the same tour, Mary attended a large evening party in Glasgow where the entertainment consisted of "music and electricity."[21]

It was in the same year, 1879, that electric lighting became a realistic proposition for domestic use with the arrival of the incandescent bulb. The physicist Joseph Swan demonstrated a version of the electric light bulb at a meeting of Newcastle's Literary and Philosophical Society in February 1879, with the armaments manufacturer William Armstrong in the chair. The following year Swan's incandescent lamps were used to light several rooms at Armstrong's country house, Cragside; Armstrong had already installed a turbine and dynamo to power an arc lamp, but the Swan lamps were much more effective. Swan claimed later that "Cragside was the first house in England properly fitted up with my electric lamps." That is open to debate, but it was certainly the first to be lit by electricity powered by a purpose-built hydroelectric station. Armstrong was himself an inveterate inventor, and Cragside was filled with innovative devices and machines. In 1869, when it was nothing more than a small fishing lodge, it already boasted what Richard Norman Shaw referred to as "wonderful hydraulic machines that do all sorts of things you can imagine," and by the time it was finished, hydraulic machinery powered lifts which moved goods and people from floor to floor, as well as the spit which turned the joints of meat in the kitchen. It rotated the heavy pots in the conservatories. An internal telephone system provided room-to-room communications. In 1879 the *World* was calling Cragside "the palace of a modern magician," a phrase which was repeated at Armstrong's death in 1900 and has stuck ever since, confirming the idea that it was primarily nouveaux riches technocrats like him who, having seen what modern technology could do in their factories and workshops, were the first to introduce it into their country houses.[22]

And that was true, but only up to a point. Armstrong wasn't the only country house owner to pioneer the use of electricity. In November 1880, the 3rd Marquess of Salisbury was on a visit to Newcastle when he saw Swan's incandescent lamps in action at Armstrong's Elswick works and heard from Armstrong that he planned to try them out at Cragside. Salisbury was impressed: "They do not flicker," he wrote to a friend, "and they are not overwhelming to look at."[23]

The marquess was an enthusiast for new technology. He had already built a gasworks and installed gas lighting at Hatfield, his Jacobean mansion in Hertfordshire, soon after inheriting the house in 1868, and in 1874 he put up electric arc lights outside the house, "mainly for the benefit of his guests' coachmen on the occasion of the annual county ball," recalled his daughter Gwendolen, but Augustus Hare, who was one of the guests, thought they provided a spectacular show, "a sea of fire and blood." Salisbury tried to introduce arc lighting into the house as well, so that, to quote Gwendolen again, "for a brief period his family and guests were compelled to eat their dinners under the vibrating glare of one of these lamps fixed in the centre of the dining-hall ceiling."[24]

Early in 1881 Salisbury began to experiment with Swan lamps in the house, powered from a sawmill a mile and a half away, with connecting cables carrying the current on telegraph poles across the park. His day job, as Conservative leader of the opposition to Gladstone's Liberal administration, didn't interfere unduly with his experiments which "for a year or two relieved the monotony of domestic life at Hatfield." There were evenings when his lights emitted no more than a dim red glow and the household had to grope around in semidarkness, and others when the bulbs burned brightly but briefly before going out completely. "One group of lamps after another would blaze and expire in rapid succession, like stars in conflagration, till the rooms were left in pitchy blackness, and the evening's entertainment had to be concluded in the light of hastily collected bed-candles." But Salisbury persevered, and within a few years all the main rooms of the house were lit by a vast array of bulbs, festooned along the panelling and suspended from ceilings. In 1890 Augustus Hare paid another visit to Hatfield, arriving just after sunset. He marvelled at the way "all the windows blazed and glittered with light through the dark walls; the Golden Gallery with its hundreds of electric lamps was like a Venetian illumination."[25]

The take-up of electric lighting was patchy but swift. Mark Girouard thought that Smallwood Manor in Staffordshire, a neo-Elizabethan mansion designed by the Prince of Wales's architect R. W. Edis and completed in 1886 for the mine owner George Hodson, was one of the first country houses in Britain, if not *the* first, to be built for electricity. Another contender is Woodlands Park in Surrey, built in 1885 for the industrialist William Bryant, who was, ironically enough, the son of the founder of the match company Bryant and May.

Gradually, existing houses were converted to take electricity. There was electric lighting throughout the late Georgian Lambton Castle in County Durham by 1887: Reginald Brett, later the 2nd Viscount Esher, was a member of a shooting party hosted by the Earl of Durham that December, and he wrote to tell his wife that the electric light was charming, especially in the bedrooms. "You touch a button, and your dressing-table is illuminated. You touch another near the *table de nuit* and your bed is as light as day."[26]

Pyrgo Park in Essex, an Italianate mansion built in 1851, was lit by electricity by 1897, even though it already had its own gasworks. Eighteenth-century Calcot Park in Berkshire was similarly lit throughout by electricity by 1899. So was Chatsworth, where the Duke of Devonshire installed a system of three water-driven turbines which generated enough power for about a thousand lamps and a set of electric ventilators which were designed to take away cooking smells from the kitchens.

By the end of the century electricity was fairly commonplace, although Mary Gladstone still made sure to pack two pounds of candles and an extra "reading candle" in her luggage when she holidayed on the French Riviera in 1897; and as late as 1915 the 5th Marquess of Bath refused to install either gas or electricity, maintaining that the rooms at Longleat had been designed for oil lamps or candlelight and that if he changed to electricity, "not only might it mutilate the ceilings and the walls but the character of the rooms would change."[27] And so each day his lamp boy had to clean, trim, and fill four hundred oil lamps. Burghley House didn't have electric lighting until the 1950s.

Where there was resistance to the new technology, it didn't always come from die-hard reactionaries like Lord Bath. Reginald Brett noted about the Earl of Durham's electrification programme at Lambton Castle that the setup costs and maintenance could be prohibitively expensive. You needed an engine, usually powered by petroleum or steam, a dynamo, an accumulator to store the electricity, mains cable, switches and regulator, and somewhere to house the plant. Then there was the cost involved in wiring the mansion, perhaps having to disrupt delicate plasterwork wall panels or ceilings in the staterooms, or at least installing conduits and making sure that they were reasonably unobtrusive. At Worsley, the Earl of Ellesmere's agent, Captain H. V. Hart-Davis, was proud of the way in which switches were concealed in the woodwork and the steel tubing carrying the wiring was fitted without damage to panelling and carving. In 1900 it was reckoned that the setup costs to provide a largish mansion with eight hundred lights, including sufficient accumulators to maintain half the lamps for nine hours after the engine stopped, would be £3,270. On top of that, annual working costs came to £168.

But Longleat and Burghley were, if not quite exceptions, then at least seen as behind the times. "In every well-appointed country house, the electric lighting is now considered to be of scarcely less importance than the water supply, the drainage, and other necessaries," declared a writer in 1899. These days, he went on, a hostess "has been forced to appreciate that her house parties are not considered up-to-date if her friends have to return to the dingy candle during their stay." And the benefits were aesthetic as well as practical. In 1907 the 5th Earl of Malmesbury installed electric lighting at his Dorset country house, Heron Court, with results that impressed courtier Sir Almeric FitzRoy when he visited the following January: "The house much improved . . . the installation of electric light having brought the fine pictures out of the walls with great effect." But then FitzRoy was quite a fan of electric lighting: he confided to his diary that the 1902 coronation of Edward VII would have been much more imposing if Westminster Abbey had been lit by electricity instead of gas.[28]

Once your country house had a supply of electricity, lighting was only one of the benefits. By the 1910s electric kettles, toasters, and coffee makers were available; so were hair dryers and irons and curling iron heaters. There were rotary floor-polishing machines and vacuum cleaners, knife cleaners and electric clocks, fans if the air was too hot and humidifiers if it was too dry. To be fair, it was only a few country house owners who leaped at the prospect of owning an electric toaster or a curling iron heater. After all, what were kitchen maids paid for if not to make the toast? Why have a lady's maid if she wasn't capable of heating the curling irons in the fire?

But some electrically powered devices did begin to appear at the beginning of the twentieth century. Minterne House in Dorset, designed by Leonard Stokes and built for the Digby family in 1902–1907, had a central vacuum cleaner system, with a powered pump in the basement connected by tubes to the main rooms and the outlets covered by brass flaps in the skirting, so that the maids could plug in a length of hose when they needed to vacuum the room. At Worsley the Earl of Ellesmere, who was clearly an enthusiast, had a dairy equipped with electricity and a granary with machinery including a wheat-grinding and sifting plant, an oat crusher, and two corn-grinding mills, all driven by two twenty-horsepower electric motors. "The offices, food-mixing places in stables and piggeries, foaling-boxes, blacksmiths' and joiners' shops are all lighted from the main power station," noted an awestruck commentator, "and a centrifugal liquid manure pump is driven by a 3h.p. motor on the 200 volt supply at a distance of 695 yards from the power station."[29]

The advantages of having an efficient communications network in a large country house were obvious, particularly when it came to summoning the servants. Wired bell systems were still in use in most houses, but alternatives were becoming available: Rousdon in Devon, built in 1874 for the grocery king Sir Henry Peek, was equipped with pneumatic bells, and the indefatigable Marquess of Salisbury introduced electric bells to Hatfield in 1868, within months of coming into his inheritance. (He wasn't quite so far ahead of the game here as he was with his other innovations: Queen Victoria and Prince Albert had installed electric bells at Osborne House as long ago as 1861.) J. J. Stevenson advocated the use of speaking tubes instead of, or as well as, a bell system, since it saved the servants considerable labour in climbing stairs. The tubes' openings "should close by a spring or plug, that they may not become a means of overhearing conversations."[30]

But as Stevenson was writing, the speaking tube was already being superseded. Alexander Graham Bell demonstrated his telephone to Victoria at Osborne House in 1878. It seems to have been only a qualified success. If she listened carefully the queen could hear the voices of Sir Thomas and Mary Biddulph, the keeper of the privy purse and his wife, who were in a nearby cottage on the estate. "But it is rather faint, and one must hold the tube close to one's ear," she wrote in her journal. She found Bell very pompous; and worst of all, he "kept calling

Arthur Lord Connaught!"[31] Bell may have been poised to change the entire nature of communication, but failing to use the proper address when talking to Prince Arthur, Duke of Connaught and Strathearn, was unforgivable.

Inevitably, the Marquess of Salisbury was one of the first adopters of the country house telephone. He was experimenting with one prototype—or rather with two, since one telephone isn't much use—in 1877, before telephones were on the market in Britain, and his daughter remembered how he laid loose telephone wires all over the house for unwary houseguests to trip over. By the early 1880s a telephone with an electric bell in Lord Salisbury's study connected directly with his steward, so that instead of summoning him to discuss some point of household or estate management, he could have a conversation at a distance.

By the end of the century, it wasn't unusual to see lines connecting a country house with its outbuildings—the porter's lodge, perhaps, or the stables and a generator house. One popular use, it has been suggested, was to issue instructions to the electrician to run the generator longer if power in the house began to fade. Lord Salisbury had a telephone line installed to run between the generator in his sawmill and the house in September 1881.

Very few country houses had external phone lines before 1914, although the telephone quickly evolved from a more efficient way of communicating with the servants into a means of talking with other members of the family, something which required either a central exchange (only seen in very grand houses) or a system which connected bedrooms and the principal reception rooms together, and connected these with the servants' hall, the gardener's cottage, the chauffeur, and so on. Each phone was numbered, and to call up someone elsewhere in the house, one simply pressed the corresponding numbered button on a board attached to the instrument. When the conversation was over the caller replaced the receiver on its hook, which released the pressed button, leaving the line clear for the next user.

It was good value, too. Installing a seventeen-instrument inter-communication system cost about sixty pounds. A much smaller system, linking the mistress of the house's bedroom with the kitchen and the kitchen with the dining room, could be had for between three and five pounds. "The telephone is now one of the usual modern conveniences found in the country house," wrote Maurice Hird in 1911, in a contribution on the telephone to architectural writer Lawrence Weaver's *The House and Its Equipment*. He went further. "If asked to prophesy as to its future, we should say that in a few years no good country house will be built without an installation of 'inter-communication' telephones."[32]

FOURTEEN

GOING TO BLAZES

T HE EARLY ADOPTION of new technology was not without its
risks. "It was no uncommon result for one of the party to be
hurled across the room in his wild endeavours to discover whether the
dynamo was performing its functions," noted one pioneering engineer, looking back from the relative safety of the late 1890s.[1] And man
of letters Hilaire Belloc wrote in 1911 of the demise of the (fictional)
Lord Finchley, who

> . . . tried to mend the Electric Light
> Himself. It struck him dead; and serve him right!
> It is the business of the wealthy man
> To give employment to the artisan.[2]

But the artisan was not immune to risk. A dance at the Marquess
of Salisbury's Hatfield in December 1881 was marred by the death of
a workman, William Dimmock, who was killed that morning by an

electric shock while setting up the lighting for the party. The dance still went ahead, though.

Less dramatic, but more common, were the unexpected blackouts. By 1893 the Earl of Derby's Knowsley Hall outside Liverpool was lit by electricity; so were the stables. Everyone was impressed by this feat, but they were less impressed when the lights failed during a big dinner party. "Happily there was gas in the passages," wrote Lady Emily Lutyens, who was one of the guests, and the lights came back on during dinner. Still, "these luxuries have their drawbacks."[3]

One drawback, in the absence of fuses, was a tendency for overheated wires to burst into flames. One evening, a house party went into the long gallery at Hatfield after dinner to find flames coming from a point where the carved panelling met the ceiling. The younger members of the party saved the day (and Hatfield House) by hurling sofa cushions at the fire until it went out.

The fusing of electrical wires was often cited as a cause of country house fires. So was carelessness with new electric devices. The fire which devastated Welbeck Abbey in 1900 was caused by an electric iron. Or, to be more accurate, it was caused by a nurserymaid who wanted to iron some sashes for one of the Cavendish-Bentinck girls to wear at a party. She switched the iron on at the plug, found there was no current, and forgot to turn it off again. Then the power returned. "I may say," recalled the Duke of Portland, "that after this I consigned most of the electric irons in the house to a watery grave in the lake."[4]

And then there was the threat posed by gas. One day in January 1909 the well-known racing driver Arthur Huntley Walker, who had recently caused a sensation by reaching a speed of 120 mph on the track at Brooklands, began to think he could smell gas in the southwest wing of his country house, Pickhurst Mead in Kent. He had estate workers searching for the leak, but without success, and eventually he ordered the furniture in the wing to be cleared out in readiness for a visit the next day from specialist workmen who were going to take up the floors to check the gas pipes.

That morning, Huntley Walker went down to the gardener's cottage with his butler to discuss whether to cut off the gas supply altogether—a prudent move in the circumstances, one feels—when there was an almighty explosion and the suspect southwest wing burst into flames. The men ran back to the house to find that a passing police constable had already broken in and rescued Huntley Walker's three young daughters (whom he had left sleeping, two of them in a room next door to the library, where the fire broke out). His wife also escaped unhurt, but the same couldn't be said for Huntley Walker's fourteen motorcars, which included Mercedes tourers, four Weigels, and three Darracqs, one of which was brand new and intended for that year's Grand Prix in France. They were all housed in a purpose-built garage next to the house, and they were all destroyed. The overall cost of the damage was reckoned at the time to be around £30,000.

There were plenty of other causes of fire: overheating flues, clothes being aired in front of open fires, curtains coming into contact with naked flames, candles being blown over or forgotten. The blaze which came close to destroying the Georgian Crosland Hall in Yorkshire in 1908 was caused by an exploding poultry incubator in the coach house. The fire that took the life of Andrew Laidlay, the owner of Seacliff, an imposing Scotch Baronial mansion in East Lothian, began in the library, where, according to press reports, Mr Laidley was in the habit of reading late into the night "by the light of a paraffin lamp."[5]

In 1899 an anonymous *Country Life* writer estimated that of the largest country houses, "those which the country looks upon almost in the light of national possessions," fire destroyed an average of twelve a

year. He (or she) cited disasters at "mansions in the first rank of interest"—
Belvoir Castle, Warwick Castle, Duncombe Park, Clumber Park,
and Ingestre Hall. The writer obviously had a long memory: the cat-
astrophic fire which destroyed James Wyatt's picturesque masterpiece
at Belvoir had happened more than eighty years earlier, in 1816.*
The other fires, though, were more recent. The Earl of Faversham's
early eighteenth-century Duncombe Park in Yorkshire, designed by
John Vanbrugh and remodelled in 1843 by Sir Charles Barry, burned
down in January 1879: there had been a hard frost, and all the taps
and water pipes were frozen, which hampered efforts to bring the fire
under control. The week after the fire one commentator noted with
pleasure that it was insured, "as it is said to have been a popular place
of resort for the people of the North Riding in the summer months."
In fact it was not rebuilt until the early 1890s, and then its architect,
William Young, failed to please. After a visit to her childhood home
in December 1893, Faversham's daughter Hermione was reduced to
tears. "I trust I may never meet Mr Young for I cannot congratulate
him on what he has done," she wrote to a friend. "[I am] fully convinced he can have no real feelings for art or he *could not* have wan-
tonly sacrificed much that was so beautiful."[6]

Ten weeks after the Duncombe disaster, a bathroom fire at the
Duke of Newcastle's Clumber Park in Nottinghamshire spread until
it engulfed the entire centre of the house. By a stroke of bad luck,
fifteen of the duke's best paintings, which had been on exhibition at
Burlington House, had come back to Clumber the previous night and
were stacked in the entrance hall waiting to be hung. The staff managed to get some of them out, but four very large still lifes by Frans
Snyders proved a problem: one was totally destroyed and another was
badly burned.

---

*   Perhaps they were confusing the Duke of Rutland's house with another Belvoir
     Castle, this the seat of the Loftus family in County Clare. That one burned
     down in 1881 and was never rebuilt.

Sandringham House: A building which, like its royal owners, radiated prosperity and an unbridled confidence in the future.

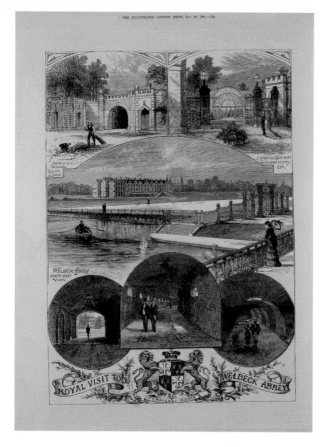

Welbeck Abbey in Nottinghamshire at the time of the Prince of Wales's visit in 1881. The 5th Duke of Portland's subterranean engineering works are much in evidence.

Henry Hetherington Emmerson's deliciously domestic portrait of the inventor and armaments manufacturer Sir William Armstrong at his country house, Cragside in Northumberland.

Andrew and Louise Carnegie. Mary Gladstone described Andrew as "a Scotch American rolling in gold."

Skibo Castle, the Carnegies' Highland home. "Like a luxurious hotel," wrote Woodrow Wilson during a visit in 1908.

'the Maharajah'

Duleep Singh

Duleep Singh, the last maharajah of the Sikh Empire, pictured by "Spy" in *Vanity Fair* in 1882.

The Punjabi designer Bhai Ram Singh at work in the Durbar Room at Queen Victoria's Osborne House on the Isle of Wight.

Paris Singer's staircase at Oldway Mansion in Devon, a faithful copy of Louis Le Vau's 1668 *escalier des Ambassadeurs* at Versailles.

Farnborough Hill House in Hampshire, remodelled in 1883 by Hippolyte Destailleur for the exiled Empress Eugénie, widow of Napoleon III.

Frank Dicksee's 1880 painting *The House Builders* depicts Sir William Welby-Gregory and his wife Victoria studying an architect's model of their new house, Denton Hall in Lincolnshire.

Devizes Castle, Wiltshire, rebuilt in the mid-nineteenth century and described rather optimistically in 1901 as "an admirable imitation of a feudal fortress."

G. F. Watts's painting of Sir Galahad. "If you cannot at once laugh at a thing and believe in it," declared G. K. Chesterton, "you have no business in the Middle Ages."

The Blenheim Palace fire engine in the 1890s.

Schloss Kranzbach in the Bavarian Alps. Called "the English castle" by locals, it was designed by Detmar Blow and Fernand Billerey in 1913, for the violinist Lady Mary Isabel Portman and her partner, Amy Hare.

THE MOTORIST'S TRIALS.

Donald McGill

The walls and things left about by the nasty middle class.

The Motorist's Trials, c.1907. The chauffeur-mechanic became an important addition to the staff at the country house in the years before the First World War.

Tranby Croft

Tranby Croft in the East Riding of Yorkshire, scene of the notorious Baccarat Case in which a member of the Prince of Wales's social set was discovered to be cheating at cards in the prince's presence.

Queen Victoria's family regularly entertained her with tableaux vivants. "Greek Poetry," in which Princess Alexandra of Edinburgh portrayed Sappho with her lyre, was performed as a surprise at Balmoral on the queen's seventy-fifth birthday.

The trial by his peers of Earl Russell for bigamy. His divorce from his first wife in Carson City, Nevada, was declared to be invalid and he was sentenced to three months in prison.

Edward VII, in the cape, inspects the bag at a shoot near Sandringham in November 1909.

Crowds cheering during a political rally at Blenheim Palace in 1912.

The Reading Room at Holkham in Norfolk. Designed by local architect Zephaniah King, it was opened in June 1886 with a concert at which Holkham Hall's Countess of Leicester played a piano solo.

Daisy Greville, the Countess of Warwick, with her son Maynard, painted by John Singer
Sargent in 1905.

A garden party at Panshanger in Hertfordshire on 23 July 1914. The United Kingdom declared war on Germany twelve days later.

The 20th Earl of Shrewsbury's Ingestre Hall in Staffordshire, described at the time as "one of the most picturesque Elizabethan mansions in England," burned down in 1882.[7] Fresh from an affair with the actress Lillie Langtry, the twenty-one-year-old premier earl of England had just caused something of a stir by eloping with the twenty-five-year-old Ellen Mundy, the wife of a Derbyshire land-owner, giving rise to all kinds of rumours: that Alfred Mundy had caught up with the couple in Strasbourg, boxed the earl's ears, and told his wife to come home and stop making a fool of herself; or that it was her five brothers who caught up with them and that between them they gave the earl a good thrashing. Whatever the truth, they dragged Mrs Mundy back to England, but she left again to live with Shrewsbury and her husband petitioned successfully for divorce. By the time she became Countess of Shrewsbury, Ellen was six months pregnant.

The newlyweds were living at Alton Towers, about twenty miles from Ingestre, at the time of the fire, while the Shrewsburys' princi-pal seat was being cleaned and redecorated in preparation for their moving in, with a skeleton staff of three female servants and a gar-dener keeping an eye on things. Fires were kept burning in most of the rooms to keep out the damp. Although there were some barbed comments in the press about the painters who had been at work near the site of the fire the previous day—"The proverbial recklessness and imbecility of painters and plasterers has added another charred heap of ruins to a long list of wanton destruction"—the papers were forced by the earl himself to publish a retraction when it turned out that the cause was a beam under the hearthstone of the state boudoir which had caught from the heat of the fireplace.[8]

Just after five o'clock in the morning on Thursday, October 13, 1882, the head housemaid was woken by a crackling noise. She went to investigate, still in her nightclothes, and, finding that the state bed-room was full of flames and smoke, she raised the alarm, and she and the other two women managed to escape. At the same time a stable-man across the park saw the flames and went for help. It was too late to save the house, but most of the earl's art objects and furniture were saved, with the exception of thousands of bottles of wine in the cellars and some large history paintings on the staircase. The total loss was reckoned at around £100,000. But although Ingestre could be, and was, rebuilt, it wasn't just about the money. The *Times* described the fire as a "grave national loss," and the *Birmingham Mail* gave full vent to a lament on the mansion's destruction:

> The gutted house is nothing . . . but a charred shell. No restorer can bring it back to what it was. A new and stately edifice may rise in its place, but it will have none of the charm of antiquity; the ivy will not cover its walls; the sombre tone of age will not be imparted to it. The indescribable halo which long centuries throw over a building will be wanting. It is impossible to regard the destruction of such a noble pile as a matter in which the Earl of Shrewsbury is alone concerned. He has lost an ancestral residence; the country has lost another of its ancient monuments. These old country seats, with their gravely quaint exteriors and rich store of treasures within, hold a place in the national heart; their very age makes them, in a sentimental sense, a national possession.[9]

That sense of a national loss was even greater when Warwick Castle burned in 1871. The castle was reputed to have Roman ancestry, and one optimistic antiquarian maintained that an Earl of Warwick had been one of King Arthur's Knights of the Round Table. That was pushing it a little, but Warwick did date back to Norman times: William I built a motte-and-bailey castle on the site circa 1068. Since then it had been the home of kings and queens, and almost every century had left its mark, remodelling, extending, rebuilding, until the

Greville family, who were given the castle by James I in 1604 and created Earls of Warwick in 1759, found themselves the owners of one of Britain's most famous historic houses, perched high on a bluff over the Avon as that river meandered past the town of Warwick. It was, to use an overused word, iconic.

And early on the morning of Sunday, December 3, 1871, it burned down.

At least, rather a lot of it did. Around 1:30 that morning the steward's room boy, Joseph Powers, and the two footmen, William Everton and William Gregory, who all slept in the castle basement, were woken by what they at first thought to be hail beating on the roof of the nearby boot room. But the sounds grew louder, and, worrying that an intruder was trying to break in, they thought they had better investigate. They found smoke coming from Lady Warwick's private apartment on the second floor, and when they opened the door to her sitting room they were confronted by a mass of flames.

They raised the alarm, and the town fire brigade was quickly on the scene, followed by another brigade from Leamington Spa, three miles away. The problem was that the private apartments directly overlooked the Avon, and the water supply wasn't powerful enough to allow the firemen's hoses to reach them from the inner courtyard, which was the closest they could get with their engines. A distraught Captain Fosbery, Lord Warwick's agent, telegraphed to Birmingham to have a more powerful steam fire engine sent down by special train; unfortunately, as the *Times* reported, "Birmingham [did] not possess a steam fire-engine, and a special train could not be procured."[10]

Most of the family was away, but two of the children, five-year-old Sidney and eleven-year-old Eva, were sleeping in the nurseries; their governess led them out to safety and the local vicar took charge of them. The only casualty was the footman William Everton, who, having realised that the gun room was in the path of the fire and that Lord Warwick, who was preparing to host his annual Christmas shooting party, had stored more than five hundred cartridges there, managed to get into the room and carry the cartridges out to a safer part of the building. According to one account, "[Everton,] who greatly exerted himself, is seriously ill, and under medical treatment."[11]

As the fire began to spread through the castle, there were frenzied scenes as tapestries were torn down from walls, paintings ripped from their frames, and furniture dragged out into the courtyard. Lady Warwick's jewels and the family plate were in a fireproof safe in the basement, and they were undamaged, as was a lapis lazuli table said to have belonged to Marie Antoinette and a precious little eighteenth-century painting of the bust of Shakespeare in the Stratford-upon-Avon church. The fire was halted just as it reached the state apartments, or things might have been much, much worse. But the private apartments and most of their contents were lost, and the Warwicks' legendary collection of early arms and armour was destroyed when the ceiling of the great hall fell in. "A page of English history has just been destroyed," declared the *Illustrated Newspaper*. "In the loss of Warwick Castle we have received a national loss—a loss no time, no labour, and no skill can ever replace."[12]

In fact, quite a lot was replaced. The Warwicks' neighbour Lord Leigh of Stoneleigh Abbey headed a list of distinguished figures who leaped in with a proposal for a national relief fund to help with repairs, since "the restoration of the building will entail a necessary outlay beyond the reach of most private fortunes."[13] A sum of £2,000 was raised immediately, enough to begin the work, and Anthony Salvin was brought in to restore the damaged hall and the east wing, which housed the damaged private apartments. Copies were quietly found of items like the buff jerkin Lord Warwick's ancestor Lord Brooke wore when he was killed fighting for Parliament at Lichfield in 1643.

There was a powerful sense that a house like Warwick belonged to the nation and that the nation had a duty to mend it. Lord Leigh emphasised that "Warwick Castle, with its art treasures, has been open to the public, with a noble generosity, for several generations." The implication was clear: it was time for the public to repay that generosity. And most people agreed. The only dissenting voice came from John Ruskin, who, when asked for a contribution to the relief fund, refused, remarking rather grumpily that "if a noble family cannot re-build their own castle, in God's name let them live in the nearest ditch till they can."[14]

Ingestre, Warwick, Clumber—these were the famous, or infamous, country house conflagrations. But a random trawl through the records for a single year, 1908, shows that at least twenty-two country houses were either badly damaged or totally gutted by fire in that year alone. The west wing roof of the Earl of Malmesbury's Heron Court in Dorset, with its newly installed electric lighting setting off the pictures so perfectly, was destroyed in April, although "owing to the energetic action of the household servants and the labourers on the estate, the fire was extinguished before the arrival of the fire engines."[15] St Anne's Manor in Sutton Bonington, Nottinghamshire, wasn't so lucky: when fire broke out in the middle of a December night, the owner, Charles Tennant, and his servants and neighbours concentrated on rescuing pictures and furniture. By the time the local fire brigade arrived, hampered by the bitter cold, and found there was no source of water for their pumps, the house was destroyed.

In 1905 fire ravaged Gaddesden Place in Hertfordshire, an imposing Georgian house designed by James Wyatt. It belonged to the local MP, Frederick Halsey, but it was then let to another MP, John Kerr. No one was hurt in the blaze itself, but after the fire had been brought under control, Kerr's butler, William Paton, became very anxious about the contents of the wine cellar. He had rescued most of it and placed it under police guard, but he was worried that it might be pilfered, so the afternoon after the fire he took a young footman, James

Jones, and started to replace the bottles in the cellar, in spite of Kerr telling him it was better to lose the wine than lose his life. Without warning, the cellar roof fell in, fatally injuring both men. Jones was dragged by firemen from the rubble, badly burned and muttering repeatedly, "The butler is in there." He died later. Paton's body was found under the wreckage the next day, his arm held up as if to protect his head.

Casualties like this were surprisingly rare considering the frequency of country house fires. Winston Churchill had a narrow escape when he was a guest at Burley House at Burley-on-the-Hill in Rutland in August 1908. Fire broke out around one in the morning, and by the time fire brigades arrived from Oakham, Melton Mowbray, and Stamford, there was no chance of extinguishing the flames. Churchill directed operations, soaking wet and in his shirtsleeves: he enlisted the aid of a couple of policemen to break down the door to the banqueting hall with a battering ram so that they could get to some of the paintings and furniture. At one point he had just emerged from the burning house carrying a couple of busts in his arms when the roof fell in behind him. A second later and the history of the twentieth century might have been quite different.

The night that Burley House burned down, there was a gas explosion at Cowfold Lodge in Sussex, and within minutes the place was on fire. The owner, Arthur Labouchere, and three of his four servants managed to escape in their nightclothes, but a twenty-seven-year-old housemaid, Lilla Clark, found herself trapped in her second-floor bedroom. Although everyone shouted to her to wait for the arrival of a long ladder which was on its way, she panicked and jumped down onto the gravel path twenty feet below, badly damaging her spine. Rudolf Valentine's wife was luckier: when the Valentines' country house, Heath End in Warwickshire, caught fire one night in March 1908, trapping the newlyweds in their bedroom, Captain Valentine dropped from the bedroom window and then caught his young bride in his arms after she jumped. They lost three hundred wedding presents in the blaze, but at least they had each other.

Prevention being better than cure, Victorian and Edwardian architects were at pains to fireproof their country houses. The standard strategy was to make use of so-called fireproof floors: iron girders supporting arches of brick or concrete, or with flat slabs of concrete supported by wood or iron frames. The disadvantage was that iron beams could crack if cold water from fire pumps hit them when they were hot; they also could expand in the heat, pushing out the walls and doing more harm than good to a structure. To counter this, they were sometimes covered with terra-cotta or plaster to protect them from the heat. The architect J. J. Stevenson in his *House Architecture* (1880) suggested that, contrary to received wisdom, wooden beams bearing the concrete were probably safer than iron, "for a wooden beam burns with difficulty, may bear its load when half charred away, and has not the dangerous character of iron."[16]

But in case the worse came to the worst, it was vital to be prepared. In theory, if not in practice, the entire household needed to know what to do in case of fire. The more farseeing owner might also work out in advance a hierarchy of rescue—which paintings in the long gallery should be saved first, which volumes in the library must at all costs be kept away from the flames. But knowing exactly what to do in an emergency could make all the difference. After a fire at his son's house in 1884, the Marquess of Hertford had a list of "Precautions Against Fire" printed on cards which were hung at strategic points all round Ragley Hall in Warwickshire. As well as exhorting family and staff to be careful with matches and candles and to "mind that the wind does not blow a curtain over a gaslight or candle," the "Precautions" set out a sensible list of things to do if fire did break out at the Hall:

1. Don't be frightened, but think calmly and quickly what is best to be done, recollecting that time is everything, and that a man's cap or a jug of water, applied promptly, or a curtain pulled down and stamped upon vigorously, may save a serious fire.

2. If this is insufficient, run and get help, closing the doors and windows as you go, and fetch the nearest hand pump, or extinctor, and apply it immediately.

3. Maidservants cannot manage the hydrants or hose, but they can fill the fire buckets and cans, and pass them from one to another in line without confusion.

4. If in the night, ring the house-bell and call up everyone, sending at once to the bailiff, the head gardener, head carpenter, the odd man, gas man, &c.

5. A groom on horseback should be sent to those living in the village, and who should then go on for the engine and the police.

6. The gas man, assisted by the stablemen, to take the fire engine from the coach-house to the nearest point where there is water, and attach the hose, nozzle, &c.

7. The hydrants and hose in the mansion should be got ready, but not let go without necessity, for fear of doing damage by water as well as by fire.

8. The engines (at the lake) to be set at work, to keep the cisterns as full as possible.

9. The odd men will get ladders, and always have saws and axes and a long rope for hauling the hose up, &c. Ladders always to be kept in the same place (viz., near the old brewery) after use, so that all may know where to find them.

   MEM. If smoke is thick, cover your mouth and nose with a wet silk handkerchief, sponge, worsted stocking or flannel, and crawl on your knees. If your clothes catch fire, throw yourself down instantly on a rug, or thick shawl, or counterpane, and roll yourself in it.

Ragley was well prepared. The marquess held regular fire drills on the first Wednesday of each month, and there were two fire engines on the estate, the more modern of which was worked by six men and could throw a jet of water to a height of seventy feet. Hydraulic rams pumped water to the house from the lake half a mile away; this fed a system of rooftop tanks and underground reservoirs. There were fire hydrants on every floor, and plenty of buckets and hand pumps on the bedroom floors and next to the servants' bedrooms.

But when a fire *did* break out at the Hall, in February 1885, it had tragic consequences. One of the chimneys caught fire in the night, and, fearing that it would spread and destroy the house, the Ragley porter, an ex-guardsman named Robert Green, went up on the roof with his wife and some buckets of water to pour down the chimney. She lost her footing and fell, breaking her arm; as he tried to grab her, he slipped and went down, landing thirty feet below on a hard pavement. He died two weeks later.

The kind of printed instructions and regular fire drills advocated by the Marquess of Hertford were common practice at the time in many country houses. The jockey and trainer Tom Cannon, owner of Danebury in Hampshire, for example, also had printed placards around the mansion, reminding everyone where the nearest water supply was and how to operate Danebury's fire engine. He opted for quarterly drills, which were held "in the presence of one of Merryweather's instructors."[17]

The Merryweather in question was the same firm of Merryweather and Sons which sold pumps and rams to increase the efficiency of water supplies to country mansions. The Merryweathers were the leading manufacturers of steam-powered fire engines at the end of the century. James Compton Merryweather and his firm supplied engines to a stream of aristocratic clients: the Duke of Norfolk for Arundel Castle, the Marquess of Exeter for Burghley, the Earl of Rosebery for Mentmore Towers, the Earl of Pembroke for Wilton House, Lord Leconfield for Petworth, and "many other noblemen and gentlemen in England and abroad, especially in India, where many of the native princes have adopted these machines." Merryweather personally drilled the Prince of Wales in the use of the Sandringham machine, a "6-inch London Brigade Manual," as used by the Metropolitan Fire Brigade. Blenheim Palace had a Merryweather engine, and the estate fire brigade, consisting of house servants and gardeners, drilled once a month. The Duke of Marlborough also had a policeman patrolling the grounds of Blenheim every night, so that, in the words of the duke's clerk of works, "if anything should break out, he would give the alarm at once, and the men servants, who are thoroughly acquainted with fire brigade drill, could be at the spot directly, before any serious damage could be done."[18]

A mansion's fire brigade was also often brought into use elsewhere in rural communities which were unable or unwilling to maintain a brigade of their own. In 1904 the Duke of Grafton bought a Merry-weather double-cylinder steam fire engine, capable of delivering 350 gallons of water per minute. It was intended for the protection of his enormous Northamptonshire seat, Wakefield Lodge, and manned by his own private fire brigade, but it was also used to fight fires at other properties in the area. And there was sometimes an element of theatre about the arrival of a new engine. In 1911 Lord Burnham took possession of a powerful steam fire engine made by another firm, Shand, Mason and Company, for the protection of Hall Barn, his country house in Buckinghamshire. Burnham's daughter, Lady Hulse, led a demonstration of the engine's efficiency in the stable yard there in November 1908, "under the supervision of the Estate Fire Brigade Chief Officer, Mr Johnson."[19] In front of a gathering of houseguests she lit the fuel under the boiler; in five minutes and twenty seconds the pressure in the boiler had reached one hundred pounds; and with a flourish she opened the steam valve, and the audience watched in awe as a jet of water was thrown 150 feet into the air.

While grand country house owners like the Duke of Marlborough and the Duke of Grafton maintained their own steam-powered, horse-drawn fire engines and trained their estate workers and servants to act as their own private fire brigade, others relied on more ad hoc arrangements. Swift and early action made all the difference: for country houses fitted with electricity, Merryweather recommended Bright's self-acting electric fire detector, a small device about an inch long which sensed a raised temperature in the room where it was installed, triggered an electric alarm bell fitted elsewhere in the house, and indicated on a board which room was threatened.

Having water to hand was, of course, essential. If there was a lake or pond nearby, the owner needed to make sure that the hoses were long enough to reach. Indoor hydrants were also recommended, gravity-fed from a tank on the roof. "The higher the tank, the better the stream of water . . . so a man who builds a high tower to his house to hold a tank is not to be looked on as a wasteful lunatic." One- or two-man hand pumps were invaluable: a good one-man pump could hold thirty gallons of water and squirt it a distance of thirty feet. Leather buckets should be kept filled and close by these pumps. Leather hoses were also preferred for use indoors, "for canvas always leaks, and spoils floors and carpets." Grenades were also popular for tackling small indoor fires around the turn of the century. These were glass globes filled with salt water (which wouldn't freeze), or a chemical liquid such as carbon tetrachloride, or a fire-retardant powder. They were hurled at the base of a fire, shattering and, one hoped, putting out the fire before it could take hold. One evening in June 1908, decorators were burning off paint on the drawing room window at White Hall near Buxton, the moorland mansion of a local JP, when they accidentally set fire to the curtains. The fire quickly spread, destroying furniture, paintings, and tapestry, but it was contained by the use of grenades. "At one time the place looked doomed," reported the *Manchester Courier*, "but the grenades, of which there was a plentiful supply, acted effectively."[20]

If the worse came to the worst and members of the household found themselves trapped on an upper floor, a little foresight could provide a means of escape. Canvas chutes with iron frames that fitted over a windowsill, rope-and-pulley systems with safety belts, and simple rope ladders were all in use. Less common was the fire escape on wheels, a system of telescoping ladders which could be manoeuvred into place by those below. "The cost of these machines is only about £50," said Merryweather.[21]

For the lucky few, there were supernatural interventions. Rev. F. H. Hawkins, vicar of Guilsfield in Montgomeryshire, told the local newspaper that several hours before fire broke out in the cellars at Garth, a nearby Gothic Revival mansion, his invalid mother-in-law woke him to say she could hear sounds of a fire engine. Was the vicarage on fire? "A remarkable story of pre-vision, or second-sight," declared the newspaper; although since Mr Hawkins didn't pay any attention to the old lady at the time, its usefulness as an early warning system seems to have been rather limited.[22]

FIFTEEN

MARVELS OF LOCOMOTION

In 1876, QUEEN Victoria was able to travel from Windsor to Baden-Baden in two days—a feat that would have seemed impossible to her Georgian uncles. Having left Windsor at 3:40 p.m., she and her retinue arrived at Portsmouth in the pouring rain at 7:00 and immediately boarded the royal steam yacht *Victoria and Albert*, where the queen dined in the saloon. Beatrice (as usual) played the piano after dinner. (It was a big yacht—2,430 tons and 360 feet long. There was plenty of room for a piano.) The *Victoria and Albert* remained at anchor overnight, getting underway after breakfast and reaching Cherbourg at 2:45 that afternoon. The party was met by the British consul, and three hours later the queen, Princess Beatrice, and two female courtiers went ashore by barge and were conducted straight to the special train that was waiting to take them on the next stage of their journey. Victoria was impressed by the "very comfortable" Brussels-built carriages, which contained "a sitting saloon, with compartment for attendants adjoining it, a little dressing room and bedroom, with compartment for maid adjoining the latter, all very prettily fitted up."[1]

The train meandered through the French countryside overnight and reaching Commercy in northeast France just before 9:00 a.m., where they stopped for coffee and breakfast. "Everything looked so strange and foreign," wrote the queen, in the best tradition of the Briton abroad, "picturesque and rather primitive."[2] They crossed the border into Germany later that morning and, after a cold lunch served in the train, the royal party arrived at Baden-Baden at 3:30 in the afternoon. The journey from Windsor to the Villa Hohenlohe had taken them forty-eight hours. That's a distance of seven hundred miles as the crow flies.

The world was getting smaller. Steamships were crossing the Atlantic in less than a week and the Channel in just over an hour. By the end of the century, an express train was leaving Charing Cross station three times a day, depositing its passengers in Paris between seven and a half and ten hours later. It wasn't cheap: a first-class return ticket cost £4 14s 9d, which is getting on for £500 in today's money. But it was a transport revolution. Engineer George Stephenson famously drove the first locomotive on the newly opened Stockton and Darlington line in 1825, pulling thirty-four coaches at a speed of twelve miles an hour. Three-quarters of a century later, there were 21,659 miles of track open in the United Kingdom and 18,616 locomotives operating on it, more than three engines for every four miles of track. The Duke of Devonshire's weekend houseguests could board a train at Rowsley station, less than four miles from Chatsworth, at 8:40 on a Monday morning and pull into London St Pancras at 1:35 that afternoon, in time for a late lunch—a journey of more than 150 miles that would have taken their grandparents several days. It is no exaggeration to say that without the railway there would have been no country house weekend.

For those country house owners who had influence and a line running through or close to their land but no railway station handy, there was always the private halt. Earl Fitzwilliam had a private station at Elsecar in Yorkshire from 1870, intended for guests to Wentworth Woodhouse. Seaham Dene railway station in County Durham belonged to the Marquess of Londonderry: built in 1875, it served Seaham Hall, one of a string of country houses owned by the Londonderrys, who had the right "to stop other than express trains within reasonable limits."[3] Ox House station in Herefordshire was another country house station, serving Shobdon Court, the seat of William Bateman-Hanbury, 2nd Lord Bateman.

Bateman was the chairman of the Leominster and Kington Railway, which no doubt helped. And the Marquess of Londonderry was a major investor in the Londonderry, Seaham and Sunderland Railway. The 3rd Duke of Sutherland went one better: in 1870 he built his own line in the Highlands, the Duke of Sutherland's Railway, which ran along the coast between West Helmsdale and Golspie, with a request stop at Dunrobin Castle, his majestic seat overlooking the Moray Firth.

Almeric FitzRoy recalled a grouse shoot at Bransdale, his uncle's Yorkshire shooting lodge, in 1890. A mineral railway skirted the moor, and "at the end of each drive we piled arms on a trolley and, with our loaders, were carried down by gravitation to the point of debarkation, sometimes at break-neck speed round sharp curves—altogether a most exciting episode in the day's amusement."[4]

In 1895 the German-born engineer Frederick Simms wrote to the *Saturday Review* with an account of a journey he had made on a sunny July day with his friend the inventor Evelyn Ellis in Ellis's new motorcar, a Panhard et Levassor. They set off from Micheldever railway station in Hampshire at 9:26 a.m., the car having been brought up from

Southampton by train, and they reached Rosenau, Ellis's villa on the Thames near Windsor, at 5:40 in the afternoon, a distance of fifty-six miles. In every village they passed through, people turned out to stare at this "new marvel of locomotion," tearing along at speeds of up to twelve miles per hour. The departure of coaches was delayed so that passengers could catch a glimpse of the pair in their horseless carriage, and cyclists stopped to gaze enviously as they took some long gradient with ease. The journey was, claimed Simms, "the first ever made by a petroleum motor carriage in this country."[5]

At the end of 1895 there were fourteen or fifteen cars on Britain's roads, but over the next fifteen years there was an explosion in car ownership: between 700 and 800 in 1900; 16,000 in 1904; over 150,000 by 1912. The so-called Red Flag Act, which had been brought in 1865 amid concerns for the safety of steam carriages and traction engines and which set a speed limit of four miles per hour and required a person with a red flag to walk at least sixty yards in front of a self-propelled vehicle, was superseded in 1896 by the Locomotives on Highways Act, which set a speed limit of twelve miles per hour and did away with the requirement for the red flag. "Slowly and surely the cult of auto-mobilism is gaining ground," declared *Country Life* in 1899. "The number of self-propelled vehicles one sees upon the road is increasing almost daily, and it is not unsafe to prophesy that before next summer has come round the auto-motor, in one form or another, will be a regular feature of our highways."[6]

Royal patronage did the motorcar no harm, although it certainly didn't come from the queen herself, who said to the Duke of Portland, her master of horse, "I hope you will never allow any of those horrible machines to be used in my stables. I am told that they smell exceedingly nasty, and are very shaky and disagreeable conveyances altogether." Evelyn Ellis gave her son, the Prince of Wales, his first ride at the 1896 Motor Car Club's exhibition in London: when they reached a speed of nine miles per hour Bertie is reputed to have cried out,

"Don't drive so fast. I'm frightened!" But he soon got over his fears, and in 1900 he acquired a Daimler Tonneau, the first car to be owned by a member of the royal family. He proved to be a great enthusiast for motoring: on the occasion of a royal visit to County Durham, the huge doors of the great hall at Raby Castle were thrown open so that he could be driven right into the house—a privilege that was granted to no one else, "for fear lest oil should drop on to the flags."[7]

Within a few years Edward VII had two big Mercedes and a Daimler, all painted a rich claret colour and trimmed with soft blue morocco leather, and all carrying the royal arms on their door panels and rear. The king also owned a smaller Renault with a folding canopy over the passenger seats in the rear—a convertible, in effect. During a visit to Germany, he saw that his cousin Kaiser Wilhelm II had a motor horn in the form of a bugle and decided he wanted one, too. His mechanic found something similar, and Bertie, having been taught to play some tunes by the conductor Herr Gottlieb, took to carrying it on his knees as he sat beside the chauffeur. Staff at the various royal residences came to recognise its distinctive tone and threw open the gates to Buckingham Palace or Balmoral when they heard its sound. Motorists—if they were wise—pulled over when they heard it blown behind them.[8]

By the early years of the twentieth century, the motorcar had gone from an adventure to an accepted mode of transport. When the Digbys held a party in the summer of 1908 to celebrate the completion of their new house, Minterne in Dorset, Lady Digby noted that about three hundred people turned up, "and my brother counted fifty-eight motors." The car had also secured a prominent place in popular culture. Tunes with titles like "A Motor Car Marriage" and "The Motor Car Polka" were performed on the stage and in the drawing room. Methuen published "a new Motoring Romance" by C. N. and A. M. Williamson, *My Friend the Chauffeur* (with eleven illustrations). "There is no more delightful mode of seeing England than driving through it on [*sic*] a motor-car," declared the *Daily Telegraph*'s "Lady Jeune."[9]

But not everyone was so enthusiastic. Coachmen, cyclists, and pedestrians all regarded the motor scorcher, or "morcher," as the enemy, driving recklessly at high speeds around country lanes, causing horses to bolt and unwary villagers to dive into ditches, running down dogs and small children. "Nothing has been so bad for the country . . . as the introduction of the motor car," said T. W. H. Crosland in his 1907 satire *The Country Life*. "If you watch [motorists] seated in fours and fives in their horrible cars, and note their smug appearance, and their utter want of interest in anything but speed, you are apt to wonder why it is that they are not taken forthwith to the nearest lunatic asylum."[10]

Women as well as men took to the roads. The *Bystander* for January 27, 1904, carried a picture of Baroness Campbell von Laurentz perched at the wheel of her six-horsepower Gardner-Serpollet and described her as "one of the first women to take up motoring in this country." Five years later the gossip columnists were noting that there were "a considerable number of ladies who drive their own cars whenever they get an opportunity." Lady Angela Forbes, half sister to Daisy Warwick, could often be seen at the wheel of Daisy's little two-seater Delage. Daisy's previous car had been wrecked in an accident which, oddly enough, had a supernatural side to it. The journalist W. T. Stead, who was friendly with Daisy, was fascinated with spiritualism, and when "a friend long since passed over" told him through spirit writing that the countess must not get into a motorcar for a week, he wrote to warn her. Unfortunately, the letter didn't arrive in time. She went for a drive; her car crashed; and she was lucky to escape unharmed.[11]

Reports of motoring accidents began to fill the columns of local newspapers, although in truth, some were more newsworthy than others. "Lord Aberdare's Car Skids" was the headline in the *South Wales Daily News* in October 1907, over an article which recounted how Lord Aberdare's car had skidded in Chepstow. That was about it. "His Lordship, except for a blow on the leg, escaped injury."[12]

A surprising number of noblemen seem to have been involved in motoring accidents in the early years of the twentieth century, an indication that car ownership in its early days tended to be confined to the wealthy. The Marquess of Downshire was summonsed to appear in Dublin Police Court in 1903 after knocking down and fatally injuring an old lady in Dublin's Lower Dorset Street; after thinking it over, the Crown authorities decided it was an accident and dropped the charge. In 1905 Lord Rosebery was on his way to catch a train in Leopold de Rothschild's car when Rothschild's chauffeur ran over and killed a young waitress. The jury recorded a verdict of accidental death, and the press reported that "in addition to paying all funeral expenses, Lord Rosebery and Mr Rothschild have bestowed a handsome gift upon the parents of the deceased girl."[13]

The Marquess of Exeter had a lucky escape in 1900 when he was thrown out of a car he was driving near Burleigh: "Somehow, when travelling at a good speed, the car got onto the roadside and was overturned."[14] He was uninjured apart from a few cuts and bruises, as was Lord Sefton, when he was thrown out of his car near Nantwich in 1904; and Lord Roberts, when his car ran into some railings and lost a wheel in 1905; and Lord Dalmeny, whose chauffeur dropped him off at a restaurant in the Strand in 1906 and then crashed into a shopfront, drunk; and Lord Curzon of Kedleston, when his car was in collision with another near Sunningdale in 1908; and Lord Lonsdale, who overturned his car on his way to his seat, Lowther Castle, in 1909. (In 1902, Kaiser Wilhelm presented Lonsdale with a Mercedes to commemorate his visit to Lowther. Lonsdale returned it to Berlin to have the chrome fittings replaced with silver.)

Lord Curzon's accident left him unconscious. When he came to, he found himself in a small room with a doctor sponging his face. The doctor dashed out of the room, returning after a while to apologise—when Curzon was brought into the house, which belonged to a local barber named Corns, he was already there attending to Mrs Corns, who was in the middle of giving birth. A little later the barber came in, said that his wife had presented him with a baby boy, and asked if his lordship would consent to be the child's godfather. The former viceroy of India agreed, and in due course the baby was christened George Nathaniel Curzon Corns.

The christening was the only lasting consequence of Curzon's accident. The 5th Earl of Carnarvon wasn't so lucky. A keen early adopter, with a fleet of cars in the stables at Highclere Castle and several convictions for speeding to his name, "Motor Car-narvon," as the press nicknamed him, nearly died in August 1909 on his way to Bad Schwalbach in Germany when he swerved to avoid two bullock carts. The Belgian Métallurgique he was driving overturned, trapping him underneath. A few days later Jack Russell, 25th Baron de Clifford, came to a tragic end. One afternoon at the beginning of September 1909 the young peer—twenty-four years old, with a baby son and a Gibson Girl wife—was driving to his Sussex country house with his chauffeur in the passenger seat when he had to brake hard to avoid two market vans coming towards him on the narrow lane. His car overturned, he and the chauffeur were both thrown out, and a projecting lamp bracket crushed his head and killed him. The chauffeur was shaken but otherwise unhurt.

Prosecutions for reckless driving mounted, and irate rural magistrates dished out heavy fines for exceeding the speed limit while secretly wishing they could still sentence culprits to a good flogging. In 1905 Lord Willoughby de Broke (master of the Warwickshire hounds) presided over a meeting in Warwick to form the Warwickshire Highways Protection League. It was carried, and local farmers supporting the motion were careful to say that if only everyone drove as carefully as the nobility there would be no need for the league. In 1907 Sudbury Hall's Lord Vernon was charged with driving his motorcar through the crowded streets of Stockport at a speed of nearly forty miles per hour. He said he wasn't going more than twenty; the magistrates said he was, and he was fined ten pounds plus costs.

What was referred to everywhere as "the motor problem" caused heated debates in bars and drawing rooms, in the House of Commons, and in the correspondence columns of the *Times*. Should the speed limit be raised or lowered? Should training for drivers be made compulsory? Should penalties for reckless driving be increased? In Parliament, feelings ran high and at times language was quite unparliamentary. In a June 1903 debate, for example, Cathcart Wason, the member for Orkney and Shetland, having declared proudly that there was not a single motorcar in the whole of his constituency, lamented the fact that "harmless men, women, and children, dogs, and cattle had all got to fly for their lives at the bidding of one of these slaughtering, stinking engines of iniquity." The House cheered. George Harwood, MP for Bolton, agreed with him that something must be done: car after car was racing along the same roads, "palpitating, throbbing, and turning the whole of the thoroughfare into chaos and confusion," he said—and again, there were cheers. "The time had come when the rich ought to be pulled up in this matter."[15]

Car owners leaped to the car's defence. Leopold de Rothschild wrote to the *Times* to say "I cannot help thinking that it would be a great mistake to allow this feeling of irritation to increase, because, in my opinion, motors have come to stay, and they are not merely, as alleged, rich men's toys." And of course Rothschild was right (although that didn't stop the irritation). By the time of the 1911 census, 23,151 people (mainly men but including a handful of women) described their occupation as domestic motorcar drivers and/or attendants, while 95,015 motorcar licences were issued during the year ending March 31, 1911.[16] Chauffeur-mechanics could command high wages—as much as four pounds a week if they combined driving skills with practical knowledge of how to repair a motor. Advertisements appeared in the columns of the *Times* offering the services of chauffeur-grooms, chauffeur-valets, chauffeur-coachmen:

Chauffeur-coachman, Dietrich Panhard. Certificated; running repairs. Thorough stableman. Age 27. Careful driver. Abstainer.[17]

Chauffeur-valet. Certificated for driving and running repairs. Single. Country preferred.[18]

Chauffeur. Thoroughly experienced gentleman, age 29, wishes to find a situation with nobleman or gentleman, thoroughly experienced in driving and engineering, knows town and country thoroughly. Highest references and abstainer.[19]

By 1904, *Country Life* was declaring that "the motor-car has won for itself a position as an almost indispensable adjunct of the country house," and Edwin Lutyens was designing elaborate Arts and Crafts garages to house it. Or rather, "them": his most interesting design was for a double garage with solid oaken doors, a steep tiled roof, and twin inspection pits—vital at a time in the history of the automobile when maintenance and repairs were almost daily requirements. Lighting was always a problem in motor houses which weren't equipped with electricity, since gas or oil lamps and petrol in a confined space invited disaster. ("Servants are notoriously careless, and a leaking petrol pipe and a lighted match thrown on the ground is a not improbable combination of circumstances.")[20] One solution was to supply the new motor house with glazed alcoves for oil lamps. Another, favoured by Lutyens but obviously not practical for every owner, was to build on steeply sloping ground, so that inspection pits could be lit by windows.

In practice, purpose-built motor houses were relatively rare as adjuncts to the country house, perhaps because it was easy enough to adapt existing coach houses. But there were some interesting examples. At Highclere Castle, "Motor Car-narvon" stabled his cars in old carriage houses in the courtyard, but he also built garages with a mechanic's pit and a separate garage with a petrol pump and a water supply for washing his cars and those of his houseguests. The 9th Duke of Beaufort had a motor house at Badminton by 1905, when it was photographed for an article in the *Motorist and Traveller*, which noted that it held two cars "and has a floor and pit covered in zinc . . . while hot water pipes keep the temperature right."[21] Edward VII commissioned a huge motor house for Sandringham from Thompsons of Peterborough in 1902; it had compartments for eight cars, a cleaning shed enclosed by revolving shutters, and living quarters above. In contrast, royal cars at Windsor Castle were kept in a converted coach house, while the garage at Buckingham Palace was just a roof slung between two existing buildings.

One of the most impressive examples was the range of motor stables built circa 1901–1902 at Broomhill in Kent, the home of motoring pioneer Sir David Salomons. Salomons, who organised the first motor show in Britain, which took place in October 1895 at the Tunbridge Wells agricultural showground, already had a two-car motor house at Broomhill by 1900, but it was little more than a shed. Within a couple of years, it had been swept away and replaced with a five-car motor stable with doors of varying heights to accommodate different sizes of vehicles and a basement which gave access to the inspection pits, a forge, a mechanics' dressing room, and a lavatory. Four of the garages, which were lit by electricity, were fitted with lifting gear. In 1909 the *Motor* described the building (which survives today and is Grade II listed), doubting "whether any other private garage is so exquisitely arranged."[22]

By 1914 motor houses were common features of the country house. They came in all shapes and sizes, from simple sheds to the gabled and barge-boarded garage added onto the stables at Daisy

Warwick's Easton Lodge in 1902 and the pantiled, weatherboarded two-storey block designed by Philip Webb's assistant, George Jack, at Rounton Grange in Yorkshire in 1904 and extended by Jack nine years later. At Beechwood Park in Hertfordshire the chapel was converted into a motor house in 1905 by Beechwood's owner, Sir Edgar Sebright, who had let the house and who, desperate to hang on to his tenant, was responding to that tenant's demands for somewhere to house his motor cars.

Newly built country houses almost always came with garaging by the early years of the twentieth century. Lutyens and Ernest George both designed country house motor stables—Lutyens at Grey Walls in East Lothian, where after the house was finished he was called back to add one, and George at Crathorne Hall in Yorkshire. Too often, though, the design of such utilitarian buildings was given to local builders, perhaps in collaboration with a motor-mad, if not aesthetically inclined, owner (or his motor-mad children).

The 6th Duke of Portland was a keen motorist. His first car, bought in September 1901, was an open Arrol-Johnston with tiller steering and large-diameter wooden wheels with solid tyres. His agent, J. Harling Turner, accompanied the car with two drivers from the factory at Paisley where it was built to Langwell, the duke's shooting estate in the Scottish Highlands, covering a distance of 296 miles in three days. They didn't see another motor vehicle the whole time. It was appallingly uncomfortable: whoever sat in front received the full force of the weather, while "the jolting one received over those roads is indescribable," recalled the duke. "It was more like the motion required to churn milk into cheese."[23]

That didn't deter him. He soon bought another equally uncomfortable Arrol-Johnston, this time a six-seater, and then a Lanchester, which at least came with a hood, although the driver's seat was directly on top of the engine, which could make for a rather hot journey. In 1902 he held motorcar races at Welbeck Abbey, straightening a stretch of road through the park specially for speed trials; the General Challenge Cup was won by a Panhard driven by Hon. C. S. Rolls, who two years later moved on to making and selling his own cars with his business partner, Henry Royce. In May 1905, Portland hosted the first provincial meeting of the Motor Union of Great Britain and Ireland at Welbeck.*

And although he didn't know it when he took possession of that first Arrol-Johnston and bounced along on those rough Highland tracks, looking back, the duke realised that "this very primitive motor car would entirely change our outlook on life." Now it would be possible actually to visit places and hills in the Highlands that before he had only gazed at through his telescope. He could drive to give a speech at some civic event and be home in time for dinner.

By 1914, Portland's experience with the motorcar was mirrored in country houses all over Britain. To be sure, motoring was still something of a gamble: socialite Cynthia Asquith, remembering life at Stanway as a teenager and trips to nearby Cheltenham, reckoned that "on an average we usually broke down six times in our ten-mile journey." But in spite of its unreliability, the car was a liberating force. Cynthia's mother, Lady Elcho, was "delighted by the extended radius brought about by motor cars," she said. The twelve miles between Stanway and Tewkesbury Abbey had once meant that a visit was quite a pilgrimage; now it was only a short drive. "We could easily go to admire the beautiful village of Bibury or the famous stained-glass

---

* Before the motorists set off from Nottingham to Welbeck the mayor of Nottingham addressed them, welcoming them to the city and then suggesting that "the motorist, the auto-driver, and the auto-cyclist were among the terrors of the road at the present time." Replying, the president of the union, Conservative politician Arthur Stanley, thanked him for the cordiality of the welcome. *Nottingham Evening Post*, May 20, 1905, 4.

windows in Fairford Church," said Cynthia, "and Stratford-on-Avon with its Memorial Theatre . . . was within easy reach."[24]

If the train had made the country house weekend possible, the car made entertaining and being entertained so much easier. A country house owner could visit neighbours twenty, thirty, forty miles away and still sleep in his or her own bed. Car-owning houseguests could come and go as they pleased, without having to give grooms and stable hands plenty of notice. Those who arrived by train were collected in shooting brakes and driven to their destination while a luggage van came along behind. If there was a shoot, the guns and their loaders might travel to it by car while their lunch came along in a van or shooting brake.

And if their host was bored with their company (or vice versa), he could pack them off for a tour of local churches or beauty spots for the afternoon, confident that they were happy with a chauffeur-mechanic and a picnic hamper as he waved them goodbye and returned to solitary pleasures in his library with, perhaps, a little sigh of relief.

SIXTEEN

ENTERTAINING ROYALLY

I N August 1872, news began to spread that the Prince and Princess of Wales planned to visit Chatsworth that autumn as guests of the 7th Duke of Devonshire. The duke was a widower—his wife had been dead for thirty-two years—but his married daughter, Lady Louisa Egerton, acted as his hostess, and house parties at Chatsworth and the duke's other country houses were common enough. Some of the most powerful aristocratic landowners in the country enjoyed Devonshire's hospitality.

But a visit from a royal houseguest changed the game dramatically. The four-night visit was scheduled to begin on Tuesday, December 17, and the duke's daughter-in-law, Lady Frederick Cavendish, arrived at Chatsworth on the Saturday before to find everyone in a frenzy of preparation.

The house is getting into order by dint of much marching about it of heads and hands: all is being pondered and prearranged in true deliberate Cavendish style; and I quite expect that when once the whole machine is given a shove on Tuesday off it will go, everything in its proper place, from the duke to the scullery-maid.[1]

The royal couple duly arrived at Rowsley station after dark on Tuesday evening, having spent the afternoon in Derby, where the prince presented the prizes at Derby Grammar School's speech day, visited the new infirmary in the town, and received loyal addresses from local councillors, Freemasons (the prince was a Mason), and the school and infirmary. Their arrival at Derby station had been announced by a fanfare from trumpeters wearing a "quaintly rich heraldic tabard," and their every step was accompanied by cheering, flag-waving crowds. At Rowsley the reception was more muted, but as the line of carriages entered the park at Chatsworth, where crowds of spectators had gathered in the twilight to see the royal party, a rocket went off and hundreds of Bengal lights illuminated the house, the cascade, the Emperor Fountain, and the surrounding woods and gardens. A twenty-one-gun salute could be heard in Buxton, fifteen miles away across the Derbyshire moors. Lady Frederick, who had a habit of finding the cloud in every silver lining, said that the hall, where everyone was waiting to receive the couple, "was unluckily as full of sulphur as it might be after a siege from the fireworks, and set us coughing." That evening there was a select dinner party for the forty-two houseguests, including two dukes, four earls, and five countesses. Dinner was followed by whist and music.[2]

The next day, Wednesday, the prince managed to get in a day's shooting, although the weather was poor and there was snow on the ground. A few of the women joined the shooting party for lunch: "All the *drinks* were forgotten and had to be fetched, and we were presented with sugar instead of salt for our pie," wrote Lady Frederick in her diary.[3] That evening the duke laid on a grand ball for four hundred of the Derbyshire gentry. ("Rather ponderous and oppressive . . . trying to the family and scrowgy [*sic*] for the royal pair.") The Chesterfield Volunteer Band serenaded the dinner guests, while for the ball itself the music was provided by Coote and Tinney's Band, a regular at royal functions—they had played at the 1870 Sandringham ball. A special train brought guests from Derby to Rowsley in sixteen saloon cars, and several hundred carriages took them through the park to the house itself.

It was a late night. Dancing was meant to begin at eleven, but the special train was late and many of the guests didn't arrive until 11:30. And although crowds had gathered in the park again to see another fireworks display, put on by Mr F. C. Copley, a pyrotechnist from Sheffield, and although it culminated in the simultaneous discharge of five hundred rockets and thirteen bombshells filled with golden rain, that wasn't enough for the spectators, who had been hoping for more and who, according to local press reports, "turned their faces homewards at last disappointed and cold."[4] Lady Frederick put it down to the fog, which crept through the park and around the gardens.

But at the ball itself, Job Jelf, the Devonshires' house steward, who was responsible for the arrangements, didn't have any reason to reproach either himself or the waiters, all in their yellow-and-silver court livery. The prince and princess led off the dancing in the state dining room, which had been decked out as a ballroom for the occasion. The duke's heir, the Marquess of Hartington, took out the princess, and the prince danced with Lady Frederick. When the royal couple went in for supper in the sculpture gallery at 12:30, the other guests formed lines of honour to watch them pass. When the signal was given that they were about to return to the ballroom, the music stopped and the company formed into two lines as before. At one point, as the princess waltzed with Earl Granville and the prince partnered one of the Misses Howard of Glossop, everyone else briefly left the floor, leaving them to put on an exhibition by themselves.

The prince and princess were allowed to relax a little the next day, but there was another big dinner for forty-odd that evening, and more dancing. On Friday, undaunted by fog and rain, thirty members of the house party set off in carriages for an excursion to Haddon Hall, one of the seats of the Duke of Rutland. The five-mile journey took them through the little village of Pilsley, where a triumphal arch swathed in flags and evergreens had been erected over the road, and into Bakewell, where, as they drove past the Union Workhouse, the children broke into song with "God Bless the Prince of Wales." ("Bakewell very enthusiastic and a little drunk," noted Lady Frederick.)[5] The cavalcade moved on through another arch, this one bearing the inscriptions "Welcome the Prince and Princess of Wales" and "Long Life to the Prince and Princess of Wales," and from there on the road was decked with flags, banners, mottoes, and smaller arches. There was a crowd in the town centre with more singing children, and as the party drove out they passed under yet another arch, this one decorated with a boar's head and a peacock, references to the coat of arms of the Dukes of Rutland.

The Rutlands' main country seat was at Belvoir Castle in Leicestershire, and medieval Haddon, one of the most romantic and picturesque of all country houses, was only rarely used by the family, although it was open to the public. (By 1906 the Rutlands were charging fourpence admission and "a fee of sixpence [was] required from users of hand cameras, and one shilling from those who [had] stand cameras.") When the party drove into the courtyard they were greeted by the duke, who was a member of the Chatsworth house party but who had gone ahead to make sure everything was ready at the hall. It was, and "after curiously examining the quaint old place" everyone settled down to lunch in the great hall, seated "in some of the fine old carved oak chairs that are considered part of the gems of Haddon" while the Buxton Pavilion Band performed a selection of appropriate pieces in the minstrel gallery above. Silver plate had been brought over from Belvoir, and, in another reference to the Rutland coat of arms, the main dish was a boar's head and the second a peacock pie.[6]

Back at Chatsworth that night, the atmosphere was much more relaxed. There were games and music. The princess completely won over Lady Frederick, who called her "our Queen of Hearts" and watched entranced as she "whisked round the billiard-table like any dragon-fly, playing at pockets. . . . Likewise at bed-time, high jinks with all the ladies in the corridors; and yet through all one has a sense of perfect womanly dignity. . . . O, bless her for a vision of enchantment!" The prince she was less enthusiastic about, calling him "fat" and announcing that "he does not get on with me, nor indeed much with any but chaffy, fast people."[7]

Then it was all over. On Saturday the duke accompanied the royal couple to Chesterfield for more speeches, more cheers, more loyal addresses before they boarded a special train back to London.* Back at Chatsworth everyone was exhausted. "We were all a little comatose," wrote Lady Frederick, "and Lou[isa Egerton] vanished to bed at 9 o'clock."[8]

National and local newspapers carried blow-by-blow accounts of the shooting party, the dinners, the seating arrangements, the ball, the decorations, the fireworks, the visit to Haddon Hall. Speeches

---

* The party continued at Chesterfield long after the couple left. That evening the local wine merchant projected a magic lantern show onto sheets hung up outside his shop, with portraits of members of the royal family, views of Sandringham and other royal residences, "and subsequently a number of comic views which created great mirth." *Derbyshire Courier*, December 28, 1872, 2. The night ended with a fireworks display by the ubiquitous Mr Copley, the pyrotechnist.

were reproduced word for word. Readers were offered potted histories of Chatsworth and Haddon. Reporters raved over the princess's ball gown, "a flood of rich lace of creamy white, looped up with cherries, over a robe of black satin, a few red roses in her hair . . ."[9]

And the same newspapers that described the royal visit to Chatsworth in such minute detail also carried another, briefer item. "The Prince of Wales intends to honour Sir Anthony de Rothschild with a visit at his seat at Aston Clinton, Bucks., on the 7th of January. Great preparations are being made . . ."[10]

The Prince of Wales often stayed at Chatsworth, with and without his wife. In 1901, for example, he was there without the princess, although his current mistress, Alice Keppel, was also a houseguest, which may explain Alix's absence. As king, Bertie went for the shooting every year between 1904 and 1907, when the 8th Duke of Devonshire's ill health and subsequent death brought the visits to an end. But he was a guest at dozens, perhaps hundreds of country houses between 1870 and his own death in 1910. A glance through court circulars and society pages shows him at Welbeck with the Duke of Portland, at Lambton Castle in County Durham with the Earl of Durham, with Lord Sefton at Croxteth Hall near Liverpool, and a guest of the Jewish financier Baron Hirsch at his recently acquired Norfolk country house, Wretham Hall near Thetford. He was an inveterate houseguest, much more dedicated than his mother or other members of the royal household, who seem to have preferred to spend their leisure time in their own houses.

There was rarely anything spontaneous about a royal visit. Entertaining royalty was bound by rules and rituals. The first intimation a hostess had that she was about to receive, say, Edward VII as a houseguest was when one of his private secretaries wrote to her to say that the king was minded to do them the honour of visiting for the weekend, or for a week's shooting, or perhaps in connection with some civic event that he was due to attend in the neighbourhood. The hostess would then submit a list of the other guests she hoped to invite, and the king instructed his secretary to cross off any who bored him or who were out of favour. And also to add the names of any who were *in* favour: it was a careless hostess who failed to include his current mistress. Daisy Warwick, who fulfilled that role with enthusiasm for some years while Edward VII was still Prince of Wales, was invariably on the list, as was her husband Francis, who had, she wrote later, "an understanding nature."[11]

In some houses, formal etiquette was observed at dinner. The king and queen (if they were both present, which wasn't often) would only come into the drawing room when all the other guests had assembled. Then the host set off for the dining room with the queen and the hostess with the king, who would already have let it be known which woman he wanted on his other hand at the table. No one spoke to royalty unless they were spoken to, and if the king was in a morose mood, that didn't make for scintillating dinner table conversation. After the meal, nobody left until the king and queen had retired, and nobody sat down if the king or the queen were standing up.

But the rules were not always observed. When Bertie and Alix entertained at Sandringham, they welcomed their guests on arrival in the hall and personally saw them off. Conversation at table was general and, as Daisy wrote, "the whole atmosphere [was] that of a gathering of friends." "Yes," said one courtier, "His Royal Highness is always ready to forget his rank—as long as everyone else remembers it."[12]

Those who played host to royalty found the honour expensive; Bertie's 1872 visit to Chatsworth must have cost the Duke of Devonshire thousands of pounds. They, or at least their agents, also had the problem of liaising with civic dignitaries and railway companies—and the local police. The protection of members of the royal family was the responsibility of the Special Branch, which had been formed in 1883 as the Special Irish Branch of the Metropolitan Police in response to a Fenian bombing campaign in London. It was made permanent at the end of 1886, when there were rumours of plots in connection with Queen Victoria's Golden Jubilee. (One or two of those rumours were well founded: for example, there was a plan to set off some dynamite in Westminster Abbey during the jubilee service.) By the beginning of the twentieth century, it was customary for members of the royal family to have at least two Special Branch detectives in tow when they went to Sandringham or Balmoral or Cowes, or when they went to the races or to the theatre. Edward VII had a travelling staff of half a dozen officers who accompanied him wherever he went in the United Kingdom but who were based at Buckingham Palace, under Chief Superintendent Percival Spencer, who had been Bertie's chief of security at Marlborough House when he was Prince of Wales. As well as ensuring that the king was adequately protected at all times by his team of detectives, Spencer, who had an office on Buckingham Palace Road and lodgings in Windsor Castle, was responsible for liaising with the king's private secretary regarding his travel arrangements, for establishing the safest route for his carriage or his motor—and for returning any speeding tickets which might have been issued to the king. (He didn't pay them, on principle.)

Queen Victoria survived no fewer than eight assassination attempts during her reign, including one incident in 1850 when a lunatic walked up to her in Piccadilly and hit her over the head with a cane. Bertie suffered only one, but it was a close call: as he and Alix were sitting on a train pulling out of Brussels-Nord station in April 1900, a fifteen-year-old anarchist, Jean-Baptiste Sipido, jumped on the carriage step and fired two shots at him from a distance of six feet, narrowly missing his target's head before he was wrestled to the ground by station staff. "If he had not been so bad a shot, I don't see how he could possibly have missed me," Edward told Daisy Warwick a few days later.[13]

In the years immediately before the First World War, it was the threat of suffragette protests rather than anarchists that gave the most cause for concern. When the prime minister, H. H. Asquith, was staying at Lympne Castle in Kent in 1909, suffragettes threw a brick at him through the dining room window. It missed, but it broke a dinner plate and, recalled Asquith's son, "scattered a lady's dress with a copious fountain of soup, and bounced off the table to the other side of the room." And George V and Queen Mary were the targets of several suffragette demonstrations. On one occasion, while they were attending a charity performance at His Majesty's Theatre in the Haymarket, the show was brought to a halt when several women in the audience jumped up and shouted in chorus, "Why don't Your Majesties stop the brutal treatment of women suffragists?" As they were being dragged away, an earnest young man tried to enter the royal box with a wad of leaflets, but he found his way blocked by Herbert Fitch, the Special Branch detective assigned to protection duty that evening, and promptly gave up his task. Fitch reflected that "a woman would never have abandoned the attempt as meekly as he had done."[14]

Fitch was also present at one of the more touching suffragette demonstrations, in the throne room at Buckingham Palace during a presentation. As the dignitaries and debutantes filed past the king and queen, bowing or curtseying as court etiquette required, suddenly a woman dropped to her knees in front of them and cried, "Oh, Your Majesties, please won't you stop all this torturing of women?" She was led away, weeping.[15]

When the king stayed in private houses, Special Branch detectives accompanied him, and Chief Inspector Spencer liaised with his hosts and with the chief constable of the county, who was responsible for the more general security arrangements, including crowd control if there were speeches to be given and royal addresses to be presented. While the Prince of Wales was staying at Chatsworth in January 1901, a few weeks before the death of his mother, police were alarmed to see a well-dressed man following the royal party through the front door and into the house. A detective grabbed the man and asked him his business; when it became obvious that he wasn't able to speak English, it seemed as if everyone's fears were confirmed and that an assassin had managed to get within touching distance of the prince. All the man would say was, "I am De Band."

And so he was: it turned out that he was one of the musicians hired by the Devonshires to provide entertainment at Chatsworth during Bertie's stay. Nevertheless, word spread through the neighbourhood that there had been an attempt on Bertie's life, that the hapless bandsman was really a foreign anarchist, and that he had been arrested carrying a stiletto. None of which was true.

Queen Victoria rarely stayed with one of her subjects after Albert's death in 1861. But she regularly spent time at her own country houses: Osborne, on the Isle of Wight, and Balmoral. Both were furnished and decorated to her own taste and the taste of her husband, whose creations they were. It was not shared by everyone: Lord Rosebery famously said he thought the drawing room at Osborne was the ugliest room in the world until he saw the drawing room at Balmoral.

The queen's set, if set it can be called, was a mixture of courtiers and relations who trailed along behind her clouds of regal glory as they followed her peripatetic movements to Windsor, Balmoral, and Osborne. Her fifth daughter, Beatrice, was her constant companion until 1885, when she dared to marry. (Her mother wouldn't speak to her for seven months after she broke the news of her engagement.) Marie Mallet, who was a maid of honour to the queen from 1887 to 1891 and then, after her marriage in that year, an extra woman of the bedchamber, thought the only reason Victoria allowed the match was because the groom, Prince Henry of Battenberg, agreed to move in with his mother-in-law.

The appointment of courtiers tended to run in families, something which reinforced the cliquish nature of the queen's household. Mrs Mallet's mother, a daughter of the 4th Earl of Hardwicke of Wimpole Hall, was a woman of the bedchamber. The 4th earl was a lord-in-waiting; his son and heir was comptroller of the royal household and then master of the buckhounds. A cousin, Lady Sarah Lindsay, was a woman of the bedchamber for more than thirty years. The queen's chaplain for forty-five years was Hon. and Rev. Charles Courtenay, who was married to the 3rd earl's granddaughter. The 3rd earl's grandson was a lord-in-waiting; the 4th earl's son Hon. Alick Yorke was a groom-in-waiting to the queen, having previously served as equerry to Victoria's youngest son, Prince Leopold, Duke of Albany.

The atmosphere in the queen's household was resolutely domestic, especially as Victoria grew older, but it was by no means dull. There were concerts and plays, with members of the household in leading roles: there was a tradition, begun by the royal children when they were young, of staging *tableaux vivants* for the queen's entertainment. In 1894, for example, the household put on five tableaux in the ballroom at Balmoral to celebrate the queen's seventy-fifth birthday. They included scenes from *King John* and *The Merchant of Venice*, and a representation of Greek poetry with Victoria's granddaughter, Princess Alexandra of Edinburgh, as Sappho playing her lyre. Princess Beatrice played the harmonium during each piece.

Christmas at Osborne House was another opportunity for *tableaux vivants*: in 1892 Alick Yorke was given the job of managing the whole, rather elaborate, affair. "All promises very well," wrote Victoria in her diary, "but it takes a good deal of arranging." A stage was erected in the Durbar Room at Osborne, and there were eight tableaux in all, beginning with an Indian bazaar, with the queen's Indian servant Abdul Karim and a selection of Victoria's Indian carpets and rugs—"The grouping and colouring was wonderfully realistic and Eastern," she wrote in her journal. It was followed by a reenactment of Charles Müller's painting of *Queen Marie Antoinette in the Conciergerie*, with Princess Helena as the unhappy queen. The rest were also mainly taken from paintings—Alfred R. Austin's *Spoils of War*, Vernet's *Rebecca at the Well*, and so on. The evening closed with an allegorical tableau, *Empire*, in which Helena posed as Victoria (wearing her borrowed diamond crown) and her sister Beatrice sat at her feet dressed as a maharanee while her maids of honour held a large peacock fan behind her head. "It was really a most brilliant spectacle," wrote the queen.[16]

If the Prince of Wales's pleasures were not quite so innocent, his favourite country house was his own, and it was one of his own making. In 1861, as his coming of age approached, Albert decided that a country estate might help to keep his erring son out of mischief. The prime minister, Lord Palmerston, suggested Sandringham Hall, an eight-thousand-acre estate eight miles northeast of King's Lynn in Norfolk. It belonged to his stepson, and although at £220,000 the price was rather high for a shooting estate, and a neglected one at that, Albert approved of the idea. He died that December, and Victoria, to whom her husband's wishes were sacrosanct, pressed ahead with the purchase. Bertie went down to inspect the place in February 1862, and after briefly considering the Somerleyton estate near Lowestoft when its owner, the railway magnate Sir Morton Peto, went bankrupt, he bought Sandringham that month. He married Alexandra of Denmark in March 1863, and the newlyweds moved in.

Built in 1771 and altered in 1836 by S. S. Teulon, who added a large conservatory, Sandringham was not beautiful. Nor was it in good repair. According to one account, "The whole estate was in the worst possible order, the house was small and dilapidated, and the demesne had been utterly neglected."[17] So in 1864 the prince commissioned some extensions from A. J. Humbert. Humbert was an architect much favoured by Prince Albert and Queen Victoria (he designed the prince consort's mausoleum at Frogmore), but he was not an inspired choice. He initially added two wings to the north and south ends, but it became plain that the old house was past saving, apart from Teulon's conservatory, which was converted into a billiard room; and by 1870 a new, rather ornate Jacobethan mansion in brick and stone had taken its place.

For a while, Bertie and Alix were happy with the new Sandringham. But by the early 1880s they decided it needed something more. Humbert had died in 1877, and they turned to R. W. Edis, a man who had once moved in exalted architectural circles—in 1862 he was with William Burges at the Red House, which Philip Webb had designed for William Morris—but who had subsequently become, in the words of his biographer, a populariser rather than an innovator. Edis designed a new wing which held telegraph and post offices but which was mainly occupied by a big new ballroom, sixty-six feet by thirty, the decoration of which was described at the time as "Elizabethan, freely treated."[18] It was inaugurated with a county ball to celebrate Bertie's forty-second birthday in November 1883; as usual, Coote and Tinney's Band provided the music.

In October 1891 Sandringham was badly damaged by fire. Bertie wasn't in residence (he was staying at Easton Lodge with Daisy Brooke—soon to be the Countess of Warwick—and her long-suffering husband), but he was planning to arrive shortly as preparations got underway for his fiftieth birthday party on November 9. Edis was telegraphed the next day, and within hours he was supervising the repairs as a hundred builders and decorators worked to patch up the damage. The party went ahead, but without Alix, who had taken herself off to Crimea, having lost patience with her husband's infidelities.

Sandringham was always the place where Bertie could act out the role of a country squire (and Alix, when she was speaking to him, could act as his lady wife). Bertie went for long solitary walks in the country, stopping to talk to estate workers and tenant farmers as he went, always followed at a discreet distance by one of his detectives. Alix would preside over afternoon tea for her guests, surrounded by her dogs and watched by a green parrot who occasionally squawked "Hip, hip, hip, hurrah! God save the Queen!" Nevertheless, tea was a full-dress meal, with all the women in tea gowns, the men in short black jackets, and a small orchestra playing in the background. Fritz Ponsonby, who was assistant private secretary to Bertie, as he had been to Queen Victoria, described a typical evening at the house. After tea, everyone was expected to play games, but those who knew better slipped off to read or talk in the library:

> Dinner was magnificent with all the women in tiaras, etc., and all the men with ribands and decorations. Bridge had just become the fashion and the King walked round to see that everyone was engaged. The Queen went to bed soon after midnight and the King between one and one-thirty. I was told that in the old days of baccarat he used to sit up till four or five in the morning and all the men of the party had to remain up whether they were playing or not. The usual practice for those who didn't play was to go to sleep in the billiard-room with a footman specially warned to wake them when the baccarat was over.[19]

The coming-of-age celebrations in January 1885 for their eldest boy, Prince Albert Victor, second in line to the throne, were held at Sandringham. Prince and princess, with their son between them, stood in Edis's ballroom at Sandringham, its windows curtained with gold-embroidered Indian silk, to receive deputations from the tenants, the major, town clerk and corporation of Norwich, the municipality of King's Lynn, the headmaster and scholars of Lynn Grammar School, and for some reason the mayor of Cambridge. Estate workers and their children assembled in front of the house to offer congratulations as the royal family appeared on the porch. They all wore their Sunday best, except for the keepers, who wore their uniforms of shiny beavers with gold tassels, dark green velveteen jackets with gilt buttons, buff breeches, and gaiters.

As if this weren't spectacle enough, that moment the circus came to Sandringham. As the birthday boy stood with his family accepting the good wishes of the villagers, music was heard in the distance, the park gates at the end of the drive opened wide, and a mighty cavalcade processed towards the house: a band perched in an enormous chariot, escorted by men dressed as knights in armour; equestriennes wearing rather less with trick horses and teams of miniature ponies; caravans and elephants and camels and a hairless horse from Egypt. John Sanger's famous circus marched past the house and began to set up their tents for a royal command performance that afternoon.

Seven years later, Sandringham was where Prince Albert Victor died of pneumonia as his mother held his hand.

Just occasionally, Bertie's country house visits were surprisingly impromptu affairs. In September 1889, when he was about to set off for Scotland, he suddenly decided he must spend a Saturday to Monday at Easton Lodge in Essex with Lord and Lady Brooke. Although the Brookes presumably had some advanced warning of the royal visit, hardly anybody else did. Accompanied by a party including his valet and Lord Loughborough, Daisy Brooke's half brother, Bertie boarded a private saloon carriage which had been added to the midday train from St Pancras. Station officials at Bishop's Stortford had been informed that an extra saloon carriage would be attached to the train and that on arrival it needed to be shunted onto a branch line and attached to another train, the 12:47 to Takeley, the station for Easton Lodge. But no one told them who was in the saloon, and they didn't find out until it arrived. The station master at Takeley hadn't been warned, either. When the prince got out he was asked in the usual way for his ticket, but he just smiled and pointed at his valet, who hurried up with a handful of tickets for the whole royal party. After a little shooting with Lord Brooke on Saturday afternoon and church parade with both the Brookes on Sunday, he set off back to London, accompanied by Daisy. There were hardly any spectators at Takeley to wave him off, since just as no one knew he was coming, no one knew he was going, either.

The reason for the Prince of Wales's lightning visit to Easton Lodge isn't hard to guess. A few months earlier Daisy, who was not yet his lover, had come to him with a tale of woe. She had been sleeping with Lord Charles Beresford (in fact she had had a child by him) until he informed her that his wife, Mina, was pregnant. Furious at what she saw as his infidelity (a bit rich, that), in January 1889 she wrote him a massively indiscreet letter which was opened and read by Mina, who was understandably rather upset. She handed the letter to her solicitor, George Lewis, and Lewis wrote to Daisy saying that if she stayed away from London she could have the letter back. Daisy appealed to the prince, who felt so sorry for her that he did his best to bully Lewis and Mina into handing it over; so sorry for her, in fact, that he began sleeping with her himself. Whenever he went to a country house for the weekend, he let it be known that he would like Daisy and her husband to be invited, too. Whenever he saw Mina's name on a guest list, he crossed it out.

The battle with the Beresfords was in full swing by September 1889, and it was presumably to discuss the latest developments that the prince made his unscheduled visit to Easton Lodge. The affair dragged on, however, and in January 1890 Beresford, who was both jealous of Bertie for stealing his mistress and furious with him for his treatment of Mina, had a blazing row with the prince at Marlborough House which ended with Bertie hurling an inkstand at Beresford's head. The following year, hearing that Alix had received Daisy, "the unabashed adventuress," at Marlborough House, a furious and still ostracised Mina circulated a pamphlet which reproduced the by-now legendary letter from Daisy to Beresford and for good measure gave some highly coloured details of her various affairs. It backfired, and the Beresfords were forced to withdraw from society for a time, while anyone whom the prince even suspected of supporting their cause was no longer welcome at a country house while he was staying there. It was a good example of the weaponisation of the country house weekend.

In September 1890 the Prince of Wales and a group of friends gathered at Tranby Croft, the recently built Italianate country house of Sir Arthur Wilson, a Hull shipowner and avid huntsman—the same Sir Arthur Wilson for whom Harold Peto designed the Villa Maryland at Cap Ferrat in 1904. Wilson and his family weren't in the prince's Marlborough House Set, but most members of the party were. There were twenty altogether, come for the Doncaster races: guests included courtiers like the Earl and Countess of Coventry and General Owen Williams, commoner friends of the prince such as Yorkshire landowner Christopher Sykes and businessman Reuben Sassoon, and Lieutenant Colonel Sir William Gordon-Cumming, a veteran of the Anglo-Zulu War and the Sudan campaigns of the 1880s. Gordon-Cumming wasn't a very likable character: arrogant and bombastic, he liked to boast in an ungentlemanly way of his "perforations," his sexual conquests, which—according to him, anyway—included Lillie Langtry, Sarah Bernhardt, and Lady Randolph Churchill. But he was a long-time friend of the prince, a dinner guest at Marlborough House and a houseguest at Sandringham. He was also reputed to lend his Belgravia house to the prince for clandestine assignations.

   After dinner on the first night there was music and general conversation, and then someone suggested a game of baccarat, which was the Prince of Wales's current obsession—so much so that he always travelled with his own set of playing cards and brightly coloured tokens with the value on one side (£10, £5, £1 or 10s) and the prince's feathers on the other. These were duly produced, three whist tables were pushed together, and the game began, lasting until well after midnight.

The next day the entire party went to the races by train, in two saloon coaches; and that night the baccarat cards and counters came out again. The game went with Gordon-Cumming on both nights, and he went away with £228 in winnings.

The following night, September 10, after another day at the races and a group photograph of the house party taken in front of Tranby Croft, Gordon-Cumming was dressing for dinner when there was a knock on his door and the Earl of Coventry and General Williams came in. There must have been an awkward pause before Coventry spoke: "There is a very disagreeable thing that has occurred in the house. Some of the people staying here object to your manner in playing baccarat."

"Lord Coventry, what do you mean?" said Gordon-Cumming.

Coventry explained that certain people in the house party—he didn't name them—claimed he had been cheating, and they had gone to the Prince of Wales. Gordon-Cumming said, "It is a foul and abominable falsehood," and he demanded to see the prince himself. The visitors said they would see about that after dinner, shook hands, and went off to dress. When dinner was over Gordon-Cumming had his interview with the prince, in the presence of Lord Coventry and General Williams. Edward was perfectly calm, but he said that five people were prepared to swear they had seen his friend cheating. What could he do?

The five were their hostess, Mrs Wilson; her son Stanley, known as Jack; her daughter Ethel; her son-in-law Edward Lycett Green; and an old friend of Jack's, Berkeley Levett, who also happened to be a subaltern in Gordon-Cumming's own regiment, the Scots Guards. That first night, Jack Wilson thought he saw Gordon-Cumming surreptitiously adding chips to his stake when he had a good hand and removing them when his cards didn't look so promising. He whispered to Levett, "This is too hot! The man next to me is cheating." Levett told him he must be mad. Then he saw it too. He was so distressed that he got up and left the room.

So did Jack. The game broke up, and he went to his mother's dressing room and told her what he had seen. He also went for a walk with his brother-in-law the next morning and told him. Lycett Green told Ethel. That night they watched and saw Gordon-Cumming cheat in exactly the same fashion. That was enough: they put the matter in the hands of Lord Coventry, as a senior courtier, one of the oldest members of the party, and their oldest friend. That was how Coventry and General Williams came to confront Gordon-Cumming.

At the end of the interview with the Prince of Wales, Coventry asked the accused man to leave them for a few minutes. When he was invited back into the room, the prince had vanished and the two men presented him with a document to sign. It read:

> In consideration of the promise made by the gentlemen whose names are subscribed to preserve silence with reference to an accusation which has been made with regard to my conduct at baccarat on the nights of Monday and Tuesday, the 8th and 9th September, 1890, at Tranby Croft, I will on my part solemnly undertake never to play cards again as long as I live.[20]

Gordon-Cumming signed. Not because he was guilty, he later insisted, but because "it would not be desirable that the name of the Prince of Wales should be associated with a game of baccarat with an officer who had been accused of cheating by his hosts or by the people of the house in which the Prince of Wales was staying." There were ten more signatures, all from men: they included Coventry, Williams, Arthur and Jack Wilson, Berkeley Levett, Reuben Sassoon, and "Albert Edward," who thus recorded for posterity his involvement in the affair—a move that he and his mother were later to regret. "The incredible and shameful thing is that others dragged him into it and urged him to sign this paper, which of course he should never have done," the queen complained.[21]

The Tranby Croft affair leaves rather a lot of unanswered questions. Why was the Wilson family so keen to pursue the matter? Why didn't Gordon-Cumming confront his accusers there and then? Levett, who was a fellow officer, made no attempt to mediate or to calm the situation. Nor did Coventry or Williams; nor did the prince, who was ready to drop his friend of ten years on the word of a nouveau riche family that he hardly knew. The mutual support network that was the Marlborough House Set had its limits.

Various theories have been put forward to explain what happened, all of them on slender evidence. Edward was piqued because he had lost so heavily to Gordon-Cumming. He wanted revenge because two days earlier he had walked into his friend's London house and found Daisy Brooke in Gordon-Cumming's arms. Gordon-Cumming was so unpopular, because of his womanising or his arrogance, that everyone was happy to see him fall from grace.

Whatever the reason, he left Tranby Croft the next morning. But if any of the protagonists really believed that would be the end of the affair, they deluded themselves. At the end of December 1890 Gordon-Cumming received a telegram from "someone who pities you" saying that his "sad adventure" was the talk of Paris and Monte Carlo. Within a few weeks the story was doing the rounds of London clubs and race meetings, and Gordon-Cumming was forced to tell his commanding officer, Henry Stracey, what had happened. With a military court of inquiry looming, he tried to get Levett and the others to retract. When they wouldn't, he sued them for slander. And he called the Prince of Wales as a witness—the first time in nearly five centuries that an heir to the throne had been summoned to appear in open court.

The case was heard by Lord Chief Justice Coleridge over seven days in June 1891, and the prince was given quite an easy time of it by both Sir Edward Clarke, the solicitor general, who was prosecuting, and Sir Charles Russell for the defence. But the trial caused a sensation—not at the thought that a member of the prince's circle might have cheated at cards but at the revelation that the prince himself was a gambler and that his friends were gamblers. "The pity of it all," declared the *Daily News*, "is in the presence of the heir to the throne at the head of the baccarat table." The *Daily Chronicle* went further: "The readiness of the Prince of Wales to dispose of himself as a 'prize guest' . . . in rich but vulgar families [rather hard on the Wilsons, this] where his taste for the lowest type of gambling can be gratified . . . has profoundly shocked, we may even say disgusted, the people who may one day be asked to submit to his rule." The *Liverpool Courier* lamented the unedifying spectacle of "the future King of England officiating as 'banker' at such a gamblers' orgy—shuffling the cards for five-pound notes." What really distressed the public, declared the *Times*, was the discovery that "the game was played to please him; that it was played with his counters, specially taken down for the purpose; that his 'set' are a gambling, baccarat playing, set." The *Dundee Advertiser* was more succinct: "The Prince of Wales is evidently not what, with such a destiny before him, he ought to be."[22]

Lord Chief Justice Coleridge's four-hour summing up didn't leave the jury in much doubt as to what he expected their verdict to be. He criticised Sir Edward Clarke for attacking the social backgrounds of the Wilsons and their friends: Arthur Wilson for being a self-made man, Mrs Wilson for being a social climber, Jack for not having a profession, Lycett Green for being the son of an engineer. He criticised the prosecution's suggestion that they were somehow less trustworthy than Gordon-Cumming, "a person of rank, gallantry, character, and position, intimate with some of the most distinguished people in the country, and visiting great houses." And finally he asked the jury whether they could believe that an innocent man "would write down his name on a dishonouring document, on a document which, in fact, stated that he had cheated, and taken money out of the pocket of the Prince of Wales by craft and sharping, simply that it might not be made known that the Prince of Wales had played baccarat."[23]

The jury took thirteen minutes to find for the defendants, and Sir William Gordon-Cumming was a ruined man. The next day he was dismissed from the army. He resigned from his clubs and retreated to his Scottish estates, taking with him a bride, American heiress Florence Garner, and her fortune. None of the Marlborough House Set had anything more to do with him.

SEVENTEEN

A SPARK OF CHIVALRY

IT WAS A scene from a silent movie—Valentino's *The Sheik*, perhaps, or Ramon Novarro's *The Arab*. While the rest of the party slept under the desert stars, with the pyramids looming large in the darkness, the English noblewoman crept from her Bedouin tent to lie with her lover, leaving her naked telltale footprints in the sand.

Mary Elcho, chatelaine of Stanway House in Gloucestershire, daughter-in-law of the 10th Earl of Wemyss and March, wife of a prominent Conservative nobleman, had known the Arabist and libertine Wilfrid Scawen Blunt since childhood. Now she was thirty-two, the mother of four children, and locked in an intense but apparently platonic relationship with the unmarried Arthur Balfour, ex–secretary of state for Ireland, ex–first lord of the Treasury, and future prime minister of Britain, while her husband Hugo was pursuing an equally intense and not at all platonic affair with an aristocratic society beauty, Hermione, Duchess of Leinster, who had already had a son by him.

Mary had arrived to spend the winter in Egypt at the beginning of January 1895, with her maid, her children, and their governess,

Miss Jourdain, in tow. Romantically decked out in Bedouin robes, she went straight to Shaykh 'Ubayd, the country estate near Cairo where the fifty-four-year-old Blunt lived with his long-suffering wife Anne, Byron's granddaughter, and their daughter, Judith. Mary and Blunt were distantly related, and at various times the indefatigable Blunt had slept with her mother, her sister, her sister-in-law, and her cousin. Now he laid siege to Mary, writing sonnets to her, telling her he loved her, begging her for a kiss. "She is an ideal woman for a lifelong passion," Blunt confided to his diary, adding rather disturbingly that she had "the subtle charm, for me, besides, of blood relationship."[1]

After ten days of this courtship, the affair was consummated one afternoon when Blunt called at Mary's lodgings to find that Miss Jourdain and the children were out riding donkeys, the maid had gone into Cairo, and Mary was alone, resting in bed. "My extremest hopes were fulfilled," he wrote.[2]

Over the next few weeks Mary opened up to Blunt about the intimate details of her private life. She hadn't slept with her husband for six years, she said, but she had sworn to be faithful to Balfour and their relationship, which was, Blunt understood, "a little more than friendship, a little less than love."[3] (While they were in bed together that first time, Blunt noticed a letter to his rival lying on the bedside table. This gave him an added frisson of pleasure in the fact that they were having revenge sex, since Balfour, as chief secretary for Ireland, had been responsible for Blunt being gaoled after speaking out at an antieviction meeting in Galway back in 1888.) The couple agreed that their affair must end when Mary went back to England in the summer. But in the meantime, they made an expedition into the desert with maid and children and governess and Arab servants. Blunt slept a little way off from the main camp beneath a blue-and-white-striped carpet shelter, and Mary came to him in the night, leaving those naked footprints in the sand. He called her his Bedouin wife and said that this was their desert honeymoon.

Ironically enough, it was on February 14, St Valentine's Day, that things began to go wrong for the two lovers. Mary announced that she had missed her period; she was sure she was pregnant. The following day a message came from her husband Hugo to say he was leaving his mistress's bedside—the Duchess of Leinster was in Menton, dying of tuberculosis—and on his way to join the party. "She is leading an odd sort of life camping out in the desert [with Blunt]," Hugo told his sister, "and I fear people may be talking about them."[4]

Every cloud has a silver lining. Mary thought that at least now she could persuade her husband to sleep with her, enabling her to pass off Blunt's baby as Hugo's. But when he arrived, the typical British nobleman abroad, arrogant, bowler-hatted, and eager to shoot things, Hugo showed no inclination to assert his conjugal rights, while Blunt exasperatingly did all he could to keep husband and wife apart. When he organised a second expedition into the desert, a caravanserai of ten camels, two Arab horses, two donkeys, and ten drivers and servants, he dictated the sleeping arrangements, putting Mary in one tent with his daughter, Judith, and Hugo in another with a friend who had recently joined them, the writer and thinker Frederic Harrison. "The Sheikh," wrote Harrison, "insisted on sleeping under a sandbank in the open air covered with fur rugs."[5] According to Blunt, the arrangement allowed Mary to sneak over to him in the night while her husband slept.

After a week or so of this Hugo left, to return to the south of France and his dying mistress, and Blunt organised one last desert expedition, a sixteen-day trek into the Eastern Desert in search of the ancient Monastery of Saint Anthony. This time, even the presence of his own wife did not deter him from persuading Mary to join him behind a convenient sandhill whenever the opportunity arose.

When they got back there was a telegram from Hugo. His duchess had died, and he was waiting for Mary at home. She left Blunt and Egypt on March 26, went home to her husband—and told him everything. She didn't have much choice, really. Then she wrote to Blunt, telling him that it was all over between them, that he had tried to wreck her life, and that "the only thing that prevents my being utterly angry with you is that I believe you *did care* for me."[6]

Hugo also wrote to Blunt, and his letter was a snorter:

> You have wrecked the life and destroyed the happiness of a woman whom a spark of chivalry would have made you protect. . . . You had known her from childhood. She was your cousin and your guest. She was a happy woman when she went to Egypt, and her misery now would touch a heart of stone.[7]

In fact, Mary didn't act like a victim. Far from it. Instead of retiring hurt, she continued to see Blunt on and off for years, even engaging in occasional sexual encounters with him, if her account of a visit to him one night in 1906 while he lay sick in bed can be believed: her "somewhat unorthodox treatment," she said, "in a few seconds turn[ed] an invalid into a distinctly rampageous young man." And it is possible, just possible, that she finally entered into some kind of physical relationship with her beloved Arthur Balfour. In 1907 she sent him a valentine on which she had drawn a birch rod, a brush, and a tin of peppermint-flavoured "squirting grease."[8] Biographers have made much of this.

Initially, Mary Elcho was annoyed with her husband because his main concern, when she told him about the pregnancy, was that the Duchess of Leinster's family would think ill of him for having sex with his wife while his mistress lay dying; but she was grateful to him for not making life unbearable. And now he knew she was capable of paying him back in kind for his frequent infidelities: "Now we can never either of us say anything to the other," he told her. She was altogether more relaxed than she had been about those infidelities, happily entertaining his various mistresses at Stanway. In the spring of 1895, with the Duchess of Leinster barely in her grave and Mary starting to show with Blunt's baby, he brought his latest lover to stay at Stanway. "I'm quite enjoying being off duty," Mary told Balfour.[9]

She gave birth to a daughter, who was named after her, on October 24, 1895. Almost exactly one year later she had a son, Yvo, the product of a temporary reconciliation with her husband, and the couple remained together in a conventionally dysfunctional relationship until Mary's death in April 1937; Hugo followed her to the grave eleven weeks later. Meanwhile, Hermione Leinster's son by Hugo had steadily moved up the ducal pecking order. She had had two sons by her husband Gerald, the 5th Duke of Leinster; when he died in 1893, the eldest, Maurice, inherited the title as 6th duke. The second son, Desmond, was killed in the First World War, and so when Maurice died in 1922, mad and unmarried, Hugo's son Edward became 7th Duke of Leinster.

Such complications were, if not common among the country house–owning classes, certainly not unique. Hilaire Belloc's savage little rhyme on the corridor-creeping habits of Edward VII and his then mistress, Evie James of West Dean, highlighted a milieu in which adultery among houseguests was an acceptable social pastime.

> *There will be bridge and booze till after three*
> *And, after that, a lot of them will grope*
> *Along the corridors in robes de nuit,*
> *Pyjamas, or some other kind of dope.*
> *A sturdy matron will be sent to cope*
> *With Lord ——, who isn't quite the thing,*
> *And give his wife the leisure to elope,*
> *And Mrs. James will entertain the King!*[10]

The convention was supposed to be that so long as a woman bore her husband one or two legitimate heirs first, he would accept later offspring as his own, whether they bore a family resemblance or not. Mary, the daughter of Mary Elcho and Wilfrid Blunt, was raised in a world where parentage was uncertain yet taken for granted. It wouldn't have occurred to her that members of her circle might have been half siblings (as indeed at least two of them were, while the conservative politician Anthony Eden bore a striking resemblance to her uncle George Wyndham, who had an affair with Eden's mother). Yet although marital infidelity is often assumed to have been an accepted feature of upper-class life, it wasn't as acceptable as all that, as proceedings in the divorce courts demonstrate.

The Matrimonial Causes Act of 1857 was the first statute to give a secular court the power to dissolve a marriage. Up until then, divorce was the province of the Church of England, which, since it held that marriage was an indissoluble union, was not inclined to allow husband and wife to remarry, although it could grant what amounted to the equivalent of a judicial separation. It was possible, but complicated and expensive, to obtain a private act of Parliament to end a marriage, and 184 private acts were granted in the first half of the nineteenth century. The 1857 Matrimonial Causes Act made the process more straightforward, although the marital dice were heavily loaded in favour of the husband, who only had to demonstrate that his wife had committed adultery. She, on the other hand, had to prove that, in the words of the act, "her Husband has been guilty of incestuous Adultery, or of Bigamy with Adultery, or of Rape, or of Sodomy or Bestiality, or of Adultery coupled with . . . Cruelty . . . or of Adultery coupled with Desertion, without reasonable excuse, for Two Years or upwards." The assumption underlying this double standard was that an unfaithful wife might foist another man's child on her husband, but an unfaithful husband "imposes no bastards on his wife."

But there was also the notion that infidelity was gendered. Sir John Bigham, the president of the Probate, Divorce and Admiralty Division of the High Court, which from 1875 onwards heard all divorce cases in England, was clear in his own mind on this. "An act of adultery on the part of a man is not inconsistent with his continued esteem and love for his wife," he declared, "whereas an act of adultery on the part of a woman, in my opinion, is quite inconsistent with continued love and esteem for the husband."[11]

So to what extent was divorce an option among the landed elite in late Victorian and Edwardian England? How likely was it that Lord Elcho might petition for a divorce from his wife Mary, citing Wilfrid Blunt as co-respondent? Taking the 1906 edition of Lodge's *Peerage, Baronetage and Knightage* as an arbitrary checkpoint, that work shows that ten living peers and fifteen living baronets had divorced their wives or been divorced by them; not many out of a combined total of around 1,500, perhaps.

More interesting, though, is the vicious vigour with which wronged husbands and wronged wives pursued their cases. The received wisdom among historians used to be that such things were arranged quietly and discreetly by members of the landed elite. A divorce was agreed on privately; then the man left his wife, who petitioned in court for the restitution of conjugal rights, even if she had no desire ever to see her husband again. He did not return, thereby demonstrating desertion, and then he took a hotel room in Brighton or Paris, spent the night in it with an obliging woman, taking care to be seen by the staff and, if the couple wanted to make absolutely sure of things, by a private detective who would if necessary camp outside their door all night, so that the woman and the detective could give evidence that she and the husband had spent the night in the same bedroom. The wife would petition for a divorce on the grounds of adultery and desertion, the husband wouldn't contest the suit, and after a statutory period the marriage would be over.

That certainly did happen. When Earl De La Warr and his wife Muriel decided to part company in 1901, Countess De La Warr wrote to "My dear Cantelupe [*sic*]" (her pet name for the earl) to say that "nearly a year has elapsed since you have lived with me as my husband, and I now write to you requesting you to come back to me and restore to me all my rights as a wife." He wrote back to say that "I have finally decided not to return to live with you." She petitioned for the restitution of conjugal rights; he refused to return to the marital home; a Miss Turner, an actress, gave evidence that she had spent the night with the earl on several occasions; and the judge pronounced a decree nisi and gave the countess custody of the couple's three young children.[12]

But rather more often, the marital breakdown was a savage and acrimonious affair, with accusations flying around the courtroom. Lady Rodney of Berrington Hall in Shropshire said that her husband punched her and went off with her lady's maid. Sir Herbert Williams-Wynn, Bt, accused his wife Louise of sleeping with his private secretary. Sir Charles Knowles's wife took him to court after discovering that "he had renewed a guilty intimacy, which he had formed some years after their marriage, with her nurserymaid."[13]

"Not in front of the servants" was a maxim which erring spouses would have done well to heed. Mary Else, who was Viscountess St Vincent's lady's maid, not only gave the name of her mistress's lover to the earl's lawyers but also stood up in court and testified that she had seen the pair in bed together on several occasions. Winifred, Lady Ross, tired of her husband Sir Charles within a few years of their marriage, as well as of living in his remote Highland fastness of Balnagown Castle. Unfortunately for her, when she began to look elsewhere for comfort, she didn't take much notice of Ross's domestic staff, the footmen and lodgekeepers and under-nurses and maids who were thus able to testify in force at her divorce trial that they had frequently seen her with her lover in compromising situations. No matter that her husband had rushed off to see another woman the day after their wedding or that he boasted to her about his sexual relations "with actresses and ladies."[14] (Note the distinction.) Ross got his divorce.

A vindictive husband was able to sue his wife's lover for damages, a course of action which wasn't open to a wronged wife in similar circumstances. The thinking behind this was set out by Justice McCardie in a case just after the First World War. "The grounds on which damages are given are: (1) the actual value of the wife lost; (2) compensation to the husband for the injury to his feelings, the blow to his honour, and hurt to his family life."[15] When Sir Henry Bayly Meredyth, Bt, divorced his wife Kathleen in 1894, after her shipboard romance with a Richard Leigh on a voyage home from Cairo turned into something more serious and she went off to New York to live with him, he demanded that Leigh not only cover the legal costs of the divorce but also pay the colossal sum of £10,000 in damages. (He later relented, after Leigh agreed to provide financially for the former Lady Meredyth.) Sir Archibald Napier, Bt, also put in a claim for damages, but since the man who was having an affair with his wife had no means of paying them, he withdrew his claim.

Napier had received a series of anonymous letters claiming that his wife was being unfaithful. He first tried to ignore them, then he confronted his wife with them. After she denied the affair he hired a private detective, Dorothy Tempest, to watch the couple, although she doesn't sound as though she was quite up to the task: when they boarded a train for the Crystal Palace one day she was unable to follow "as the railway officials would not allow her into the train without a ticket."[16] After he discovered that Lady Napier was holidaying in Biarritz with her lover, a man named Kirklinton, he consulted his solicitor—who advised him to break open her writing desk while she was out of the country. There he discovered a bundle of letters "which were absolutely conclusive as to the relations which existed between them" and which were couched in such language that learned counsel didn't feel he could read them aloud in open court. Neither Lady Napier nor her lover appeared in court to defend themselves.

The co-respondents in these aristocratic divorce cases came from a variety of different social backgrounds. At least three were titled peers. The Earl of Shrewsbury we have already met, when he eloped to the Continent with the wife of Alfred Mundy of Shipley Hall. When Lord Zouche's young wife Anne disappeared from their country house, Parham in Sussex, after only three months of marriage, the Earl of Mayo was blamed. (So was Wilfrid Blunt, incidentally, although Zouche dropped his suit against Blunt when it came to court.)

Henry Wellesley, the 3rd Earl Cowley, appeared not once but twice in the role of co-respondent. In 1902 Sir Charles Cradock-Hartopp, Bt, tried to divorce his wife Millicent on the grounds of her adultery with the earl, who was often in Leicestershire for the hunting season and had met Lady Hartopp, a keen rider, in the hunting field—which seems to have set the scene for the start of quite a few adulterous relationships. In the course of a marathon thirteen-day trial, plenty of evidence was heard that the pair met alone both at Lady Hartopp's cottage (she was already living apart from her husband) and at Baggrave Hall, the earl's country house, while Lady Hartopp countersued for divorce on the grounds that that her husband had been violent towards her and had himself committed adultery with a Mrs Sands. A picture emerged of a hedonistic set of people who spent their lives hunting, gambling, and dining alone with members of the opposite sex. Yet at the end of the trial the jury decided that Cowley and Lady Hartopp had not committed adultery; that Sir Charles Hartopp and Mrs Sands had not committed adultery; and that Sir Charles was not guilty of cruelty to his wife. As the *Times* said in an angry editorial, "Before rushing into a thing of this kind it would surely be wise for people to see that they have grounds more relative than the gossip and the distorted apprehension of servants, the suspiciously clear recollections of cabmen, and exaggerated inferences suddenly drawn from the free and easy manners which all concerned normally accept as a matter of course." Worst of all, this kind of thing fuelled class prejudice by offering "fair evidence of the moral depravity of all the upper classes of society."[17]

Rather more evidence of moral depravity was offered three years later when Sir Charles had another shot at divorcing his wife, this time having prudently hired private detectives. They gave evidence that Lady Hartopp had visited Cowley at a house in South Audley Street on several occasions, staying till after midnight. "I have heard quite enough," said the judge, who was clearly not prepared to sit through another lengthy trial. He granted Sir Charles his divorce, and Earl Cowley and Lady Hartopp decamped to Ceylon, where they were married at the end of the year.

Earl Cowley, whose family seat was Draycot House in Wiltshire, was no stranger to the divorce courts. In 1897, five years before Sir Charles Hartopp's first, unsuccessful attempt at divorce, Violet, Countess Cowley, petitioned for divorce on the grounds of the earl's desertion and adultery with a married woman, Monica Charrington. The earl strenuously denied the charge, as did Mrs Charrington, but just as she was about to be called as a witness Cowley dramatically announced to the court that he had indeed committed adultery, not with her but with a prostitute in Brighton some years before, and Violet was given her divorce and custody of their seven-year-old son, Viscount Dangan. And Earl Cowley appeared in the divorce court yet again in 1913 when Millicent Hartopp, now Countess Cowley, divorced him for desertion and adultery with another divorcée, a Mrs Buxton.

Another member of the landed elite whose matrimonial ups and downs give the lie to the idea that the Upper Ten Thousand would go to any lengths to avoid scandal and public scrutiny was Harcourt Lees, the son and heir of Rev. Sir Harcourt Lees, Bt. Lees was named as co-respondent when an Indian army officer called Moore successfully sued his wife Harriet for divorce in 1869. Lees was married at the time, and now his own wife (who had borne him six children) divorced him, and he married Harriet. But in 1887 he put in a third appearance, or rather nonappearance, before the president of the Probate, Divorce and Admiralty Division. Harriet said he had deserted her (and the three children they had raised together) and contracted a bigamous marriage with a woman called Flora Nelson. Taking one of their daughters with her, she tracked the couple down to a Hamburg hotel, where she, the daughter, her husband, and her husband's wife had what must have been a rather awkward meeting at the table d'hôte. According to Harriet, she told Harcourt that a warrant was out for his arrest. "I am safe here," he said, but the next day he fled to America. She was granted her decree nisi, although it was rescinded seven months later when the court discovered that Harriet had been living with another man on the Continent for years and had given birth to another three children after Lees left her.[18]

In 1898 Flora left Lees, who had succeeded to the baronetcy that year, in Washington, DC, and in spite of not being legally married to her he filed for divorce. By the early years of the twentieth century he was living in Ireland, where he was described in the nationalist press as "perhaps the foremost bigot of his time."[19] His bigamy seems never to have caught up with him.

The same can't be said for the unfortunate John Francis (Frank) Russell, 2nd Earl Russell, whose protracted matrimonial battles with his first wife, Mabel, gripped the attention of the public throughout the 1890s and beyond. Russell, the older brother of philosopher Bertrand Russell, was raised in a succession of country houses, the most impressive of which was his grandmother's house, the Georgian Pembroke Lodge in Richmond Park, where he recalled being raised in an atmosphere of "doubts, fears and hesitations, reticences and suppressions, and of a sort of mournful Christian humility."[20] After a spell at Winchester College he went up to Oxford, only to be sent down because of an unspecified and unsubstantiated allegation that he had written an inappropriate letter to a fellow student.

In 1887 the twenty-two-year-old Russell bought Broom Hall, "an old-fashioned house, not very well built, but it had lovely grounds and a long frontage to a wide and smooth piece of the river [Thames] just above Teddington Weir."[21] He kept a very modest establishment—just his old nurse, Mrs Billings, and her two daughters, Jennie and Emma—and spent his time pottering about on the river in his steam-powered launch, the *Isabel*. Two years later he was introduced to a neighbour, Mabel Scott, the twenty-year-old daughter of a baronet, who with her widowed mother had moved into a house nearby. He fell in love with Mabel, and in February 1890 the couple were married.

The marriage lasted three months. Then Mabel ran home to her mother, having first persuaded her husband to sell Broom Hall and buy a rather ordinary house in Maidenhead because she said the hall was gloomy. Russell was not an easy man: by his own admission he was fussy about little things and full of the arrogance of youth. The philosopher George Santayana, who knew him well at this point in his life, said of the couple rather darkly that "in their intimate relations he was exacting and annoying."[22] And he had seduced young Emma Billings, who was suing him for breach of promise.

But all in all, Russell was a man more sinned against than sinning. Mabel's mother was eager to have an earl for a son-in-law. The Russell name would provide both cachet and cash, and Lady Scott was in need of both. Her creditors were hounding her, and with a chequered past (she had left her husband for another man years before) she was not quite welcome in the best circles. Or as Santayana put it, she spent her life "scouring the borderland between the *monde* and the *demi-monde*."[23] She would be declared bankrupt in 1892.

When the marriage broke down, Lady Scott realised that she might have to forgo the cachet, but she certainly wasn't going to forgo the cash. She persuaded Mabel—now a countess—to sue for a judicial separation on the grounds of the earl's cruelty, with a view to obtaining a hefty settlement. Among a long list of complaints put before the court, which ranged from insulting language and physical violence to making her clean the servants' water closets at their Eaton Square town house, one stood out. Mabel maintained that on two occasions when an old friend of the earl, a mathematics teacher named Herbert Roberts, was staying with them, Russell had dressed for bed and then disappeared into Roberts's bedroom and stayed there for some hours. "No doubt a very serious suggestion might appear to be raised," said Mabel's QC, but he was not going to raise it. Mabel was: when asked by her husband's counsel if she meant "to make an imputation upon [Roberts] and your husband," she replied, "Yes."[24] Her counsel also brought up the circumstances of Russell's abrupt departure from Oxford, suggesting that this confirmed his homosexual tendencies. After Roberts and Russell had both denied the accusation under oath, Mabel's lawyers abruptly dropped the charge. But the damage was done.

It is quite likely that Russell experimented with homosexuality at Winchester. His greatest friend there was the poet Lionel Johnson, who looked, Russell recalled later, "like some young saint in a stained-glass window."[25] And Johnson certainly was part of a gay circle at the time. But being outed in open court like this could have fearful consequences, as Mabel and her mother well knew. Only six years before, the Criminal Law Amendment Act had extended the law to punish with two years' imprisonment any man found guilty of gross indecency with another male. And even if Mabel's accusations didn't lead to prosecution, for someone in Russell's position this kind of no-smoke-without-fire innuendo could mean social ostracism: indeed, as his uncle had already helpfully suggested to him when he was forced to leave Oxford, the best course would be for him to blow his brains out.

However, Mabel was a bad witness, and it became obvious during her cross-examination that she was either exaggerating or inventing her allegations. The jury didn't believe her—nor did the judge, if his summing up was anything to go by—and Russell won the case. As he left the court he was "warmly congratulated by numerous persons in the corridor and outside, who followed him from the door of the court, cheering as they went."[26]

But Mabel and Lady Scott weren't finished yet. They had Russell followed by detectives and tried to persuade his servants to provide evidence of his homosexual activities. Mabel gave an interview to the *Hawk*, a popular newspaper, in which she repeated her suggestion that her husband was gay. She threatened to have all the documents in the case published in pamphlet form and accused him of sodomy. Then in 1894, after an acrimonious exchange of letters between husband and wife in which Mabel threatened to go on the stage if Frank wouldn't give her any money, she abruptly changed tack and sued for restitution of conjugal rights. Russell countersued for a judicial separation, on the grounds that her allegations of homosexuality amounted to cruelty.

This second case began on April 4, 1895, on the very day that Oscar Wilde was appearing at the Old Bailey, down the road from the Royal Courts of Justice, and losing his libel action against the Marquess of Queensberry for accusing him of "posing as a somdomite [*sic*]."[27] The stakes were high. Within weeks, Wilde would be convicted of committing acts of gross indecency with other men and would be sentenced to two years in prison with hard labour.

Mabel's problem was how to convince a jury that, having accused her husband of "an abominable crime" and saying that she could never live with him because of it, she was now asking the court to force him to come back to her. She did this by the simple expedient of saying she hadn't understood exactly what it was she was accusing him of; now that she knew, she was sure he hadn't committed any such act. Her mother, Lady Scott, when asked in the witness box why she had employed ten private detectives to follow her son-in-law, claimed it was all done out of her "extreme desire to prove his innocence."[28] (She had a rather difficult time explaining how she was able to pay so many detectives when she was an undischarged bankrupt with a list of creditors as long as her arm.) It took the jury twenty minutes to find that Mabel was not acting in good faith and that she was guilty of cruelty against Earl Russell.

At this point the sorry saga switched to the police courts. Lady Scott printed libels "of a most obscene and degrading character" which were meant either to force the earl to stump up some cash or to make him institute proceedings for criminal libel, rather as Wilde had been manoeuvred into suing Lord Queensberry. And that is what he did. But for Lady Scott, at least, the move went catastrophically wrong. Along with two associates, she had persuaded a young soldier named Frederick Kast, who had been a cabin boy on Russell's yacht years before, to testify that he had been a witness—in fact a party—to homosexual acts with Russell and Herbert Roberts. But Kast died before he could give evidence. Lady Scott's defence of justification collapsed, and after she gave an impassioned speech to the court—"I trust all you gentlemen, and your lordship included, will never see any daughter of yours suffer as my darling has done"—she was sentenced to eight months in prison.[29]

A sympathetic press applauded the verdict. Lady Scott's sole object, said one newspaper, was "to ruin a nobleman, the woman's own son-in-law, and at the same time to force him to pay a large sum of money." Earl Russell, said another, "can fortify himself with the assurance that no sensible person will henceforth attach the slightest importance to the unclean ravings of a weak and vengeful mind."[30]

Which brings us, at last, to the bigamy. Russell had his countess watched, but although he was convinced "that both she and her mother were earning their living by men" his detectives could find no evidence, so he was unable to divorce her. Nor could Mabel divorce him, because her claims of cruelty and desertion had already been rejected by the courts and she needed at least one of these grounds to make her case. But the earl had met someone else, an activist and suffragette named Marion "Mollie" Somerville, and he wanted to marry her. The pair decamped to America, where, after taking legal advice, Earl Russell obtained a divorce from Mabel in Carson City, Nevada, on the grounds of her desertion, and three days later he and Mollie were married in Reno. They came back to England in May 1900 and Russell bought a four-roomed cottage on the South Downs, which was called Telegraph House on account of its having originally been an admiralty semaphore station. He pulled it down and replaced it with a much roomier villa equipped with a tower that gave magnificent views. "I now had a beautiful and perfect house," he wrote, "protected from the weather outside by a cement coating like a coastguard station, and protected inside by hollow walls and double glass windows, and warmed throughout by steam radiators."[31]

In the meantime, the earl persuaded Mabel (by offering her £5,000) to sue him for divorce in the English courts, on the grounds that he had technically committed bigamy. She agreed, but unfortunately for this most unfortunate earl, the authorities didn't consider the bigamy to be technical. One morning in the spring of 1901, he and his new wife were getting out of a train at Waterloo station when they were approached by a man who asked if he was speaking to Lord Russell. When told that he was, the man produced a warrant for his arrest and carted him off to Bow Street Police Station. "One is not in the habit of being arrested," said the earl, "and it appeared almost an impertinence."[32]

It turned out that English law did not recognise his Nevada divorce, although bizarrely, it did recognise his Nevada marriage. He never knew what made the authorities decide to prosecute after he had been back in England for a year, but decide they did. And so on the morning of Friday, July 19, 1901, for the first time in sixty years and almost the last time in English history, a nobleman was tried by his peers in the House of Lords. As Black Rod led the prisoner—wearing a grey frock coat and a bright-red tie—to the bar of the House, around two hundred of his peers were crammed into the Royal Gallery, where the trial took place, to hear what he had to say. They included the prime minister, the Marquess of Salisbury; four dukes; three more marquesses; and the Archbishop of York. The bewigged judges—all eleven of them—who had been summoned to advise the peers, sat in the body of the room, while the other peers in their state robes were ranged to either side. The whole was presided over by the Lord High Chancellor of Great Britain, a forbidding criminal lawyer named Hardinge Giffard, 1st Earl of Halsbury.

It was all rather an anticlimax. The charge was read, that on April 15, 1900, "at the Riverside Hotel at Reno, in the County of Washoe, in the State of Nevada, in the United States of America," Russell "feloniously and unlawfully did marry and take to wife" Mollie Somerville while his first wife was still living. The earl's counsel, W. S. Robson KC, argued that the American divorce was legal; Halsbury said it wasn't.

And that was that. Russell had no option but to plead guilty. He addressed the House before sentencing, pleading ignorance, which was of course no defence, and explaining, "Twelve years ago this month, my Lords, when only twenty-three years of age, that series of misfortunes began of which this trial today is the crown." He was sentenced to three months in gaol, an outcome which enraged him. "The whole thing appeared to me so monstrous, so incredible, such a piece of arrant stupidity, that I found it difficult to realize," he wrote later. "Fortunately, after a few weeks I calmed down and found the rest of my imprisonment restful and agreeable."[33]

In 1902 Mabel married a young man who said he was a wealthy Bavarian prince, a member of the Austrian royal family called Athrobold Stuart de Modena. He turned out to be a footman from Frimley named William Brown. After a short career in the music halls, Mabel died of consumption in 1908.

EIGHTEEN

AN HONEST FEELING
OF SATISFACTION

B OTH WHEN HE was Prince of Wales and when he was king,
Bertie's country house weekends usually involved shooting. At
Sandringham, there were four weeks' shooting every year, the main
two weeks coinciding with his birthday, November 9, and then with
Alix's birthday, December 1. He also had a week or two of shooting
at Balmoral every October. Whenever there was a partridge drive, an
equerry had the job of asking each gun how many birds he had got.
"This may have been very amusing for the good shots," recalled his
assistant private secretary, Fritz Ponsonby, "but it seemed to hold up
the bad shots to ridicule when the totals were read out at luncheon."[1]

It would be hard to exaggerate the impact that shooting had on
country house life. Although men (and it was an overwhelmingly
male pursuit) had been firing at all manner of wildlife since the end
of the sixteenth century, Victorian developments in the design of the
gun revolutionised the sport. Until the nineteenth century, game was

always walked up—that is, a small group of men moved forward in a line over open countryside with their dogs, carrying muzzle-loading guns. The dogs were trained to zigzag over the ground until they located a bird, when they stopped and pointed to it.

It was a cumbersome business: the guns, which had barrels perhaps forty inches long, were susceptible to damp and awkward to load with powder, wadding, and shot; the charge had to be seated with a ramrod; there was a delay between ignition and firing; and when the gun did go off it enveloped the shooter in a cloud of powder smoke which was slow to clear. As a result, bags were tiny in comparison with the big aristocratic shoots of the Edwardian period.

In 1851 a French invention, the breech-loading shotgun, was shown at the Great Exhibition in London, and within a few years it had been adopted by British sportsmen along with the all-in-one cartridge which contained charge and shot. The chokebore, which appeared in the early 1870s, increased the killing power of the gun, while smokeless gunpowder, which arrived around the same time, meant that one could shoot repeatedly and swiftly from the same location without having to wait for the smoke to clear.[2]

These technological advances all helped to popularise the most fundamental innovation in British game shooting: the driven shoot, or grand battue. Driven shooting, where the guns stayed in the same place and the birds were driven towards them by beaters, was already happening on several estates in the northwest of England by the 1820s: the Earl of Derby's Knowsley in Lancashire, for example, and the Marquess of Westminster's Eaton Hall in Cheshire. But from the 1850s onwards, helped along by the support of Prince Albert, who was an enthusiast, the driven shoot grew into a major social event on estates all over the country, with the exception of some of the Midland counties, where fox hunting still reigned supreme. The two were generally regarded as incompatible: preserving foxes so that they could slaughter pheasant chicks was something that was frowned on by the shooting fraternity, while shooting foxes to protect those birds came in for criticism from the hunt. Tenants were even forbidden to shoot game on their own fields: that right belonged to the landlord. Nor were they allowed to do anything to discourage birds, even if those birds were gobbling up their crops.

More effective firearms and the careful management of game led to a dramatic increase in the size of the bag. In 1859 eight shooters using muzzle-loaders and walking in line at Buckenham in Norfolk killed 704 partridges. Ten years later, on the Earl of Leicester's Holkham estate in the same county, with the shooters still walking in line but using breech-loading shotguns, 3,385 and 3,308 partridges were shot in two successive seasons. In 1885, when the grand battue was firmly established at Holkham, 8,100 birds were shot in a single season. On a single day at Elveden in Suffolk in September 1876, Maharajah Duleep Singh single-handedly killed 780 partridges, which was regarded as something of a record.

With fifty or a hundred liveried beaters, seven or eight guns with their loaders and their dogs, game wagons and ammunition carts and hundreds of spectators from local villages, an army of servants laden with food and drink for a shooting lunch which was more like a corporation banquet, and wives and other nonshooting houseguests traipsing across the fields to join the guns in devouring it, the set piece grand battue was a piece of theatre with something for everyone (except the birds). By the turn of the century the shoot had become a numbers game, and one which to modern sensibilities was rather grotesque. Even the dedicated Edwardian gun felt a little unease at the contemporary desire to rack up more kills than the next man:

So long as your interest in figures remains subjective [wrote the author of the 1911 *Partridges and Partridge Manors*], so

long as it is but an honest feeling of satisfaction that your science and skill have not been applied in vain, all is well; but,
alas, from that happy state it is but a step, or rather a grada-
tion of almost imperceptible steps, to the objective interest,
the desire to outshine your neighbours, the longing to hold or
break the record for your county or country.[3]

The writer, a retired soldier and a veteran of the Boer War named
Aymer Maxwell, went on to contrast two different approaches to
the shoot. On one type of estate, shooting was carried on over many
weeks, and guests were invited because they were friends, not because
they were famously good shots. The keepers were instructed not to
reveal the bag at the end of the day, and no one referred to numbers.

On the other estate, "a vast tract of country is devoted to the great
driving week."[4] The guns were semiprofessional, and they weren't
there to socialise. Everyone went to bed early and rose early so that
they were in position for the first drive by the time the sun came up.
Women were banned from the house party in case they distracted
the men from the business of the week. And that business was to kill
more birds than anyone else in a given time, with scores meticulously
recorded and published.

For Maxwell, there was a middle way. The pleasure of entertaining
friends shouldn't be ignored, but it was as well if the guns one invited
out were reasonably competent and took the business seriously. Chat-
ting with each other as the birds flew by was enough to dishearten the
best of keepers.

On the Castle Ashby estate, a bag of eight hundred pheasants in a
day was regarded as modest. At Lambton Castle, the Earl of Durham's
nineteenth-century country house south of Newcastle upon Tyne, it
was the proud boast that game was so plentiful that four thousand
head could be disposed of in a single day. When the Prince of Wales
was a member of a shooting party there in November 1897, the eight

guns managed a mere 1,186 pheasants on the first day, plus an unspecified number of ground game. "In the evening Herr Gottlieb's Vienna
Orchestra of stringed instruments played at the Castle."[5] Perhaps Herr
Gottlieb's waltzes spurred the guns on to greater efforts. The next day's
bag totalled 2,218, including more than 2,000 pheasants, and another
1,200 hit the ground on the next and last day's shooting.

Killing birds, rabbits, hares, and the occasional beater at this level
was small change to some of the most famous guns of the period. The
Duke of Portland, who took a keen interest in such matters—in 1906,
at one of the many shooting parties he hosted at Welbeck Abbey, the
guns killed 1,478 partridges in one day—reckoned that one of the
best shots he ever met was the 2nd Marquess of Ripon, who until he
inherited the title from his father in 1909 was known as Earl de Grey.
Once at Sandringham, Ripon killed twenty-eight pheasants in a minute. In 1900 he showed Portland a list of all the game he had killed
in the previous thirty-three years: it included 56,460 grouse, 97,759
partridges and 142,343 pheasants.*

Portland's own game books were impressive enough. Pre–First
World War partridge bags at Welbeck peaked in the 1906 season, when
6,183 were shot. Over three days in December 1909, shooting over
two more of his estates in Derbyshire and Nottinghamshire, a party
of ten guns, including His Royal Highness the Duke of Connaught,
killed 7,789 creatures. The vast majority were pheasants, but they also
managed fifty hares, twenty-two rabbits, and seven jays. "When I look
back at the game book I am quite ashamed of the enormous number of
pheasants we sometimes killed," he recalled much later.[6]

As battue shooting grew in popularity, it attracted its own legends
and literature, not all of it involving four-figure kills, and memoirs
of the time are full of such tales, some more amusing than others.
The Duke of Portland, who revelled in the anecdotal literature of the

---

*   The Duke of Portland's wife was the first president of the Royal Society for the
Protection of Birds. She was also a vegetarian.

shoot, described how, during a partridge shoot in the eastern counties, a distinguished nobleman shot a royal equerry and his loader. "The noble lord was so disgusted with himself that he returned home and went straight to bed!" chuckled Portland, without thinking to mention how things turned out for the equerry and the loader.[7]

Shooting was a dangerous sport. Prince Christian of Schleswig-Holstein, Queen Victoria's son-in-law, lost an eye while he was out with the Duke of Connaught and a shooting party at Osborne in December 1892. The same year a gun in Bedfordshire fired at a wounded partridge and managed to hit eight beaters, which must have been some kind of record.

Beaters were shot and killed with surprising frequency. They got into the line of fire or were hit by stray shot. One man was shot dead after one of the shooters aimed at a rabbit and shouted to the beaters, who were between him and his prey, to lie down; the beater raised his head to see what was going on as the man fired and was killed. A groom who was acting as a beater on a Warwickshire estate was handing one of the guns across a fence when the trigger caught and both cartridges were discharged into his stomach, killing him instantly. Another unfortunate went to pick up a grouse brought down by one of the guns when a second bird rose near him. Someone fired at it and shot him in the back of the head. He died.

Portland recalled seeing a woman spectator knocked out cold by a dead pheasant falling on her head. She "did not really recover from the blow for three or four months." Something similar very nearly happened to Edward VII, who was out with the shoot at Welbeck but temporarily confined to a wheelchair, having injured his foot. The Marquess of Ripon killed a high-flying bird which fell on the king, bursting open and covering him with blood and feathers. "Naturally, H.M. was none too pleased," said Portland, with a gift for understatement.[8]

After Ripon, Portland's other candidate for best shot at that time was Thomas de Grey, 6th Baron Walsingham. A little after five in the morning on August 30, 1888, Walsingham went shooting on his Blubberhouses Moor estate in Yorkshire. By the end of the last drive, just over thirteen hours later, he had shot 1,057 red grouse, working with a team of loaders. He potted thirteen more that he happened to see on his walk home. That bag, 1,070 game birds shot on a single day, remains a world record, albeit a rather inglorious one.

On Tuesday, December 16, 1913, George V left Buckingham Palace by motorcar, accompanied by Fritz Ponsonby and his equerry, Lord Charles Fitzmaurice. Their destination was Hall Barn in Buckinghamshire. Since 1880 the house and its four-thousand-acre estate had belonged to Edward Levy-Lawson, the proprietor of the *Daily Telegraph* and one of Edward VII's many Jewish friends, and as both Prince of Wales and king, Edward often visited Hall Barn for the shooting; he had given Levy-Lawson a title, Lord Burnham of Hall Barn, in 1903.

George V was not on such close terms with Lord Burnham.* As the *Tatler* rather nastily pointed out when the news of the king's two-day visit to Hall Barn came out, "Hosts of Lord Burnham's nationality entertain royalty but seldom under the present *régime*, for the possession of gold untold together with business acumen galore is somehow not now the social passport it was—not in royal circles anyway."[9] But Burnham had assembled an interesting and eclectic bunch of guests to meet the king during his two-day stay. There was

---

* There is a Max Beerbohm caricature of Burnham walking along a corridor in Buckingham Palace with Alfred and Leopold de Rothschild, Sir Ernest Cassel, and Arthur Sassoon, with the caption, "Are we as welcome as ever?" And the answer, as George V's biographer Jane Ridley points out, was "No."

the dramatist Arthur Wing Pinero, now calling himself Sir Arthur Pinero, having been knighted in 1909, and the actor and comedian Sir John Hare, who also was knighted by the king's father. The press was represented by J. L. Garvin, editor of the *Observer*, and the critic and philosopher W. L. Courtney, who wrote for Burnham's paper. The prison reformer Sir Evelyn Ruggles-Brise was there. So was the all-round athlete and sportsman Willie Grenfell, Lord Desborough, and the Liberal politician and ex–cabinet minister the Marquess of Lincolnshire. The nineteen-year-old Prince of Wales didn't stay the night (this wasn't due to one of his clashes with his father but simply because Edward VII had instituted a policy by which the king and his heir never stayed overnight together as guests in a country house) and joined the party on the morning of December 18.

George V hadn't come to Hall Barn to meet interesting people. He was there to shoot pheasants, an occupation which his son declared to be "one of [his] father's greatest pleasures in life." Even more than his father, King George was addicted to the sport: for years, his public functions were arranged around the shooting season, which always took precedence. In a single season, the winter of 1896–1897, he shot a total of 11,006 creatures, including 2,509 partridges and nearly 6,000 pheasants. He once threatened not to attend his brother-in-law's wedding because it clashed with his shooting; and when he was staying at Elveden in Suffolk in October 1897 and a telegram came from his wife saying she was heartbroken because her mother had just died and begging him to join her at once, he was heard to mutter as he stepped into the waiting car, "It is very hard on me: as it knocks all my shooting on the head."[10]

Although Lord Burnham expended huge amounts of money on the pheasants at Hall Barn, he didn't shoot with the king on this occasion, perhaps because he was getting on a bit—he was only a couple of weeks away from celebrating his eightieth birthday. The shoot was organised by his son Harry, who was also one of the guns on the first day, when 1,475 birds were killed. The next day, Harry gave his place to the Prince of Wales. Apart from the king, the other five guns were the equerry Lord Charles Fitzmaurice; groom-in-waiting Henry Stonor, who was one of the best game shots in England at the time; the Earl of Ilchester and the Earl of Dalhousie; and Lord Herbert Vane-Tempest, director of Cambrian railways and another famous shot.*

That morning, the seven guns and their loaders went out and began their day's sport. They were six hours in the field, with a break at one o'clock for lunch in a large marquee which Lord Burnham had filled with twenty or so guests from London, invited up to meet the king and to join in what the Prince of Wales described as "a baronial repast of the choicest of victuals and the rarest of wines."[11] Afterwards, a story went round that a guest with simpler tastes had caused anguish to the majordomo by asking for a glass of iced water—which was about the only thing he hadn't thought to provide.

After lunch, the slaughter continued. The birds kept on coming— so many that the prince reckoned Burnham must have brought in hundreds to supplement his own coverts and released them purely for the king's benefit. George used three guns and had a distinctive style, his left arm straight down the barrel and both eyes open. One spectator reported he saw the king bring down thirty-nine pheasants in a row without missing a single bird.

When the shoot was finally over and the seven guns stood down, half deafened from the noise, their shoulders aching and their hands shaking, the whole place was a sea of feathers and spent cartridges. The carcases were laid out in rows of a hundred, and there were nearly forty rows. The king had shot more than a thousand birds, and his son—who was not a particularly good shot—had downed over three hundred. A total of 3,937 pheasants had been killed that day—still a record. Driving back to London that evening, the king

---

* Ten months later Lord Charles Fitzmaurice died at Ypres.

turned to his son and said, "Perhaps we went a little too far today, David."[12]

Shoots on this apocalyptic scale were very expensive. "Up goes a guinea, bang goes a penny halfpenny, and down comes half-a-crown" was the old adage. And they demanded careful management by land agents and keepers. Pheasants were lovingly hand-reared and fed grain. Birds were bought in; live hares were imported to bolster numbers. Eggs were protected from predators by being removed from the nest and placed under domestic hens before being put back into the wild. Head gamekeepers on the biggest estates kept a small army of keepers, each of whom had responsibility for a particular beat. As far back as the eighteenth century the Duke of Richmond, who was then employing twenty gamekeepers, imported more than a thousand partridge eggs a year from France to be hatched under hens on his Goodwood estate, a practice that came to a halt with the French Revolution.

And then there were the poachers. Apart from their nightly patrols, gamekeepers resorted to all sorts of tricks to confound them. They fixed trip wires between trees and tied threads of cotton between bushes on paths which they suspected of being used illegally. One keeper who thought a local character was stealing his pheasant's eggs and selling them on to a particular game-breeding farm, wrote his name in invisible ink on every single pheasant's egg he knew of. Then, because he was also buying in when he needed to, he put in an order with the farm and dipped these eggs into a special fluid, at which his signature appeared as if by magic. Confronted with the evidence, the breeder gave up the name of the thief, who was duly prosecuted.

As the importance of preserving game for sport grew, so did the legislation. The draconian game laws of the eighteenth and early nineteenth centuries, with their mantraps and spring guns and spikes set in hare runs at a height which allowed a hare to pass but impaled the pursuing dog, had been relaxed a little: mantraps and spring guns were made illegal in 1827. But an "Act for the more effectual prevention of Persons going armed by Night for the Destruction of Game," the 1828 Night Poaching Act, remained on the statute books: the penalty for a first offence was three months' hard labour; for a second, six months; and for a third, transportation "beyond Seas for Seven Years," or two years' hard labour. Any poacher who tried to resist arrest by a keeper or who attacked one could expect the maximum penalty, even for a first offence.

The laws were labyrinthine. (The 1877 edition of *Oke's Handy Book of the Game Laws*, the standard work on the subject, ran to 683 pages.) The Night Poaching Act was amended in 1844 to apply to anyone taking game or rabbits on any public road, highway or path. The Poaching Prevention Act of 1862 made it lawful for "any Constable or Peace Officer" to stop and search anyone they suspected of having been poaching, and to bring them up for the petty sessions, where they could be fined five pounds and have guns, nets, and other equipment confiscated.

Various arguments were put forward in defence of the game laws. If tenants were allowed to kill game on their land, farmers and their sons would spend so much time shooting that they would neglect their farming. An increase in gun ownership would pose a threat to public order. And there would be nothing left for the gentleman sportsman, who would be discouraged from taking an interest in local affairs if their sporting pleasures were removed. In a parliamentary debate in 1880 on a proposition to allow tenants to kill game on land which they occupied, Sir Walter Barttelot, who owned a 3,633-acre estate in Sussex, declared that any relaxation of the game laws would be disastrous. "If they did not give gentlemen some amusement to attract them to the country and to keep them there, they would have absenteeism, which was so much complained on in Ireland." In the same debate Earl Percy, who was heir to Alnwick Castle and his father the Duke of Northumberland's vast estates in the north, went further. "That which distinguished this country was what was called our country life, under which a body of gentlemen possessed of property, and having the interests of the people at heart, took part in the sports and directed the local affairs of their district, thus showing that they were of use and influence in the world."[13] Any attempt to relax the game laws would undermine the very fabric of British rural life. The bill passed into law, but it was confined to ground game: a farmer could kill hares and rabbits, but the right to shoot birds still belonged to the landlord. And there were restrictions: only one other person beside the occupier was allowed to use firearms; the terms of an existing lease stayed in force until the end of that lease; and guns could only be used in daylight hours.

These terms were enforced, too. In 1881, James Moore, who farmed at Bittadon in Devon, decided that the Ground Game Act allowed him to hunt rabbits over his farmland, and he invited three friends to join him. A keeper found the men in the act of netting a rabbit in the middle of the night, and the owner of the sporting rights over the land brought Moore and the others before the bench. Their lawyer argued that the Ground Game Act permitted them to hunt rabbits, but the prosecution pointed out that Moore's old lease was still in force, and even if it wasn't, the Night Poaching Act would have caught them out. They were fined five pounds each plus costs, with the unpalatable alternative of one month's hard labour.

Most poachers weren't particularly concerned with the finer points of the Ground Game Act. Judging from the frequency with which offenders came up before the courts, it seems that snaring, trapping, netting, and shooting wild animals and birds was a favourite pastime in rural Britain. Their judges, the local justices of the peace, usually came from the landed classes whose game was being pilfered. In fact, on more than one occasion, the JP was actually the victim, although when that happened it was considered good form to leave the case to one's colleagues (and fellow landowners).

But what stands out is not the poaching, which was usually handled with a telling off, a fine, and the option of a month in jail. It is the frequency with which keepers, policemen, and poachers were caught up in violent assaults, sometimes in pitched battles with clubs, knives, and guns. Policemen were found lying bleeding and unconscious, having tried to arrest a gang. Poachers were shot. Masked men with dogs launched vicious attacks on lone keepers. In one nighttime encounter between salmon poachers and keepers in Applecross Bay, Ross-shire, in 1886, one of the poachers held a keeper's head under water and tried to drown him. He would have succeeded if another keeper hadn't come to the rescue and knocked him senseless with a blow to the head with the butt of his gun. It is not surprising to know that in 1886 an organisation was founded, the Keepers' Benefit Society, to provide for the widows and families of gamekeepers who lost their lives in the protection of game. (The Duke of Portland was its president.)

And there were fatalities. About three o'clock one Sunday morning in November 1881 a party of twenty keepers came on four poachers who were shooting on High Legh in Cheshire, an estate belonging to a Colonel Henry Legh. The poachers were all armed with guns, while the keepers had only sticks—or so they claimed later. They rushed the poachers, who fired at them, missed, and then used their guns as clubs, shattering one man's jaw and knocking him senseless. Initial reports said that one of the poachers was also knocked down and died while he was being carried to the local police station. In fact he had been shot, and the keepers maintained that he must have been hit by one of his comrades, who were duly charged with wilful murder. But it turned out that the raid on the poachers had been carefully planned and the head keeper, a local farmer, and Colonel Legh's agent were all carrying revolvers, in spite of denying the fact in court; and it was one of these revolvers which had killed the man. At the Chester Assizes the poachers were tried for intent to do grievous bodily harm, but the judge spoke up for them in his summing up and they were each sentenced to eighteen months' hard labour. The three young men who had perjured themselves were denounced by the same judge, who said that if he thought they had lied under oath in an attempt to get the poachers hanged, no sentence he could pass would have been too severe. As it was, he gave them the benefit of the doubt and gave them the same sentences as the poachers—eighteen months' hard labour.

It wasn't only the judge whose sympathies lay with the poachers. When the jury found them guilty, with a recommendation for mercy on account of the treatment they had received from the keepers, the court cheered. The *Graphic* used the case to attack game preserving and the grand battue: "One man dead, several more or less severely wounded, and six men shut up in prison for a year and a half. And all for what? Why, that a few rich men may have a few hours' annual indulgence in battue-shooting, an amusement which has very little of the true sportsmanlike element to recommend it."[14]

When men blundered about in the woods with loaded guns, the consequences could be terrible. One afternoon in January 1904 Harry Osmond, an under-keeper on Lord Falmouth's Tregothnan estate in Cornwall, went out with his gun and his dog and didn't come back. By nightfall his wife was anxious and a search party was organised. Eventually Osmond was found dead in woods on the estate with a chest wound, his dog lying at his side, his gunstock badly damaged, and parts of his watch and chain lying about twenty yards from the body.

Police followed a trail of blood in the direction of the village of Probus, two miles away. That night a Dr Bonar was called to a house in Probus belonging to thirty-five-year-old Robert Bullen, a known poacher, who was in great pain with a shotgun wound to his upper leg.

When Dr Bonar mentioned that Osmond was missing, Bullen admitted firing at the gamekeeper, but he said that Osmond shot first and he was acting in self-defence. "I was in the wood and saw the keeper," he said, "and I attempted to run away. He fired at me, and I turned round and fired at him. I heard a noise, but I did not go back to see if he was living or dead."[15]

A witness later claimed to have heard *three* shots fired in rapid succession that night, coming from the Nance Mabyn Woods, where the body was found. It seemed that Osmond had surprised Bullen poaching in the woods; Bullen had fired and hit the keeper, who kept on coming and shot Bullen in the hip, at which point Bullen fired again at point-blank range, hitting Osmond in the chest and killing him, before dragging himself home on his hands and knees. A postmortem showed the keeper had about a hundred pellets in one lung and a hole in his heart big enough to poke a finger in.

For some weeks it seemed as though Bullen wouldn't survive his injuries. But at the end of February, he had recovered sufficiently to be carried to the inquest in a police ambulance. The jury returned a verdict of wilful murder against Bullen, but when the case came to court at the Cornwall Assizes in June, the charge was reduced to manslaughter, since the judge said that the shot which killed the keeper was undoubtedly provoked by the shot which Osmond fired at Bullen. He was sentenced to ten years' penal servitude.

He hanged himself in his cell at Bodmin Prison three days later.

NINETEEN

LADY BOUNTIFUL

O UTWARDLY," RECALLED DAISY Warwick, looking back in the 1930s on life at the turn of the century, "it was a life of idle pleasure, and was condemned in consequence. This was only true in part, for duty was a big word in those days. We took a personal interest in our tenants, their families, and their affairs":

> In the old days the châtelaine played the part of Lady Bountiful, and gave of her time, and dispensed her charity with a free hand. The sick and the poor looked up to her as a source of "dole," and I think that it is only fair to say that she was kind at heart and well-meaning, even where the gods had not blessed her with any special measure of intelligence. But the system for which she stood was founded on something akin to serfdom; the rising tide of democracy has carried it away—unwept, unhonoured and unsung, except by those in whose blood there is something of the flunkey strain.[1]

The balance between kindness and condescension was hard to achieve. Late Victorian and Edwardian rural society was a world in which villagers were expected to show deference to those at the big house, not only because it was politic to do so—although it certainly was—but also because it was in the nature of things to respect your betters, although it was rather harder to respect the company director who had just bought the estate than it was to tug one's forelock to the peer whose family had overseen your community for the past five hundred years. And relationships with even the kindest and most liberal of those betters operated in the context of a shared knowledge that they had the power to dismiss and evict out of hand, with no possibility of appeal.

There were attempts to empower the smallholder or the occupant of a tied cottage, but they were not a success. The Town Planning Act of 1909, for example, made provision for tenants to petition for an enquiry if they believed that their cottage was below standard. By 1912, 153 new cottages had been built as a result, but 1,689 more had been served with closure orders. As critics pointed out at the time, agricultural labourers preferred sleeping under a leaky roof to sleeping under no roof at all.

When John Picton-Turbervill inherited Ewenny Priory in Glamorgan in 1892, his nineteen-year-old daughter Edith played the organ in church, trained the choir, taught in the Sunday School, and, as she wrote, "undertook the duties that generally fall to a squire's daughter . . . not because I had any qualifications for teaching spiritual truths, but because it was expected that one of us should do it." In a 1909 essay on "The Position of Women," Consuelo, Duchess of Marlborough, explained the duties and responsibilities that were still incumbent on the chatelaine of a country house, remnants of feudal obligations. She oversaw the distribution of blankets and coal to villagers in winter and organised the entertainment of schoolchildren in summer. She was the head of all the village organisations and events, from the annual flower show to the beekeeping society. "She will have to attend and preside at numberless meetings, flower-shows and bazaars, visit hospitals and workhouses, care for the poor and destitute, and get to know everyone, and his and her wants individually." And if she didn't live up to expectations, everyone from the local gentry to an old blind widow would let her know of it.[2]

As Consuelo suggested, the pressure on the woman of the country house to conform to traditional expectations of her came from all sides: from her peers and from the recipients of her good offices. But she was not powerless. She could exert social control over estate workers and their families, withholding largesse at will, arbitrating over moral matters, and, in partnership with her husband or, more often, her husband's land agent, removing families who failed to live up to her standards.

Describing this process, the social commentator F. G. Heath gave the example of Wilcot, an estate hamlet near Marlborough in Wiltshire. Writing in 1880, he applauded the way that Wilcot was managed by its landlords, a retired admiral and his wife. Rents were kept low. The standard of housing was exemplary. "But 'conduct' [was] the key to admission." The village inn remained closed on Sundays—not because the admiral (who was also the owner of the inn) required it, but because there was apparently no demand among the uniformly pious inhabitants of Wilcot for strong drink on Sundays. Gardens were kept neat and tidy—not because the admiral and his wife demanded it, but because they let it be known that they liked neatness and tidiness, "and the cottagers [took] the hint." If any member of a Wilcot family was found to be drunk, he or she was told to leave the village. "If the daughter of a labourer proves to be 'unfortunate' on returning from service or otherwise, the family to which she belongs are also required . . . to leave the house they occupy." By no means did every country house owner exert this draconian level of control. But the knowledge that they *could* was a strong incentive to conform.[3]

And there were unexpected perks to patronage. Strolling into an unnamed West Country village at dusk, the writer W. H. Hudson decided to visit the church, where he was struck by the figure of a female saint in stained glass which filled the west window. She was "a lovely young woman in a blue robe with an abundance of loose golden-red hair, and an aureole about her head. Her pale face wore a sweet and placid expression, and her eyes, of a pure forget-me-not blue, were looking straight into mine."[4]

The vicar told Hudson that this was a portrait of "our generous patroness," Lady Y——, who had contributed a huge sum towards rebuilding the church a few years before. Hudson knew her—but as a "funny old woman" rather than a beautiful girl. The vicar explained that, as she owned most of the parish and had done so much for it, he was happy to grant her wish "that the future inhabitants of the place shall not remember her as a middle-aged woman not remarkable for good looks."[5]

Who said philanthropic endeavours couldn't be fun? At Christmas 1889, for example, the younger members of the Devonshire clan staged two farces, John Oxenford's *Twice Killed* and William Dean Howell's *The Mouse-Trap*, to benefit the reading room in the Chatsworth estate village of Beeley. The performance took place in the coach house at Chatsworth, which was decked out for the occasion with a stage, footlights, and a red baize proscenium arch festooned with orchids; props included several paintings brought over from the house. There was an invited audience of around 470, drawn largely from the county, and the event raised £21 6s 6d—not a huge amount at less than a shilling a head, but no doubt the reading room welcomed it; and the dress rehearsal, which took place two days before the performance proper, doubled as a Christmas treat for the pupils of schools on the Chatsworth estate, with a sit-down tea afterwards. The children put on a show of their own in the interval, "the Edensor boys gaining much applause for a song with a whistling chorus."[6]

Owners sometimes offered their houses, or more often their gardens and parks, to organisations with which they were associated: that was one of the perks of having a prestigious landowning patron or patroness. It might mean no more than lending a corner of the park for the annual Sunday school outing, or it might mean something much more ambitious. In August 1898 the Duke of Marlborough, who was president of the recently formed National Fire Brigades Union, threw open the grounds of Blenheim Palace to an enormous gathering of around eight hundred firemen. Delegates came from France, Belgium, South Africa, Australia, and Germany as well as all parts of United Kingdom, camping out in a sea of bell tents that stretched across the park and almost reached the palace, and taking part in a programme of events which ran with military precision over four days. There were tug-of-war competitions; hose races, in which each man had to run twenty yards, pick up, unstrap, and run out with a fifty-foot length of hose; ladder and bucket races; parades and drills; concerts and dancing in the evening; and a procession to the palace lit by petroleum torches. On the Sunday there was church parade attended by the Duke and Duchess of Marlborough and their houseguests. The rector took the text for his sermon from the Epistle of James, "Behold how great a matter a little fire kindleth." Firemen in full uniform were allowed to see the palace staterooms, but only for an hour on a single afternoon.[7]

The grounds of country houses were convenient settings for big political rallies. In September 1896, for example, the Duke and Duchess of Marlborough hosted a one-day rally of around two thousand Conservatives at Blenheim. Lunch was served in a vast marquee put up on the front lawn, and afterwards parties of visitors were shown over the house while a band played outside and, in the Long Library, an organist from Birmingham Town Hall gave a recital on the four-manual Henry Willis organ which had been installed five years earlier, before the inevitable speeches exhorting the party faithful to greater efforts.

Similar gatherings in aid of the Liberals were less earnest, if the "Liberal Demonstration and People's Fete in Support of Home Rule" held at Althorp in August 1893 was anything to go by. There were still the speeches, notably from home secretary and future prime minister H. H. Asquith, and music was supplied by the Northampton Temperance Silver Band; but the ten-thousand-strong crowd was also entertained by the Ladderites, a troupe of acrobats; by trapeze artists; and by "Edie and Annella, two pretty children, [who] gave a pleasing entertainment on the double tight wires."[8] A local pub landlord ran a beer tent (in competition with a temperance café, which was also in residence for the day), and special excursion trains were laid on to bring in the visitors, who were charged threepence each for admission and a penny for children, with parking at sixpence for two-wheeled carriages and a shilling for four-wheelers.* The evening culminated in a spectacular firework display with a giant fire portrait of Gladstone and the flaming motto "Long live our leader."

As lord lieutenant for Northamptonshire, Althorp's owner, the 5th Earl Spencer, thought it prudent to stay away on the day, in case he was accused of political bias: although since he was a well-known Liberal politician and was currently serving as first lord of the admiralty in Gladstone's government, nobody was fooled. The local paper noted that he "allowed" his wife and his sister-in-law to be there to represent him.

---

* At Jesmond Dene, Sir William Armstrong regularly hosted the Newcastle Temperance Union's annual "monster picnic," which attracted between ten thousand and fifteen thousand people. Temperance was big in Victorian Newcastle, although in 1864 one enterprising chap set up a barrel of beer at the entrance to the grounds to fortify abstainers as they went in.

Standing somewhere between the private fundraising theatricals aimed at an elite invited audience and the mass rallies of the party faithful, complete with beer tents and trapeze artists, were the public garden parties and fetes and bazaars and sales of work, usually directed at raising money for local causes. Sometimes a country house owner's involvement might amount to nothing more than lending the park for the day; more often, if the cause was dear to their heart, they would play a more active role.

In 1886 the Earl and Countess of Leicester, of Holkham Hall in Norfolk, gave a reading room to their estate workers in Holkham village. Rural reading rooms enjoyed quite a vogue in the second half of the nineteenth century, as the Chatsworth theatricals in 1889 in aid of the reading room at Beeley testify. Part of a movement to provide rational recreation for the labouring classes, they were frequently seen as more palatable alternatives to the village inn (more palatable to the landed elite, at least), in that they were a means of affording their tenants "a rational occupation and diverting them from mere sensual indulgence." As one Norfolk landowner claimed, by donating a reading room to his village, he enabled the villagers "to pass some of their evenings rationally and profitably, without being driving to the bar or to the tap room as the only place of resort."[9]

Because they were seen as replacements for the village pub—itself a gendered space in Victorian and Edwardian Britain—rural reading rooms tended to be male domains, equipped not only with newspapers and journals but sometimes also with all the paraphernalia of the pub: dominoes, draughts, cribbage boards, and, in one case, eight spittoons. Some boasted billiard tables; others had pianos. Cricket clubs and bowling clubs were sometimes attached, and rifle clubs in several Gloucestershire villages were only open to reading room members.[10] There were a few attempts to be more inclusive: the committee running the reading room at Necton in Norfolk, which doubled as a hostel for young male workers, decided in 1872 to admit local women, five of whom promptly paid their subscription of sixpence a quarter and joined as full members. But two only lasted a year, and by 1878 all but one had dropped out.

Rural reading rooms were often supported by local landowners who, like the Leicesters, might donate a site and pay for fitting it out. At Sandringham, the Prince of Wales opened a reading room for the use of "servants and workmen employed on the Sandringham estate." The Earl of Elgin donated land at Broomhall near Dunfermline for the erection of a reading room and public hall for the benefit of people living on his estate there; his sister, Lady Louisa Bruce, offered to pay for building it and fitting it out. In 1884 the evangelically inclined Earl of Tankerville built a reading room on his Chillingham estate for the use of Irish navvies working on a new railway nearby; his countess oversaw the project when she wasn't busy organising "prayer meetings, bible classes, children's and mother's meetings, [and] young men's tea gatherings at Chillingham." The earl also employed a Protestant missionary specifically to work with the navvies, while one of his estate stewards gave them educational classes.[11]

The Holkham reading room was said to have cost £1,500. It is an eccentric piece of Old English architecture, very much of its time, with tall Jacobethan brick chimneys and a spiky timber-framed turret, all hovering incongruously over pedimented windows. Described by a contemporary as "a beautiful building in the Swiss cottage style" (neither of which was true), it was designed by a Norwich-born architect, Zephaniah King, and opened in June 1886 with a concert at which the Countess of Leicester played a piano solo.[12] She played again at an entertainment in the new reading room that Christmas, accompanying a "Children's Band" composed of the Leicester children and grandchildren, and over the next twenty years or so she was indefatigable in her efforts to support the venture.

Once they were up and running, rural reading rooms were meant to be self-supporting, with members paying a small weekly, monthly, or quarterly subscription. But those with a small membership couldn't hope to cover all their running costs this way: Holkham had only around fifty members (out of a village population of under five hundred), and the countess's fundraising efforts were relentless. In the summer of 1891, for example, she held a tennis tournament at Holkham in aid of reading room funds, with a bazaar in the Egyptian Hall at the house where she and her children presided over stalls selling fancy goods, fruit, and sweets, aided by four or five other noblewomen. The proceeds were most encouraging, reported the local paper, helped along by sales of teas in the hall at sixpence a head. "The admission also included the privilege of viewing several of the adjoining rooms." The countess opened another bazaar and sale of work in the reading room itself in 1899, when the stalls were once again presided over by members of her family and guests staying at the hall, who were also recruited to do a turn when sales began to flag. They sang, they gave violin solos, and the Leicesters' sixteen-year-old son Reginald "delighted the audience with exhibitions on a powerful gramophone."[13]

The annual reading room bazaars became a regular feature of Holkham life, and when the reading room committee staged a fancy dress dance in 1903, the countess was there providing the band and making sure the room was decorated with plants and flowers from the Holkham gardens.

The Countess of Leicester's activities at Holkham offer a good example of aristocratic community engagement. She paid for an annual treat for the village schoolchildren and bought each of them a present. As president of the Norfolk branch of the Soldiers' and Sailors' Families Association, a welfare organisation set up in the 1880s to support military families, she hosted its meetings in the Egyptian Hall at Holkham. She lent the house for gatherings of the Church of England Waifs and Strays Society. She opened fetes and bazaars and hospitals and, with her husband, took an active interest in a range of good causes. "Her interest in local matters was of the keenest," declared one obituarist.[14]

Aristocratic chatelaines came in many forms. Before she married the 2nd Earl of Leicester, the countess was Hon. Georgiana Caroline Cavendish, daughter of William George Cavendish, 2nd Baron Chesham and a member of the extended Cavendish clan headed by the Duke of Devonshire. Her mother, Henrietta, was the niece of the Earl of Harewood. One of her sisters was married to the Duke of Westminster; another, to Viscount Cobham. Anyone who felt the need to look up the countess's pedigree in *Debrett's Peerage and Baronetage* would be impressed.

The same could not be said of every countess in *Debrett's*, as the Earl of Clancarty discovered to his cost. Richard Somerset Le Poer Trench was an eminent Victorian, the 4th Earl of Clancarty in the Irish peerage and Marquess of Heusden in the Netherlands. His ancestral seat, Garbally, stood at the heart of a twenty-five-thousand-acre estate in Galway and Roscommon. In London, where he had a residence in Knightsbridge, his was a familiar face at royal levees, state concerts, and Buckingham Palace balls, along with his wife Adeliza, the impeccably aristocratic daughter of a marquess and granddaughter of a duke. Lineage and class mattered a very great deal to the 4th Earl of Clancarty.

So when, in July 1889, he read in the *Pall Mall Gazette* that his twenty-year-old son and heir had just married a burlesque actress named Belle Bilton, the earl was understandably dismayed. She was two and a half years older than Freddie but, in the words of the QC who appeared for him in the resulting court case, she was "many years his senior in experience of the world."[15] When Clancarty heard that Belle, who performed a song-and-dance act on the halls with her sister Flo, had an illegitimate one-year-old son and that the father, a married man called Weston, was serving eighteen months in Pentonville Prison for fraud, he was apoplectic.

Freddie, who went by the courtesy title of Viscount Dunlo, was already something of a disappointment to him. He was a "weak-faced, beardless boy" who was not blessed with brains and whose main interests lay not in the military career that his father had arranged for him but in gambling clubs and racecourses and weekends in Brighton.[16] Clancarty's reaction to the news of the nuptials was to pack the boy off to Australia without his new wife and to set a pack of private detectives on the viscountess in the hope of finding evidence for a divorce.

They found it. Or perhaps it would be fairer to say, they invented it. Left alone after only nine days of marriage (five or six of which the couple had spent apart), and with no means of support other than the ten pounds a week that she and Flo earned on the stage at the Alhambra, Belle accepted the protection of an old friend named Isidor Wertheimer, the son of a New Bond Street antique dealer, who had been in love with her for years and who had paid her medical expenses when she had her child. After she was attacked at her lodgings by Weston, her ex-partner, newly released from gaol and determined to get some money out of her, Wertheimer offered her the use of a furnished house in St John's Wood. He visited her there regularly, took her to the theatre, dined with her at the Café Royal, and generally accompanied her about town, furnishing Clancarty's team of detectives with a mountain of circumstantial evidence. Detectives claimed to have seen the couple together standing at Belle's bedroom window; servants claimed they turned the key in the drawing room door when they were alone together; and by the end of the year Clancarty was in a position to send a packet of evidence to his son in Australia, ordering him to begin proceedings for divorce.

If the quotes appearing in the Australian press are anything to go by, Dunlo—"a not very promising twig of the English nobility," said one paper—wasn't too upset about the enforced separation from his bride. He spent his time racing, going to balls and supper parties, hunting, playing tennis and cricket, "and nearly always drunk."[17]

Believing he wouldn't have to appear in court—and thus be confronted by his deserted bride—Freddie agreed to the divorce, but he hedged his bets by writing immediately to Belle, telling her he didn't believe a word of the detectives' statements.

The case of *Dunlo v. Dunlo and Wertheimer* was one of the most notorious causes célèbres in late Victorian England. In the course of a trial lasting six days in July 1890, the private lives of the three people concerned were ruthlessly dissected and paraded before the public in a horribly unedifying manner. Dunlo, who had been mistaken in thinking he could stay safely out of the way on the other side of the world, was made to appear and came across as a pathetically weak young man with no backbone and no morals. He and his dubious friends had apparently tossed for who should have Belle, and he had won. And after his father found out about the marriage he wrote him a snivelling letter, begging his forgiveness and saying he wanted to go abroad and stay there for as long as possible. "I now see clearly what an awful thing I have done," he wrote three days after his marriage. "What is to become of her I must leave to you."[18] In the witness box, Lord Clancarty said unequivocally that he didn't care what happened to Belle.

Isidor Wertheimer's guilt was taken for granted by the earl's team. Why would a man be so kind to a girl unless she was sleeping with him? And Belle herself was obviously guilty. She was a fallen woman, a single mother. She was an *actress*. Of course she must be Wertheimer's mistress.

But as the trial wore on, something happened. Clancarty's vindictiveness alienated the jury. His son's desertion of his bride was repeatedly held up as an example of unmanly behaviour. The detectives who testified to having seen Belle and Isidor Wertheimer together in compromising situations had destroyed their notebooks in the days leading up to the trial and were unable to provide an explanation as to why they had done so. One of the witnesses failed to turn up and later admitted to having been paid a guinea to incriminate Belle. And Belle herself cut an imposing and dignified figure, sitting calmly at her solicitor's table and passing notes up to her QC, Frank Lockwood, as he cross-examined her husband, and answering Sir Charles Russell, Dunlo's QC, quietly and articulately. She had been forced to leave one set of lodgings because Weston attacked her; she had had to leave another because her landlady objected to the fact that she was being watched and followed by Clancarty's detectives. She had been left destitute when her husband fled to Australia. And in spite of all this she had been faithful to him.

Lockwood gave a masterly closing statement. Belle was a woman more sinned against than sinning. Except for her relationship with Weston, "her life was without reproach." The judge, Sir James Hannen, in summing up the case, blamed Clancarty for doing his best to expose Belle to temptation, and he blamed Dunlo, who he said was "a puppet in the hands of his father," for deserting her.[19]

It took the jury just fifteen minutes to find "that Lady Dunlo had not committed adultery with Mr Wertheimer." The court broke into applause, and when Belle appeared outside the court she was greeted by a cheering crowd. Men clambered on omnibuses to get a glimpse of her, traffic in the Strand came to a standstill and hundreds of people shouted "Bravo, Lady Dunlo!"[20]

Over the following days, the press in Britain and across the world followed up on the story. They duly acknowledged what one paper called "the highly ambiguous outward relations between Lady Dunlo and her platonic admirer." But they were merciless in their condemnation of Lord Dunlo and his father. "The youthful heir to the Earldom of Clancarty is obviously not overburdened with brains," declared the *Daily Telegraph*, attacking him for his weakness in deserting his bride before attributing the earl's attempts to fabricate evidence to "an essentially artificial and perverted estimate of the relative importance of his family dignity." The *Times* went further: Clancarty's behaviour towards his daughter-in-law was hard and unfeeling. "Hardly had the marriage taken place when he sent his son on a voyage round the world, apparently careless of the terrible temptations that assail a handsome woman, deprived of her husband's protection, and marked out by her calling for the attentions of every wealthy libertine." It was the earl's own fault if his conduct was seen as "a piece of sharp practice, intended to bring to pass as quickly as possible what it should have been his anxious care to avert." In Ireland, the *Freeman's Journal* called Dunlo a "dishonourable coward," adding contemptuously, "He is but a poor creature, this scion of nobility, and it is almost a waste of space to have devoted so much to him." *Reynolds's Newspaper* went further still, declaring, "In all the disgraceful records of the British peerage we doubt if anything can be found that surpasses in sheer unadulterated blackguardism the conduct of Lord Clancarty in the matter," and adding that "if Lord Dunlo is a contemptible dolt it is little to be wondered at when he is the son of such a father."[21]

And now something rather unexpected happened. The hapless and useless Lord Dunlo, having aided and abetted his father in trashing his wife's reputation all over the English-speaking world, decided he wanted her after all. He put it about that the divorce case was really a friendly action, designed to clear his wife's name, although no one believed him.

Even more surprisingly, Belle agreed to take him back.

The earl's response was to stop his son's allowance and change his will. The new will, drawn up days after his humiliation in court, made his wife, rather than his son and heir, his executor, because only she would "religiously carry out what she knows to be my wishes." Those wishes were that she should have his personal estate, valued at £53,000 and including the family seat at Garbally. He created a trust fund for his younger son, Richard, and his daughter, Katherine, and he ordered that "whatever furniture, pictures and plate with the Clan-carty crest at Garbally or Coorheen [the dower house] at the time of his death should be sold and the proceeds given . . . two thirds to his son Richard John and one third to his daughter Katherine Anne."[22] He couldn't bequeath away from Dunlo the settled estates, but he could, and did, put them in trust, so that Dunlo, who would succeed as the 5th Earl Clancarty, would have to apply to trustees, who would give him an allowance, so long as he behaved reasonably and didn't try to mortgage the Galway property. After his father's death he went to court to have the will overturned, without success.

There's no doubt that this was how the 4th earl meant to punish his son and, by extension, his daughter-in-law. But there was more to it than a father's revenge on a wayward son. Even as a teenager Dunlo was quick to rack up substantial debts—during the divorce case Belle's counsel suggested that he agreed to leave his wife on condition that his father pay off his many creditors—and the earl feared for the future of the family estates. He was right to do so: the 5th earl was declared bankrupt in 1907, although this didn't prevent him from signing cheques and obtaining credit. At one stage he bought a diamond ring from a London jeweller with a cheque for £400 and pawned it the same day for £300. He got himself into the hands of moneylenders, continued to spend, and finally in 1920 was summoned to appear at the Old Bailey, where he was charged with incurring debts without disclosing the fact he was an undischarged bankrupt and obtaining money under false pretences. Half an hour late for his trial, he was convicted and sentenced to three months in gaol.

Belle, his countess, wasn't there to see this final humiliation. When her husband succeeded to the earldom in 1891 she gave up the stage—she was actually appearing as Venus in burlesque at The-atre Royal Plymouth when she heard the news of her father-in-law's death—and she retired to Garbally, where she settled comfortably into life as a noblewoman in rural Ireland. She rode with the Galway hounds; she entered her colts and mares in the local horse show at Ballinasloe, where she also won rosettes for her driving; she entertained pupils from the local school and doled out pieces of fruit to each one. In 1897 she was one of a gaggle of aristocrats who turned up to support the Galway Hunt's Kennel Fund at the local town hall, watching an evening of musical entertainment.

Her marriage seems to have been happy enough, given its inauspicious beginnings. She gave birth to four sons and a daughter, and although there were periodic rumours that she was about to return to the London stage, her connection with the theatre was confined to turning up at the local town hall along with other dignitaries to watch an evening of "music, dancing, conjuring and theatricals" and once, in 1901, taking part herself in a fundraising concert organised by the Sisters of Mercy in aid of the poor of Ballinasloe.* "The Countess of Clancarty sang most sweetly 'The Old Brigade' and 'Old England and the New,'" reported the local paper. One wonders what she thought, what memories that performance conjured up of footlights and fame and a time when Belle Bilton's portrait photographs were on sale all over London and her name featured on playbills and posters.[23]

In 1904 Belle was diagnosed with cancer. She went to Paris for treatment by specialists, but in 1906, on the evening of the last day of the year, she died at Garbally with her family at her bedside. Her husband walked behind her coffin as it was taken to the family vault in the nearby Protestant church, and his wreath of lilies, forget-me-nots, and asters lay on the casket, with the inscription "To my darling Belle, from her sorrowing husband, Freddie."

---

* Her first, illegitimate, child was packed off to America. Given her long association with Isidor Wertheimer, it may or may not be significant that he too was named Isidor.

TWENTY

TWO TRIBES

IN 1870 THE fifteen-year-old William Lanceley left his home in the Cheshire village of Malpas, where he lived with his widowed mother and eight siblings. He had with him a carpetbag containing an extra pair of trousers, a change of underclothes, and some apples; and with a few pennies in his pocket, he walked for five miles until he reached Carden Park, an imposing half-timbered country house belonging to a long-lineaged hunting squire, John Hurleston Leche, and his wife Eleanor. He had never been away from home before.

Lanceley had come to Carden to take up a job as hallboy. He was met at the door by a footman who took him through to meet the butler, a "portly and dignified" character named Joseph Loges who explained the boy's duties, which began at six in the morning:

First light the Servants' Hall fire, clean the young ladies' boots, the butler's, housekeeper's, cook's and ladies' maids, often twenty pairs altogether; trim the lamps (I had thirty-five to look after, there being no gas or electric light in the district

in those days); and all this had to be got through by 7.30. Then
lay up the hall breakfast [and] get it in.[1]

The food usually consisted of stew—served on pewter—with
cold beef, bread, and cheese. The menservants still had beer with
their breakfast, drawn from seventy-gallon casks into a big leather jug
and dispensed into pewter tankards and drinking horns. (There was
a penny fine for any manservant caught drinking from a glass.) The
women had tea, and so did the new hallboy, who to his chagrin was
considered too young at fifteen to be drinking beer.

After he had cleared up the servants' hall breakfast, Lanceley's next
tasks were to clean knives and silver, to clean the windows and mirrors, and to tidy the housekeeper's room. There were a dozen indoor
servants at Carden, plus several liveried grooms who lived above the
stables and a coachman who presided over the meals in the servants'
hall, and the rest of Lanceley's day was spent waiting on them—
setting the table for the servants' hall dinner, bringing it in, taking
it out and washing it up, and doing the same for the servants' hall
supper. He came into contact with the Leches only at the daily family
prayers and in the evening, when he had to help carry their dinner up
to the dining room and, if there were guests, wait at table. He usually
got to bed around midnight, a sixteen-hour working day. For this he
had eight pounds a year, payable annually in arrears; clothes were provided except for boots and underwear, which he had to find out of his
wages. That wasn't bad, considering that an adult labourer might only
make ten pounds a year, and Mr Loges told Lanceley that if he paid
special attention to the needs of visiting ladies' maids, cleaning their
boots nicely and bringing up the luggage promptly, he might make a
tidy sum in tips, "which proved correct," he recalled years later. "I seldom felt tired as the work was so varied and the food of the best, and
we generally got a little leisure in the afternoons." Most of that leisure
was spent fishing in the lake in the park.[2]

Lanceley's experience of domestic service was fairly typical, although life for the country house servant was not always filled with domestic bliss. One Saturday night in November 1891 Oliver Skittiwell, an under-footman at Hassobury House in Essex, walked into the butler's pantry there to find the first footman Charles Keller, who had been at Hassobury for just three weeks. Keller closed the door and locked it. Then he produced a revolver, told Skittiwell to put up his hands—and shot him. Skittiwell, who survived the attack, staggered and turned in time to see Keller put the muzzle of the gun into his own mouth and shoot himself dead. The cause was said to be "a slight quarrel between the two footmen."[3]

Augustus Venables-Vernon, 6th Lord Vernon, was away from home on Sunday, April 2, the night of the 1871 census. He and his valet were in London, staying at his brother's Grosvenor Place house. Lady Vernon was absent, too: she was in Torquay, visiting some cousins. Their two sons, George and William, were away at school.

But Lord Vernon's ancestral seat of Sudbury Hall in Derbyshire was far from empty. It still held the Vernons' five daughters, who ranged in age from Diana, the eldest at nineteen, down to little Adelaide, who was just five months old. Their French governess, Josephine de Lolaine, was there to keep an eye on Diana and her eighteen-year-old sister, Mildred, and Lady Vernon had left behind her lady's maid, Matilda Tabbey, to help them with their toilette. The younger girls, Margaret (five), Alice (three), and Adelaide were in the day and night nurseries at the top of the house, looked after by their Scottish nurse, Margaret Mitchell, and an under-nurse, Martha Kent.

Whether Lord and Lady Vernon were in residence or not, meals at Sudbury were prepared by their French chef, Julius Riveri, who was helped by two kitchen maids and a stillroom maid. Those meals were served by two footmen, who were supervised by an under-butler, a young widower named Herbert Woolley. The smooth running of the hall and its staff, which also included three twentysomething housemaids and two laundry maids, was entrusted to two people: the Vernons' housekeeper, Esther Price, and their butler, a Yorkshireman named George Kirton.

A domestic staff of eighteen (nineteen, including Lord Vernon's absent valet) was about right for a reasonably large country house in 1871. That excluded the servants who lived out in Sudbury village—a lodgekeeper, at least three gardeners, two gamekeepers, and various grooms and stable hands. And there were the specialists who managed the Sudbury estate for Lord Vernon: his land agent, who had an assistant and a young clerk, and the estate surveyor and clerk of works.

Sudbury is a scattered rural parish on Derbyshire's southwestern border with Staffordshire, with an estate village built by the Vernons in the seventeenth century at its heart. In 1883, John Bateman's *Great Landowners of Great Britain and Ireland* reckoned the 6th Lord Vernon owned 6,154 acres in Derbyshire and another thousand acres in Staffordshire (plus a further 2,578 acres in Cheshire, where the family owned extensive collieries as well as another country house, Poynton Hall). And although Lord Vernon complained that Bateman's estimates were "grossly wrong," it was certainly true that the village of Sudbury was his, as was much of the surrounding farmland. The population of the parish—102 households in all—consisted mostly of small farmers and tradespeople, shopkeepers and agricultural labourers, with a smattering of professional men: a doctor, a veterinary surgeon, a curate. Some of the farms were little more than smallholdings; even the largest were no more than 285 acres, and although most of Sudbury's better-off farmers kept a general servant, typically a teenage girl, and perhaps a cook or a housekeeper, the only other inhabitant of the parish who could be said to maintain an establishment was Lord Vernon's widowed stepmother, who had a dower house in the village where she lived in some style with a staff of her own: her lady's maid, housekeeper, cook, footman, and housemaid.

Finding appropriate living accommodation and workspace for his staff posed something of a problem for Vernon. The hall was put up in the second half of the seventeenth century by his ancestor George Vernon, an ambitious young member of the Derbyshire gentry with a happy knack of marrying heiresses (three, in fact). Raised up on a half basement and topped with a hipped roof, dormer windows, and a central cupola, it was very beautiful but also very much of its time as far as the domestic arrangements were concerned: servants slept in the attics and lived and worked in the basement. That time was past, and at some point in the nineteenth century one of the Vernons built a low gabled service wing connecting the main house to a courtyard containing a range of stables and other outbuildings. The kitchen was moved into this wing, along with food storage and preparation areas—scullery, pantry, fish, game and meat larders, stillroom, and so on.

We don't know the architect or the precise date for this rather ordinary extension: it may possibly have been commissioned by the 6th Lord Vernon, who as Hon. Augustus Henry Venables-Vernon moved into the hall on his marriage in 1851 to Lady Harriet Anson, daughter of the Earl of Lichfield. His father, a Dante scholar, was living in Italy and was content to remain there while his son and heir managed the family estates. (More than content, in fact: in 1842 he had left his wife and set up house with an Italian woman, who bore him four children.) In 1866 the 5th Lord Vernon died and Augustus came into the title and decided it was time to take the modernisation of Sudbury Hall more seriously. Edward Middleton Barry, the son of the distinguished architect Sir Charles Barry and a well-known architect in his own right, was a houseguest at Sudbury in 1869, as he was completing the rebuilding of another seventeenth-century country house, the Jacobean Crewe Hall in Cheshire, after a fire; and by 1871 Vernon had commissioned him to reroof the main house. At the same time, Barry came up with some ideas for remodelling the service wing.

By choice, architects and clients preferred Victorian service wings to be tucked away out of sight: no owners wanted to be confronted with reminders of exactly how domestic miracles were performed. (The old service wing at Sudbury was notably lacking in this respect, with the doorway to the men's lavatories in full view of visitors to the house.) At Lanhydrock in Cornwall in the 1880s, Lord Robartes's architect, Richard Coad, went to great lengths to screen his new and vastly complicated service block from the drive. Robert Kerr advised that "the Servants' Department" should be tucked away on the north side of a house "to avoid sunshine on the windows, which is seldom if ever welcome to business."[4] The problem at Sudbury was that the wing connecting the main house to the stable court was plainly visible from the front lawn: it was of necessity part of the entrance facade, an asymmetrical addition to what was a supremely symmetrical building.

The existing wing was vaguely Tudorish, all sharp gables topped with spiky finials, with no attempt at all to blend with the seventeenth-century hall. It looked odd. But although Barry produced several schemes, Vernon wasn't happy with any of them, to judge from his forthright pencilled scribblings all over them: "I do not like . . . ," "These not wanted . . . ," and plenty more in the same tone. One reason for his disenchantment may have been that he was coming into contact with another architect whose style and flexible approach to design were more to his taste. At the end of September 1871, he was in Kent, staying with the Liberal politician Sir Walter James, whose wife Sarah was Vernon's aunt. Kinship was still important in High Victorian Britain, and family ties were things to be cultivated. The Jameses' country house, Betteshanger, had started out as a Georgian villa but had been transformed over the past fifteen years into a delightful jumble of towers and turrets and tall chimneystacks by their architect, George Devey, a man with a romantic passion for the buildings of the past but with none of the earnestness that characterised the more ardent Gothic Revivalists.

Devey, who had become a great friend of the Jameses, happened to be staying at Betteshanger that weekend. We don't know if the house party marked the beginning of a productive relationship (Vernon's brother William had already employed Devey to carry out £162 worth of alterations at his town house in Grosvenor Place back in 1869), but what *is* clear is that by the end of 1872 Barry had disappeared from the scene and Devey had taken his place at Sudbury. More than that: between 1872 and 1875 he designed stables, kennels, and cottages for the Meynell Hunt just outside the village, at a cost of over £10,000. He modernised the Sudbury church (1875–1883); he designed an attractive little coal-gas plant which serviced the hall and a number of houses in the village (1874); he made alterations to the village inn, the Vernon Arms; and between 1874 and 1877 he virtually rebuilt the hall's service wing.

There were two interesting features of the new wing. First, Devey paid homage to Sudbury Hall's Caroline roots by giving the extension an understated seventeenth-century look, linking it tactfully to the old building through a series of different roof lines and carrying on the theme of diapered brickwork, which was a feature of the old house (and was almost certainly a reference to frets on the Vernon coat of arms). That respect for the architecture of the Restoration was in itself quite unusual for the 1870s.

And second, the new work was not a domestic service wing in the strict sense of the term. Devey put the housekeeper's room, cook's room, scullery, stillroom, and larders in the basement—presumably where most of those workspaces had been situated when the hall was built. The new wing included a servants' hall and a steward's room next to the plate safe—normal practice, so that the steward could keep an eye on it—but otherwise the servants had to come and go via a new entrance at the end of the wing, screened from general view, and then walk down a long corridor to get into the basement, which held their work areas. The floor above contained extra family accommodation—a boudoir, bedrooms, and dressing rooms for the Vernons and their visitors, with servants' bedrooms at the far end of the wing and reached via a new back stair. The strict segregation which Victorians expected to exist between family and servants, Robert Kerr's underlying idea that "the family constitute one community, the servants another," that "the Servants' Department shall be separated from the Main House, so that what passes on either side of the boundary shall be both invisible and inaudible on the other," was maintained, but the division was between floors rather than between the house and its new wing—literally an upstairs-downstairs separation of the two tribes.

The truth is that the vast self-contained servants' wing, so lovingly described by Kerr in the 1860s, was being challenged almost as soon as his book appeared. Writing in his two-volume *House Architecture* of 1880, John James Stevenson complained about the overelaborate planning of the domestic offices advocated in *The Gentleman's House*. "I venture to doubt if a house should be planned as Mr. Kerr recommends," wrote Stevenson, "so that the servants may shut themselves off from the family in a separate establishment, where the mistress feels herself an intruder." Why should servants stay in their places for years and express loyalty and affection for their employers when they were kept in what amounted to a separate building, never meeting the family? And wasn't the big servants' wing a ridiculous extravagance? asked Stevenson. "All these places, with the interminable passages connecting them, have to be kept in order; and, if they increase the facility of doing the work, they increase labour of the house, and necessitate a greater number of servants."[5]

And as the number of servants had grown, so had the wage bill that country house owners were forced to pay if they wanted to maintain an impressive complement of staff. In 1890 *The Duties of Servants:*

A Practical Guide, by the anonymous author of *Manners and Rules of Good Society* (a manual for the socially insecure), carefully listed the number and type of domestic servants required for different sizes of household. Beginning at the top, with those who had an annual income of "considerably over £40,000," the author suggests an establishment of over thirty servants, excluding gamekeepers and gardeners. The menservants in these big establishments, "those of noblemen and commoners of great wealth," should include a house steward, a groom of the chambers, a butler, a valet, a "man cook," three footmen, a steward's room boy, and a servants' hall boy. If there were big stables attached to the house, the family might also keep a stud groom; a pad groom, who escorted his master or mistress when they went out riding; and a couple of under-grooms. The list of female servants is even longer:

> A housekeeper, a head lady's-maid, an under lady's-maid, young ladies'-maids, according to the number of young ladies in the family, a head nurse, a cook (if a man cook is not kept), a head house-maid, two or three under house-maids, a head laundry-maid, two under laundry-maids, a head kitchen-maid, a scullery-maid, a vegetable-maid, one or two stillroom-maids, an under nurse, a nursery maid, and a schoolroom-maid.[6]

In case anyone was in any doubt, the author was clear that "the staff of servants here enumerated is considered requisite, both in town and country."[7]

This was a colossal household, and it came at a colossal expense. *The Duties of Servants* suggests pay scales for each member of the household staff, and based on these figures, a big household employing thirty domestic servants would face a wage bill ranging from £764 to £1,047 a year—well over £400,000 in today's money. The highest earner was the "man cook"—a male chef could earn as much as

£150 a year, plus perks. Female servants' wages were generally around two-thirds those of men's.

Wages varied according to the experience of the servant and the wealth of the employer: better-off employers could offer more money to secure the best servants. But the expenses didn't stop there. There were suits of livery for the footmen, knee breeches, silk stockings, and powdered hair, and black dress coats and white ties for the groom of the chambers and the butler. They all had to be fed: "In large households a hot dinner for the servants is a matter of course . . . [and] both the upper and under servants are allowed puddings every day." Every servant had an allowance of a pound of tea and two pounds of sugar per month, and although the old practice of providing beer for the men was on the wane in towns, it was still common in the country, "where beer [was] home-brewed by the butler."[8]

Then there were the outdoor servants: A head gardener might have £75 or £80 a year, plus a rent-free house. A good head gamekeeper earned £100 a year. And in a sign of the times, a head chauffeur might earn £200 a year "in a large establishment where three or four cars and an assistant chauffeur [were] kept."[9] Few owners of country houses in the 1890s were prepared to reduce their riding establishment in the hope that the motorcar would take the place of the horse, so the employment of chauffeurs (and chauffeur-mechanics) increased the wage bill still further. That bill, if it was for a large, well-trained, experienced domestic staff, indoor and outdoor, could easily approach £1,500 or even £2,000 per year.

The later nineteenth century saw the appearance of a lot of advice on the duties of servants, both in the form of individual manuals and also incorporated in the flood of general works on household management that aimed to trade on the success of Isabella Beeton's 1861 bestseller, which sold two million copies in its first seven years of publication. Her *Beeton's Book of Household Management* (the "Mrs" was added to later editions) was followed by titles like *Warne's Model Cookery and*

Housekeeping Book (1871) and the monumental eight-volume *Book of the Home* (1900). Some of these manuals were aimed directly at the servants, although whether or not they were enthusiastically consulted by those servants is another matter, considering the hectoring tone they usually adopted. *A Few Rules for the Manners of Servants in Good Families*, published in 1901 by the Ladies' Sanitary Association, an organisation which had been founded in 1857 to promote health education and "to encourage the study of domestic economy," was typical in its determination to reinforce difference and deference:

> When meeting any ladies or gentlemen about the house, stand back and move aside for them to pass.
>
> Always answer when you receive an order or a reproof, either "Yes, Ma'am," or "I am very sorry, Ma'am," to show that you have listened.
>
> Never sing or whistle at your work where the family would be likely to hear you.
>
> Should you be required to walk with a lady or gentleman, in order to carry a parcel, or otherwise, always keep a few paces behind.[10]

Other manuals were aimed at inexperienced employers. *The Servants' Practical Guide: A Handbook of Duties and Rules*, which first appeared in 1880 and ran through several more editions before the end of the century, began by claiming that "paradoxical as it may appear, this work is expressly written for the use of Masters and Mistresses." But fascinating though these manuals are, their core readership tended to be members of middle-class households and young inexperienced wives rather than the owners of country houses. It is hard to imagine a Duchess of Devonshire reaching for volume four of her *Book of the Home* to discover that "on Monday mornings it is the housemaid's task to collect, sort, and prepare the soiled linen—household and personal—for the wash." Or to visualise a Marchioness of Bath leafing through her well-thumbed copy of *Warne's Model Cookery* to find out that she should learn "by personal observation which are the best shops for different articles, and what are the fair rates of payment for them." That was what the servants were for. Even those owners who were relatively new to country house life and its protocols—the brewers and the railway magnates and the cotton lords and their wives, the chorus girl who captured the heart (and more importantly the hand in marriage) of a young landowner—didn't need to read a book to work out the best kind of washstand for servants' use or the timing of dinner in the servants' hall. They had stewards and butlers and housekeepers to do that for them.[11]

The demand for domestic servants grew steadily throughout the nineteenth century, until by 1901 1.33 million women were in service in private homes in England and Wales, making service one of the largest occupational groups. It is hard to pinpoint any single reason for the increase, although a growing and prosperous middle class with higher aspirations and different expectations certainly had something to do with it. As the authors of the census reports for 1871 had it, "Wives and daughters at home do now less domestic work than their predecessors: hence the excessive demand for female servants and the consequent rise of wages."[12]

This clearly didn't apply to wives and daughters who inhabited country houses. They had never done any domestic work, so it wasn't possible for them to do less. But that hadn't stopped the builders of country houses from planning for armies of servants. Beyond a certain point, the size of those armies didn't make life easier for the family: having five or six housemaids instead of three or four didn't make much difference. But it did make a statement about status, as did the matched pairs of liveried footmen hovering in the entrance hall and the French chef in the kitchen and the Swiss lady's maid who accompanied her mistress when she went away for the weekend.

Service in a big house, with its strict lines of demarcation, its plentiful food, and the chance it offered to accompany the family to London or even to Europe, was a good deal more attractive than working as a general servant in a middle-class home, where one had to prepare and cook the meals, wait at table and wash up afterwards, blacklead the grates and lay the fires, dust and clean every room, carry the hot water up to the bedrooms, and remove the contents of the chamber pots. Rachel Ketton, who moved with her husband into Felbrigg Hall in Norfolk in 1863, recorded in her diary that there were twenty-nine applications for a sewing maid's place and twenty-six for a footman's.[13]

While in the grander households men continued to occupy the more visible roles—butler, under-butler, groom of the chambers, coachman, chauffeur, and, of course, the footman in his livery and powdered wig—women were thought by virtue of their sex to be peculiarly suited to domestic work. They worked for lower wages than men, and with fewer employment opportunities, service was a conventional career path for girls, who typically went into a household when they were fourteen or so, changed jobs every couple of years, and then married in their midtwenties, an act which usually precluded them from continuing as a servant. Against that figure of 1.33 million female indoor servants, there were only 64,146 men in indoor service in 1901.[14]

The gender imbalance had been given extra impetus, if it were needed, by the Revenue Act of 1869, which stated that anyone employing a *male* servant was required by law to obtain a licence for that servant, costing fifteen shillings and renewable every year. The term "male servant" was pretty comprehensive. It included a house steward, master of the horse, groom of the chambers, valet de chambre, butler, under-butler, clerk of the kitchen (did anyone employ a clerk of the kitchen in 1869?), confectioner, cook, house porter, footman, page, waiter, coachman, groom, postillion, stable boy or helper in the stables, gardener, under-gardener, park keeper, game-keeper, under-gamekeeper, huntsman, and whipper-in. And the same act levied a duty of one guinea on anyone who used or wore armorial bearings of any sort, two guineas if they had those bearings displayed on their carriage.

There was quite a lot of confusion about this new legislation, which placed a butler and a coat of arms in the same category as a dog (dog licences had been introduced two years earlier). If someone employed a jobbing gardener for a few hours a week, did they need a licence? If a farmer asked one of his labourers to pitch in and help with domestic work every now and then, did *they* need a licence? If a trades-man had a coat of arms printed on his letterhead, did that constitute the using of armorial bearings?

The answer to all these questions turned out to be no. But that didn't stop employers from falling foul of the act, and the law was no respecter of persons. In 1884 the vicar of Littlebourne in Kent, Rev. Nicholas McGachen, was hauled in front of the bench and charged with employing a manservant without a licence. He pleaded guilty but said it was entirely through ignorance. Ignorance was no defence, and since the magistrates suspected McGachen was being economical with the truth when he claimed he had only just taken on his servant a couple of months previously, he was fined twenty shillings. Twenty years later an officer from the Inland Revenue paid a visit to Rev. George Robinson in his rectory at Whitchurch in Herefordshire. Pre-sumably acting on a tip-off, he found a gardener at work, and a dog. When quizzed, the gardener happily admitted that he was employed full-time by Mr Robinson and that the dog belonged to the rector. Sentence: a fine of eight pounds with nineteen shillings costs for keep-ing a manservant without a licence, and another two pounds with nine shillings costs with respect to the dog.

It wasn't only the clergy who felt the full force of the law. Major General J. P. Brabazon, veteran of the Second Anglo-Afghan War, the Nile expedition of 1884–1885, and the Boer War, was fined five pounds for keeping unlicenced stable hands at his house in Northamptonshire. And when the famous cricketer Ranjitsinhji, Maharajah of Nawanagar, rented a shooting estate in Norfolk for the season in 1897 and engaged a gamekeeper and three dogs, he discovered too late that they all needed licences and was fined two pounds with costs.

The prince offered no defence. Not so Princess Sophia Duleep Singh, daughter of Maharajah Duleep Singh. Princess Sophia, an active suffragette, lived at Faraday House, an eighteenth-century grace-and-favour house in Hampton Court. In 1911 she was summoned for keeping five dogs without licences, for employing a manservant without a licence, and for using armorial bearings—a coronet and the letter *S*—without a licence. She instructed her lawyer to enter a protest in court, saying that she considered it "a gross injustice and incongruity that women, who were not represented in any office in the management of the country, should be subject to taxation."[15] The magistrates ignored her protest, although they did dismiss the summons relating to armorial bearings, saying that *S* and a coronet weren't subject to taxation—much to the annoyance of Middlesex County Council, which, like other county councils, received the proceeds of the licencing arrangement.

Although the 1869 Revenue Act spurred employers to reduce the size of smaller households, or at least to employ fewer men, it didn't have much effect on the grandest. In the 1870s the Duke and Duchess of Marlborough kept an indoor staff of twenty-six at Blenheim Palace. By the early twentieth century that had risen to thirty-five (including an electrical engineer). At the same time the Marquess and Marchioness of Bath were employing forty-three indoor servants at Longleat, although when they migrated to their town house in Grosvenor Square they made do with a mere seventeen. The full complement included eight housemaids, three liveried footmen, a fourth footman who waited on the steward's room, and a tiger—a young boy whose role in life was to sit in his livery on the box of the carriage when the family went out for a drive. And the fact that the domestic staff at Edwardian Chatsworth included the post of "seventh housemaid" suggests that retrenchment wasn't exactly the order of the day with the Devonshires, either.

TWENTY-ONE

TRUE CRIME

I T WAS ALMOST axiomatic—among employers, at any rate—that servants would cheat you if they could. And no doubt there were masters and mistresses who stooped to the time-honoured trick of hiding money behind cushions or under rugs. If a housemaid found the money and didn't hand it over, she was a thief; if she didn't find it, she wasn't doing her job properly. The dishonesty of servants ranged from sneaking out at night to meet a boy or a girl, to petty pilfering, to major crime. A housekeeper left a bedroom window open at night so that her accomplices could steal jewels belonging to a houseguest; butlers stole the family silver and went to great lengths to suggest the job was done by outsiders. Ex-butlers, harbouring a grudge against their employers and thoroughly acquainted with the layout of their old homes, broke in at night and took cash and plate. Footmen ransacked guest bedrooms and housemaids turned up at pawnbrokers with suspiciously valuable diamond pins and inlaid snuffboxes.

Most of these men and women were not career criminals, and some were plain stupid. Take James Morrison, for example, a footman at a house in Lancashire who ransacked his mistress's bedroom one night and stole her jewellery. A search of the house proved it to be hidden up the chimney in his bedroom. He got three years.

Whenever there was a theft at a country house, the servants were the first to be suspected. One of the great causes célèbres of 1877 was a daring robbery that took place at Battle Abbey in Sussex, a country house converted from the ruins of the medieval abbey that had been erected on or near the site of William the Conqueror's defeat of King Harold in 1066. At the time of the crime, it belonged to the Duke and Duchess of Cleveland, and on the night of Thursday, February 15, 1877, they were in residence and entertaining some houseguests. The servants were having their own supper and there was no one on the upper floor of the house, until at half past ten one of the housemaids went to check the duchess's dressing room, which was about twenty feet up and overlooking the terrace. She found the door was locked on the inside, so she called a footman, who broke the door down and went in to find empty jewel cases scattered over the floor, drawers forced open, and the duke's travelling case, where he kept his ready cash, lying empty. The window had been forced open and two ladders, lashed together with rope, were lying on the terrace.

It was an audacious raid. Altogether the thieves got away with some £10,000 worth of necklaces, bracelets, earrings, and other items, chief of which was a pearl necklace which alone was worth £3,000. Police and press were swift to say that the robbery "if not perpetrated by, was, at all events, instigated by persons who must have known the premises well, and been acquainted with the customs of the family."[1] The servants were questioned. The duke offered a reward. The duchess ordered a sturdy safe which was drillproof, fireproof, and unpickable, although it was a little late for that, perhaps. And neither the burglars nor the jewels were ever found.

It was left to the *Daily Telegraph* to challenge the insinuations that a member of the domestic staff must have been in on the raid and to blame the Clevelands for their sloppy security arrangements. "If servants cannot or will not regularly shut and secure the windows and fasten alarm bells inside; if there is no watch-dog in the grounds, and no prowling little terrier in the corridors or passages," then at least the valuables should be locked in a heavy strongbox. But "the real secret of burglars' success in these cases . . . is that in all households of any extent and pretension too much is left to the servants."[2] In other words, if the servants were dishonest, it was because their employers were careless. Either way it was their fault.

If it is possible to generalise about such things, it seems that housemaids of a criminal turn of mind tended to engage in petty larceny; footmen went for valuable jewellery; butlers were attracted by the family silver. In general, employers preferred to deal with minor acts of dishonesty themselves, without recourse to the courts. In an age in which most members of the landed elite regarded any kind of publicity with abhorrence, it was considered far better simply to dismiss the offender, usually without a reference. And for most servants that was punishment enough, although there was a ready market in fake references for those who knew where to look.

The fear of publicity didn't mean that employers would avoid publicity at any cost. When one of the palace housemaids was caught shoplifting in 1885 at a draper's on Buckingham Palace Road, for example, the queen's master of the household appeared in court to give evidence of her good character. (She still got two months.)

Some of these thefts by servants were pure opportunism; others were carefully planned. Having embarked on a life of petty crime while employed at Stocks House in Hertfordshire as a servant to the novelist Mrs Humphry Ward, from whom he stole various bits and pieces without being caught, the eighteen-year-old George Finn went as second footman to the Montagu family of Melton Park in Yorkshire, a substantial country house thought to have been designed by James Paine and dated 1757. Finn's brain having been turned, as his defence lawyer was to put it later, "by reading foolish types of imaginative literature," one evening at the beginning of January 1908, when he had been at Melton for a couple of months, he found himself alone in the butler's pantry, where the key to the Montagus' safe was kept. Seizing the opportunity, he opened the safe and extracted a diamond tiara worth £1,300, a wedding present from Frederick Montagu to his wife Louisa. Then he crept out of the house and hid the thing beside a tree at the roadside about half a mile away. Finn's career as a master jewel thief nearly came to an end there and then. A passing policeman saw him lurking behind a haystack and challenged him; Finn lied that he had been out cycling but had a puncture, so he had to walk back to the mansion. He explained the lurking by saying he was out of the wind and trying to get a light for his cigarette.

Five days later Frederick Montagu received an anonymous letter:

A diamond head ornament which was taken from your house on Thursday, 2nd, is quite safe, and we will return it whole for the sum of £500. If you want it put advertisement in personal column of *Daily Mail* on Monday or Tuesday, under X.Y.Z., and you will hear from us.[3]

The letter was postmarked Kentish Town in London, but Montagu noticed that it was sealed with the same shade of magenta sealing wax that his wife Louisa kept in her boudoir. He removed the stick of wax and substituted a stick of vermilion wax. Then he—or rather the police, in the shape of a Superintendent Hicks—replied to the letter, and Hicks, who had temporarily moved into Melton Park, saw Finn grab the *Daily Mail* and immediately turn to the personal column. Three days later a second letter arrived, again with a Kentish Town postmark but now sealed with exactly the same shade of vermilion wax which Montagu had left in his wife's boudoir, and written on notepaper of the type used by the Montagus. Hicks found out that Finn's parents lived in Kentish Town, and when the police went round to their home his mother told them her son had sent her two letters, containing sealed and stamped envelopes addressed to Montagu, and asked her to post them locally.

That was enough for Superintendent Hicks. Finn was arrested at the hall and made a full confession. He said he wanted the £500 to buy himself an apprenticeship as a marine engineer. He took the police to the tiara, still hidden in the field, and, in a last attempt to play the debonair master criminal of countless halfpenny comics, told them, "I have played the game, and I have lost."[4]

Finn must have had something about him. When he appeared in the dock, smartly dressed and pleading guilty to the theft of the Montagu tiara, his previous employers, the Wards, came forward to say they would help him to a new start in life, in spite of the fact that various possessions of theirs had been found in his room at Melton Park; and Frederick Montagu, who had apparently missed several other items besides the tiara, declined to press charges in relation to them. The judge sentenced Finn to twelve months in Borstal, where, he said, "you will have an opportunity of learning some trade, and of beginning an honest life."[5] He also observed rather unnecessarily that he didn't think Finn would get a job as a footman again.*

The publicity surrounding the Montagu tiara case was considerable and, no doubt, painful for the Montagus. The judge criticised them for not keeping the tiara locked up more securely, and defending counsel said that "great temptation had been put in the way of the prisoner by the manner in which the jewellery was kept."[6] But worse than the criticism was the plain fact that their names were in the newspapers associated with a court case.

---

* Unnecessarily and mistakenly, in that Finn turned up in Cuba in 1919 working as a valet.

Taking a servant to court was fraught with risks, as Philip and Louisa Yorke of Erddig discovered to their cost. The Yorke family had an unusual relationship with their servants, dating back to the 1790s when Philip Yorke I commissioned a local artist, John Walters, to paint portraits of several of them, including the gamekeeper, the kitchen man, and the estate carpenter, accompanied by doggerel verses composed by Yorke. His son Simon II (all the male Yorkes were Philip or Simon, hence the need to number them) continued the tradition, and by the later nineteenth century, the oil paintings were being supplemented by photographs, still with verses by the Yorkes.

It used to be thought that this uniquely coherent process of memorialising the servants was evidence of the Yorkes' respect for their domestic staff. It was Merlin Waterson, in his classic 1980 history of Erddig, *The Servants' Hall*, who pointed out that the staff they recorded were the successes, "those whose virtues, loyalty and long service were held up as an example to other staff. . . . Their verse describes the relationship as the Yorkes wanted it to be; not necessarily as it was."[7]

There certainly were plenty of successes, but there were plenty of failures, too. In the 1780s the Erddig agent was sacked after the Yorkes found out that he was helping himself to their money and adjusting the accounts accordingly. In 1897 their housekeeper, Miss Harrison, was dismissed after she was found to be selling estate pheasants on the side. In her defence, the Yorkes paid their servants below the going rate, which is perhaps why, at the turn of the century, they managed to get through eight housekeepers and cooks in the space of eight years.

That may also go a little way to explaining the behaviour of Ellen Penketh, who in 1903, when she was thirty-two years of age, was taken on as cook-housekeeper at Erddig at a salary of forty-five pounds per year. She was fond of drink, something that the almost teetotal Yorkes found difficult to swallow; but they put up with it for nearly five years, until in 1907 they discovered that she was fond of their money, too.

The arrangement at Erddig for paying tradesmen was that Ellen kept a book in which she entered housekeeping expenses—basically a list of tradesmen's accounts. Each month Louisa Yorke went through the accounts with Ellen and gave her a cheque to cash at the bank in Wrexham, so that she could pay the tradesmen. Only she didn't. Not all of them, anyway. She later claimed that her mistress scolded her because the housekeeping costs kept rising, and that as a result she took to keeping back some of the bills and then using the following month's cheque to pay them late. Whatever the truth of the matter, she clearly got into a muddle and tried rather desperately to cover her tracks. She "lost" her account books, and when she found them again and handed them to Louisa Yorke, there were pages torn out. Then a grocer in Wrexham complained to the Yorkes that his bill hadn't been paid, and Louisa sat down with Ellen and the Erddig agent to try and get to the bottom of things. Between them, the grocer, a butcher, and a draper were owed £201 12s 1d. How was it that Miss Penketh had not paid the bills? Louisa asked. The unlikely reply was that seven months earlier, in May 1906, Ellen had gone to the Hope Street Bank in Wrexham to cash the Yorkes' cheque, but when she came out her bag had flown open and £130 in gold had fallen out and rolled away. She hadn't dared to tell the Yorkes it was lost, and she had been juggling the accounts ever since.

A couple of days after this interview Ellen travelled to Manchester and Liverpool in search of her parents, taking with her an elderly solicitor's clerk, Henry Davies, who had befriended her. She said she needed £200 in a hurry, but neither her father nor her mother was inclined to help. Her mother simply said, "Didn't we warn you of what it would come to?" When they got back to Wrexham, Davies charged his expenses to the Yorkes.

Ellen Penketh was sacked, although the rest of the Erddig servants clubbed together to pay her rail fare, which may say something about where their sympathies lay. Philip and Louisa Yorke also decided to prosecute her for converting money to her own use. But when it became clear that instead of dealing with the matter themselves, the Wrexham magistrates wanted to send her for trial at the North Wales Assizes, with all the publicity that this might entail, they tried to have the charges dropped. It was too late: the magistrates declared that it was in the public interest for the case to go ahead. To make matters worse, they suggested that Philip Yorke might like to stand bail for his ex-housekeeper, a request that he found impossible to refuse. There was public applause at his decision, although after he left the court, he withdrew the offer and Ellen Penketh went to jail to await trial.

The housekeeper came up at the assizes at the beginning of December 1907, for what should have been an open-and-shut case. She could offer no clear explanation for the missing £201 12s 1d. Her lawyers wouldn't allow her to give evidence in her defence—a point which usually told against a defendant. And the judge made a point of commenting to the jury on the improbability of her story about losing all that money outside the bank. "It was not every day, he remarked, that £130 in gold rolled about the streets of Wrexham without the police hearing a word about it."[8]

But the jury returned a verdict of not guilty, and Ellen Penketh left the dock smiling.

The Yorkes were beside themselves with rage. They had been presented as gullible fools—the defence claimed that Louisa didn't understand household accounts and made much of the fact that when Philip Yorke withdrew his offer to stand bail, "this woman was dragged handcuffed from Wrexham to Manchester." The Yorkes were sneered at as "idlers on the pathway of life."[9] And Philip was left to vent his anger privately in doggerel, describing Ellen as one who

> *Did for five years our substance waste,*
> *As foul a thief as e'er we saw,*
> *Though whitewashed by Un-Civil Law.*[10]

Burglary was as much of a worry as careless housekeepers losing 130 gold sovereigns. If the servants and ex-servants weren't conspiring to ransack the plate safe or make off with the mistress's jewel case, then any strangers in the neighbourhood were suspect. Rag-and-bone men who called were probably there to look for weak points in the country house's security. "The man who travels about the country with a piano accordion and a monkey is also engaged very often in spying out the land for the purpose of paying a nocturnal visit. . . . The calling of painter and decorator is one that is frequently adopted by men whose real vocation is burglary."[11]

Police divided burglars into dinner thieves and first-sleep thieves. The former were those, like the Battle Abbey burglars, who waited until family and guests were downstairs at dinner before using a ladder to climb into a promising upstairs bedroom. They would then lock the bedroom door so they wouldn't be disturbed, just as the thieves had done at Battle, and hunt for jewellery and any other valuables that might be lying about. In September 1908 Jean Ward, the daughter of the American ambassador, was staying with friends at Worplesdon Place near Guildford. Mrs Ward went up to bed around eleven and found her door locked. She went into another room and rang for her maid, who tried and failed to force the door. When the servants finally managed to get it open she found that a gold purse set with diamonds was missing, and a ladder was discovered hidden in the shrubbery. The dinner thief's mate might wire up the front door to delay pursuers, and he would sometimes stretch wires across the garden paths for the same reason, "a circumstance that it is as well to bear in mind in case of any attempted pursuit," noted one late Victorian commentator.[12]

It could be argued (and usually was) that the best way to thwart the dinner thief was not to leave jewellery lying around and to bolt the bedroom windows securely. The first-sleep thief was harder to deal with. This was the man who broke into the house, usually through a window, when the household had just gone to bed and was lost in its first, and reputedly its soundest, sleep. One night in May 1910 thieves broke into Sewardstone Lodge in Essex, a country house belonging to a nitrate merchant named W. P. Robertson. The window of Mrs Robertson's ground-floor boudoir, where they gained entry, was protected by indoor shutters which were secured by an iron crossbar, but this didn't deter the burglars. They smashed two panes of the window, battered in the shutters, and ransacked the room, taking Mrs Robertson's furs, silver, and other bits and pieces. They loaded their booty into a wheelbarrow they found in the garden, carried it off to an outbuilding in the grounds, and parcelled it up before vanishing. The house was nearly full: the only unoccupied bedroom, in fact, was immediately above Mrs Robertson's boudoir, which suggested inside knowledge. The thieves were never caught.

What precautions could country house owners take to safeguard their property from thieves? One solution was to store valuables off-site. The royal furriers, Debenham and Freebody, offered to "undertake the Storage of Furs and Fur Garments upon very moderate terms" in specially prepared cool chambers.[13] (You should have listened to them, Mrs Robertson.) Jewellery might be kept in a safety-deposit box at the bank, or least in a fireproof and burglarproof safe in the house. Internal doors could be locked at night; windows should be shuttered and barred. Plate glass was preferable because it made more of a noise when it was broken: picturesque leaded panes offered very little protection against the experienced burglar, who was adept at prising up the leads and simply removing the glass.

It was theoretically possible to make every window safe by installing massive iron shutters, but it was important to maintain a sense of proportion. "After all," pointed out one writer, "one lives in a house, not—unless one is a burglar suffering under misfortune—in a prison." Better to hang burglar bells on the shutters to jangle if a shutter was moved, or to fit what were called "alarm strings," wires attached to bells. Having a telephone installed with a connection to the local village was a good idea, too, if only for sounding the alarm when the burglary was discovered. Owners of a particularly nervous disposition might be comforted by the presence of a revolver under their pillow, although the advice was to keep it unloaded. "The prospect of challenging a burglar is not one to be keenly anticipated, while the pleasure derived from having shot and, perhaps, killed him, must be of a very questionable quality."[14]

Keeping a dog or two on the premises was a good idea. But letting the Hound of the Baskervilles loose in the grounds at night had its drawbacks: "The dog with a penchant for human throats is likely to get you into more troubles than the burglaries he will prevent."[15] And he wasn't the deterrent that owners believed him to be: there were several cases of guard dogs being fed poisoned meat by well-prepared burglars. The best advice was to keep a yapping terrier actually in the house and tie the creature up at night, so that thieves couldn't tempt it to the door and give it drugged food through a keyhole.

Ironically, considering the way that servants were usually the first to be suspected when a crime was committed, the most effective safeguards against theft in the country house were those same servants. It was much better to give them the pleasure of challenging a burglar than to risk one's own skin. The grandest families, like the Devonshires and the Marlboroughs, employed watchmen to patrol the house and grounds each night. The Duke of Portland employed three nightwatchmen at Welbeck Abbey. But even more modest households relied on the staff to be alert to possible break-ins. It was common practice for the butler to sleep next door to the plate safe, and it certainly wasn't unknown for him to be equipped with a big stick or even a revolver, loaded or otherwise.

The appearance of a servant frequently cut short a burglary. In 1912, Count de Ramirez de Arellano, a Portuguese nobleman with a country house in Surrey, lost thousands of pounds' worth of paintings and silver when thieves broke into his house one night, using the time-honoured method of sticking brown paper to the drawing room window with treacle to deaden the sound of breaking glass. The losses would have been much greater, but the count's footman was woken by a sound and disturbed the thieves. In another incident a Swiss footman named Leutwyler was commended for his bravery after he was disturbed in the middle of the night by the sound of something falling. Seeing a light in the pantry, he half dressed, grabbed his sword stick (although quite why he had a sword stick to hand isn't clear), and attacked two men with blackened faces whom he found gathering up his master's plate.

Perhaps the most sensible precaution against country house crime was insurance. Until the 1890s, very few insurance companies would provide cover against burglary. When they did, their rates were high, and they only covered loss after forcible entry. By the early 1900s, however, almost every company offered comprehensive policies covering housebreaking and burglary, loss by larceny, and theft by servants "and other persons lawfully on the premises." Policies also covered damage done to furniture and fittings in the commission of a crime—a useful addition if thieves had broken windows and forced doors. Rates for insuring furniture, household goods, "pictures, articles of value, wearing apparel, cycles, gold or silver plate, jewellery and the usual contents of a mansion" were around two shillings per £100 on the full value, or 0.1 per cent; and there were policies available to cover valuables against loss while they were lodged with a bank, a jeweller, or a safety-deposit company, or when in transit.[16]

Every once in a while, there was a case of country house crime that no amount of precautions could have prevented. The Mansion Mystery, as the newspapers dubbed it, was just such a case. It was also one of Edwardian England's most notorious unsolved murders.

Gorse Hall stood in an isolated spot overlooking moorland between the mill towns of Dukinfield and Stalybridge on the border of Cheshire and Lancashire. A solid neoclassical mansion built in the 1830s, in the late summer of 1909 it belonged to a middle-aged building contractor and mill owner named George Storrs, who lived very modestly with his wife Margaret, their twenty-six-year-old niece, Marion Lindley, and three servants—a coachman, a cook, and a maid. The gardens were neglected, the entrance portico was dilapidated, and the family lived in only part of the house, leaving the rest unfurnished. George was described by contemporaries as "simple and lonely in his tastes, avocations, friends, and mode of life." Every evening at five o'clock he drove home in his brougham from his mill, and he rarely left again until the next morning. In the summer he pottered about in his greenhouses; in the winter he read and talked with his wife.[17]

One night in September 1909 George and Margaret Storrs were sitting together in the dining room at Gorse Hall when they heard a shot. A moment later the dining room window was smashed, a gun barrel poked through the broken pane, and someone outside shouted, "Hands up, or I'll shoot!" Storrs, a giant of a man, went to tackle the intruder but his wife held him back and by the time he got outside the man had vanished. The Storrs reported the incident to the police and gave a description, but they could offer no explanation. The local consensus was that it must have been one of the local youths, larking around. All the same, the family was shaken enough to install an alarm bell at the hall, to ensure doors and windows were locked and bolted at night, to have shutters fixed to the window—and to ask for police protection. All this was done, George's brother James claimed later, not because George was nervous but simply "to pacify the ladies of the house."[18]

Whatever the reason, a police guard was put on Gorse Hall, and it was maintained for more than seven weeks. But on Monday,

November 1, 1909, there were local elections in Stalybridge, and with the chief constable anticipating trouble, the police patrolling the grounds of the hall were called off and sent to provide support for their colleagues in the town.

At around 9:30 that night, with the house shrouded in a thick fog, George, Margaret, and Marion were eating supper in the dining room. Their cook, Mary Evans, went down into the cellar to fetch a bowl of milk, and when she came back up, she saw a man by the outer kitchen door (which she had forgotten to lock). He pointed a revolver at her and said, "If you speak a word, I'll shoot you." Mary ran into the hall, pulling the inner kitchen door closed behind her, and burst into the dining room, shouting "There's a man in the house." In the meantime, the Storrses' maid, Ellen Cooper, came out of the dining room, saw the man coming after the cook, and ran through the scullery and out into the garden to find the coachman, John Worrall, who lived in a cottage in the grounds. Margaret and Marion tried to bar the dining room door, but George told them to move out of the way and went into the hall, where he came face to face with the intruder, who was advancing towards them and pointing his gun as though to shoot. "Now I've got you," he said to George, but the enterprising Margaret grabbed a Zulu knobkerrie which was hanging on the wall and brandished it at him, at which he dropped the revolver and cried out, "Don't strike!" The two men began to wrestle with each other, with Margaret and Marion trying to part them. Then George told his wife to "run and ring the alarm bell," and she ran upstairs to trigger the alarm, taking the revolver with her. (It was later established that it was unusable.) She stayed there while Marion and the cook dashed out of the house and down the mile-long drive to summon help.

After some minutes Marion reached the Liberal Club in Dukinfield, so breathless that she could hardly speak. Eventually she managed to say that there was a burglar at Gorse Hall, and eight men who were drinking in the club dashed out and ran to the mansion, where they found the alarm bell ringing, the kitchen door open, and George Storrs lying on the kitchen floor in a pool of blood with multiple stab wounds. George was conscious, and the men asked him who had done this to him. All he could do was to ask for his wife. Then he died.

The police were at a loss as to the motive for the attack. Premeditated murder seemed unlikely, since if the intruder had entered the house intending to kill, why was he waving a revolver that wouldn't shoot? Theft was discounted—if only because, as the newspapers at the time tactfully hinted, the Storrs had nothing worth stealing. Margaret Storrs swore that her husband had no enemies—no recently dismissed servants, no disgruntled employees at the mill. Blackmail or extortion was mooted, but George Storrs seems to have led a blameless life: "His personal character was regarded by those who knew him, both as a married man and a single man, as beyond the slightest suspicion," declared the *Manchester Guardian*.[19] The police brought in bloodhounds, which couldn't pick up any scent; they dragged ponds in the grounds; they called on Scotland Yard for assistance. The chief constable of Cheshire, Colonel John Hamersley, circulated a polite but rather naive note to police forces all over the country:

> I should be greatly obliged if you would . . . let me have the names and description of any persons of homicidal tendency or of violent character who may have been absent from their usual place of abode at or about the time of this murder, or of any person that in the opinion of your officers is likely to have committed the crime.[20]

Eleven days after the murder the Storrses' coachman, John Worrall, was found dead in the stables at Gorse Hall. He had hanged himself, a fact which might have suggested a guilty conscience. However, the police were at pains to say he had been in Stalybridge at the time

of the murder and hadn't returned to the hall until after it was discovered. Margaret Storrs said he had been "greatly attached" to his master
and suffered from depression as a result of his death.[21]

The real reason why the police didn't regard Worrall as a person of
interest was that they thought they already had their man. Cornelius
Howard, a cousin of George Storrs, had come out of the army in April
1909 and taken up a new career in the district as a housebreaker. He
fitted the description of the killer given to the police by Margaret,
Marion, and the two servants, and the police made it known they
would like to interview him. On November 17 he was found breaking
into a Co-operative Store, and although he initially gave a false name
and a false address, he eventually admitted that he was Howard. He
had cuts and bruises on his legs, and the constable who arrested him
found a knife and a pair of blood-drenched socks in his pocket. When
Margaret Storrs, Marion Lindley, and the two servants all identified
him as the man they saw fighting with George, he was charged with
the murder and sent for trial at Chester Assizes.

The trial, which took place at the beginning of March 1910,
attracted national attention. Howard, who had initially explained the
cuts on his legs by saying that he was helping his landlord to fit a
window and the glass fell on him, now said that he had received the
injuries when he was breaking into a wholesale grocer's in the district. It also transpired that he had been in prison for shop-breaking in
September 1909, when the first break-in at Gorse Hall occurred, and
yet everyone had assumed the two incidents were connected. There
was also the question of identity. Although Marion Lindley was quite
clear that Howard was the man she saw at Gorse Hall on the night of
November 1, Margaret Storrs picked out the wrong man in one of the
identity parades.

That was enough to cast doubt on Howard's guilt. But even more
telling was the fact that four witnesses swore Howard had been drinking with them at a hotel in Huddersfield, twenty miles away, at the

time of the murder. The jury was out for only twenty minutes before returning a verdict of not guilty, and there was uproar in court. People in the public gallery cheered and applauded. Howard's solicitor leaned into the dock to shake his client's hand. "The shouting and clapping and handwaving was quite wild," reported the *Guardian*.[22]

The crowd's reaction to the verdict is intriguing. George Storrs was a popular man; Cornelius Howard was a thief and a liar. Yet public opinion was not on the side of the angels, a point heralded even before the trial by the fact that local people in Stalybridge and Dukinfield organised a fund to pay for his defence. Was it simply a case of standing up for the working man against the landed elite? (Not that Howard seems to have done much work.) A case of the public siding with the underdog, as had happened with Ellen Penketh and the Yorkes at Erddig five years earlier? Or was there a genuine and widespread belief that Howard was innocent?

Undeterred, the police reopened their investigations, and over the summer suspicion fell on a labourer and ex-soldier, Mark Wilde, who lived less than a mile from Gorse Hall. He was in possession of a knife—at least, he had been, until one night in June when he threatened a pair of young lovers with it and the man took it from him. As a result of this incident he received a visit from Inspector Brewster of the Stalybridge police, who noticed dried blood on his vest and coat and asked him for an explanation. He said he had got into a fight with a man outside a pub in Ashton-under-Lyne on November 1, the night of the murder. He was sentenced to two months' imprisonment in Knutsford Prison for the assault on the lovers, and when he was released on August 30, he found the police waiting to arrest him on suspicion of murder. He had owned two revolvers but said that after the murder he was frightened that he might be accused, so he had dismantled them both and thrown the parts into the canal. It turned out that he couldn't account for his movements on September 10, the night when the Storrs were threatened by an intruder: he was supposed to be at his job at the railway station in Stalybridge, but he didn't turn up and was sacked as a result.

Things looked rather bleak for Wilde, and they looked a good deal worse when Marion Lindley, Ellen Cooper, and Mary Evans all picked him out in a thirteen-man identity parade staged at Knutsford Gaol. Several of Wilde's old army colleagues identified the unusable revolver left at the scene as having belonged to him, and the single bullet in it corresponded to bullets found at his home.

His trial took place in the last week of October 1910, again at Chester Assizes. Witnesses swore the revolver belonged to Wilde; other witnesses swore it didn't. No one came forward to corroborate Wilde's story that he had been in a fight on the night of the murder, but no one came forward to contradict it, either. Marion Lindley, Ellen Cooper, and Mary Evans all swore Wilde was the man they saw grappling with George Storrs that night nearly a year earlier. But as defence counsel was swift to point out, they had already sworn that Cornelius Howard was that man, and this was perhaps the most telling point in Wilde's favour. Cross-examined by Wilde's counsel, Margaret Storrs broke down in tears and "pleaded piteously that she had lived a lifetime since these events." "You don't know what I have gone through," she told the judge, before fainting in the witness box and having to be revived with smelling salts.[23] The prosecution argued that the two men looked so much alike that it was a natural mistake for the women to have made, and in a moment of high drama, the judge had Howard brought into the court to stand silently side by side with Wilde in front of the jury while the lights in the courtroom were turned full on.

Wilde was acquitted. And once more the public galleries broke into cheers and applause. Once more there was wild cheering outside the court. No one was ever convicted of George Storrs's murder, no motive for it was ever established, and the Mansion Mystery was never solved. Margaret Storrs had Gorse Hall demolished.

EPILOGUE
—————

AND THE BAND PLAYED ON

T HIS STORY BEGAN with a ball. Let it end with a garden party, one of the last that this golden age of the country house ever saw. On August 3, 1914, the Earl and Countess of Warwick opened the grounds of Easton Lodge in Essex to the annual cottage garden show, as they did every year. Frances Maynard, as Daisy then was, had inherited the enormous Gothic Revival mansion, and a fortune to go with it, from her grandfather back in 1865, when she was just three years old. (The surprising news of her good fortune arrived while the rest of the family was sitting in the morning room at Easton, with breakfast things still on the table. They were so cross at the bequest that they hurled pats of butter at their grandfather's portrait.) Under Daisy's skilful management, Easton's house parties had become the stuff of legend, attracting the cream of British society.

On this particular summer's day, the sun shone, the stalls were crowded, and the band of the Essex Yeomanry played on as the villagers strolled around in their Sunday best, admiring the prize marrows and the embroidered antimacassars and the fancy table decorations. Daisy's friends came down from London for the day and drew admiring glances as they sat under the trees or strolled around in pairs, the women in huge picture hats, the men in white with Panama hats and elegant walking sticks.

And as they basked in the afternoon sun and enjoyed Easton's delights, it seemed as though the party would last forever. Daisy glided from one group of guests to another, exchanging pleasantries, complementing Mrs Cozens on her sweet peas and Mr Chanin on his prize-winning ducks, politely clapping for the winners of the tennis tournament on the lawn, smiling as the crowds gasped at the spectacular display of fireworks as evening fell.

The next day, Germany invaded Belgium. And very soon, the grand pyrotechnic displays would be all too real, the gentlemen would swap their elegant walking sticks for service revolvers, and the band of the Essex Yeomanry would play "Keep the Home Fires Burning" as it marched into hell.

There were still garden parties that summer, still country house weekends. The week after war was declared, shooting expert Aymer Maxwell contributed an article to *Country Life* on the prospects for grouse on the Glorious Twelfth and Lawrence Weaver wrote at length on the Earl of Strathmore's Glamis Castle.

But there was no escaping the war. The *Tatler* carried a full-page photograph of a uniformed Prince of Wales brandishing a rifle. He had joined the Grenadier Guards two days after Britain declared war, and the photo was captioned "A Royal Example to the Young Unmarried Men of the Empire."[1] Noting that the weekly "circulate[d] enormously among the more prosperous members of the community," it published a list of societies looking for funds, from the British Red Cross to the Friends of the Poor, which appealed for funds to support London families whose men were being called to active service.

Owners rushed to offer their country houses to the war effort as hospitals and convalescent homes. The 4th Marquess of Bute lent the government Cardiff Castle. Nancy Astor offered Cliveden, and Lady Sackville fitted up the great hall at Knole to receive wounded soldiers. Other society hostesses opted for a more active approach. Viscountess Castlereagh, who upon the death of her father-in-law in 1915 became the Marchioness of Londonderry, opened Londonderry House on Park Lane to wounded officers and also served as colonel in chief of the Women's Volunteer Reserve before leaving to found her own breakaway organisation, the Women's Army Auxiliary Corps. Her marquess, Charlie, was serving in France and occasionally wrote home to ask her to forward his letters to his various mistresses. "Put a stamp on it and just send it off," ran one of his notes to his wife. "That would be very sweet and dear [of] you."[2]

Within days of the outbreak of war, the Duchess of Westminster gave £1,000 and guaranteed £400 a month to fund a hospital she was organising. She was not the first: on August 15 Lady Dudley, wife of the former governor-general of Australia, established the Australian Voluntary Hospital, which was staffed by Australian doctors and nurses in the United Kingdom. Staff and equipment left for France at the end of the month. Winston Churchill's aunt Lady Sarah Wilson, a veteran of the siege of Mafeking in the Boer War, took money and nurses out to France days later and set up a base hospital at Boulogne. Mary Elcho, now the Countess of Wemyss, was keen to set up a convalescent home at Stanway, a plan which was steadfastly resisted by her husband Hugo, who nevertheless ordered the Stanway menservants to join up. "I shall have no chauffeur, no stableman, no odd man to carry the coals!" complained Mary.[3] The shortage of staff didn't worry Hugo: he spent most of his time at Gosford in East Lothian, another family seat where he had set up house with his current mistress, Angela Forbes.

The 6th Viscount Hawarden was the first British peer to be killed. A lieutenant in the Coldstream Guards, he died of wounds on the night of August 25–26 during the retreat from Mons. On September 20, 1914, Lord John Spencer Cavendish, brother of the Duke of Devonshire, was killed in France. Mary Elcho's nephew Percy had died six days earlier, at the First Battle of the Aisne.

In October, a notice appeared in *Country Life*. "Our readers will learn with very great regret of the death of Captain Aymer Maxwell, who was killed in action at Antwerp on October 8th."[4] The following month, Lady Sarah Wilson was running her hospital in Boulogne when she heard that her husband Gordon, a lieutenant colonel in the Royal Horse Guards, had been shot dead whilst leading his men in a counterattack near Ypres.

Mary Elcho would lose two of her sons to the war. Yvo, a second lieutenant in the Grenadier Guards, was killed on October 17, 1915, when he was just nineteen. In the spring of 1916 his older brother Hugo, who was married to Violet Manners, daughter of the Duke of Rutland, was serving in the Middle East with the Royal Gloucestershire Hussars, defending the Suez Canal against the Turks, when his unit was overrun. For two months the family believed he had been wounded and taken prisoner, but in July they received a telegram from Ankara confirming that he'd died in the battle.

As the casualties began to mount, so did the stories of heroism, sometimes bordering on the foolhardy. The fifty-year-old Earl of Longford of Packenham Hall in County Westmeath was killed at Gallipoli on August 21, 1915, while leading a cavalry charge over open ground. A brigadier general, his last words to his officers were, "Don't bother ducking. The men don't like it and it doesn't do any good."[5] His body was never found. Rudolf Valentine, who with his bride had so narrowly escaped death when fire broke out at his Warwickshire country house in 1908, was killed nine years later in another famous cavalry charge, this one against Turkish forces at Huj in Palestine. Lord Bute's brother, Lieutenant Colonel Lord Ninian Crichton-Stuart, died at the Battle of Loos while rallying his troops. He stood up above the parapet of his trench, in full view of the enemy, shouting, "Steady, men," before a German sniper shot him in the head.

There was a surge in country house sales immediately after the war. Daisy Warwick put her five-thousand-acre Easton Lodge estate up for sale in the autumn of 1918, and Lympne Castle in Kent came on the market at the same time, as did the three-thousand-acre Hassop Hall in Derbyshire, which boasted its own water-powered cotton mills and an annual rent roll in excess of £3,500. The number of sales grew dramatically over the next few years, until it seemed that the end of the war meant the end of country house life.

It didn't. New mansions were built and old ones cherished after 1918. Friends were entertained and shooting parties were organised, just as they had been before the war. Perhaps there were fewer servants to hand round the cocktails and carry up the breakfast trays. Perhaps it made financial sense to shut up the London house or to sell off that awkward outlying piece of land. But high wartime prices meant that those families who still depended on the land were doing rather well.

But there are different kinds of ending. The war memorials on countless village greens, the stained-glass tributes in countless country churches, were reminders of loss at a time when no reminders were needed. For many, it wasn't the war which marked a change: it was a death, the death of a father or a son or a brother.

In 1918 Sir Edwin Lutyens's masterpiece of a country house, the modern-medieval Castle Drogo in Devon, was still unfinished, although the project had been ongoing for eight years. The Drewe family, for whom Lutyens was building Drogo, were still living in their old home, Wadhurst Hall in Sussex, a big Victorian mansion bought by Julius Drewe in 1898.

But not all the family. When war broke out the Drewes' eldest son, Adrian, was studying medicine at Barts Hospital. He gave up his studies and took a commission in an artillery regiment which went out to Flanders in the spring of 1915. At 6:00 a.m. on July 12, 1917, a shell hit his command post in the little village of Vlamertinge, and he was killed.

His heartbroken parents reacted by turning his old bedroom at Wadhurst into a shrine filled with mementoes of his time at Eton and Cambridge—group photographs, oars and cricket bats and house colours, a makeshift wooden grave marker from Flanders with the inscription "He was a gallant gentleman." They hung a full-length portrait of their son in uniform and placed before it a bronze figure of Victory, with his battle honours engraved around its base.

Other families commemorated their fallen sons in much the same heartbreaking way, although few memorial rooms have survived intact. But perhaps the most poignant thing about this particular example is that when the Drewes finally moved into Castle Drogo in 1928, eleven years after Adrian's death, they brought the contents of the Wadhurst Hall bedroom with them and carefully arranged them in another room that they had set aside for the purpose.

Drogo, a magical symbol of a faith in a postwar future for the country house, could not, would not, leave its ghosts behind.

ACKNOWLEDGEMENTS

So many people have helped me with the writing of this book, and I owe a debt of gratitude to them all. I would particularly like to thank my students at the University of Buckingham, who asked the right questions and came up with the right answers; Patricia Lankester and Michael Clements, both of whom read an early draft of the book and made many helpful comments; Professor Terence Dooley, whose kind welcome to Maynooth University will not be forgotten; my agent, Sally Holloway, and her assistant, Katerina Lygaki, who took a weight from my shoulders; Tony and Jane French, Sinéad Gallagher, Linda Rogers, and Kirsty Wallace, who gave kindness and hospitality; Cherry Ann Knott, who generously shared her encyclopaedic knowledge of Sudbury Hall and George Devey; and Paul Hawthorne, who took the time to show me round Oldway Mansion and shared his insights into Oldway and the Singer family.

Last, first, always, my thanks to Helen.

Tullaghanbaun, February 2024

ILLUSTRATION CREDITS

While every effort has been made to trace copyright holders, if any have been inadvertently overlooked the publishers would be happy to acknowledge them in future editions.

Sandringham House © Print Collector / Contributor via Getty Images

Wellbeck Abbey Tunnels © Illustrated London News Group. Image created courtesy of the British Library Board or Look and Learn

Cragside © National Trust Images

Andrew and Louise Carnegie © Bettmann / Contributor via Getty Images

Skibo Castle © Jon Furniss / Contributor via Getty Images

Maharaja Duleep Singh © National Portrait Gallery, London

Bhai Ram Singh © Heritage Images / Contributor via Getty Images

Oldway Mansion by Ianmacm: at English Wikipedia

The Empress Eugenie's New Residence for Illustrated London News by Look and Learn History Archive

The House Builders © Christie's Images / Bridgeman Images

Devizes Castle © Adrian Sherratt / Contributor via Alamy Stock Photo

George Frederic Watts, Sir Galahad, Harvard Art Museums/Fogg Museum, Bequest of Grenville L. Winthrop, Photo © President and Fellows of Harvard College, 1943.209

Blenheim Palace Fire Engine © Blenheim Palace

Schloss Kranzbach © dpa picture alliance / Alamy Stock Photo

Picture Postcard by Donald McGill © Greaves and Thomas

Tranby Croft © East Riding Photos—Picture Archives

Royal Collection RCIN 2980067 (Balmoral Tableaux-Vivants: "Greek Poetry." 24—24 May 1894), Royal Collection Trust / © His Majesty King Charles III 2023

Earl Russell trial for Illustrated London News by Look and Learn History Archive

King Edward VII at a shoot © Topical Press Agency / Stringer via Getty Images

BIBLIOGRAPHY

PERIODICALS

Aberdeen Press and Journal

Alnwick Mercury

Architect

Barnsley Chronicle

Belfast Newsletter

Birmingham Mail

Bromley Journal and West Kent Herald

Bucks Advertiser and Aylesbury News

Builder

Building News

Buxton Advertiser

Bystander

Chard and Ilminster News

Chelsea Mail

Cheltenham Chronicle

Cheshire Observer

Civil and Military Gazette (Lahore)

Country Life

Daily Gazette for Middlesbrough

Daily Mirror

Daily Telegraph

Derbyshire Courier

Dundee Evening Telegraph

Eastern Post

English Lakes Visitor

Eton College Chronicle

Express

Freeman's Journal

Garden

Gardening World

Gentlewoman

Graphic

Herts Advertiser

Hexham Courant

Hull Daily News

Illustrated London News

Illustrated Newspaper

Inquirer and Commercial News (Perth, Western Australia)

Jackson's Oxford Journal

John Bull

Leeds Mercury

Leicester Daily Post

Liverpool Mail

London Evening Standard

Manchester Courier

Manchester Guardian

Mansfield Reporter

Marlborough Times

Morning Post

Newcastle Journal

Newcastle Weekly Chronicle

Norfolk News

Northampton Mercury

Northern Echo

Northern Ensign and Weekly Gazette

North Star and Farmers' Chronicle

North Wales Times

Norwich Mercury
Nottingham Evening News
Nottingham Evening Post
Oxfordshire Weekly News
Pall Mall Gazette
Pall Mall Magazine
Reynolds's Newspaper
Salisbury and Winchester Journal
Saturday Review
Sheffield Daily Telegraph
Sketch
South Wales Daily News
Sporting Gazette
Tatler

Thomson's Weekly News
Times (London)
Tuam Herald
Ulster Echo
Warder and Dublin Weekly Mail
West Cumberland Times
Westerham Herald
Western Daily Press
Westminster Gazette
Worcestershire Chronicle
Yarmouth Independent
York Herald
Yorkshire Post and Leeds Intelligencer

BOOKS AND OTHER SOURCES

Abdy, Jane, and Charlotte Gere. *The Souls*. Sidgwick and Jackson, 1984.

Alexander, Michael, and Sushila Anand. *Queen Victoria's Maharajah: Duleep Singh, 1838–93*. Phoenix, 2001.

Allfrey, Anthony. *Edward VII and His Jewish Court*. Weidenfeld and Nicolson, 1991.

Allibone, Jill. *George Devey: Architect 1820–1886*. Lutterworth, 1998.

Aslet, Clive. *The Last Country Houses*. Yale University Press, 1982.

Asquith, Cynthia. *Haply I May Remember*. James Barrie, 1950.

———. *Remember and Be Glad*. Charles Scribner's Sons, 1952.

Asquith, Herbert. *Moments of Memory: Recollections and Impressions*. Charles Scribner's Sons, 1938.

Asquith, Margot. *Margot Asquith: An Autobiography*. 4 vols. George H. Doran, 1920–1922.

Astor, William Waldorf. "Free in a Faraway Land." *Pall Mall Magazine*, August 1903.

———. "The Wraith of Cliveden Reach." In *Pharaoh's Daughter and Other Stories*, 127–147. Macmillan, 1900.

Baedeker, Karl. *South-Eastern France . . . Handbook for Travellers*. 2nd ed. Karl Baedeker, 1895.

Bailey, John, ed. *The Diary of Lady Frederick Cavendish*. 2 vols. Frederick A. Stokes, 1927.

Bailey-Denton, E. *The Water Supply and Sewerage of Country Mansions and Estates*. E. & F. N. Spon, 1901.

Baillie Scott, M. H. *Houses and Gardens*. George Newnes, 1906.

Bance, Peter. *The Duleep Singhs: The Photographic Album of Queen Victoria's Maharajah*. Sutton, 2004.

Bateman, John. *The Great Landowners of Great Britain and Ireland*. 4th ed. Harrison, 1883.

Battersea, Connie. *Reminiscences*. Macmillan, 1922.

Bedoire, Fredric. *The Jewish Contribution to Modern Architecture, 1830–1930*. KTAV, 2004.

Belloc, Hilaire. *More Peers*. Alfred A Knopf, 1924.

Bielenberg, Andy. "Late Victorian Elite Formation and Philanthropy: The Making of Edward Guinness." *Studia Hibernica* 32 (2002–2003): 133–154.

Blomfield, Reginald. *A Short History of Renaissance Architecture in England, 1500–1800*. George Bell, 1900.

Blomfield, Reginald, and F. Inigo Thomas. *The Formal Garden in England*. 2nd ed. Macmillan, 1892.

Blunt, Wilfrid Scawen. *My Diaries: Being a Personal Narrative of Events 1888–1914*. 2 vols. Alfred A. Knopf, 1922.

Boutell, Charles. *Arms and Armour in Antiquity and the Middle Ages*. Gibbins, 1902.

Brandon, Ruth. *A Capitalist Romance: Singer and the Sewing Machine*. J. P. Lippincott, 1977.

Brett, Maurice V., ed. *Journals and Letters of Reginald Viscount Esher*. 4 vols. Ivor Nicholson and Watson, 1934–1938.

Brittain-Catlin, Timothy. *The Edwardians and Their Houses: The New Life of Old England*. Lund Humphries, 2020.

Burdett-Coutts, Baroness, ed. *Woman's Mission: A Series of Congress Papers on the Philanthropic Work of Women by Eminent Writers*. Sampson Low, Marston, 1893.

Burges, William. *Art Applied to Industry: A Series of Lectures*. John Henry and James Parker, 1865.

Burns, James. *Sir Galahad: A Call to the Heroic*. James Clarke, 1915. Online at the Camelot Project: A Robbins Library Digital Project, University of Rochester. https://d.lib.rochester.edu/camelot/text/burns-sir-galahad-a-call-to-the-heroic.

Cammaerts, Emile. *The Laughing Prophet: The Seven Virtues and G. K. Chesterton*. Methuen, 1937.

Cardigan, Earl of. *The Wardens of Savernake Forest*. Routledge and Kegan Paul, 1949.

Carey, Agnes. *Empress Eugénie in Exile*. Century, 1920.

Carnegie, Andrew. *Autobiography of Andrew Carnegie*. Houghton Mifflin, 1920.

Casey, Brian. "The Decline and Fall of the Clancarty Estate, 1891–1923." *Journal of the Galway Archaeological and Historical Society* 67 (2015): 171–183.

Cecil, Lady Gwendolen. *The Life of Robert, Marquis of Salisbury.* 4 vols. Hodder and Stoughton, 1921–1932.

Census of England and Wales for the Year 1871, General Report. Vol. 4. George Edward Eyre and William Spottiswoode, 1873. https://www.visionofireland.org /census/EW1871GEN/5.

Census of England and Wales for the Year 1911, General Report. Vol. 4. His Majesty's Stationery Office, 1911. https://www.visionofireland.org/census /EW1911GEN/5.

Chadwick, Owen. *The Victorian Church.* 2 vols. Adam and Charles Black, 1965–1970.

Chesterton, G. K. *Alarms and Discursions.* Methuen, 1910.

Coleridge, Christabel. *Charlotte Mary Yonge: Her Life and Letters.* Macmillan, 1903.

Collins, W. Lucas. "King Arthur and His Round Table." *Blackwood's Edinburgh Magazine,* September 1860, 311–337.

Cowper, Katrine, Countess of. *Earl Cowper, K. G.: A Memoir.* Privately printed, 1913.

Crook, J. Mordaunt. *The Rise of the Nouveaux Riches: Style and Status in Victorian and Edwardian Architecture.* John Murray, 1999.

———. *William Burges and the High Victorian Dream.* John Murray, 1981.

Crosland, T. W. H. *The Country Life.* Greening, 1906.

Cundall, Frank, ed. *Reminiscences of the Colonial and Indian Exhibition.* William Clowes and Sons, 1886.

Dakers, Caroline. *Clouds: The Biography of a Country House.* Yale University Press, 1993.

———. *The Countryside at War 1914–18.* Constable, 1987.

Davidson, H. C., ed. *The Book of the Home: An Encyclopaedia of All Matters Relating to the House and Household Management.* 4 vols. Gresham, 1905.

Davis, Charles, comp. *A Description of the Works of Art Forming the Collection of Alfred de Rothschild.* 2 vols. Privately printed, 1884.

Davis, Richard W. "'We Are All Americans Now!': Anglo-American Marriages in the Later Nineteenth Century." *Proceedings of the American Philosophical Society* 135, no. 2 (June 1991): 140–199.

Dawes, Frank. *Not in Front of the Servants: Domestic Service in England 1850–1939.* Wayland, 1973.

de Courcy, Anne. *Circe: The Life of Edith, Marchioness of Londonderry.* Sinclair-Stevenson, 1992.

Desborough, Ethel, Baroness. *Pages from a Family Journal.* Privately printed, 1916.

Ditchfield, P. H., and George Clinch, eds. *Memorials of Old Kent.* Bemrose and Sons, 1907.

Ditchfield, P. H., and Fred Roe. *Vanishing England.* 2nd ed. Methuen, 1911.

Dooley, Terence A. M. *The Decline and Fall of the Dukes of Leinster, 1872–1948: Love, War, Debt and Madness.* Four Courts, 2014. Digital edition.

Dooley, Terence, and Christopher Ridgway, eds. *Sport and Leisure in the Irish and British Country House.* Four Courts, 2019.

Duff Gordon, Lucy, Lady. *Discretions and Indiscretions.* Jarrolds, 1932.

Duncan, Isadora. *My Life.* Victor Gollancz, 1928.

The Duties of Servants: A Practical Guide to the Routine of Domestic Service. Frederick Warne, 1890.

Ellmann, Richard. *The Trial of Oscar Wilde.* Penguin, 1996.

Escott, T. H. S. *King Edward and His Court.* T. Fisher Unwin, 1908.

———. *Society in the Country House.* T. Fisher Unwin, 1907.

Fea, Allan. *Nooks and Corners of Old England.* 2nd ed. Martin Secker, 1911.

———. *Old English Houses: The Record of a Random Itinerary.* Martin Secker, 1910.

———. *Picturesque Old Houses: Being the Impressions of a Wanderer Off the Beaten Track.* S. H. Bousfield, 1902.

———. *Recollections of Sixty Years.* Richards Press, 1927.

———. *Secret Chambers and Hiding-Places.* 3rd ed. S. H. Bousfield, 1904.

Festing, Sally. *Gertrude Jekyll.* Penguin, 1993.

Filon, Augustin. *Recollections of the Empress Eugénie.* Cassell, 1920.

Fitch, Herbert T. *Memoirs of a Royal Detective.* Hurst and Blackett, 1936.

FitzRoy, Sir Almeric. *Memoirs.* 6th ed. 2 vols. Hutchinson n.d. [1926?].

Forbes, Lady Angela. *Memories and Base Details.* Hutchinson, 1921.

Foreign Resident [T. H. S. Escott]. *Society in the New Reign.* T. Fisher Unwin, 1904.

Franklin, Jill. *The Gentleman's Country House and Its Plan, 1835–1914.* Routledge and Kegan Paul, 1981.

———. "Troops of Servants: Labour and Planning in the Country House 1840–1914." *Victorian Studies* 19, no. 2 (1975): 211–239.

Gaffney, T. St. John. *Breaking the Silence: England, Ireland, Wilson and the War.* Horace Liveright, 1930.

Gathorne-Hardy, Robert, ed. *Ottoline: The Early Memoirs of Lady Ottoline Morrell.* Faber and Faber, 1963.

Gaunt, Ian, and John Tory. "Mary Portman's Violin, 1877–1931." Blandford Town Museum website. Posted 2010; updated 2014. https://blandfordtown museum.org.uk/theme-content/uploads/2021/10/MARY-PORTMAN .pdf.

Geraghty, Anthony. *The Empress Eugénie in England: Art, Architecture, Collecting.* Paul Holberton, 2022.

Girouard, Mark. *Life in the English Country House.* Yale University Press, 1978.

————. *The Return to Camelot: Chivalry and the English Gentleman*. Yale University Press, 1981.

————. *The Victorian Country House*. Yale University Press, 1979.

Glenconner, Pamela. *Edward Wyndham Tennant: A Memoir by His Mother*. John Lane, the Bodley Head, 1919.

Glyn, Eleanor. *Romantic Adventure*. Ivor Nicholson and Watson, 1936.

Green, Abigail, and Juliet Carey. "Beyond the Pale: The Country Houses of the Jewish Elite." *Journal of Modern Jewish Studies* 18, no. 4 (2019): 393–398.

Grimmett, Gordon. "The Lamp Boy's Story." In *Gentlemen's Gentlemen: My Friends in Service*, ed. Rosina Harrison, 9–88. Arlington Books, 1976.

Hare, Augustus. *The Story of My Life*. 6 vols. George Allen, 1896–1900.

Harrison, Frederic. *Autobiographic Memoirs*. 2 vols. Macmillan, 1911.

Hartwell, Clare, Nikolaus Pevsner, and Elizabeth Williamson. *Nottinghamshire*. Yale University Press, 2020.

Heath, Francis George. *Peasant Life in the West of England*. Sampson Low, Marston, Searle, and Rivington, 1880.

Heindel, Richard Heathcote. *The American Impact on Great Britain 1898–1914*. Octagon, 1968.

Henriques, U. R. Q. "The Jewish Emancipation Controversy in Nineteenth-Century Britain." *Past and Present* 40 (July 1968): 126–146.

Hignett, Sean. *Brett: From Bloomsbury to New Mexico*. Franklin Watts, 1983.

Hirshfield, Claire. "Labouchere, Truth and the Uses of Antisemitism." *Victorian Periodicals Review* 26, no. 3 (1993): 134–142.

Historic Houses of the United Kingdom. Cassell, 1892.

Holmes, Ann Sumner. "The Double Standard in the English Divorce Laws, 1857–1923." *Law and Social Inquiry* 20, no. 2 (1995): 601–620.

Holroyd, Michael. *Lytton Strachey: A Critical Biography*. 2 vols. Holt, Rinehart and Winston, 1968.

Hoole, Kenneth. *A Regional History of Railways of Great Britain*. Rev. ed. Vol. 4, *The North East*. David St John Thomas, 1986.

Hudson, W. H. *Afoot in England*. J. M. Dent and Sons, 1941.

Hyamson, Albert M. "The First Jewish Peer." *Transactions (Jewish Historical Society of England)* 17 (1951–1952): 287–290.

Ingram, John H. *The Haunted Homes and Family Traditions of Great Britain*. Gibbings, 1897.

Jackson, Sir Thomas Graham. *Recollections: The Life and Travels of a Victorian Architect*. Edited by Sir Nicholas Jackson. Unicorn Press, 2003.

James, Henry. *English Hours*. Houghton, Mifflin, 1905.

James, M. R. *Ghost Stories of an Antiquary*. Edward Arnold, 1904.

Jekyll, Francis. *Gertrude Jekyll: A Memoir*. Jonathan Cape, 1934.

Jekyll, Gertrude. *Colour in the Flower Garden*. Country Life, 1908.

Jennings, H. J. *Our Homes and How to Beautify Them*. Harrison and Sons, 1902.

Jessopp, Augustus. *Trials of a Country Parson*. T. Fisher Unwin, 1890.

Jewry, Mary, ed. *Warne's Model Cookery and Housekeeping Book*. Frederick Warne, 1871.

J. M. *Thomas Robinson Woolfield's Life at Cannes and Lord Brougham's First Arrival*. KeganPaul, Trench, Trübner, 1890.

Keep, Carolyn. "F. W. Meyer (1852–1906): Landscape Gardener for Robert Veitch & Son, Exeter." *Garden History* 42, no. 1 (Summer 2014): 64–88.

Kelly's Handbook to the Titled, Landed and Official Classes. Kelly's Directories, 1909.

Kerr, Robert. *The Gentleman's House; or, How to Plan English Residences*. 2nd ed. John Murray, 1865.

———. *The Newleafe Discourses on the Fine Art Architecture*. J. Weale, 1847.

King, Carole. "The Rise and Decline of Village Reading Rooms." *Rural History* 20, no. 2 (2009): 163–186.

Kornwolf, James D. *M. H. Baillie Scott and the Arts and Crafts Movement*. Johns Hopkins University Press, 1972.

Lanceley, William. *From Hall-Boy to House-Steward*. Edward Arnold, 1925.

Lasic, Barbara. "'Dignity and Graciousness': Mewès and Davis and the Creation of *Tous les Louis* Period Rooms." *Furniture History* 48 (2012): 193–210.

———. "A Display of Opulence: Alfred de Rothschild and the Visual Recording of Halton House." *Furniture History* 40 (2004): 135–150.

Leslie, Anita. *Edwardians in Love*. Hutchinson, 1972.

Lethaby, W. R. *Philip Webb and His Work*. Oxford University Press, 1935.

Liddell, A. G. C. *Notes from the Life of an Ordinary Mortal*. John Murray, 1911.

Lodge, Edmund. *The Peerage, Baronetage, Knightage and Companionage of the British Empire*. Kelly's Directories, 1906.

Login, E. Dalhousie. *Lady Login's Recollections: Court Life and Camp Life 1820–1904*. Smith, Elder, 1916.

Login, Lady. *Sir John Login and Duleep Singh*. W. H. Allen, 1890.

Longford, Elizabeth. *A Pilgrimage of Passion: The Life of Wilfrid Scawen Blunt*. Tauris Parke, 2007.

Lutyens, Emily. *A Blessed Girl: Memoirs of a Victorian Girlhood*. Heinemann, 1989.

Machin, G. I. T. "The Last Victorian Anti-Ritualist Campaign, 1895–1906." *Victorian Studies* 25, no. 3 (Spring 1982): 277–302.

Macpherson, Angus. *A Highlander Looks Back*. Oban Times, 1900.

Marlborough, Consuelo, Duchess of. "The Position of Women." *North American Review* 189, no. 639 (1909): 11–24, 180–193, 351–359.

Marsh, Edward. *A Number of People: A Book of Reminiscences*. William Heinemann, 1939.

Martin, John. "British Game Shooting in Transition, 1900–1945." *Agricultural History* 85, no. 2 (2011): 204–224.

Masterman, Lucy. *Mary Gladstone (Mrs. Drew): Her Diaries and Letters*. E. P. Dutton, 1930.

Mawson, Thomas H. *The Art and Craft of Garden Making*. Batsford, 1900.

———. *The Life and Work of an English Landscape Architect: An Autobiography*. Scribner, 1927.

———. *The Life and Work of a Northern Landscape Architect: Thomas H. Mawson 1861–1933*. Exhibition catalogue. University of Lancaster, 1976.

———. "On the Designing of Gardens." In *The Studio Year-Book of Decorative Art*, iii-x and ills. The Studio, 1908.

Maxwell, Aymer. *Partridges and Partridge Manors*. Adam and Charles Black, 1911.

McCarthy, Patricia Alice. "To Whom Belongs the Land: Change and Reform on a North Riding Estate, 1889 to 1914." *Yorkshire Archaeological Journal* 92, no. 1 (2020): 131–153.

Merryweather, James Compton. *Fire Protection of Mansions*. Merritt and Hatcher, 1884.

Middlemass, Barbara, and Joe Hunt. *John Corbett: Pillar of Salt 1817–1901*. Saltway, 1985.

Mills, Ernestine. *The Life and Letters of Frederic Shields*. Longmans, Green and Company, 1912.

Mills, John. *The British Jews*. Houlston and Stoneman, 1853.

Mills, J. Saxon. *The Life and Letters of Sir Hubert Herkomer*. Hutchinson, 1923.

Montgomery, Maureen E. *Gilded Prostitution: Status, Money, and Transatlantic Marriages 1870–1914*. Routledge, 1989.

Murdoch, Tessa. "Sir Ernest Cassel, a 'Jew of Taste.'" *Journal of the History of Collections* 34, no. 3 (2022): 399–412.

Muthesius, Hermann. *The English House*. Edited by Dennis Sharp. Translated by Janet Seligman. BSP Professional Books, 1987.

Nairn, Ian, and Nikolaus Pevsner. *Surrey*. Penguin, 1999.

———. *Sussex*. Penguin, 1991.

Nevill, Ralph. *The Life and Letters of Lady Dorothy Nevill*. Methuen, 1919.

———, ed. *Leaves from the Note-Books of Lady Dorothy Nevill*. Macmillan, 1907.

———, ed. *The Reminiscences of Lady Dorothy Nevill*. Edward Arnold, 1906.

O'Neill, Daniel. *Sir Edwin Lutyens' Country Houses*. Lund Humphries, 1980.

One of the Old Brigade [Donald Shaw]. *London in the Sixties (with a Few Digressions)*. Everett, 1908.

Ottewill, David. *The Edwardian Garden*. Yale University Press, 1989.

Oxford and Asquith, Earl of. *Memories and Reflections*. 2 vols. Cassell, 1928.

"Park Lane." Chapter 15 in *Survey of London*, vol. 40, *The Grosvenor Estate in Mayfair, Part 2 (The Buildings)*, ed. F. H. W. Sheppard, 264–289. London County Council, 1980. Online at http://www.british-history.ac.uk/survey-london/vol40/pt2/pp264-289.

Pevsner, Nikolaus. *Bedfordshire and the County of Huntingdon and Peterborough*. Penguin, 1968.

———. *Berkshire*. Penguin, 1966.

———. *South and West Somerset*. Penguin, 1958.

Pevsner, Nikolaus, and Edward Hubbard. *Cheshire*. Penguin, 2001.

Pevsner, Nikolaus, and David Lloyd. *Hampshire and the Isle of Wight*. Penguin, 1990.

Picton-Turbervill, Edith. "Childhood in Brighton and Bruges." In *Myself When Young*, edited by Margot Asquith, 313–360. Frederick Muller, 1938.

A Pictorial and Descriptive Guide to Matlock, Dovedale, Chatsworth, Haddon Hall, Derby etc. Ward, Lock, 1906.

Pinney, Thomas, ed. *The Letters of Rudyard Kipling*. 6 vols. Macmillan, 1990–2004.

Ponsonby, Sir Frederick. *Recollections of Three Reigns*. Eyre and Spottiswoode, 1951.

Portland, Duke of [William Cavendish-Bentinck]. *Men, Women and Things*. Faber and Faber, 1937.

Pullan, R. P. *The House of William Burges A.R.A.* Privately printed, 1885.

Quest-Ritson, Charles. *The English Garden Abroad*. Penguin, 1996.

Rajabzadeh, Shokoofeh. "Is Your Bread White Enough? King Arthur Baking Company's Racist Marketing History." *Medium*, November 24, 2020, https://medium.com/the-sundial-acmrs/is-your-bread-white-enough-king-arthur-baking-companys-racist-marketing-history-e070df0dd13a.

Renton, Claudia. *Those Wild Wyndhams: Three Sisters at the Heart of Power*. William Collins, 2014.

Ridgway, Christopher. "A Privileged Insider: George Howard and Edward Burne-Jones." *British Art Journal* 3, no. 3 (Autumn 2002): 4–18.

Ridley, Jane. *Bertie: A Life of Edward VII*. Vintage, 2012. Digital edition.

———. *Edwin Lutyens: His Life, His Wife, His Work*. Pimlico, 2003.

———. *George V: Never a Dull Moment*. Vintage, 2023. Digital edition.

Ridley, Jane, and Clayre Percy, eds. *The Letters of Arthur Balfour and Lady Elcho, 1885–1917*. Hamish Hamilton, 1992.

Robinson, William. *The English Flower Garden*. 3rd ed. John Murray, 1893.

———. *Garden Design and Architects' Gardens*. John Murray, 1892.

———. *The Wild Garden*. John Murray, 1870.

Roth, Cecil. "The Court Jews of Edwardian England." *Jewish Social Studies* 5, no. 4 (1943): 355–366.

Rothschild, Ferdinand de. "French Eighteenth-Century Art in England." *Nineteenth Century* 31 (1892): 376–390.

———. *The Red Book*. Privately printed, 1897.

Rothschild, Mrs James de. *The Rothschilds at Waddesdon Manor*. Collins, 1979.

Russell, Earl [John Francis Stanley Russell, 2nd Earl]. *My Life and Adventures*. Cassell, 1923.

Saint, Andrew. *Richard Norman Shaw*. Yale University Press, 1976.

Santayana, George. *The Middle Span*. Charles Scribner's Sons, 1945.

Savage, Peter. *Lorimer and the Edinburgh Craft Designers*. Paul Harris, 1980.

Scott, George Gilbert. *Personal and Professional Recollections by the Late Sir George Gilbert Scott, R. A.* Sampson Low, Marston, Searle, and Rivington, 1879.

———. *Remarks on Secular and Domestic Architecture*. John Murray, 1857.

The Servants' Practical Guide: A Handbook of Duties and Rules. Frederick Warne, 1880.

Shore, W. Teignmouth, ed. *The Baccarat Case: Gordon-Cumming v. Wilson and Others*. Notable Trials Library. Butterworth, 1932.

Sinclair, Jill. "Looking for Monsieur Lainé." *Historic Gardens Review* 29 (October 2013): 11–15.

Singh, Prince Frederick Duleep. *Portraits in Norfolk Houses*. 2 vols. Jarrold and Sons, 1927.

Singh, S. Ganda. "Some Correspondence of Maharaja Duleep Singh." *Journal of Indian History* 27 (April 1949): 1–23.

Smith, Pete. *The Motor Car and the Country House: Historic Buildings Report*. Research Department Report Series no. 94-2010. English Heritage, 2010.

Spring, Eileen. "Landowners, Lawyers and Land Law Reform in Nineteenth-Century England." *American Journal of Legal History* 21, no. 1 (1977): 40–59.

Stammers, Thomas. "Old French and New Money: Jews and the Aesthetics of the Old Regime in Transnational Perspective, c. 1860–1910." *Journal of Modern Jewish Studies* 18, no. 4 (2019): 489–512.

Stead, W. T. *The Americanization of the World*. Horace Markley, 1902.

Stevenson, J. J. *House Architecture*. 2 vols. Macmillan, 1880.

Strong, Roy. *"Country Life," 1897–1997: The English Arcadia*. Boxtree, 1999.

Tennyson, Alfred Lord. *Idylls of the King*. Macmillan, 1904.

Teulié, Gilles. "World War Two Iconoclasm: The Destruction and Reconstruction of Memorials to Queen Victoria and Edward VII on the French Riviera," *e-Rea* 14, no. 2 (2017), https://doi.org/10.4000/erea.5809.

Thom, Adam Bisset. *The Upper Ten Thousand: An Alphabetical List*. George Routledge and Sons, 1875.

Thomas, F. Inigo. "The Garden in Relation to the House." *Journal of the Society of Arts* 44 (1896): 241–266.

Tilden, Philip. *True Remembrances: The Memoirs of an Architect*. Country Life, 1954.

Tinniswood, Adrian. *The Arts and Crafts House*. Mitchell Beazley, 1999.

———. *Behind the Throne: A Domestic History of the Royal Household*. Jonathan Cape, 2018.

———. *Historic Houses of the National Trust*. National Trust, 1991.

————. *The Long Weekend: Life in the English Country House Between the Wars.* Jonathan Cape, 2016.

Tomlin, Maurice. *Ham House.* Victoria and Albert Museum, 1986.

Trevelyan, Raleigh. *Grand Dukes and Diamonds: The Wernhers of Luton Hoo.* Faber and Faber, 2013. Epub.

Twisleton, Ellen Dwight. *Letters of the Hon. Mrs Edward Twisleton, Written to Her Family, 1852–1862.* John Murray, 1928.

Tyack, Geoffrey. "Buckler, John." In *Oxford Dictionary of National Biography.* Oxford University Press, 2004; online ed., 2011. https://doi.org/10.1093/ref:odnb/3863.

Vandal, Pervaiz, and Sajida Vandal. *The Raj, Lahore, and Bhai Ram Singh.* National College of Arts, Lahore, 2006.

Vernon, William Warren. *Recollections of Seventy-Two Years.* John Murray, 1917.

Victoria. Journals, 1832–1901. 141 vols. Royal Archives, Windsor Castle. www.queenvictoriasjournals.org.

Vincent, John, ed. *The Crawford Papers: The Journals of David Lindsay, 27th Earl of Crawford and 10th Earl of Balcarres, 1871–1940, During the Years 1892 to 1940.* Manchester University Press, 1984.

Visitor [William Waldorf Astor?]. "Hever Restored." *Pall Mall Magazine,* January 1907, 2–15.

Wall, Joseph Frazier. *Skibo.* Oxford University Press, 1984.

Warwick, Frances [Daisy], Countess of. *Afterthoughts.* Cassell, 1931.

————. *Life's Ebb and Flow.* Hutchinson, 1929.

————. *Warwick Castle and Its Earls.* 2 vols. Hutchinson, 1903.

————. *William Morris: His Homes and Haunts.* T. C. & E. C. Jack, 1912.

Washington, Booker T. *My Larger Education: Being Chapters from My Experience.* Doubleday, Page, 1911. Electronic edition, https://docsouth.unc.edu/fpn/washeducation/washing.html.

Waterson, Merlin. *The Servants' Hall: The Domestic History of a Country House.* National Trust, 1990.

Watson, Mrs Andrew. *The Story of Bamba.* Women's General Missionary Society, 1890.

Waugh, Evelyn. *Brideshead Revisited.* Little, Brown, 1945.

Weaver, Lawrence, ed. *The House and Its Equipment.* Country Life, 1912.

Whalley, Robin. "Peto, Harold Ainsworth." In *Oxford Dictionary of National Biography.* Oxford University Press, 2004; online ed., 2011. https://doi-org.lonlib.idm.oclc.org/10.1093/ref:odnb/96721.

Wilde, Oscar. "The Canterville Ghost." In *The Complete Works of Oscar Wilde,* 193–214. Barnes and Noble, 1994.

Wilkinson, William. *English Country Houses: Forty-Five View and Plans.* James Parker, 1870.

Wilson, Derek. *The Astors, 1763–1992: Landscape with Millionaires.* Weidenfeld and Nicolson, 1993.

Wilson, John R. A. "Paris Singer: A Life Portrait." *Torquay Natural History Society Transactions and Proceedings*, February 1997, 142–171, and February 1998, 254–279.

Wilson, R. G. "Bass, Michael Thomas." In *Oxford Dictionary of National Biography*. Oxford University Press, 2004; online ed., 2011. https://doi-org.lonlib .idm.oclc.org/10.1093/ref:odnb/1631.

Wilson, R. G., and A. L. Mackley. "How Much Did the English Country House Cost to Build, 1660–1880?" *Economic History Review* 52, no. 3 (August 1999): 436–468.

Windsor, Edward, Duke of. *A King's Story: The Memoirs of the Duke of Windsor.* Cassell, 1951.

Wohl, Anthony S. "'Ben JuJu': Representations of Disraeli's Jewishness in the Victorian Political Cartoon." *Jewish History* 10, no. 2 (1996): 89–134.

NOTES

INTRODUCTION: ALL THAT GLITTERS

1. Spring, "Landowners," 51.
2. Spring, 54.
3. Cardigan, *Wardens*, 311.
4. *Ulster Echo*, October 5, 1887, 4.
5. Cardigan, *Wardens*, 40.
6. Cardigan, 39.
7. Cardigan, 44.
8. *London Evening Standard*, January 17, 1891, 2.
9. *Times*, August 8, 1891, 3.
10. *Times*, August 8, 1891, 3.
11. Cardigan, *Wardens*, 47.
12. *Daily Telegraph*, April 17, 1894.
13. Liddell, *Notes*, 300.
14. United Kingdom, *Parliamentary Debates*, House of Lords, July 26, 1894, vol. 27, col. 964–65 (Duke of Devonshire), https://api.parliament.uk/historic-hansard/lords/1894/jul/26/second-reading.
15. United Kingdom, *Parliamentary Debates*, House of Lords, July 26, 1894, vol. 27, col. 953 (Earl of Feversham); col. 996 (Lord Halsbury), https://api.parliament.uk/historic-hansard/lords/1894/jul/26/second-reading.
16. McCarthy, "To Whom Belongs," 133.
17. *Country Life*, January 9, 1969, 69.

CHAPTER ONE: POWER AND PRIDE

1. *Northern Ensign and Weekly Gazette*, January 1, 1880, 3.
2. *Historic Houses*, 6, 8.
3. Gathorne-Hardy, *Ottoline*, 73.
4. Gathorne-Hardy, 73.

5.   Hartwell, Pevsner, and Williamson, *Nottinghamshire*, 685.

6.   Gathorne-Hardy, *Ottoline*, 74.

7.   Hartwell, Pevsner, and Williamson, 75, 74.

8.   *Sheffield Daily Telegraph*, December 13, 1879, 3.

9.   *Daily Telegraph*, December 8, 1879, 3.

10. *Historic Houses*, 12.

11. Gathorne-Hardy, *Ottoline*, 76.

12. Portland, *Men, Women and Things*, 42.

13. Portland, 56.

14. Portland, 247.

15. Portland, 54.

16. Thom, *Upper Ten Thousand*, iii.

17. Thom, ix.

18. *Kelly's Handbook* (1909), 7.

19. *Kelly's Handbook* (1909), 1070, 1117, 283.

20. *Newcastle Journal*, July 19, 1864, 2.

21. This description of Cragside first appeared, in a slightly different form, in my *Historic Houses of the National Trust*, 247–254.

22. *The Onlooker*, January 2, 1901; quoted in Girouard, *Victorian Country House*, 317.

CHAPTER TWO: MONEYBAGS

1.   *Hull Daily News*, August 10, 1895, 25; *Marlborough Times*, October 20, 1894, 7; *Daily Telegraph*, August 27, 1887, 5; *Liverpool Mail*, February 3, 1877, 8; *Truth*, January 6, 1881, 9.

2.   Jessopp, *Trials of a Country Parson*, 36.

3.   Jessopp, 37.

4.   Crosland, *Country Life*, 99–100.

5.   *Illustrated London News*, October 21, 1881, 429.

6.   *Illustrated London News*, October 21, 1881, 429.

7.   *Country Life*, June 2, 1900, xxvii.

8.   *Country Life*, June 9, 1900; June 16, 1900.

9.   *Country Life*, May 11, 1901, 592.

10. Middlemass and Hunt, *John Corbett*, 48.

11. *Country Life*, May 11, 1901, 594.

12. *Worcestershire Chronicle*, April 19, 1879, 6.

13. *Worcestershire Chronicle*, July 16, 1887, 5.

14. Middlemass and Hunt, *John Corbett*, 93.

15. Wilson, "Bass, Michael Thomas."

16. Bielenberg, "Late Victorian Elite Formation," 141.

17. Census return for Impney Hall, March 31, 1901, Public Record Office RG 13/2797, *Census of England and Wales*, 1901, "Impney Mansion, Dodderhill, Worcestershire"; *Cheltenham Chronicle*, April 27, 1901, 8.

CHAPTER THREE: KINGS OF THE GILDED AGE

1. Carnegie, *Autobiography*, 216.
2. Carnegie, 215.
3. Masterman, *Mary Gladstone*, 258; Hay is quoted in Carnegie, *Autobiography*, 216fn.
4. Wall, *Skibo*, 42.
5. Aslet, *Last Country Houses*, 188.
6. *Aberdeen Press and Journal*, January 30, 1902, 4; Macpherson, *Highlander Looks Back*, 32.
7. Quoted in *Country Life*, February 8, 1996, 65.
8. Washington, *My Larger Education*, 257, 258.
9. Aslet, *Last Country Houses*, 187.
10. Escott, *King Edward*, 196–197.
11. FitzRoy, *Memoirs*, 2:463.
12. Nevill, *Leaves*, 33; R. Davis, "'We Are All Americans,'" 140–199. Twenty-two of these marriages ended in divorce.
13. Quoted in Heindel, *American Impact*, 347, 346.
14. Stead, *Americanization*, 323.
15. *North Star and Farmers' Chronicle*, July 19, 1906, 6.
16. *Country Life*, July 11, 1903, xiv; January 21, 1899, v.
17. *Belfast Newsletter*, March 13, 1905, 9.
18. R. Davis, "'We Are All Americans,'" 153; *Leicester Daily Post*, November 6, 1888, 3.
19. *Herts Advertiser*, September 21, 1895, 7.
20. *Herts Advertiser*, May 27, 1899, 3; Hignett, *Brett*, 92.
21. *West Cumberland Times*, April 15, 1893, 6; *Bucks Advertiser and Aylesbury News*, April 15, 1893; *English Lakes Visitor*, April 22, 1893, 2.
22. Wilson, *Astors*, 145.
23. Astor, "Wraith of Cliveden Reach," 127.
24. *Westerham Herald*, February 4, 1899, 5.
25. Astor, "Free in a Faraway Land," 434.
26. "Hever Restored," 6, 8.
27. "Hever Restored," 12, 9.
28. Wilson, *Astors*, 142; Tilden, *True Remembrances*, 114.
29. "Hever Restored," 4.

CHAPTER FOUR: COSMOPOLITANS

1. *Country Life*, February 16, 1989, 83.
2. Cowper, *Earl Cowper*, 278–279; Warwick, *Afterthoughts*, 40. In her second sentence Countess Cowper was quoting the society artist Henry Weigall, with approval.
3. Allfrey, *Edward VII*, 54.
4. Ridley, *Bertie*, 329.
5. Allfrey, *Edward VII*, 102; Ridley, *Bertie*, 328.
6. FitzRoy, *Memoirs*, 1:97.
7. FitzRoy, 389.
8. "Park Lane," 265.
9. M. Asquith, *Autobiography*, 4:127–128.
10. *Tatler*, June 21, 1905, 4; and February 6, 1907, 2.
11. Allfrey, *Edward VII*, 32.
12. M. Asquith, *Autobiography*, 1:14; Henriques, "Jewish Emancipation Controversy," 133.
13. John Mills, *British Jews*, iii, 352.
14. Wohl, "'Ben JuJu,'" 102; *Newcastle Weekly Chronicle*, April 1, 1876, 1.
15. Vincent, *Crawford Papers*, 600; FitzRoy, *Memoirs*, 2:551.
16. Victoria, journal entry, October 1869; Hyamson, "First Jewish Peer," 288; FitzRoy, *Memoirs*, 2:495, 2:516.
17. Russell is quoted in Trevelyan, *Grand Dukes*, loc. 2989; *Country Life*, January 23, 1992, 51.
18. *Country Life*, January 23, 1992, 52.
19. Trevelyan, *Grand Dukes*, loc. 2853.
20. Pevsner, *Bedfordshire*, 121.
21. Trevelyan, *Grand Dukes*, loc. 3027.
22. Quoted in Trevelyan, loc. 2606.
23. FitzRoy, *Memoirs*, 2:516.
24. Vincent, *Crawford Papers*, 599; Beatrice Webb, diary entry, July 2, 1906, London School of Economics Digital Library, https://lse-atom.arkivum.net/uklse-dl1wd01002.
25. Webb, diary entry, July 2, 1906.
26. Bedoire, *Jewish Contribution*, 8.
27. According to Historic England's Grade II listing for the Lodge, the Rothschilds had owned property in the area since the early nineteenth century, "using it as a staging point for couriers and carrier pigeons for their communication system with the Continent." "Shorncliffe Lodge," Historic England, accessed January 29, 2024, https://historicengland.org.uk/listing/the-list/list-entry/1344161?section=official-list-entry.

28. *Bromley Journal and West Kent Herald*, July 2, 1909, 4.

CHAPTER FIVE: BRITISH RAJ

1. *Western Daily Press*, October 23, 1880, 7, for quotes 1 and 3; Portland, *Men, Women and Things*, 234, for quote 2.
2. Victoria, journal entry, August 22, 1854.
3. E. D. Login, *Lady Login's Recollections*, 114; *Western Daily Press*, October 23, 1880, 7.
4. E. D. Login, *Lady Login's Recollections*, 249.
5. Ponsonby to "Babs," April 27, 1897, BL MSS Eur F 84 126a, British Library.
6. *Country Life*, May 13, 1939, 502.
7. Nairn and Pevsner, *Sussex*, 440; *Illustrated London News*, February 15, 1845, 101.
8. *Builder*, November 18, 1871, 904.
9. E. D. Login, *Lady Login's Recollections*, 239.
10. *Builder*, November 18, 1871, 904.
11. Bance, *Duleep Singhs*, 54.
12. Bance, 68.
13. One of the Old Brigade, *London in the Sixties*, 303, 302.
14. Victoria, journal entry, June 25, 1894.
15. Cundall, *Reminiscences*, 11.
16. Cundall, 113, 27.
17. Cundall, 28.
18. *Illustrated London News*, January 6, 1877, 17.
19. Victoria, journal entry, August 22, 1890.
20. Vandal and Vandal, *Raj, Lahore*, 159.
21. Victoria, journal entry, February 4, 17, March 21, 1891.
22. Vandal and Vandal, *Raj, Lahore*, 163.
23. Vandal and Vandal, *Raj, Lahore*, 164; Victoria, journal entry, February 8, 1893.
24. Victoria, journal entry, March 31, 1891.
25. *Daily Telegraph*, January 5, 1898, 11.
26. *Civil and Military Gazette*, October 15, 1898, 6.
27. *Daily Mirror*, September 28, 1904, 7; *Morning Post*, April 8, 1903, 9.
28. Singh, *Portraits*, 2:xi.
29. Singh, 2:xiv.
30. Alexander and Anand, *Queen Victoria's Maharajah*, 248.

CHAPTER SIX: FIRE FROM FRANCE

1. Duncan, *My Life*, 261.
2. Brandon, *Capitalist Romance*, 184.
3. *Chard and Ilminster News*, October 30, 1875, 4; Brandon, *Capitalist Romance*, 189.
4. Stammers, "Old French and New Money," 8.
5. *London Evening Standard*, May 14, 1898, 4; *Aberdeen Press and Journal*, March 10, 1902, 5; *Daily Telegraph*, July 5, 1899, 7; Wilson, "Paris Singer," 146.
6. Duncan, *My Life*, 250, 257.
7. Jennings, *Our Homes*, 183–184.
8. Lasic, "'Dignity and Graciousness,'" 193.
9. Nevill, *Leaves*, 206.
10. "Wrest Park House and Service Block Comprising Pavilions, Clock Tower and the Dairy," Historic England, accessed January 29, 2024, https://historicengland.org.uk/listing/the-list/list-entry/1311484?section=official-list-entry.
11. *Northern Echo*, June 11, 1892, 4.
12. Mrs J. de Rothschild, *Rothschilds at Waddesdon Manor*, 19; F. de Rothschild, *Red Book*, 7.
13. F. de Rothschild, 3.
14. Nevill, *Leaves*, 208; Masterman, *Mary Gladstone*, 361.
15. Masterman, *Mary Gladstone*, 197.
16. Nevill, *Leaves*, 207, 208; "Samuel Glendening Payne & Son," Genealogy in Hertfordshire (website), accessed January 26, 2024, http://www.hertfordshire-genealogy.co.uk/data/postcards/publisher-payne-aylesbury.htm; Lasic, "Display of Opulence," 136.
17. Warwick, *Afterthoughts*, 89, 90.
18. Pevsner and Lloyd, *Hampshire*, 230.
19. *Morning Post*, January 10, 1888, 5; *London Evening Standard*, January 10, 1888, 3.
20. Geraghty, *Empress Eugénie*, 44.
21. Filon, *Recollections*, 309.
22. Duncan, *My Life*, 254.
23. Duncan, 262.
24. Duncan, 265–266.

CHAPTER SEVEN: MANSIONS OF OLD ROMANCE

1. *Country Life*, January 8, 1897, 17–20.

2. *Country Life*, January 8, 1897, 22.

3. *Country Life*, February 13, 1897, 156.

4. *Country Life*, February 20, 1897, 186, 188.

5. *Country Life*, March 4, 1916, 300.

6. Strong, *"Country Life," 1897–1997*, 29.

7. Fea, *Recollections*, 166, 171, 167.

8. Fea, 172.

9. Fea, 190; Pevsner, *Berkshire*, 187.

10. Fea, *Picturesque Old Houses*, 1; Fea, *Nooks and Corners*, 139, 140, 201, 212.

11. *Country Life*, November 20, 1897, 552.

12. *Country Life*, December 4, 1897, 635–636.

13. Hare, *Story of My Life*, 5:231.

14. Quoted in Tomlin, *Ham House*, 104.

15. Hare, *Story of My Life*, 5:233.

16. Hare, 5:233n1.

17. Hare, 5:234.

18. Hare, 6:495. The guides still show this stain to visitors today.

19. Ingram, *Haunted Homes*, vi; Fea, *Secret Chambers*, 73.

20. James, *Ghost Stories*, 59; Wilde, "Canterville Ghost," 203.

21. Wilde, "Canterville Ghost," 203.

22. Fea, *Recollections*, 232, 233.

23. The quote about believing in anything is attributed to Chesterton but has not been traced to him: quoted in Cammaerts, *Laughing Prophet*, 230; Ingram, *Haunted Homes*, 419; Fea, *Nooks and Corners*, 229.

24. *Country Life*, August 29, 1903, 320.

25. Fea, *Old English Houses*, 224–225.

26. *Jackson's Oxford Journal*, April 21, 1894, 8.

27. *Pall Mall Gazette*, April 18, 1894, 7; *Jackson's Oxford Journal*, April 21, 1894, 8.

CHAPTER EIGHT: GENTLEMEN'S HOUSES

1. *Country Life*, May 29, 1897, 1.

2. That figure of 270 is arrived at by combing through Mark Girouard's gazetteer in his *The Victorian Country House* and Clive Aslet's gazetteer in his *The Last Country Houses*. Neither author pretends his list is comprehensive. One suspects the true figure might be two or three times larger.

3. *Builder*, October 29, 1904, 435.

4. Kerr, "Preface to the First Edition," *Gentleman's House*, v.

5. Kerr, *Gentleman's House*, 99.

6. Kerr, 177.

7. Kerr, 64, 180, 182.

8. Kerr, 185, 195.

9. Ford Manor is now called Greathed Manor. Nairn and Pevsner, *Surrey*, 267; Girouard, *Victorian Country House*, 271.

10. Quoted in Girouard, *Victorian Country House*, 272.

11. Jackson, *Recollections*, 55.

12. O'Neill, *Lutyens' Country Houses*, 93; *Country Life*, March 24, 1923, 398.

13. Dakers, *Clouds*, 135; Lethaby, *Philip Webb*, 128.

CHAPTER NINE: CAMELOT

1. Chesterton, *Alarms and Discursions*, 29.

2. *Eton College Chronicle*, June 17, 1897, 370; Burns, *Sir Galahad*.

3. "The Villain in Our Berkshire Midst," Royal Berkshire Archives website, February 9, 2022, https://www.berkshirerecordoffice.org.uk/news/article/villain-our-berkshire-midst.

4. Tennyson, *Idylls*, 292.

5. Collins, "King Arthur," 311; Rajabzadeh, "Is Your Bread White Enough?"

6. *Salisbury and Winchester Journal*, July 6, 1889, 4.

7. Scott, *Remarks*, 14, 15. I owe both quotes in this paragraph to Girouard's *Victorian Country House*, 154–155.

8. Quoted in Girouard, *Victorian Country House*, 157.

9. *Country Life*, November 14, 1903, 694; Pevsner, *South and West Somerset*, 157.

10. Savage, *Lorimer*, 105.

11. Ridley and Percy, *Letters*, 199.

12. Home page, Devizes Heritage website, accessed January 26, 2024, devizesheritage.co.uk; *Warder and Dublin Weekly Mail*, March 2, 1901, 1.

13. *Sporting Gazette*, July 7, 1888, 4; *Eastern Post*, August 25, 1888, 3.

14. Victoria, journal entry, December 2, 1846.

15. This is from John Martin Robinson's 1991 articles for *Country Life*, May 23, 1991, and May 30, 1991. I have relied heavily on these two articles for my account of Arundel.

16. *Country Life*, May 23, 1991, 98; Tyack, "Buckler, John"; Nairn and Pevsner, *Sussex*, 91, 92, 93.

17. FitzRoy, *Memoirs*, 1:85.

18. Crook, *William Burges*, 234.

19. Crook, 234.

20. Crook, 239, 240.

21. Girouard, *Victorian Country House*, 278.

22. Crook, *William Burges*, 261.

23. Crook, 267.

24. Crook, 34.

25. Holroyd, *Lytton Strachey*, 339.

CHAPTER TEN: A MODERN EDEN

1. James, *English Hours*, 230.

2. *Country Life*, February 24, 1900, 236.

3. *Country Life*, March 10, 1900, 293.

4. *Country Life*, February 1900, 236–237.

5. Robinson, *Wild Garden*, 7.

6. Robinson, *English Flower Garden*, 13.

7. Blomfield and Thomas, *Formal Garden*, 1.

8. Robinson, *Garden Design*, 2, 3, 13, xiii.

9. Blomfield and Thomas, *Formal Garden*, vii, xviii, vi; Thomas, "Garden in Relation," 242.

10. Thomas, "Garden in Relation," 241; Blomfield, *Short History*, 302, 142.

11. *Country Life*, September 2, 1922, 275.

12. Whalley, "Peto, Harold Ainsworth."

13. Quoted in Ottewill, *Edwardian Garden*, 13–14.

14. *Country Life*, August 14, 1909, 236.

15. *Country Life*, January 18, 1902, 84.

16. *Country Life*, May 17, 1984.

17. *Country Life*, September 2, 1899, 275.

18. *Country Life*, May 24, 1984, 1480.

19. Mawson, "Designing of Gardens," iv.

20. *Country Life*, May 24, 1984, iii; Mawson, *Art and Craft of Garden Making*, 3, 154, 165.

21. [Mawson,] *Life and Work*, 64; Mills, *Herkomer*, 165; Mawson, *Art and Craft of Garden Making*, 209.

22. Francis Jekyll, *Gertrude Jekyll*, 7.

23. This paragraph and the one preceding it first appeared (in a slightly altered form) in Tinniswood, *Arts and Crafts House*, 111.

24. *Garden*, vol. 62, 1902, 326–327, 343–344; *Garden*, vol. 79, 1915, 300–301.

25. Gertrude Jekyll, *Colour*, vi.
26. Festing, *Gertrude Jekyll*, 133, 143.
27. *Gardening World*, April 5, 1890, 495.
28. *Country Life*, June 29, 1912, xvii, xviii.
29. *Country Life*, June 1900, 836.
30. *Garden*, July 26, 1879, 87; *Country Life*, April 9, 1898, ii; March 26, 1898, x; September 14, 1907, xxx.
31. *Country Life*, February 3, 1900, 134.

CHAPTER ELEVEN: ARRANGED WITH GREAT TASTE

1. J. M., *Woolfield's Life at Cannes*, 50.
2. J. M., 15.
3. Masterman, *Mary Gladstone*, 277.
4. Victoria, journal entry, March 25, 1882.
5. Victoria, journal entry, March 25, 1882; Quest-Ritson, *English Garden Abroad*, 70.
6. Victoria, journal entry, March 15, 1895.
7. Victoria, journal entry, May 1, 1899.
8. *Times*, January 31, 1883, 5.
9. Baedeker, *South-Eastern France*, 236, 241.
10. *Country Life*, July 16, 1910, 97.
11. *Country Life*, December 10, 1910, 870.
12. *Country Life*, July 16, 1910, 97.
13. *Country Life*, July 16, 1910, 90; Teulié, "World War Two Iconoclasm"; *Times*, April 15, 1912, 6.
14. *Architect*, October 28, 1871, 214; *Building News*, August 26, 1881.
15. Muthesius, *English House*, 51.
16. Baillie Scott, *Houses and Gardens*, 235.
17. Baillie Scott, 139.
18. Kornwolf, *Baillie Scott*, 177.
19. Kornwolf, 436.
20. Gaunt and Tory, "Mary Portman's Violin."
21. Gaffney, *Breaking the Silence*, 60.
22. Victoria, journal entry, March 29, 1876.
23. Victoria, journal entry, April 5, 1872.
24. Victoria, journal entry, March 29, 1876.
25. Victoria, journal entry, April 15, 1880.

CHAPTER TWELVE: GOD IS IN THE HOUSE

1. Warwick, *Life's Ebb and Flow*, 26.
2. Asquith, *Autobiography*, 1:56; Nevill, *Reminiscences*, 31.
3. Masterman, *Mary Gladstone*, 68.
4. Twisleton, *Letters*, 41, 41–42.
5. Lanceley, *From Hall-Boy*, 19, 19–20.
6. Lanceley, 37–38.
7. Quoted in Coleridge, *Yonge*, 309.
8. *Illustrated London News*, May 20, 1882, 501.
9. Pevsner and Hubbard, *Cheshire*, 208; Mills, *Life and Letters*, 225–226.
10. *Cheshire Observer*, April 12, 1890, 5.
11. *Building News*, October 18, 1878, 394.
12. Waugh, *Brideshead Revisited*, 38–39.
13. Ridgway, "Privileged Insider," 15.
14. *Leeds Mercury*, July 3, 1889, 8; *John Bull*, July 20, 1889, 466.
15. Chadwick, *Victorian Church*, 2:151.
16. Machin, "Last Victorian Anti-Ritualist," 282, 286; Protestant Alliance home page, accessed April 15, 2024, www.protestant-alliance.org.
17. *Nottingham Evening Post*, January 3, 1889, 2; and October 8, 1889, 2.
18. *Manchester Guardian*, October 23, 1889, 8.
19. *Manchester Guardian*, October 23, 1889, 8.
20. *Times*, November 5, 1889, 9.

CHAPTER THIRTEEN: MAGICIANS

1. Lanceley, *From Hall-Boy*, 38.
2. *Builder*, January 24, 1880, 87.
3. *Builder*, January 24, 1880, 88.
4. *Builder*, January 24, 1880, 88.
5. Franklin, "Troops of Servants," 229.
6. *Country Life*, Electrical Supplement, March 9, 1912, xvi; *Country Life*, September 26, 1906, xliv.
7. Aslet, *Last Country Houses*, 109.
8. Stevenson, *House Architecture*, 2:213; Weaver, *House and Its Equipment*, 30.
9. *Country Life*, April 4, 1908, lvi.
10. *Country Life*, December 1, 1900, xxx; and April 11, 1908, xli.
11. *Country Life*, August 14, 1897, viii; and February 4, 1905, 168.
12. *Country Life*, February 4, 1905, 170.

13. *Country Life*, December 27, 1913, 8.

14. *Country Life*, December 27, 1913, 11.

15. *Country Life*, December 27, 1913, 7.

16. *Country Life*, April 3, 1909, lii.

17. Stevenson, *House Architecture*, 2:276; Bailey-Denton, *Water Supply and Sewerage*, 52.

18. Bailey-Denton, *Water Supply and Sewerage*, 51.

19. Kerr, *Gentleman's House*, 152–153.

20. *Country Life*, May 25, 1912, xiv.

21. Masterman, *Mary Gladstone*, 180, 181.

22. Alan Sykes, "Palace of a Modern Magician to Glow Once More with His Water-Powered Light," *The Northerner* (blog), *Guardian*, March 15, 2013, https://www.theguardian.com/uk/the-northerner/2013/mar/15/newcastle-energy; Saint, *Richard Norman Shaw*, 69; *Westminster Gazette*, December 28, 1900, 4.

23. Cecil, *Life of Robert*, 3:4.

24. Hare, *Story of My Life*, 4:223; Cecil, *Life of Robert*, 3:3–4.

25. Cecil, *Life of Robert*, 6; Hare, *Story of My Life*, 6:236.

26. Brett, *Journals and Letters*, 1:136.

27. Grimmett, "Lamp Boy's Story," 21.

28. *Country Life*, October 14, 1899, 472; FitzRoy, *Memoirs*, 1:336.

29. *Country Life*, November 7, 1908, ix.

30. Stevenson, *House Architecture*, 2:279.

31. Victoria, journal entry, January 14, 1878.

32. Maurice Hird, "House Telephone Installations," in Weaver, *House and Its Equipment*, 124.

CHAPTER FOURTEEN: GOING TO BLAZES

1. *Country Life*, October 14, 1899, 472.

2. Belloc, "Lord Finchley," in *More Peers*, 22–23.

3. Lutyens, *Blessed Girl*, 250.

4. Portland, *Men, Women and Things*, 53n.

5. *Norfolk News*, August 3, 1907, 16.

6. *Country Life*, August 26, 1899, 234; *Daily Gazette for Middlesbrough*, January 20, 1879, 3; Hermione, Duchess of Leinster, to Evelyn de Vesci, undated, in Dooley, *Decline and Fall*, 104, digital edition.

7. *Daily Telegraph*, October 13, 1882. It was actually Jacobean.

8. *Nottingham Evening Post*, October 18, 1882, 2.

9. *Birmingham Mail*, October 13, 1882, 2.

10. Quoted in Warwick, *Warwick Castle*, 2:809.

11. Warwick, 2:813.

12. *Illustrated Newspaper*, December 9, 1871, 11.

13. Warwick, *Warwick Castle*, 2:816.

14. *Westminster Gazette*, February 13, 1895, 2.

15. *London Evening Standard*, April 20, 1908, 7.

16. Stevenson, *House Architecture*, 2:199.

17. *Country Life*, August 26, 1899, 235–236.

18. Merryweather, *Fire Protection*, 56, 69.

19. *Bucks Advertiser & Aylesbury News*, November 28, 1908, 2.

20. *Country Life*, August 26, 1899, 235; *Manchester Courier*, June 23, 1908, 8.

21. Merryweather, *Fire Protection*, 95.

22. *Thomson's Weekly News*, October 31, 1908, 10.

CHAPTER FIFTEEN: MARVELS OF LOCOMOTION

1. Victoria, journal entry, March 28, 1876.

2. Victoria, journal entry, March 29, 1876.

3. Hoole, *Regional History of Railways*, 157.

4. FitzRoy, *Memoirs*, 1:xvi.

5. Frederick R. Simms, "A Trip in a Road Locomotive," *Saturday Review*, July 11, 1895, https://www.ellisjourney.co.uk/ellis-history.

6. *Country Life*, October 21, 1899, xxii.

7. Portland, *Men, Women and Things*, 316, 27.

8. Portland, 109.

9. Smith, *Motor Car*, 2; *Times*, August 18, 1905, 6; *Daily Telegraph*, October 21, 1899, 5.

10. Crosland, *Country Life*, 94.

11. *Bystander*, January 27, 1904, 7; *Gentlewoman*, September 18, 1909, 54; Warwick, *Life's Ebb and Flow*, 121–122.

12. *South Wales Daily News*, October 14, 1907, 5.

13. *Daily Mirror*, November 3, 1905.

14. *Yorkshire Post and Leeds Intelligencer*, September 12, 1900, 4.

15. *Times*, June 12, 1903, 6.

16. *Times*, October 1, 1902, 10; *Census of England and Wales*, 1911, "IV. Occupations and Industries."

17. *Times*, October 28, 1903, 16.

18. *Times*, February 10, 1904, 16.

19. *Times*, March 4, 1904, 14.

20. *Country Life*, July 2, 1904, xlviii.
21. Quoted in Smith, *Motor Car*, 16.
22. Quoted in Smith, 27.
23. Portland, *Men, Women and Things*, 316.
24. Asquith, *Haply I May Remember*, 221; Asquith, *Remember and Be Glad*, 15.

CHAPTER SIXTEEN: ENTERTAINING ROYALLY

1. Bailey, *Diary of Lady Frederick*, 2:142–143.
2. *Buxton Advertiser*, December 21, 1872, 3; Bailey, *Diary of Lady Frederick*, 2:144.
3. Bailey, *Diary of Lady Frederick*, 2:144.
4. *Buxton Advertiser*, December 21, 1872, 3.
5. Bailey, *Diary of Lady Frederick*, 2:145.
6. *Pictorial and Descriptive Guide*, 82; *Times*, December 21, 1872, 5.
7. Bailey, *Diary of Lady Frederick*, 2:143, 146.
8. Bailey, 2:146.
9. *Sheffield Daily Telegraph*, December 21, 1872, 3.
10. *Derbyshire Courier*, December 28, 1872, 2.
11. Warwick, *Life's Ebb and Flow*, 178.
12. Warwick, *Afterthoughts*, 256; Ridley, *Bertie*, loc. 2724.
13. Ridley, *Bertie*, 408.
14. Asquith, *Moments of Memory*, 158; Fitch, *Memoirs*, 60.
15. Fitch, *Memoirs*, 72.
16. Victoria, journal entry, January 7, 1892.
17. *Nottingham Evening Post*, November 10, 1891, 2.
18. *Norwich Mercury*, November 10, 1883, 4.
19. Ponsonby, *Recollections of Three Reigns*, 201.
20. Shore, *Baccarat Case*, iv.
21. Shore, *Baccarat Case*, iv; Ridley, *Bertie*, 149.
22. All the newspaper quotations in this paragraph are taken from Shore, *Baccarat Case*, v–vi.
23. Shore, *Baccarat Case*, 287–288.

CHAPTER SEVENTEEN: A SPARK OF CHIVALRY

1. Longford, *Pilgrimage of Passion*, 310.
2. Longford, 311.
3. Longford, 312.

4. Dooley, *Decline and Fall*, 112.
5. Harrison, *Autobiographic Memoirs*, 2:177.
6. Longford, *Pilgrimage of Passion*, 315.
7. Longford, 315.
8. Renton, *Wild Wyndhams*, 189–190; Ridley and Percy, *Letters*, 236.
9. Longford, *Pilgrimage of Passion*, 317; Ridley and Percy, *Letters*, 124.
10. Quoted in Leslie, *Edwardians in Love*, 153.
11. Holmes, "Double Standard," 602, 605, 607.
12. *Times*, March 20, 1902, 7.
13. *Times*, January 13, 1876, 11.
14. *Times*, May 22, 1897, 14.
15. Quoted in Holmes, "Double Standard," 618.
16. *Times*, June 20, 1903, 14.
17. *Times*, December 17, 1902, 10.
18. *Times*, October 26, 1887, 3.
19. *Freeman's Journal*, July 18, 1921, 4.
20. Russell, *My Life*, 33.
21. Russell, 115.
22. Santayana, *Middle Span*, 73.
23. Santayana, 72.
24. *Times*, December 2, 1891, 4.
25. Russell, *My Life*, 90.
26. *Times*, December 5, 1891, 7.
27. Ellmann, *Wilde*, 8.
28. Russell, *My Life*, 191.
29. Russell, 206; *Times*, January 9, 1897, 10.
30. Russell, 213.
31. Russell, 233, 264.
32. Russell, 280.
33. Russell, 283, 287.

CHAPTER EIGHTEEN: AN HONEST FEELING OF SATISFACTION

1. Ponsonby, *Recollections*, 201.
2. Martin, "British Game Shooting," 207.
3. Maxwell, *Partridges and Partridge Manors*, 309.
4. Maxwell, 310.
5. *Hexham Courant*, November 27, 1897, 2.
6. Portland, *Men, Women and Things*, 237.

7. Portland, 248.

8. Portland, 246.

9. *Tatler*, December 17, 1913, 4.

10. Windsor, *King's Story*, 85. The story about George V reluctantly returning to his wife, along with the other anecdotes about George V's obsession with shooting, is in Jane Ridley's brilliant biography, *George V*, 96.

11. Windsor, *King's Story*, 86.

12. Windsor, 87.

13. United Kingdom, *Parliamentary Debates*, House of Commons, March 2, 1880, vol. 251, col. 160–94, https://api.parliament.uk/historic-hansard /commons/1880/mar/02/game-laws-resolution.

14. *Graphic*, February 18, 1882, 2.

15. *Daily Mirror*, January 30, 1904, 4.

CHAPTER NINETEEN: LADY BOUNTIFUL

1. Warwick, *Afterthoughts*, 37, 242.

2. Picton-Turbervill, "Childhood in Brighton and Bruges," 335; Marlborough, "Position of Women," 354–355.

3. Heath, *Peasant Life*, 286, 288.

4. Hudson, *Afoot in England*, 14.

5. Hudson, 15.

6. *Mansfield Reporter*, December 27, 1889, 6.

7. *Oxfordshire Weekly News*, August 24, 1898, 8.

8. *Northampton Mercury*, September 1, 1893, 5.

9. King, "Rise and Decline," 163–164, 165.

10. King, 182.

11. King, 167; *Alnwick Mercury*, December 13, 1884, 8.

12. *Kelly's Directory of Norfolk*, 1896, quoted at "Holkham," Forebears, accessed April 15, 2024, https://forebears.io/england/norfolk/holkham #sid14355.

13. *Norwich Mercury*, August 15, 1891, 7; *Norfolk News*, September 2, 1899, 14.

14. *Yarmouth Independent*, March 6, 1937, 21.

15. *Daily Telegraph*, July 24, 1890, 8.

16. Casey, "Decline and Fall," 172.

17. *Inquirer and Commercial News* (Perth, Western Australia), February 19, 1890, 7. It should be noted that besides publishing this letter, the Australian papers also claimed that Belle was a ballet dancer with three children and that Wertheimer was "a bric-a-brac dealer."

18. *Daily Telegraph*, July 25, 1890, 2.

19. *Daily Telegraph*, July 31, 1890, 2.

20. *Daily Telegraph*, July 31, 1890, 2.

21. *Times*, July 31, 1890, 7; *Daily Telegraph*, July 31, 1890, 3; *Times*, July 31, 1890, 7; *Freeman's Journal*, July 31, 1890, 4; *Reynolds's Newspaper*, August 3, 1890, 4.

22. Casey, "Decline and Fall," 177.

23. *Tuam Herald*, February 20, 1897, 4.

CHAPTER TWENTY: TWO TRIBES

1. Lanceley, *From Hall-Boy*, 14.

2. Lanceley, 13, 14.

3. *Yarmouth Independent*, December 5, 1891, 6.

4. Kerr, *Gentleman's House*, 203.

5. Stevenson, *House Architecture*, 2:79, 80.

6. *Duties of Servants*, 2.

7. *Duties of Servants*, 2.

8. *Duties of Servants*, 25, 26.

9. *Duties of Servants*, 20.

10. Quoted in Dawes, *Not in Front of the Servants*, 35.

11. *Servants' Practical Guide*, v; Jewry, *Warne's Model Cookery*, 1; Davidson, *Book of the Home*, 4:229.

12. *Census of England and Wales*, 1871, "III. Occupations of the People."

13. Franklin, "Troops of Servants," 212.

14. *Census of England and Wales*, 1911, "IV. Occupations and Industries."

15. *Westminster Gazette*, May 22, 1911, 13.

CHAPTER TWENTY-ONE: TRUE CRIME

1. *York Herald*, February 19, 1877, 5.

2. *Daily Telegraph*, February 19, 1877, 5.

3. *Express*, March 14, 1908, 8.

4. *Barnsley Chronicle*, February 1, 1908.

5. *Express*, March 14, 1908, 8.

6. *Express*, March 14, 1908, 8.

7. Waterson, *Servants' Hall*, 3.

8. *North Wales Times*, December 7, 1907, 3.

9. *North Wales Times*, December 7, 1907, 3; Waterson, *Servants' Hall*, 193.

10. Waterson, *Servants' Hall*, 193.
11. *Country Life*, October 30, 1909, 582.
12. *Country Life*, March 24, 1900, 363.
13. *Country Life*, June 27, 1903, liii.
14. *Country Life*, March 24, 1900, 362; and August 3, 1912, 34.
15. *Country Life*, June 9, 1900, xxviii.
16. *Country Life*, August 3, 1912, 34.
17. *Daily Telegraph*, November 5, 1909, 11.
18. *Manchester Guardian*, March 4, 1910, 4.
19. *Manchester Guardian*, November 1909, 7.
20. *Daily Telegraph*, November 8, 1909, 13.
21. *Dundee Evening Telegraph*, November 15, 1909, 3.
22. *Manchester Guardian*, March 5, 1910, 6.
23. *Manchester Guardian*, October 25, 1910, 4.

EPILOGUE: AND THE BAND PLAYED ON

1. *Tatler*, August 12, 1914, 188.
2. De Courcy, *Circe*, 103.
3. Ridley and Percy, *Letters*, 311.
4. *Country Life*, October 24, 1914, 538.
5. Lexden, Alistair, Lord, "The House of Lords and World War One," *The House Magazine*, June 27, 2014, 35-7, 37.

INDEX

Note: Page numbers with * indicate a footnote.

CREDIT: HELEN ROGERS

Adrian Tinniswood is professor of British cultural history at the University of Buckingham, adjunct professor in history at Maynooth University, and the author of many books on British history, including *Noble Ambitions* and the *New York Times* bestseller *The Long Weekend*. He was awarded an OBE for services to heritage by Queen Elizabeth II and lives in Ireland.